STEEL CITY GRIDIRONS

Stories of all things football
from the high schools, the colleges, the
pros, and the earliest days of the game.

David Finoli
Chris Fletcher

TOWERS
MAGUIRE
PUBLISHING

Pittsburgh, Pennsylvania, USA

Published by
Towers Maguire Publishing
(an imprint of *The Local History Company*)
112 North Woodland Road
Pittsburgh, PA 15232-2849
www.TowersMaguire.com
Info@TowersMaguire.com
www.TheLocalHistoryCompany.com
info@TheLocalHistoryCompany.com

Cover and title page photo credits: Front cover photo of football by Tom Altany. Background image within the *Steel City* text on the back cover and title page from Pitt Panther photo with Hugh Green and teammates, courtesy of University of Pittsburgh. Back cover background image from Robert Morris University Colonials photo of Tim Hall and teammates courtesy of Robert Morris University. Photos not otherwise credited are from the collections of the authors.

Library of Congress Cataloging-in-Publication Data

Finoli, David, 1961-
Steel City gridirons / by David Finoli and Chris Fletcher.—1st North American ed.
p. cm.
Includes bibliographical references.
ISBN-13: 978-0-9770429-1-3 (softcover : alk. paper)
ISBN-10: 0-9770429-1-X (softcover : alk. paper)
1. Football—Pennsylvania—Pittsburgh Metropolitan Area—History.
2. Pittsburgh Steelers (Football team)—History. 3. University of Pittsburgh—Football—History. 4. Pitt Panthers (Football team)—History.
5. Youth league football—Pennsylvania—Pittsburgh Metropolitan Area—History. I. Fletcher, Chris (Christopher E.), 1961- II. Title.

GV959.53.P58F56 2005
796.332'09748'86—dc22

2005022256

Printed in USA

dedication

To my father Domenic and my Uncle Vinny who first anointed me as part of the Steeler Nation in 1970 when they took me to my first game: a Steeler thumping of the hated Browns 28-9. It's a membership I treasure to this very day. A thank you to my loving wife Viv and kids Matt, Tony and Cara who put up with me during the writing of this book. Also to my extended family: my mother Eleanor, father Domenic, brother Jamie, his wife Cindy, my sister Mary, her husband Matt, my nieces Marissa and Brianna; Tom D., Gary, Amy, Linda, Fran, Luci, Flo, Beth, Tom A., Amanda, Claudia, Vinny, Richard, Diane, Ginny Lynn, Eddie, Pam, Debbie, Maryanne, Betty, Mary, Louise, Evie and the memory of Vince, Jeannie, Norma and Libby. My wife's wonderful parents who have always made me feel a part of the family, Vivian and Salvatore Pansino. And finally, to Chris with whom I have had the honor of sharing many tales of the steel city gridiron for over 20 years.

DF

Thanks to Linda for understanding the obsession and even finding a Steelers bar for me in Kalispell, Montana, so that I wouldn't miss a game. And to Dylan: someday you'll rejoice in two of the greatest words in the English language—Touchdown Steelers. Thank you both for being patient as I spent many hours holed up in the home office. One day, Dylan, you'll learn to love the game, or at least I'm still holding out hope. Also, to my uncles Vince, Bruce, Joe, and especially Fran for instilling a lifelong love of football. To my mom—even though she never allowed me to play football—for her love and support. To Dave for pulling me in to this project. I look forward to the next one. To all of the good folks at DirecTV for beaming the NFL into my home each weekend. And finally, to Joe Namath for making it cool to be from Beaver Falls.

CF

contents

SECTION I

introduction

Quarterback John Brallier was the first player ever to admit being paid to play the game. He was proud of his title as the first professional player until the day he died. A couple years following his death it was discovered that Pudge Heffelfinger was paid in 1892, three years before Brallier, taking his title as the first professional player. (Courtesy of the Latrobe Historical Society.)

The French love Jerry Lewis. Pittsburghers love football. (And we use "Pittsburgh" as the shorthand for a region that sprawls well outside the city limits.) There are no pratfalls in our devotion, but there is something in our collective consciousness that views the donning of pads and helmet as a sacred rite of fall and winter. Oh, how our calendars change.

Want to hold an event? Don't even think of scheduling it for a Friday night—that's high school football night. It's a pageant that reaches into all the communities of southwestern Pennsylvania, with more than bragging rights on the line. In one match-up, the game even determines the name of a bridge. Should Monaca win, you cross the Monaca-Rochester bridge. A loss carries you across the Rochester-Monaca bridge.

Saturdays also bring a veritable smorgasbord of pigskin pleasures. If you crave Division I fare, there's the University of Pittsburgh, where fans can get their fill of a top-20 program. Or they can nibble at a number of smaller college programs—new powerhouses like Duquesne University and the traditional tastiness of Washington & Jefferson, Carnegie Mellon and Indiana University of Pennsylvania.

And finally, for many, Sundays are religious holidays that don't involve traditional churches or temples. They worship at Heinz Field. . . Our Lady of the Three Rivers. It's with great zeal and fervor that the congregation prays for the pilgrims in black and gold to bless them with victory and make all right with the world. Can we get an amen?

This is what football in Pittsburgh is all about. Go to any other city in the nation and you won't find another one that combines four Super Bowl titles, nine national championships, several small college titles and a myriad of high schools that have spawned the likes of Joe Montana, George Blanda, Joe Namath, Iron Mike Ditka and Jim Kelly to name only a few.

Football spurs emotion in Western Pennsylvania and it has for more than 100 years. The pages of this book capture the emotion of just about every aspect of what is the new national pastime. From the birth of the professional version of the sport, which happened right here when the Allegheny Athletic Association paid William "Pudge" Heffelfinger $500 to play a game against their rivals from the Pittsburgh Athletic Club, to Franco's immaculate reception to Tony Dorsett's single-handed destruction of the Notre Dame Fighting Irish, *Steel City Gridirons* tells the stories of the players, teams and games that make football a true obsession in the Steel City—and throughout Southwestern Pennsylvania.

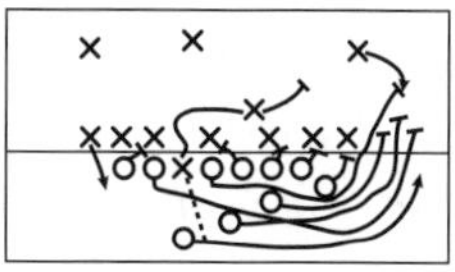

ONE

21 Reasons We Love Steel City Football

A Manifesto

How do we love football? Let us count the ways. Well, we came up with 48 ways. Some are serious. Others are not. After all, football in Western Pennsylvania is equal parts pastime, religion, event and entertainment. Let's break huddle and line up. And if we've called a play you'd like to see more of, we refer you to another chapter in this book.

Ready. . . on three. Break.

1. *Weekends were made for football.*

It starts at the end of August, and with any luck doesn't end until the beginning of February. For five-plus months in Western Pennsylvania we bask in the glory that is football season. It becomes a regional obsession—but one of those good obsessions not like those goofballs who dress up in Star Trek gear and go to conventions. But we digress.

Any given football season draws 3 million fans to their gridiron of choice. Think that number is high? Not here in the hotbed of football, where the game is enjoyed on the pro, large college, small college and high school level. (We're not including sandlots—only games where people pay to go.) Consider a *Pittsburgh Post-Gazette* story in the fall of 2004 extrapolated (a fancy word for projecting) that more than 1 million people attend WPIAL high school football games on Fridays.

"I've been told that if you like to play the slot machines," says New Brighton athletic director Joe Ursida, "Friday nights are the nights to go to Mountaineer

[Race Track & Gaming Resort], because no one's there. They're all at high school football games."

Event planners take note. Scheduling on a fall Friday night isn't a good idea.

High school football grabs a hold of the area in so many ways. For the students it's about pep rallies, the band, mascots, cheerleaders and bus rides to the away games. It's about putting those uniforms on, the same design that dads, uncles, cousins and brothers wore before you. And it's about creating memories.

Even the pros remember their high school games. Bill Cowher, head coach of the Pittsburgh Steelers, offers this memory: "I remember my Carlynton team… 22 guys on the team… there were some days we didn't have enough to practice 11 on 11," he says. "But I still remember that we went 7-2, and that we were all very close. Because we didn't have a lot of guys, we had this 'us against them' attitude. We fed off of it."

And the surrounding communities feed off of high school football, too. "You can go up and down the [Steel] valley, from community to community and it's the same thing—Fridays mean high school football," says Steelers chairman Dan Rooney. "It goes back to the mill days, but communities identify with their football teams. It's something that unites them."

For Ursida, it's a similar recognition. He's been involved with the high school game for 40 years, including time spent as a head coach at Seneca Valley and New Brighton. High school football reaches outside the school. For instance, the New Brighton Quarterback Club—the booster group that gets together for fundraising and other activities centered around the high school team—is made up of adults who no longer have children playing the game. "But they still get together and come out and support the team."

He likes that kind of quarterback club compared to others that can be more politically motivated. "You

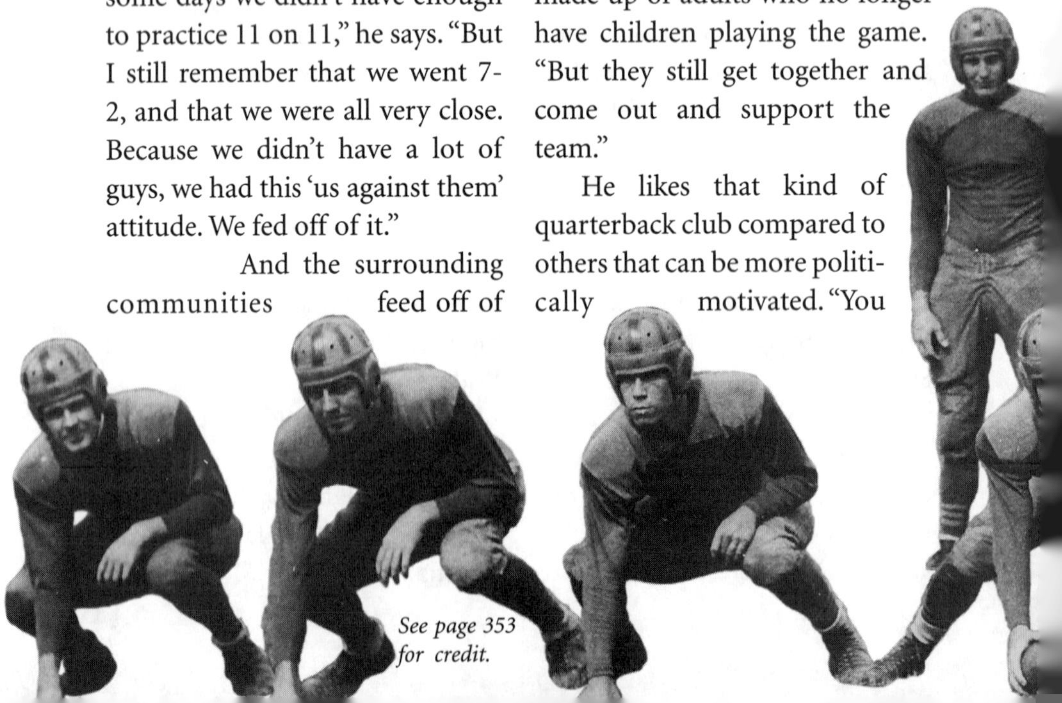

See page 353 for credit.

get some parents who get involved in them, thinking it will help their kids get more playing time. You get a lot of ulterior motives."

When author H.G. Bissinger was studying places to write a book about high school football and the community that surrounds it, he reportedly stopped in Aliquippa, Massillon, Ohio, and Odessa, Texas—places with a well-known fervor for the high school game. When he saw the palaces that held 15,000 fans in Texas, he headed there for his book *Friday Night Lights.* In passing on Aliquippa, he chose the flash over the grit, which is probably best. *Friday Night Lights* didn't offer Odessa in the best possible way with its tales of racism and misplaced educational priorities, although it did make a damn fine movie.

But here in Pennsylvania, we can have a script of our own. At around 7 p.m., it begins. Traffic picks up a bit along the roads leading to the high school field. Lines are at the concession stands as people—many wearing team colors and hats with team logos—talk about past games. "Remember when... " is a frequent start to conversations. Of course, as the years go by, stories are embellished. Runs that originally gained 15 yards are now closer to 30 or 40 as the retellings continue.

Soon the players break through the decorated hoops and set off to create a whole new set of memories that will be embellished years in the future as well. It's kickoff for the players lined up on the manicured field, freshly painted with yard lines. Two sets of grandstands are packed. The home side is larger, while across the field, the visitor's stand is less roomy but still filled. It's football under the

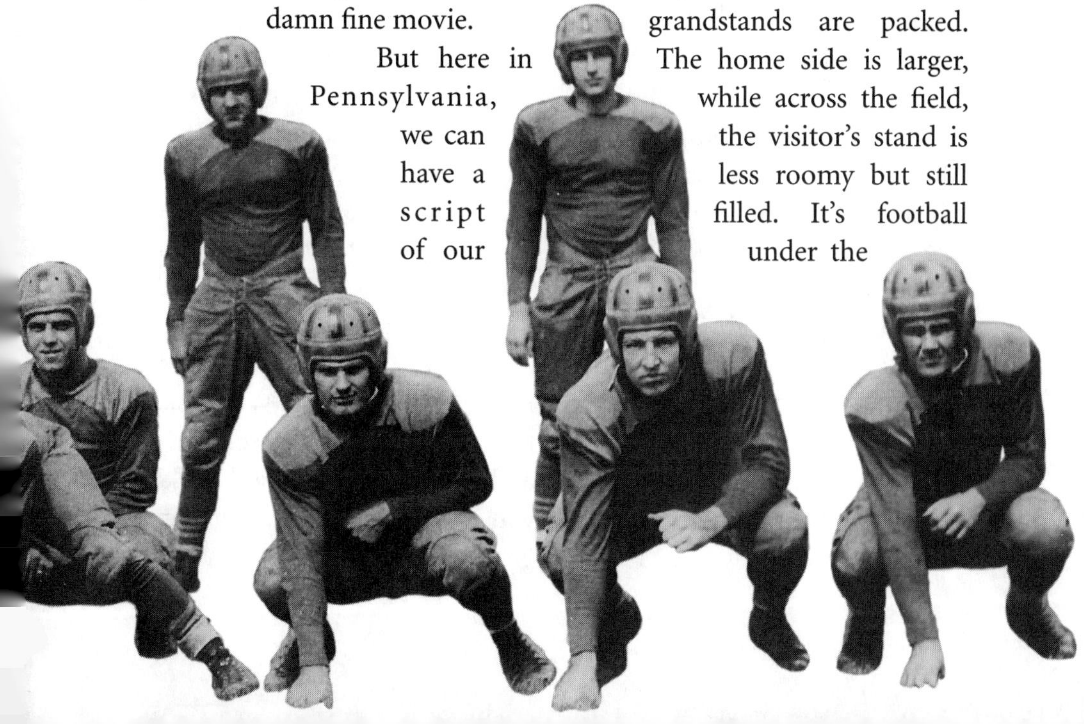

lights watched by your friends and neighbors. What a way to start the weekend.

Come Saturday, it's football of a different kind. The college game takes front and center. At the University of Pittsburgh, buses leave to transport the students to Heinz Field, the state-of-the-art complex the team shares with its professional cousins. Tailgating is in full swing. Fraternities and sororities reunite. For Andrea White, a Pitt grad who won't disclose her year of graduation, it's a chance to relive some of her college times. "I miss Pitt Stadium, but not the walk up that damn hill," she says. "But you come down here and you see some people you went to school with and you reconnect. And the sausage is really good."

So is the football. Each week you see some players who will eventually line up for the NFL upon graduation. Other players went this route to get a college education. But at other schools like Duquesne University, the concept of the student athlete not only survives, it thrives. There, students walk to on-campus fields to watch their teams play. The crowds rarely get above the low thousands, but it only serves to provide a more intimate football experience. Duquesne has been a powerhouse in the small college ranks of late, capturing an NCAA Division I-AA Mid Major championship—a lot of words to describe a good team.

At Robert Morris University, there's a coach who had been at football's highest level—the NFL and in the media capital of New York—but is happy to be competing at the small-college level. "Some of my best football experiences have happened on this campus," he says. "We play some good football here. I don't miss the NFL." (For more on Walton's transition, see Chapter 31, "No Ordinary Joe.")

And that brings us to Sundays. And the NFL. And the Steeler Nation. And it truly is a nation, based in Pittsburgh, but spread throughout the country. In California, there's the Black And Gold Brigade, which bills itself as "the world's largest nonprofit Steelers' fan club." It even has a hotline to keep displaced Steelers fans abreast of the latest happenings, although you wonder how much it's called now that the Internet is here.

But the capital of the Steeler Nation is Heinz Field. Want season tickets? Get your name on the list and the Steelers will get back to you in a decade or so. Fans rarely give up their seats. Keep in mind, of course, that *fan* comes from the word *fanatic*. It fits, when you're talking about the Steelers, or "Stillers" in Pittsburghese. Chants of "Here we go Steelers" are heard in the restrooms, which is a little unsettling proposition when you think about it.

Although it offers wonderful panoramas of the city, Heinz Field is lacking certain aspects of the Steelers' former home, Three Rivers Stadium (See Chapter 15), besides championships, of course. It's much more spartan. With its open end zone, sound escapes Heinz Field. It never seems to be as rollicking as Three Rivers. And Steelers fans do like to rollick, with their team jerseys and Terrible Towels. There's probably never been a study done, but productivity on Mondays in Pittsburgh probably fluctuates with the performance of the team of Sunday. (Hmmmm, perhaps some grant money is in order. . .)

There are the occasions when the football weekend does extend to Monday. If the Steelers play on *Monday Night Football*, it's often an even greater spectacle. The city will plan Light-up Nights. The Terrible Towels twirl a little faster. And the rest of the country finds out what we know—Pittsburgh is made for football.

2. *We have great rivalries on all levels.*

What is football without rivalries? Practice maybe? Thankfully, we don't have to worry about it, because Steel City gridirons are filled with them. At the pro level there are the Steelers and the hated Cleveland Browns. It's one of the longest-running rivalries in the league, with the two teams playing more than 100 times—many of them hard fought grudge matches. There was only one break in the hatred Steelers fans felt for the Browns. When Cleveland briefly lost its NFL franchise in a move to Baltimore, many Steelers fans actually felt bad. It passed, but there were a few moments of genuine empathy. Of course that hatred traveled to Baltimore in the form of the Baltimore Ravens. And when the Browns got their new franchise four years later, the Steelers were there to welcome them back with a 43-0 whipping.

In the '70s there was another great Steelers rivalry with the Oakland Raiders. This one was born out of respect. From 1972-76 the teams met each year in the playoffs. They were the foes you loved to hate.

At the college level, there's a rivalry so great it has a name: The Backyard Brawl. Nice name, better rivalry with West Virginia University. The Panthers and Mountaineers have had some great shootouts in a series that pits teams 75 miles apart against each other. There was the 31-31 tie coming on last-second field goal by Pitt kicker Ed Frazier before a record Mountaineer crowd of nearly 70,000 in 1989. And then there was the overtime classic at West Virginia, a 41-38 thriller in 1997 that vaulted Pitt into a bowl game for the first time in eight years.

Unfortunately for Pitt, one of the great rivalries of the past is no more. Pitt and Penn State used to have some historic match-ups, much to the delight of alums from both schools. But Penn State czar of football and increasingly crotchety old man Joe Paterno has doggedly refused a renewal of the series. (Hey, this is a book about Pittsburgh football, so we can be mean to the old guy). Apparently, JoePa has hurt feelings about Pitt rebuffing his efforts to form an Eastern football conference in the days before the Big East Conference. Joe, get over it already. But such is the thinking with rivalries. It becomes emotional rather than logical.

For small colleges, there's a new rivalry to keep an eye on—Duquesne University versus Robert Morris University. *Two* non-scholarship programs led by two coaches who teach football the right way are a joy to see.

And what would high school football be without its rivalries? New Brighton athletic director and former coach Joe Ursida likes to think of the Beaver Valley as the epicenter for rivalries. "You have Monaca and Rochester, the bridge game [see Chapter 40, "Football Over the Bridge"], Aliquippa and Ambridge, and for us, Beaver Falls and New Brighton," he says. "And then there's Moon and Blackhawk—a new and pretty good rivalry. All of this is happening in the Beaver Valley. That's hard to beat."

But then again at the high school level, each team has its own rivals. That's what engages the whole community to come out on a Friday night. And that's why football is so ingrained in our consciousness.

3. Professional football was invented here.

It makes sense that, given our love of football, the pro game started here. Visit Latrobe Stadium and you'll see a marker that honors the spot where John Braillier accepted $10 to quarterback the Latrobe club in 1895, a moment that was originally thought to be the first documented payment given to a football player. That honor eventually went a little west, right smack dab in the heart of Pittsburgh as an expense sheet was found in the early 1960s proving that Pudge Heffelfinger, who played for the Allegheny Athletic Association, was actually the first paid professional. According to the document, he received $500 from the AAA in 1892 for a game against the Pittsburgh Athletic Club at Recreation Park, not far from where Heinz Field currently sits today. (See Chapter 3.)

Professional football had rough origins. Many fans preferred the "purity" of the college game. But the region's rough-and-tumble steel workers had a lot to do with the acceptance of the pro game in Western Pennsylvania.

Steelers chairman Dan Rooney gives this historical perspective: "A lot of the mills had football teams that were started by the companies to promote harmony. And a lot of the time they hired people who could play football." Often, he adds, there were "ringers" brought in, who didn't

Art Rooney, Sr., (far right) joins several Latrobe dignitaries in dedicating the plaque commemorating the 1895 Latrobe club, the team that included among its members John Brallier, thought to be the first professional player until the early 1960s. (Courtesy of the Latrobe Historical Society.)

"The Frozen Tundra of Greensburg". Offutt Field in Greensburg has been the home of Greensburg-Salem High School since 1890. Formerly known as Athletic Field, these grounds perhaps played home to the first professional football game ever when Greensburg met Latrobe in 1897. (Courtesy of Tom Aikens.)

actually work at the companies, but somehow they showed up for the football games.

That intensity fed throughout the communities of Western Pennsylvania and helped bolster fan interest in the Steelers at a time when wins were few and far between.

4. *Art Rooney was a true sportsman.*

While his first 40 years as the owner of the Steelers were marked by one embarrassing losing season after another, Art Rooney, Sr., or "The Chief," as he was affectionately known, had a history of excellence in athletics in several sports. He was the "Jim Thorpe" of Pittsburgh, if you will.

As a boxer, Rooney was at his best capturing the welterweight and middleweight AAU (the preeminent amateur athletic association in the country) championships simultaneously. He was awarded a spot on the United States Boxing Team for the 1920 Olympic games in Antwerp, which he turned down to pursue his studies.

In baseball, he played in the minors from 1920-1925, hitting .361 for the Wheeling Stogies of the Middle Atlantic league in his best season. Unfortunately, injuries prematurely ended his promising career. Art was so enamored with the national pastime it prompted him to name his NFL franchise the Pirates, in honor of the city's baseball team, from 1933-1940 before changing it to the Steelers.

And of course, he stood out on the gridiron as the starting quarterback of the Duquesne University Dukes in the 1920s. The Chief, whose name adorns the current Duquesne football stadium, Rooney Field, was described as a "resourceful little quarterback" by the school's monthly magazine. Before playing on the Bluff, Rooney was heavily recruited to play at Notre Dame by the greatest collegiate football coach ever to grace the sidelines, Knute Rockne.

Even though it was on the playing field that Rooney excelled, it was at the horse track where he was most at home. Perhaps the most famous story about Rooney's exploits betting the ponies took place in the 1930s. On a junket to New York City, the Chief began with $300 in his pocket. He quickly grew it to $21,000, but rather than settle for that he went to Saratoga Springs the next day. His hot streak continued, and by the time the dust settled, Art Rooney's $300 investment became approximately a quarter of a million.

The family's love of horse racing continues today, as his son, Tim, is currently the president of Yonkers Raceway, a position he's held since 1972.

5. Even when the Steelers sucked, they still beat the living snot out of their opponents.

They didn't win a lot in the early years or even the middle years, for that matter. But teams knew they'd played the Steelers, particularly on Mondays when the aches and pains settled in. This was a team that reveled in big hits, particularly in the rough-and-tumble NFL of the '50s, an era when there were few rules to protect ball carriers.

"I think our players in those days were a lot like the steelworkers and other blue-collar folks of Pittsburgh," Rooney says. "They were tough. Even though we didn't win a lot, I don't think teams looked forward to seeing us on their schedules."

Even now as the Steelers have enjoyed success, physical play is still a big part of their game, says head coach Bill Cowher. "Big hits can really get fans in the game," he says. "And that makes it tougher for the other team."

6. And even as lovable losers, the Steelers were entertaining.

The best story of how hapless the Steelers were: In 1956, the team selected 26-year-old Colorado State quarterback Gary Glick with the first overall pick in the draft after someone in their brain trust had read a favorable article about him in the annual *Street & Smith's College Football Guidebook*. They converted Glick to a kicker/defensive back/half back. In seven pro seasons in the NFL with the Steelers, Redskins and Colts, and one season in the AFL with the San Diego Chargers, Glick picked off 14 passes.

By selecting Glick, the Steelers bypassed running back Lenny Moore, offensive tackle Forrest Gregg, linebacker Sam Huff, defensive end Willie Davis and quarterback Bart Starr—all of whom would become Hall of Famers. It was part of the Steelers' tradition of bad draft-day decisions that would last until the Chuck Noll years. (For more on the best draft in Steelers'—and NFL—history, turn to Chapter 10, "A Picture-Perfect Draft.")

7. "The Steeler Way" makes for great football.

And the team is recommitted to it. Run the ball to set up the pass. Attack on defense. Control the clock. Now that's a formula we can get behind. And it's one that has led to success. Never should you use the dreaded "F-word" to describe Steeler football—you know, finesse. Ick.

"I think it's a ball-control offense for the most part," says head coach Bill Cowher, describing his philosophy. "It allows you to control the tempo of the game. It opens up the play-action passing game. It's a physical approach to playing football."

Cowher studied under one of the leading practitioners of that approach. As a coach on Marty Schottenheimer's staff in Cleveland and Kansas City, he was schooled in the brand of physical play that he adapted upon his arrival in Pittsburgh. Cowher teams were physical and wore their opponents down by the fourth quarter. They hung in and won tough games. They kept other teams' offenses off the field.

On offense, the Steelers have had some strong running backs in the Cowher years. Barry Foster was the first, rushing for a franchise-record 1,690 yards in 1992. Then came Jerome Bettis, a first-ballot Hall of Famer, and a back who would dish out more punishment to would-be tacklers than he would absorb.

On defense, his team stopped the run. Quick linebackers like Greg Lloyd, Kevin Greene, Jason Gildon, Joey Porter and Kendrell Bell flew around the field to make plays. And all was right with the world.

But Cowher admits he got away from that approach in 2003 when the team finished a disappointing 6-10. His offense became pass happy. For the first time in his tenure with the Steelers, his team was near the bottom of the league in rushing offense. The Steelers didn't work on the running game as much in practice that season, concentrating more on developing the intricacies and sharp timing required to properly execute the passing game. Did that shift in the offense in practice affect the defense? "Yeah, I think it goes hand in hand," Cowher notes. "When the approach to the game is more run-oriented it increases the physicality of the practice. It's a much more physically demanding practice."

The defense also had a philosophical change. Gone were the different array of blitzes that Cowher's team had used under defensive coordinator Dick LeBeau, the architect of the zone blitz that revolutionized pass coverage. Under LeBeau, the Steelers created "Blitzburgh," an attacking defense that kept quarterbacks guessing where the pressure would be coming from. In 2003, under coordinator Tim Lewis, Cowher's defense reacted more than it attacked. It was his defenders who tired.

Cowher took responsibility for that change during a press conference, saying "I am as guilty as anybody of getting a little enamored with the wide-open part of it when you have a little bit of success. Then, all of a sudden, you don't have that immediate feedback from running the ball... you're only getting 3 or 4 yards. You have one of those games where you don't run it and you start to deviate a bit and say, 'Let's go ahead and throw it.'"

For the 2004 season, Cowher returned to his roots. He brought back LeBeau to be his defensive coordinator. His new offensive coordinator Ken Whisenhunt went back to the basics of the running game, eschewing the trick plays and wide-open passing game. The Steelers are playing the physical brand of football that we enjoy again. Finesse be damned.

8. *The Immaculate Reception happened here.*

It was the greatest play in NFL history, and the one that signaled that perhaps, just perhaps, nearly 40 years of misfortune for Pittsburgh's professional football franchise was over with a capital "O."

Oh sure, there are other plays or series of plays that you know by their names—The Catch, The Drive, The Motor City Miracle, for example. But what adds to the lure and the lore of the Immaculate Reception is that there is no good existing footage that shows conclusively what happened. However, famed Steelers' broadcaster Myron Cope swears that soon after the game he saw video from local station WTAE that shows once and for all that Terry Bradshaw's desperation, fourth-down pass bounced off of Jack Tatum and not Frenchy Fuqua. Why is that so crucial? Remember that NFL rules at the time, since changed, stated that an offensive player could not catch a pass that hit off of another offensive player without first touching a defensive player. NFL Films has an often-shown clip, taken by a telephoto lens, that shows the ball floating softly until Franco Harris makes the catch at his ankle. Unfortunately, NFL Films doesn't offer a good view of the impact zone—the key to the play. So where is the Cope video that would provide those missing answers? According to Myron, it's locked somewhere, unmarked, in storage. Or, as an alternative he offers this: since stations didn't keep stock like they do now, the footage could have been destroyed. Either way, it's the Holy Grail of football video.

Recently, Timothy Gay, a physicist from the University of Nebraska-Lincoln and author of *Football Physics: The Science of the Game*, spends a chapter addressing the play. In "The Steelers Get Lucky," he surmises that principles of physics suggest that the Steelers caught a break on this one. I may lack a doctorate, and it was 25 years since I pulled down an A in physics in high school, but let me try it here. The ball and Frenchy Fuqua are knocked backwards during the impact. According to Newton's Law (and that has nothing to do with the fact that Fig Newtons always taste better when accompanied by milk), Tatum's momentum is transferred to the prone Fuqua and to the ball. Had the ball hit Fuqua, it's doubtful that it would have bounded so far backwards toward the line of scrimmage. It's Tatum's force that is transferred to the ball. Physics says so, as do I. And, Gay grew up rooting for the Cincinnati Bengals, thus clouding any semblance of good judgment he might claim to have.

(For more on the NFL's Greatest Mystery: The Immaculate Reception, turn to Chapter 9.).

9. *We had Myron and the Terrible Towel.*

From the "only in Pittsburgh" file: Myron Cope is the voice of the Steeler Nation. And, oh what a voice. Melodious, it ain't, as Cope would tell you. The Steelers' venerable broadcaster has added phrases like "yoi" and "double yoi," "you betcha," and "the dear (fill in player's name here)" to the local vernacular. Many home viewers have taken to the habit of turning the sound off on the TV and listening to Myron instead, although the advent of satellite television makes it difficult to do so without thinking that perhaps Cope is a bit clairvoyant. He does claim to have some mystical powers through his invention, the "Terrible Towel." Cope claims that banner of black-and-gold fandom is charged with secret powers to sap the will and energy of Steelers' opponents. Who are we to argue? Plus, it's quite a sight to see a stadium full of towel-waving fanatics. Even the players have taken up towel twirling.

Above all, Myron makes football fun, and he reminds us that it's just a game, lest we take things too seriously. A man of self-deprecating wit, he doesn't take *himself* too seriously. That's too bad, because his considerable talents are often overlooked. Before taking the airwaves, Cope was a sportswriter of great renown. In fact, in the '60s, only two special contributors were listed on the masthead of *Sports Illustrated.* George Plimpton was one. Myron was the other.

10. *We have the coolest uniforms.*

Maybe it's the three hypocycloids on the one side of the helmet. Maybe it's just that understated elegance where black meets gold. But the Steelers have the best unies in the NFL hands down. We'll give you the fact that the Dallas Cowboys have classy threads. So will shoppers. According to Dan Rooney, at the high point of the two franchises' Super Bowl rivalries, the Steelers and the Cowboys accounted for a whopping 72 percent of all league merchandise sold. We give the Steelers' stuff the nod, not just because we're homers, but because the black is rather slimming.

Pittsburgh's defunct pro team also had great uniforms. Though they lasted only one season, the USFL's Pittsburgh Maulers made a fashion statement—regal purple and a bold helmet design with hammer and anvil. Too bad their play on the field (detailed in "Defending the Honor of the Steeler Nation: The Maulers' Home Opener," Chapter 14) wasn't as attractive.

But for our money, the best look came from the University of Pittsburgh in the '70s and up to the stylishly horrible Steve Pedersen years. When he came to Oakland as athletic director, Pedersen hoped to reinvent the Panthers' program, right down to their on-field look. Gone were the classic script Pitt helmets. Gone also were the blue-and-gold jerseys and pants. With retro being the fashion craze, won't someone bring back that classic Pitt look?

11. *Our football made great TV and movies.*

OK, so the Immaculate Reception footage is missing in action. But there's no shortage of great Steelers moments in video and celluloid. Take the best television commercial ever made. A young fan gives an obviously pained Mean Joe Greene his Coke, which he proceeds to chug down in about three seconds (I burp just thinking of what that must have been like). In return, Greene tosses the kid his jersey, which I hope he washed later since Greene was dripping with sweat. Still it's a great TV moment, and when the smiling kid gushes, "Thanks, Mean Joe," who can help but get a lump in the throat. Grown men cried. Coke sales soared.

And speaking of tearjerkers, there was the TV movie, *Fighting Back*, based on Rocky Bleier's inspirational tale of coming back from wounds suffered in Vietnam so serious that doctors doubted his ability to walk let alone to play in the NFL. Get past the bad soundtrack music and enjoy some great performances—Robert Urich as Bleier and Art Carney as The Chief, Art Rooney, Sr. (Although would it have hurt the writers to have him say, "To the moon, Rocky!"?)

Later, Bleier and Greene parlayed those TV moments into a hilarious cameo on *SCTV*, the cult late-night comedy show on NBC. Their sketch, "Mean Joe Greene Playhouse: Big Dude and The Kid" spoofed PBS' *Masterpiece Theater* and the Coke commercial. It was a football player's tour de force. I laughed. I cried. Etc.

And the Steelers were well represented on the big screen, too. Terry Bradshaw, when he wasn't making classic albums like *I'm So Lonesome I Could Cry*, was a fixture in movies with his pal, Burt Reynolds. His ability to take a hit came in handy in *Smokey and The Bandit*, paving the way for a post-football career in shilling products.

And something must have rubbed off from those Bradshaw-Reynolds movie moments. It moved to the small screen, as Burt starred as an ex-pro football star (a Steeler, natch) who returns to his Arkansas home to coach the high school football team that hadn't won a game in two years. Although the wins were few, Reynolds lasted five seasons in the sitcom *Evening Shade.*

High school football had a starring role elsewhere, too. In 1983's *All The Right Moves*, Tom Cruise played a Milltown high school football player who runs afoul of his overbearing coach, played by Craig T. Nelson (was it a coincidence that Nelson would star in the TV sitcom, *Coach*, years later?). Filmed in Johnstown, the movie features a cameo by Don Yanessa, at the time the coach of Aliquippa's high school team.

The area didn't always have to be the star. The Steelers also provided great background footage in two movies. In *Black Sunday*, footage of the Steelers playing the Dallas Cowboys provides the backdrop for a terrorist takeover on Super Bowl Sunday. It's a chilling moment in a pre-9/11 world. For lighter fare, the Steelers were featured in another Super Bowl, this time in a losing effort against the Los Angeles Rams in *Heaven Can Wait.* Warren Beatty's character, plucked from the beyond when he was mistakenly pronounced dead by one of the afterlife's middle managers, comes back to lead the Rams to a championship. Great movie, but we all know it's implausible since God is a Steelers fan. Have a doubt about that? See "Immaculate Reception, The."

12. There are other great pop-culture moments, too.

Who could forget the Charlie Daniels Band picking the Steelers as a symbol of toughness in its song "In America"? Even this southerner appreciated the boys in black and gold. "You just go and lay a hand on a Pittsburgh Steeler fan and I think you'll understand." It just wouldn't have sounded right if he'd substituted Cleveland Browns or Atlanta Falcons now, would it?

There was also a classic poem by Randall Jarrell in the late 1960s that told the sad tale of perhaps the most dominant defensive lineman in the pre-Steel Curtain days (except for Ernie Stautner, of course), Big Daddy Lipscomb. We would have included it in this book, except Jarrell's publishers want an arm and a leg for the rights. Trust us, it's moving.

13. We welcome back our heroes.

October 21, 2002: It was an emotional night at Heinz Field. After 21 years of being away from the city and the team he quarterbacked to four Super Bowls, Terry Bradshaw was back in town again to be honored at half time of a Monday night game against the Indianapolis Colts. Bradshaw had been in self-exile, mired in a feud—created in his own mind—with the city. As the years went by, that gap only seemed to grow bigger, often cited in books he and collaborator David Fisher wrote about his life in and out of football. There were similar stories of a rift with his head coach, Chuck Noll, and a fan base that he thought all but chased him out of town.

The truth of the matter was that Bradshaw was one of the more beloved players in Steelers' history. And the irony is only one quarterback since Bradshaw has truly been accepted; rookie quarterback Ben Roethlisberger had a magical regular season, but Steelers fans had yet to see him lose. And when it comes to winning, Bradshaw is the quarterback against whom all others are compared. Yet somehow, he couldn't see that.

There were hints along the way. Because of his television duties, hosting the NFL pregame show for the Fox Network, Bradshaw was unable to join the Steelers who came back for one last Steel Curtain call at the final game played at Three Rivers Stadium. However, he did send a video greeting, that when played on the Jumbotron, caused the fans to go crazy. Cheers and chants of "Bradshaw! Bradshaw!" filled the stadium. Whatever slights might have been there—real or imagined—were gone, from the fan perspective at least.

Steelers chairman Dan Rooney thinks the media fueled a lot of the controversy. "My relationship with Terry has always been good," he says. "Sometimes the media like to make a story of things like this and just keep adding to it."

Given the Jumbotron reception, Rooney decided it was time to honor Bradshaw for his achievements with the franchise. He called his reluctant ex-quarterback, the prodigal son of four Lombardi Trophies, to talk about it.

Bradshaw had mixed feelings, but at the urging of Rooney agreed to come back to Pittsburgh. It was nerve-wracking, preparing to walk onto Heinz Field. He told local sports talk host Stan Savran: "I was a little nervous that day. . . no, make that a *lot* nervous. I was afraid the fans would boo me terribly after all the things that had been said and written."

Instead, all Bradshaw heard was thunderous applause that made the reaction to his Jumbotron message seem like a mere murmur. For Rooney, it was one of his prized memories. "That was Terry's day and he deserved it," he says. "The roar of the crowd was incredible. It gave you goosebumps."

Perhaps what was even more gratifying to Bradshaw was having his daughters there with him for that special moment. He struggled to hold back tears, especially during a video tribute. During the highlights, his oldest daughter Rachel turned to him and said, "Daddy, you were awesome."

"I know, honey," he replied with a laugh and that trademark Bradshaw grin. And it was like he never left.

14. *Pittsburgh postseason football is filled with unlikely heroes.*

Everyone points to the Immaculate Reception as the greatest moment in postseason football in this area, and rightfully so. This may be a bit sacrilegious, but the IC was a lucky bounce that went into the hands of a player who just happened to be in the right place at the right time. Lucky? Absolutely. But it's one of those things that, if *we're* lucky as fans and viewers, seem to happen in big games. What makes it even better is when the players who make those memorable plays are the last people we would expect to do so. That's entertainment.

Take nothing away from Franco Harris. He had a Hall of Fame career, is among the most celebrated running backs in NFL history. But there's something just a bit cooler about Merril Hoge's run in the 1989 playoffs. Run being the key word. In successive weeks, Hoge rushed for 100 yards on 17 carries against the Houston Oilers in the first round and 120 yards on 16 carries against the Denver Broncos the following week. He was the only back in Steelers history to have two straight 100-yard games in the postseason. A late fumble by Dwight Stone kept Hoge and the Steelers from winning and setting up a chance for Hoge to continue his streak.

And then there's Willie Williams. On a defense that had such names as All-Pros Greg Lloyd, Kevin Greene and Rod Woodson, it was Williams who made one of the biggest plays in Steelers' postseason history. Trailing the Indianapolis Colts 16-13 in the 1995 AFC championship game, the defense was facing a third-down-and-1 play with only 3:57 left. A Colts first down would enable them to run more clock and probably win the game.

Cornerback Williams knifed in from the left side and brought down the Colts running back for no gain. No big deal? Think again. Williams wasn't even supposed to be there. The Steelers had called for a blitz, but there was confusion when safety Myron Bell didn't come up for it. Seeing this, Williams came in from the opposite side of the field—completely ignoring the play that was called—to make the play. Wrong place. Right time again. The Colts were forced to punt to the Steelers and another unlikely hero emerged.

Yancy Thigpen was the Steelers' big-name receiver. But it was Andre Hastings who leaped high for a reception to convert a fourth down. It was Ernie Mills who hauled in the pass to set up the winning score.

The Steelers aren't the only local team with late-game heroics from unlikely players in the postseason. Consider Jan. 1, 1982, and the University of Pittsburgh's come-from-behind victory in the Sugar Bowl. Pitt quarterback Dan Marino found a little used tight end, John Brown, for a 33-yard touchdown strike with just 35 seconds left. Brown wasn't the primary receiver. The play was designed to go to an outside receiver like game-breaker Julius Dawkins. The tight end was there to stretch the defense and allow Dawkins to run free. The decoy was the hero.

In 1989, Pitt scored another win on a late pass play. This time it was an Alex van Pelt toss to Henry Tuten that brought a 31-28 victory over Texas A&M in the John Hancock Bowl. Van Pelt was a record-setting quarterback. But Tuten? Unlikely, but very exciting.

15. The Steelers kept the 49ers from going undefeated.

Each year when the surviving members of the 1972 Miami Dolphins, the only team in NFL history to go through an entire season with a perfect record, get together to toast the fact that the last remaining undefeated team of the current calendar year has fallen, Don Shula's boys should have one in honor of the 1984 Steelers. That Steelers team provided the only blemish for the San Francisco 49ers, which would wind up with an 18-1 record.

The Steelers traveled to Candlestick Park and upset the favored 49ers, 20-17. They won by playing Steelers football: they controlled the clock, thanks to an efficient outing by quarterback Mark Malone (11 of 18 passing for 156 yards), whose 6-yard touchdown pass to John Stallworth turned out to be the game winner, and the rushing of Frank Pollard (105 yards rushing). The Steelers' two touchdown drives consumed more than 14 minutes, leaving 49ers quarterback Joe Montana, the NFL's master of the comeback, unable to rally the team on that day. And so we say, this round is on you, Miami.

16. We also ended the longest winning streak in NFL history—and then kept going.

Coming into Heinz Field for a 2004 Halloween match-up, the New England Patriots had won an NFL-record 21 straight games (both in the regular season and playoffs). But like Charlie Brown trick-or-treating, they got a rock. The Steelers, thanks to great offensive line play, an attacking defense (see above) and some great running by Duce Staley, stoned the Pats 34-20. Ben Roethlisberger came dressed as a franchise quarterback and led a dominant effort. Patriots head coach Bill Belichick summed it up this way: "We got killed. We didn't do much of anything right. They outplayed us. They outcoached us." The Steelers were downright frightening.

So what do you do for an encore? How about going out and beating another previously undefeated team the next week? This time it was the Philadelphia Eagles, sporting a 7-0 record, who came into Heinz Field. The Steelers ran wild again, this time Jerome Bettis doing the damage in a 27-3 rout. It marked the first time in NFL history that a team beat previously undefeated teams in back-to-back games so late in the season.

17. We had the two most successful rookie quarterbacks in NFL history.

Rookie signal callers are supposed to take their lumps, build some character and learn the game the hard way. They're not supposed to win. But the Steelers had two record-setting performances by rookie quarterbacks, Mike Kruczek and Ben Roethlisberger, who set the standard for wins to start a career. Subbing for an injured Terry Bradshaw, Kruczek rolled off six straight wins for the Steelers in 1976. (See Chapter 12, "The Defense Never Rests") Strangely, he never threw a touchdown pass during that winning streak.

But as amazing as that stat is, Big Ben took Pittsburgh and the NFL by storm. In 2004, Roethlisberger won his first 13 starts and provided a preview of what

Steelers fans hope will be a long and glorious career. Roethlisberger had perhaps the best year of any quarterback in NFL history—going 13-0 and posting rookie records for quarterback rating (98.1) and completion percentage (66.4). And he had at least three sandwiches named after him. You never heard of anyone chomping down a Bubby Burger.

18. We made them change the rules.

So physically dominant was Steelers cornerback Mel Blount that the league had to change the rules. Blount manhandled receivers. He punished them and wouldn't allow them to get into their pass routes. If they did get by him he caught up and continued the physical onslaught.

"He was the greatest bump-and-run cover man ever," effuses Dan Rooney.

In an effort to open up the passing game (chicks dig the long ball, you know), the NFL instituted the 5-yard chuck rule that said defenders could only touch receivers within the first 5 yards of the scrimmage line. Anything after that would be a 5-yard penalty and an automatic first down. Okay, we could live with the rule change. But why not call it the 5-yard Mel rule? Still, many in the league referred to it as the "Mel Blount rule."

19. We brought "turf toe" into the sports lexicon.

Oh, the irony of it all: Jack Lambert, perhaps the toughest Steeler of all-time, had his career prematurely ended by what at the time seemed to be a pansy-type injury—turf toe. Who knew anything about this injury in the pre-artificial turf days? Now every football fan worth his or her salt knows that turf toe is a serious thing.

Technically, in doctor speak, turf toe is an injury to the joint capsule and ligaments that connect the big toe to the foot. In its most severe form, it is a complete tear of the capsule and ligament. And never underestimate the importance of the toe—it may be small, but it's a crucial weight-bearing area for your balance and gait.

Part of the problem in Lambert's day was that artificial turf was a fairly new surface. Players were complaining about the grab that it had, and often opted for lighter and lighter shoes as a way to increase speed. However, those lighter shoes offered little in the way of support, resulting in an increase in turf toe injuries.

Now, sports docs have a better strategy for treating turf toe. Icing (not of the cake frosting variety but rather the use of a cold pack), rest and anti-inflammatory medicine will usually do the trick. A hard plate or insert is also placed in the shoe. There are also better surgical procedures to fix the joint capsule. Ultimately, the best treatment is not playing on artificial turf. Although the turf at Three Rivers Stadium brought us many great memories, it also ended the career of one of the most popular Steelers three to four years too early. That's why we should lobby to have this injury renamed "Jack Lambert toe."

20. Joe Greene is a Steeler again.

He is arguably the greatest player in franchise history and he's on the payroll again. (See Chapter 19, "The Ultimate List".) In 2004, 12 years since he last served as a defensive line coach for the team, Greene returned as special assistant/pro and college personnel.

"It's very important to have Joe back," says Steelers' chairman Dan Rooney. "He makes quite an impact and is recognized by the players as one of the greatest defensive players in the history of the game. When he talks, people listen, and he's a great evaluator of what it takes to be successful at this level."

Greene had interviewed for the head coaching position in 1992, a job that eventually went to Bill Cowher. From there, Greene joined the Miami Dolphins as a defensive line coach for four years before accepting a similar position with the Arizona Cardinals for eight years. When a new coaching staff came to Arizona, Greene was in contact with the Steelers and the deal was announced in the 2003 offseason.

Rooney tells this story of Greene's first camp with the team in this new position: "We're in Latrobe doing drills and one of the young rookies plowed right into Joe on the sidelines. Joe apologized to him. But the kid said, 'Listen, you're Joe Greene. It's an honor for me to even be on the same field with you.' I just happened to be there to overhear that."

Rooney places another factor in the decision to put Greene in a position of scouting. "He knows the kind of people we like to have on the team," he says, pausing for a second. "People like Joe Greene."

21. Character counts.

The Steelers have a practice of not putting up with problem

players. Those who aren't good citizens on the field and off don't stay in black-and-gold for long. "Integrity is very important for us," Dan Rooney says. "That's what we built this franchise on."

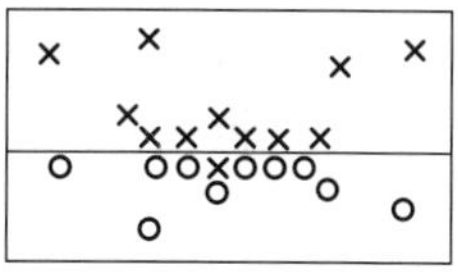

TWO

27 More Reasons We Love Steel City Football

Call it a 2-minute warning, but we thought you needed a little break.

Okay, let's get back in the game.

22. We're a quarterback factory.

Perhaps the greatest legacy Western Pennsylvania football has given to the sport is its uncanny knack to provide outstanding quarterbacks to the National Football League. Hall of Fame names like Unitas, Montana, Marino, Namath, Blanda and Kelly all got their starts on the area high school gridirons, and that's only the beginning. (To see just how many NFL quarterbacks got their start here, check out Chapter 39 "The Quarterback Factory.")

23. We do well with receivers, too.

Pittsburgh football, both at the collegiate and the pro level, has been marked with great wide receivers. Larry Fitzgerald may have been the best receiver in Pitt history. In only two seasons with the Panthers he made his mark, setting an NCAA record by hauling in touchdown receptions in 16 consecutive games. Fitzgerald was a consensus All-American and took home his fair share of hardware: the Biletnikoff Award as the nation's top receiver and the

Walter Camp Player of the Year Award. Following his career at Pitt, Fitzgerald was reunited with Dennis Green, head coach of the Arizona Cardinals. Fitzgerald had served as a ball boy in Minnesota, when Green was the head coach of the Vikings.

Antonio Bryant is Pitt's all-time reception leader in terms of yardage (3,061) and is second in number of catches (173). Like Fitzgerald, who followed him, Bryant won the Biletnikoff Award as a sophomore. (The only other sophomore besides Fitzgerald and Bryant to win the award was Randy Moss). He was also a dangerous return man for the Panthers. Unfortunately, Bryant's college success has yet to translate to the NFL level. He's been a serviceable receiver, but not yet the impact player that the Dallas Cowboys thought they had drafted, prompting the Cowboys to deal him to the hated Cleveland Browns before the trade deadline in the 2004 campaign.

In the glory days at Pitt during the 1970s and '80s, two receivers helped balance the Panther offense: Gordon Jones and Dwight Collins. Jones was a sophomore in the national championship season of 1976 and was the ying to Tony Dorsett's yang. While Dorsett was churning up incredible amounts of yardage on the ground, Gordon was Matt Cavanaugh's deep threat, making the Pitt offense devastating to opposing defenses. Perhaps his most memorable catch came in the Sugar Bowl that season when "Too Much," as Jones was called, took a short pass and turned it into a 59-yard touchdown en route to the Panthers 27-3 destruction of Georgia. Gordon finished his career with 133 catches, the Pitt record at the time, and was named All-American in 1978.

Collins was a very talented sprinter coming out of Beaver Falls and took his magic to Oakland as Danny Marino's deep threat at Pitt in 1980. While the Panthers' national championship hopes were dashed at Florida State that year 36-22, Collins had perhaps the greatest game a Pitt receiver ever had, snagging six passes for an unbelievable 183 yards. He finished his career with 133 catches, tied for the all-time Pitt lead, ironically with Gordon "Too Much" Jones.

On the NFL level, the Steelers are probably best known for their great tandems. In the '70s, Lynn Swann and John Stallworth made opposing defenses pick their poison—particularly when the Steelers opened up the offense at the end of the decade. Swann was the high-flying aerialist, who would make the aesthetically pleasing catches. And no receiver was better in the big games. Swann virtually stole the show in Super Bowl X against the Dallas Cowboys. Stallworth, however, was no slouch either. He was also a big-play receiver and dangerous after he caught the ball. Stallworth retired as the franchise reception leader.

That mark may soon be eclipsed by one of the members of the Steelers' current tandem. Hines Ward is on his way to rewriting the team's record books. He's the only receiver in club history to surpass 1,000 receiving yards three straight seasons. Ward is second only to Stallworth in receptions. Besides grabbing any pass in his direction, he's known for his grit. Ward is a devastating blocker and a key to the success of the Steelers' running game. A former college quarterback, his number is often called for reverses and run/option plays.

His former receiving mate, Plaxico Burress, was often as frustrating as he was talented. Blessed with great height and explosive acceleration, Burris prevented opposing defenses from game-planning Ward out of the game. He also had a couple of 1,000-yard seasons under his belt, but consistency remained a question. Burress may have ultimately showed his value in 2004 by not playing. Forced to miss four and a half games with a hamstring injury, Burress' absence hurt the offense. It meant the Steelers no longer had a true deep threat, and opposing defenses took advantage by double-and even triple covering Ward.

There are other receivers who have left their marks as Steelers. In the early '60s, Buddy Dial was a favorite target of quarterback Bobby Layne. Later in the decade it was Roy Jefferson, who was the team's deep threat, including the 1968 season when he led the league in receiving yards. Ronnie Shanklin was another Steeler league leader in yards per catch for the pre-Super Bowl teams of the early '70s. After the glory years, Louis Lipps was their most dangerous receiver and ranks third in receptions in team history. The 1997 Super Bowl team was paced by another scoring threat, Yancy Thigpen, a two-time Pro Bowl selection.

24. There have been great backfields, too.

It's one thing to have one threat at running back, but what do you do when you have two—or even more—backs who can carry the pigskin? Consider the Pitt Panther's so-called "Dream Backfield" of 1937. There was consensus All-American tailback Marshall Goldberg, the master of the single-wing. Goldberg split time with sophomore Dick Cassiano. Then there was Curly Stebbins, one of the most explosive halfbacks of the era. Quarterback John Chickerneo was more of a runner/blocker, but the threat of his aerials kept defenses honest. These four players received almost as much notoriety as did Notre Dame's Four Horsemen. And add one more—Frank Patrick, the bruising fullback who starred in the Panther's rout of Washington in the Rose Bowl.

The Steelers also had multiple threats, but never as devastating a running game as the 1976 performances of fullback Franco Harris and halfback Rocky Bleier. Harris shook off early injuries to rush for 1,128 yards and a league-leading 14 touchdowns. Bleier was the perfect complement to Harris' power running. Bleier darted for 1,036 yards as the Steelers became only the second team in NFL history to have two backs top the 1,000-yard mark. That ground game enabled the team to overcome a 1-4 start and pull together a string of 10 consecutive victories. (See Chapter 12, "The Defense Never Rests".)

25. We fill the Hall of Fame.

Maybe they didn't build the Professional Football Hall of Fame in Latrobe (okay, we're still sore about that one. See Chapter 3 for why), but there wouldn't be much of a Hall without Pittsburgh's contributions. Pennsylvania is the birthplace of more Hall of Famers than any state—25 to be exact—and the majority of them are from Western Pennsylvania. Add to that the 20 Steelers who are enshrined in Canton, and we should lay claim to our own wing.

We're well represented on the college level, too. Pitt has 22 players and coaches in the College Football Hall of Fame, from Jimbo Covert to Hube Wagner. Carnegie Mellon has three inductees—coach Chuck Klausing, tackle Lloyd "The Plaid Bull" Yoder (he should make the nickname Hall of Fame, too) and quarterback Howard Harpster. Indiana University of Pennsylvania is represented by defensive end Jim Haslett, better known now as the head coach of the New Orleans Saints. Washington & Jefferson can claim two players—offensive lineman Edgar Garbish and tackle Wilbur "Fats" Henry—and three coaches, including John Heisman, the man for whom the trophy is named.

26. Some of the greatest college coaches walked the sidelines in Pittsburgh.

John Heisman is only one of the Hall of Famers who coached in Pittsburgh. A Shakespearean actor in the offseason, Heisman was known for his impassioned half time speeches and would often slip into exaggerated stage English to deliver them to his Washington & Jefferson team (like we could make that up). He was also a leading proponent of the forward pass and lobbied for its inclusion in the rules.

Greasy Neale, another W&J coach, was the first man enshrined in both the College and Pro Football Halls of Fame as a coach. He led W&J to an undefeated season and a Rose Bowl appearance.

Elmer Layden parlayed a successful college playing at Notre Dame to success as a coach at Duquesne University—leading the Dukes to an undefeated season in 1929. Layden would later serve as the first commissioner of the NFL.

Pop Warner's coaching career spanned more than 40 years, and his career victories total was tops until the 1980s. He was the architect of offensive innovations, including the screen pass and the naked reverse. The one-time Pitt coach is credited with the football axiom: "You play the way you practice."

That philosophy was carried by a much more modern coach, Chuck Klausing, who led teams at Indiana University of Pennsylvania and Carnegie Mellon. The former Marine instilled a sense of discipline for his players while posting a career college record of 124-25-2.

27. Since 1969, the Steelers have had only two head coaches.

Sports have entered the realm of instant gratification, particularly for coaches. Win now or you're gone. It's a cliché that "you're hired to be fired." But increasingly it's true. Former Pitt athletic director Steve Pederson, who moved to take the same post at Nebraska, fired Frank Solich *after* the coach posted a winning record. In the professional ranks, there's also a revolving door.

That's what makes the fact that the Steelers have only made two head coaching changes in 35-plus years astounding and unmatched. A lot of that credit needs to go to chairman Dan Rooney, who upon taking control of the day-to-day operations of the franchise established an important mandate: Stability starts at the top.

"Stability is a key factor in the making of a good team," he says. "Just because your coach loses a game or two doesn't mean you run them out. There's no sense in going and retreading by getting coaches that have been other places. Everything doesn't always go right. You learn more about the character of people when there's some adversity."

Adversity was the name of the game before the Steelers hired Chuck Noll, the architect of their most successful run. But it didn't start off as a success. Noll was 1-13 in his first season with the team. Again, many teams would have cut their losses at that point, especially given that it was Noll's first time as a head coach. However, the Steelers believed, and so did their players as Noll took the team to its highest level ever—four Super Bowls in six years.

There were hard times as well. The last 7 of his 23 years with the team were fraught with disappointments and a 52-61 record. Still, it was Noll who triggered the move to step down, according to Rooney, who wanted his coach to stay. Noll was tired, telling the *Pittsburgh Post-Gazette*, "39 years in professional football [he started in the Baltimore Colts organization before coming to Pittsburgh] is a goodly time."

Enter Bill Cowher. Unlike Noll, Cowher enjoyed success immediately. He brought his team to the playoffs his first six years as a head coach—only the second coach to ever do so (Paul Brown was the other). By year three, the Steelers were in the AFC championship game; the following year they were in the Super Bowl.

There were no championships, however. And after missing the playoffs for three consecutive years—1998 to 2000—there were calls on the radio talk shows for Cowher's job.

But Rooney didn't heed those calls. The Steelers were a team that judged a coach on his body of work, not just the latest season. For Cowher, that kind of support allows him to be a more effective coach.

"I have been blessed to be a part of the Steeler organization," he says. "The fact that there have been only two coaches here is a direct reflection of Mr. Rooney. He's a very grounded person. He values loyalty. And that's so important in this business."

Rooney showed that loyalty before the 2004 season, signing Cowher to a contract extension, even though the team had missed the playoffs in 2003 and the coach still had two years remaining on his contract. It raised a few eyebrows.

Rooney explains the team's decision to re-up Cowher: "No. 1, he wins a lot more games than he loses. Certainly, we looked at that first. There's only one thing left for him to do, and that's to win a championship. We want him to do it here." As do we.

28. *We've produced successful professional coaches.*

Sure, Western Pennsylvania is a hotbed of quarterbacks. We all know that. But just as impressive is the number of NFL coaches who hail from the region. The 2004 season started with five of the league's 32 head coaches hailing from the Pittsburgh region.

Obviously, Steelers' coach Bill Cowher is a local boy (graduate of Carlynton High). That's an easy one. Also on the list are Cowher's mentor Marty Schottenheimer, the Cannonsburg native who is head coach of the San Diego Chargers. He held similar posts with the Cleveland Browns and Kansas City Chiefs but continues to be plagued by knocks that he hasn't brought home a championship.

Dave Wannstedt of Brookline was the first NFL coach to step down in 2004, as his Miami Dolphins endured an absolutely terrible season. (However, we were glad to see him sign up to replace Walt Harris as the headman at the University of Pittsburgh at year's end).

Former IUP standout and Avalon High graduate Jim Haslett leads the New Orleans Saints, and, like Wannstedt, he had a rather challenging 2004 season with the club.

Marvin Lewis, from Fort Cherry High School in nearby McDonald, has managed to bring some respectability to the Cincinnati Bengals, once the laughing stock of the NFL. Lewis, the architect of the Baltimore Ravens' Super Bowl-winning defense, has brought that same mentality to this assignment. Somewhere, Paul Brown looks on with approval.

These coaches are a natural extension of some of the other great NFL coaches with local roots. Mike Ditka, who starred at Aliquippa High and then at the University of Pittsburgh, is the only member of the regional fraternity with a Lombardi Trophy. His 1985 Chicago Bears won Super Bowl XX with a physical defense that mirrored the personality of its coach.

Beaver Falls' Joe Walton, now at Robert Morris University (see Chapter 31, "No Ordinary Joe"), never made it to the Super Bowl. His 1986 New York Jets started the season 10-1, before a series of debilitating injuries caused them to falter a bit down the stretch. Still, they came within an overtime field goal of reaching the AFC championship game that season.

Sewickley-born Chuck Knox didn't make it to the Super Bowl, either. However, he did take over three franchises, leading them to playoff appearances—the Los Angeles Rams, the Buffalo Bills and the Seattle Seahawks.

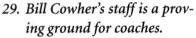

Pitt's Mike Ditka became perhaps the greatest tight end in NFL history with the Chicago Bears. (Courtesy of Graule Studios.)

29. Bill Cowher's staff is a proving ground for coaches.

If there's any doubt that "the Steeler way" isn't the formula for successful football, consider this: six NFL head coaches got their starts as part of Bill Cowher's coaching staff.

Cincinnati's Marvin Lewis was a linebackers' coach for Cowher's first Steelers team. He replaced former Cowher defensive coordinator (now current Steelers' defensive coordinator) Dick Lebeau.

In fact, being one of Cowher's coordinators is a good path to follow for obtaining a head coaching job. It's worked for Jim Haslett (New Orleans Saints) and Dom Capers (Carolina Panthers and Houston Texans).

But lest we typecast Cowher as a defensive guy, his former offensive coordinators have garnered head coaching gigs, too—Chan Gailey (Dallas Cowboys) and Mike Malarkey (Buffalo Bills).

It's no surprise that these coaches have grown under Cowher and the Steelers organization's tutelage, according to chairman Dan Rooney. "We believe in hiring good people and giving them an opportunity to succeed," he says. "If a coach gets an inquiry from another organization, we try to go over it with them. And there have been cases where we've told them that 'this might not be a place that you want to go.' But because we encourage people to grow, there's trust that we can have that kind of conversation.

"And," he continues, "Bill [Cowher] is a good judge of coaching talent."

30. We produce broadcasters.

They say Syracuse University is the breeding ground for sports journalists. Sure, it's given us big names, including Bob Costas, Ted Koppel, Marv Albert, Dick Stockton, Len Berman, Sean McDonough and Mike Tirico. But you can make a serious argument for Pitt when it comes to football analysts. How's this for a list? Dan Marino quarterbacks the pregame show for CBS and is a co-host of HBO's *Inside The NFL*. Teammate Mark May is a staple on ESPN's college football coverage, anchoring highlights and analysis. Tony Siragusa, as might be expected, is in the trenches. He's a sideline reporter for the NFL on Fox. His Panther's teammate, Bill Maas, is also in the booth for Fox's NFL coverage and is part of the network's longest tenured broadcasting team. John Congemi, Marino's understudy, is a color commentator often heard on Big East football broadcasts. The latest entrant to the Pitt broadcasting fraternity is Bill Fralic, who calls Panthers games. He replaced former wide receiver Billy Osborne, who has since moved on to announce for the Comcast Network.

31. We had a Supreme Court justice play football here.

Long before he was making rulings at the nation's highest court, Byron "Whizzer" White ruled the local gridirons. Well, he didn't exactly rule in his lone season with the Steelers in 1938. After a spectacular college career in Colorado, the Steelers signed the future justice as one of a long line of would-be saviors. White wasn't able to duplicate his playmaking skills in the pros. As a Steeler he tossed 2 touchdown passes and was intercepted 18 times, compiling a passing rating of 27.2. He also gained 567 yards on the ground, rushing for an unspectacular 3.7 yards per carry before spending two ordinary seasons with the Detroit Lions. But then again, had his football career gone better, would he have been a Supreme Court justice?

32. The Steelers have great "on-hold" music.

Call the Steelers' administrative offices and when you're on hold, you're treated to some of the great music from NFL Films. And another cool thing: If the switchboard is jammed and you get placed into voice mail, you'll get a greeting from Tyrone Ryan, who refers to himself as "the Steelers' director of first impressions." Every business should copy that for receptionists and those who answer the phone.

33. John Facenda loved us.

The late, great voice of NFL Films—and what we all imagine God would sound like if He talked to us—uttered some of his greatest lines in Steelers highlight films. "There are 27 teams in the National Football League, and then there are the Pittsbuuuuurgh Steelers" is one. Another is his description of middle linebacker Jack Lambert, snarling and missing some of his front teeth: "He looks like Count Dracula in cleats... " Okay, admit it. You can hear the voice, and you have chills.

34. We've had great nicknames.

Besides the aforementioned "Count Dracula in cleats," Pittsburgh football is the repository of great nicknames. There were the ones for size—Eugene "Big Daddy" Lipscomb and Ernie "Fats" Holmes. By the way, if you think Holmes was big when he played, he has ballooned in retirement. We kid, Ernie, we kid. Don't hurt us.

And speaking of hurting, there were the nicknames that seemed to have to do with bad dispositions—"Mean" Joe Greene and Dwight "Mad Dog" White. However, having met both of them, they're among the nicest and most gracious athletes we've encountered.

There are the nicknames that connote titles of leadership: Art Rooney, Sr., was "The Chief." Chuck Noll was "The Emperor." All hail two of the greatest names in Steelers history.

On the international side was John "Frenchy" Fuqua (more on him later). That nickname came at a time when some Americans didn't take offense to all things french. John "Freedom" Fuqua just wouldn't have the same ring to it.

There are those linked with viscous substances: Johnny "Blood" McNally ran through opponents, making them see red. And who could forget Earl "Greasy" Neale? But then again, I'm not sure I'm in favor of nicknames that suggest bad hygiene. It's sort of like being called "Stinky."

In a similar vein, the nickname "Dirt" is oft-used. In the '70s, it was attached to linebacker Dennis Winston and center Dermontti Dawson had it in the '80s and '90s as a sign of their hard-nosed play. Interestingly it was also given to their former groundskeeper Dirt DiNardo. But how much dirt did he actually deal with at Three Rivers Stadium with its artificial turf?

Other nicknames are kinetic: Byron "Whizzer" White. And when 255-pound running back Jerome Bettis runs over you, you feel like you've just been hit by "The Bus." More fun with physics—force equals mass times acceleration.

On the violent side, there have been players who took their monikers from munitions. Jack "Cannonball" Butler exploded on the scene in the defensive backfield of the Steelers of the '50s. Two decades later, rifle-armed quarterback Terry Bradshaw was "The Blonde Bomber." But since he created that one for himself, it never really caught on. It's unlike the cool nicknames that just sound good. Kordell "Slash" Stewart was a triple threat as a runner/receiver/quarterback—or at least two of the three. And then there was Johnny Cloud, known simply as "Mister O." That has some Rat Pack cool to it.

Another cool one that we never understood was L.C. "Hollywood Bags" Greenwood. What the hell does that mean? Who knows, but it's a nickname that you have to love saying.

Some nicknames overtook given names. Award yourself 20 points if you knew that quarterback "Bubby" Brister's real name is Walter. Then take away 19 of those points if you cared.

35. We had a quarterback named "Bubby."

A nickname so memorable it had to be repeated.

36. Carson Long is a great name for a kicker.

It's no nickname. Go figure. What's a better name for a strong-legged kicker? Certainly we couldn't get behind a kicker named Carson Wide or Carson Short. But we didn't have to. The Ashland, Pennsylvania, native was as close to a sure thing as the University of Pittsburgh Panthers had in the '70s. He set an NCAA record for most points by a kicker.

37. Frenchy Fuqua knew how to dress.

Told you we'd get back to him. Cue wah-wah guitar. "Who's the back who won't dress down, when there's tacklers all around? Frenchy. Right on. That dude Frenchy is one bad mutha. . . shut your mouth. I'm just talkin' 'bout Frenchy's threads. We can dig it."

Oh, yes we can. He was the Shaft, the Super Fly of Steelers sartorial splendor. The capes that flowed in the wind, the hats with their wide brims that blotted out the sun, the glass shoes with goldfish swimming in them. Plaxico, if only you had shared a tailor with Frenchy, we, the Steeler Nation, would have finally embraced you. Really, we would have.

38. Bobby Grier broke down barriers.

When Jackie Robinson signed with the Brooklyn Dodgers in 1945, becoming the first African American to play major league baseball since Moses "Fleet" Walker in 1884, it was the beginning of true integration in sports in this country. There were several pioneers that would one by one break down the walls of prejudice on this country's playing fields—and eventually in the world outside sports. At the University of Pittsburgh, that player was Bobby Grier.

Grier was a fullback and defensive back of note coming out of the football factory of Massillon, Ohio. He had his day in the national spotlight in 1956 when he became the first African American to play in the Sugar Bowl. That bowl game was played in New Orleans, deep in the heavily segregated south. The Panthers' opponent that day was the Georgia Tech Yellow Jackets and this game would mark the first time a southern school played a team from the north with a black player on its roster.

So offended was Georgia Governor Marvin Griffin at the prospect of his sons of the Confederacy playing against a black man that he demanded Georgia Tech turn down the bid. Luckily for all involved, Griffin did not get his way and the game went on as scheduled, a 7-6 Pitt loss, coming at the hands of a very controversial pass interference call against none other than Bobby Grier himself. (You can read more about it in Chapter 24, "Bobby Grier, Reluctant Pioneer.")

39. We brought football games to the evening hours.

Imagine life without night sports. Until contests after dark first became en vogue during World War II as a way to boost morale, giving workers a chance to see more games, night contests were about as common as Bubby Brister throwing for 300 yards.

The first night game on the gridiron in Pittsburgh history wasn't of an NFL variety, but a collegiate match-up between Duquesne University and Geneva College. The brainchild of Dukes' graduate manager John Holohan, both schools took the field under the floodlights at Forbes Field on November 2, 1929, for the historic tilt. While the lights made the contest historic, the game was not, as 27,000 fans were treated to a 27-7 Duquesne rout.

40. There are other football firsts—many taken for granted—that started here.

Oh the things that make football enjoyable, like being able to figure out who made the big play out there. Credit the 1908 University of Pittsburgh Panthers for being the first college team to wear numbers, thus also giving birth to the spotter—the guy in the press box who tells the announcers who the ball carrier was and who made the tackle.

Speaking of announcers, there's another first in Pittsburgh: The debut of college football on the radio waves. KDKA broadcast Pitt's 21-14 win over West Virginia on October 8, 1921. It was the second pioneering sports moment by the station in three months. In August, KDKA offered the first broadcast of a major league baseball game, a contest between the Pirates and Phillies. But that's baseball, and a different book.

Back to the gridiron, Elmer Layden was quite the innovator. He came up with the hand signals that officials would use to signal penalties that debuted in November 1928 when his Duquesne Dukes took on Thiel at Pitt Stadium. League merchandising folks have another reason to thank Layden, who would go on to be the first commissioner of the NFL. Layden introduced the concept of having his team wear different colored jerseys for home and away games while at Duquesne.

And on the sidelines—and this is a shocker—the Steelers were the first NFL team to have cheerleaders. Don't believe us? See "Rah Raw," Chapter 7.

41. The Steelers and Monday Night Football: *A grand marriage.*

In terms of broadcasting, it doesn't get much better than *Monday Night Football*—an event that has changed the viewing habits of Americans since ABC debuted it in 1970. And the

Steelers have played pretty well on Monday nights, posting a 31-20 record. Coach Cowher should lobby for the team to schedule all its games on Mondays. Under him, the Steelers are 16-6.

"Monday nights are a great showcase," he says. "The rest of the league is tuning in to see that game." And so are Pittsburghers. Whenever the Steelers are on *MNF*, the broadcast gets some of its best market penetration of all NFL cities.

And Steeler fans have been treated to some great performances: In their first appearance in the series' inaugural year, the Steelers opened their rivalry with the Cincinnati Bengals with a 21-10 win over their new AFC Central foes. It was a game memorable only by the fact that rookie quarterback Terry Bradshaw was a meager 4 for 12 as the Steelers were down 10-7 going into the final frame. In came Terry Hanratty, who tossed a 72-yard TD pass to Dennis Hughes and then led Pittsburgh on a 59-yard drive, culminating with a 2-yard blast by the memorable Warren Bankston. You could tell it was the first year of *MNF*. Now the network showcases match-ups between strong teams—well, at least that's the goal on paper. The 1970 Steelers finished the season 5-9, while the Bengals were 8-6. Still it was a showcase of the newly created AFC.

There were more great division moments against the Houston Oilers. In 1978 and '79, the Steelers wound up on the short end of two memorable games. The Oilers rode punishing running back Earl Campbell to two close victories over the Steelers in the Astrodome, 24-17 and 20-17. The 1979 contest was, at the time, the second most watched game in *MNF* history (it's now sixth). Two years later, the teams met again, this time the Steelers winning 26-13.

Some of Cowher's most impressive victories have come on Monday nights. And defense keyed the wins. In 1992, his first year, the Steelers crushed the Bengals 20-0. The next year, the victims were the Buffalo Bills, 23-0, in a game dominated by defensive back Rod Woodson.

And one of the more rollicking nights had the Steelers holding off the Green Bay Packers, 27-20. The Packers' Reggie White, the NFL's all-time sack leader, was held in check by Steelers' oft-forgotten Jamain Stephens (unfortunately the only guy Stephens would ever neutralize) while the rejuvenated Steel Curtain kept future Hall of Famer Brett Favre under control before what may have been the loudest Monday night crowd in the history of Three Rivers Stadium.

42. The Steelers on Thanksgiving: Pass the turkey.

Some fans might see it as a downside. The Steelers are awful when playing on Thanksgiving Day. There was the 45-3 drubbing at the hands of the Detroit Lions in 1983. In '91, Chuck Noll's final season as head coach, the Dallas Cowboys did the stuffing, beating the Steelers 21-10 in a game that wasn't as close as the score suggests. And then there was the coin-flip debacle of '98: To start overtime, the Steelers' Jerome Bettis called "tails" but the ref heard "heads." Detroit won the toss and the game after kicking a field goal on their first and only possession in overtime for a 19-16 win.

What upside could there be in this? The Steelers' performance frees you up to concentrate on other matters—specifically turkey, mashed potatoes, gravy and cranberry sauce.

43. The '70s marked a decade of unprecedented excellence in pro football.

Oh, those pre-parity days of the NFL. How we miss our dynasties, particularly the Steelers of the '70s. Eight straight playoff appearances. Four Super Bowl victories in six years. These are unsurpassed numbers by an unsurpassed team (but keep your eye on the current New England Patriots).

"When you talk about sustained excellence," says Steelers' chairman Dan Rooney. "there just isn't any comparison."

44. For more sustained excellence, look to CMU.

We came across this one while doing our research: Carnegie Mellon University put together a string of 27 consecutive winning seasons, from 1975-2001 (30 non-losing seasons as the Tartans were 5-5 in 2002). We all knew of the school's excellence in the classroom, often appearing in the rankings of the top 10 colleges academically. But the Tartans' on-field success flew under the radar a bit.

45. This area has its share of football championships.

Besides the Steelers' four Super Bowl victories and one AFC crown, we have a lot to celebrate. Pitt has claimed nine Division I NCAA football championships (1915, 1916, 1918, 1929, 1931, 1934, 1936, 1937 and 1976). That total ranks sixth in NCAA history, trailing only Notre Dame, Yale, Princeton, the

University of Southern California and Alabama.

More recently, small college powerhouses Duquesne University and Robert Morris University have flexed their muscles, pulling in three Division I-AA Mid Major championships between them. (For more area small colleges and their championship seasons, see Section IV of this book, "On Campus: Western Pennsylvania's Small College and High School Heroes.")

In high school, Gateway reached the lofty heights of a No.3 national ranking in the USA Today high school poll in 1986 after defeating top ranked North Hills 7-6 in the Quad A WPIAL championship tilt. It was the same North Hills club that won the national championship a year later in 1987. In a USA Today poll of the top 25 high school football programs in the country between 1982-2003, North Hills was ranked 18th.

46. There's a hidden giant at Greensburg-Salem.

While Westmoreland County football may not have the pedigree of other Western Pennsylvania counties, it does boast two of three schools in the WPIAL that have achieved the rarified air of 600 wins. New Castle in Lawrence County leads the way with 656 wins. The most recent addition is Westmoreland's Jeannette, joining the 600-club in 2004.

And then there's Greensburg Salem High. Despite the fact the Lions have not won any WPIAL titles in 77 years, they stand second all time in victories with 631 (a 639-304-39 record to be exact) through the 2004 campaign—a Red Sox of the Western Pennsylvania high school world if you will. Their futility has come into play recently, even with the Red Sox finally ending their curse after 86 fruitless seasons, with the Lions going to the WPIAL playoffs four years in a row, each time being ousted in the first round.

The beginnings of their legendary, yet heartbreaking, program came over 100 years ago in the 19th century. Football in the 1890s was alive and vibrant in Westmoreland County with Greensburg and Latrobe often battling for the county championship among club teams, the forefathers to the current day NFL. In 1894, Greensburg High School decided to get into the act and took up the sport, quickly becoming one of the strongest high school teams in the Western Pennsylvania area.

According to the foremost Westmoreland football historian Bob Van Atta, the Lions never won any WPIAL championships during their successful run because the school did not have the "prestige" to be invited to the playoffs. (Co-author Fletcher says, "Oh, boo-hoo".) For the record, Fletcher's alma mater Blackhawk High School in Beaver County not only has won four WPIAL crowns since the school district began in 1974, but put a beating on the Lions in the first round of the 2004 AAA playoffs, 38-9, at Offutt Field. However, Greensburg rose up in 1927 to capture its one and only WPIAL crown.

Despite the fact they have not won another title, Salem has nonetheless continued its successful program over the years, churning out several good players such as Ed Bortz, who played in the early 1910s, amassing several school records and finishing as perhaps the greatest star in school history; Bob Mitinger, who went to Penn State and then on to the San Diego Chargers; Wayne Wolfe, a Wake Forest man before taking his game to the old AFL and the New York Titans; John Andress, the starting quarterback of the 1975 Penn State Sugar Bowl squad; and more recently Adam Bostick, quarterback of the Lions in the late 1990s who took them to the AAAA quarterfinals, where they were upended by none other than the school that sits above them in the all-time WPIAL standings, New Castle.

Bostick went on to carve out his career in baseball rather than football. The lefty is currently in the Oakland A's organization with Greensboro of the South Atlantic League. Adam, picked in the sixth round of the 2001 draft, led the league in strikeouts with 163 and finished second in all of the minor leagues with 12.87 Ks per nine innings.

Such would be the luck of a high school program more comparable to the Red Sox and Cubs (much success; few titles), turning out football players who succeed on the diamond rather than the gridiron.

47. And then there's Offutt Field.

It is the Fenway Park of high school football in Western Pennsylvania, a classic old facility that has not been home to a champion since phones and electricity were new and exciting developments (Greensburg's last football title was in 1927, only nine years after the Red Sox won their last). Except for a few years in the early 1900s, when the city was debating whether or not to turn the stadium into a racing venue, the Greensburg-Salem Lions have called Offutt Field home.

Originally named Athletic Field, the facility was also home to the classic Greensburg club football teams at the turn of the 20th century that helped usher in the new national pastime, professional football.

As the story goes, Lemuel Offutt, a local physician, owned the land where the field was located; when he passed away, the field was donated to the community and Athletic Field was renamed Offutt Field.

Located in the heart of downtown Greensburg, Offutt Field, one of the oldest if not the oldest facility of any stadium in Western Pennsylvania, was built in the 1890s and not only played home to several high school teams that included Greensburg-Salem and Greensburg Central Catholic (the official alma mater of *Gridirons*' co-author Dave "I Bleed Maroon and White" Finoli, until their own on campus facility was built in the 1990s), but of all things, Greensburg's lone professional baseball team.

From 1934 to 1939, Offutt Field played host to the Greensburg franchise, (changing names no less than four times in their six-year existence, Trojans to Red Wings to Green Sox and finally Senators) in the old Pennsylvania State Association, a D league, which is akin to A ball today. They not only won the league championship in 1934, but as a member of the St. Louis Cardinals farm system, hosted the famed Gashouse Gang at the classic facility in an exhibition game.

Although pro baseball left Greensburg in 1939, Greensburg High, the precursor to Greensburg Salem, played baseball there until the 1950s. For those of you with Greensburg knowledge, home plate was in front of the Sunset Cafe (a place that's still in existence today and serves Finoli's favorite pizza) and the famed park included a classic old-time covered grandstand and a wall. It also had a strangely shaped track that, according to Westmoreland County Historical Society Executive Director James Steeley, was neither oval or round, but asymmetrical. The track, covered grandstand and wall were replaced in the 1970s as the field took the football-only form that it is currently configured in today.

Offutt Field used to have another distinguishing feature, a creek running along the sideline. Jack's Run Creek ran parallel to the home sideline (underneath where the press box sits today) and often times people would joke about a player being driven into the creek by a tackler. Strangely enough the water also came into play when the field was set up for baseball running along the third base line.

While the new modern facilities are in vogue today, even in the high school world (i.e. the meccas recently built at Gateway and Norwin), Offutt Field endures, bringing fans a glimpse of the past when Greensburg was one of the epicenters of the football world.

48. *Oh, and by the way, the first pro football game was played at Offutt Field.*

At least that's what we're claiming. Follow our logic here: In the 1890s Greensburg and Latrobe were at the forefront of the club football world. Despite admissions to the contrary, the club football movement was secretly changing. So-called amateur players were actually beginning to be paid for their services.

It was in 1897 that the two Westmoreland County combatants both claimed (although it was years later that they would stake their declaration) to be the first to field all-professional clubs for an entire season.

According to the book *Pro Football: From AAA to '03*, Greensburg's claim is shaky. It questions Greensburg's pro legitimacy because there were 27 players on their roster at the time—an incredible amount for the era and a rather expensive proposition. However, historians figure it was likely they had 11 paid professionals on the field at one time, but it was unlikely that they paid all 27 players.

Latrobe's claim to have the first, fully paid team, on the other hand, was not questioned. Van Atta, the leading authority on Westmoreland County football, asserts that Latrobe's roster was completely made of up professionals who played together for an entire season.

The teams were bitter rivals and when they met for the first time of the season on November 20th, 1897, the championship of Western Pennsylvania was on the line. It would be safe to assume that each club would play their best players for this titanic match-up, meaning there was a good chance Greensburg was fielding *all* professionals. More than 5,000 rabid fans showed up at Athletic Field (aka Offutt Field) to see Latrobe score 12 second half points en route to a 12-6 victory. The large throng saw 22 players battling to the bitter end, 22 players who just might have been the first collection of professional players ever to grace the gridiron at one time.

SECTION II

Black and Gold Legends

(and purple and orange ones, too)

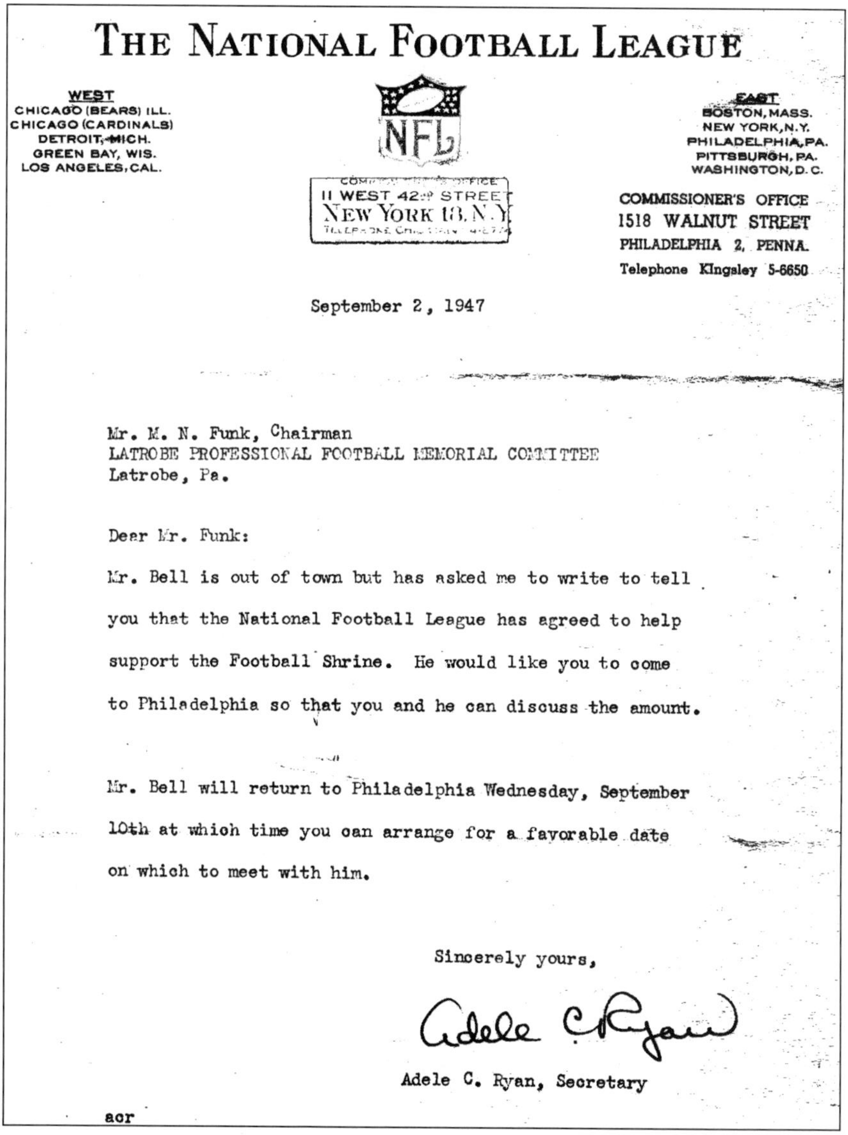

THE NATIONAL FOOTBALL LEAGUE

WEST
CHICAGO (BEARS) ILL.
CHICAGO (CARDINALS)
DETROIT, MICH.
GREEN BAY, WIS.
LOS ANGELES, CAL.

NFL

COMMISSIONER'S OFFICE
11 WEST 42ND STREET
NEW YORK 18, N.Y.

EAST
BOSTON, MASS.
NEW YORK, N.Y.
PHILADELPHIA, PA.
PITTSBURGH, PA.
WASHINGTON, D.C.

COMMISSIONER'S OFFICE
1518 WALNUT STREET
PHILADELPHIA 2, PENNA.
Telephone Kingsley 5-6650

September 2, 1947

Mr. M. N. Funk, Chairman
LATROBE PROFESSIONAL FOOTBALL MEMORIAL COMMITTEE
Latrobe, Pa.

Dear Mr. Funk:

Mr. Bell is out of town but has asked me to write to tell you that the National Football League has agreed to help support the Football Shrine. He would like you to come to Philadelphia so that you and he can discuss the amount.

Mr. Bell will return to Philadelphia Wednesday, September 10th at which time you can arrange for a favorable date on which to meet with him.

Sincerely yours,

Adele C. Ryan

Adele C. Ryan, Secretary

acr

This letter shows that the National Football League did in fact originally commit money to Latrobe's Hall of Fame effort. Not having the finances that it has today, the NFL never came through with its support. (Courtesy of the Latrobe Historical Society.)

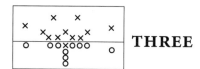

THREE

Latrobe's Troubled Place in Pro Football History

A Tale of What Could Have Been

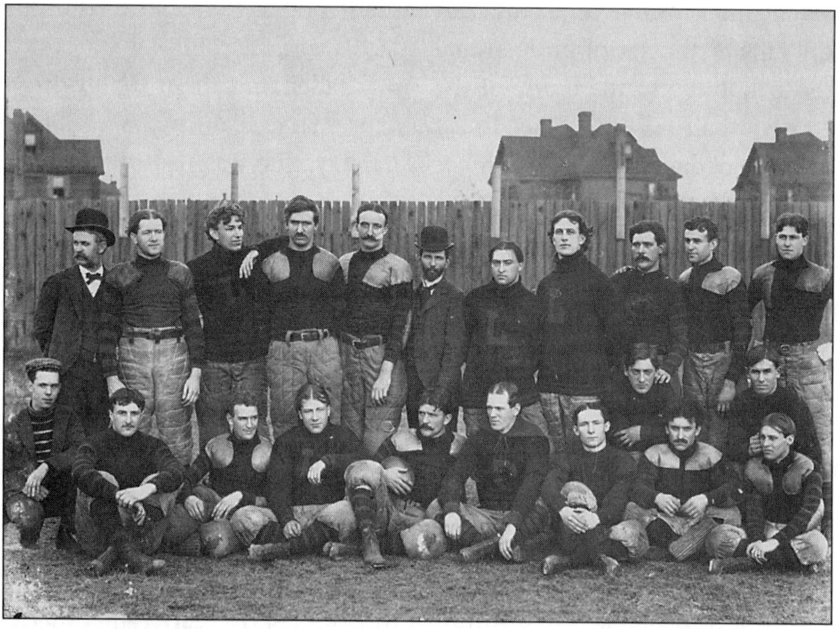

The 1897 Latrobe football club is considered to be the first all professional team in the history of the sport. (Courtesy of the Latrobe Historical Society.)

Imagine if you will, a summer drive down route 30 through the Laurel Mountains in scenic Westmoreland County on a hot, sweltering July day. The temperature hovers around 90 with a humidity that rivals the swamplands in Florida. Hopefully the air-conditioning in the car works, as the traffic approaching the Arnold Palmer Regional Airport will backup well over a mile. As you finally make the left turn at the light, you enter the small hamlet of Latrobe, Pennsylvania, and the anticipation is now at a fever pitch. You're entering not only the birthplace of professional football, but also the home of the Pro Football Hall of Fame. Today is a special day as the first member of the Steelers is about to be inducted into the hallowed halls, Mel Blount. There is an enormous sea of black and gold in the crowd as this quaint town is nestled only 45 minutes from the Steel City.

Overhead, one captures the wonderful scent of beer hovering in the air from Latrobe's other jewel, the Rolling Rock brewery. Blount enters the podium, pointing over the hill as he recounts those days in the boot camp they call Steeler training camp that annually occurs in the local place of higher education, Saint Vincent College. The day is perfect, one that you will excitedly anticipate every year, as a slew of Steelers are about to be inducted into Pro Football's mecca.

Yes, the above story sounds like a wonderful fantasy, but believe it or not it was a fantasy that came ever so close to coming true; that is until everything came crashing down as Latrobe not only lost the bid for the Pro Football Hall of Fame, but unfortunately its proud identity as the birthplace of professional football.

As the story goes, nearby Greensburg had fielded one of the strongest football teams in the 1890s, and Latrobe was interested in challenging them for gridiron supremacy. Team manager David J. Berry, who was also editor of the local paper, the *Latrobe Clipper*, had what he felt was an equally strong squad that began the 1895 campaign against Jeannette. Unfortunately, they were going to be forced to play the contest without their starting quarterback, Eddie Blair, who was already committed that day to playing for Greensburg in baseball.

Desperate for someone to fill the bill, Berry had remembered seeing a 16-year-old QB who played for a high school in Indiana, PA, and contacted him, offering to bring the youngster to Latrobe and pay for his expenses, which

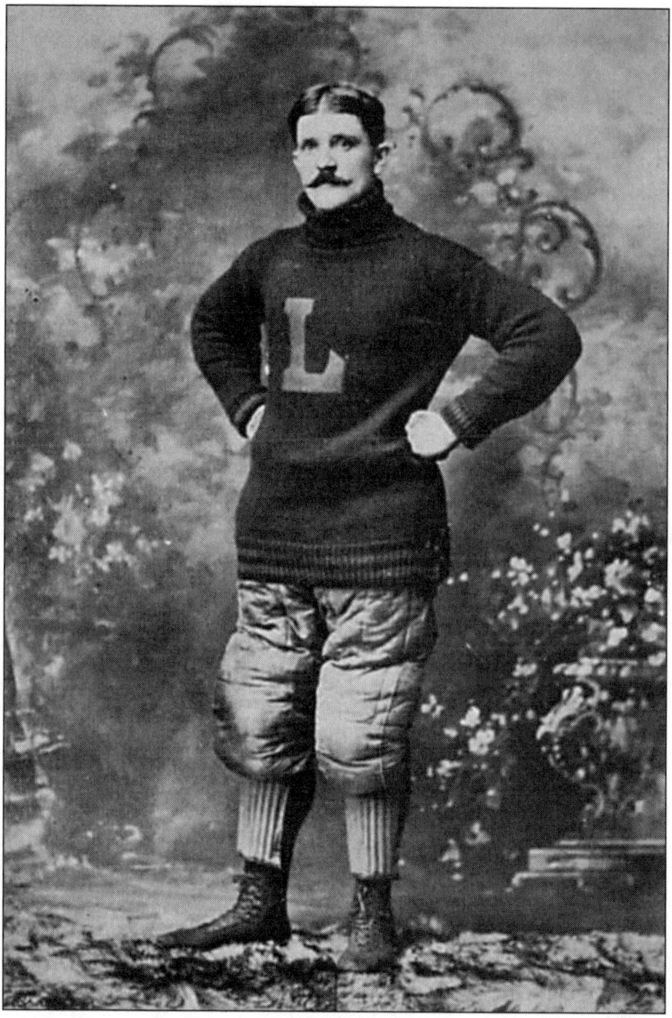

Harry Ryan was the heart and soul of the historic Latrobe football teams in the late 19th century.(Courtesy of the Latrobe Historical Society.)

were called "cakes" at the time. The quarterback's name was John Brallier, and the high school star declined Berry's offer. With time running short, the head of the Latrobe club decided to sweeten the offer by adding $10 on top of the expenses, trying to coerce Brailler into joining his club for "$10 and cakes." Ten dollars in those days was a generous offer, one that the young signal caller could not pass up (he eventually spent his new found "wealth" on a pair of pants to go to college).

Brallier joined the club as they entered their first contest clad in orange and maroon uniforms, and he proved to be well worth the money. He directed Latrobe to their first scoring drive after a Jeannette fumble and kicked the extra point, giving his club a 6-0 lead (TDs were 4 points at that time and the extra point was actually good for two). The Indiana native once again brought his team down the field to increase the advantage to 12-0, which ended up being the final score of the game. Berry's $10 investment proved to be well worth it, as the world of professional football seemed to be born on that date, September 3rd, 1895, when Brallier was given his bounty.

Fifty years after this momentous occasion, the citizens of Latrobe were so proud of their place in pro football history that they set out, with the help of then Pennsylvania Governor David Lawrence, to secure not only the official title of "The Birthplace of Professional Football," but to also be the permanent home of the Pro Football Hall of Fame.

With baseball opening the doors to its mecca only eight years earlier, in 1939, the time seemed right for the powers that be to do the same in football. The problem was there lacked a single supreme governing body over the sport to make that decision; there were two organizations battling for pro football supremacy: the NFL and the upstart All American Football Conference (AAFC).

The AAFC had been a financial thorn in the side of the more established National Football League, causing salaries to rise in a bidding war for players' services. The new association also had some powerful teams, including the Cleveland Browns, San Francisco 49ers and the Baltimore Colts, while also showing its financial power with several large stadiums, such as Cleveland's Municipal Stadium, which helped the Browns produce larger gate receipts than any NFL team had garnered in its history.

Looking for a way to distance itself from its new rival, the NFL sought ways to help establish its supremacy as the true power of professional football, and decided to use the city of Latrobe in its quest. Being the birthplace of a sport carried a lot more weight in the '40s than it does today, so the NFL made a deal with the fine citizens of Latrobe, giving them the official designation as the "Birthplace of Professional Football" as well as the bid for the sport's Hall of Fame. NFL Commissioner Bert Bell told the Latrobe committee that he would try and get money from the league to help build a facility that would include a new stadium with the Hall of Fame located underneath, as well as areas for other sports. In exchange for the NFL's magnanimous gesture, Latrobe agreed to recognize the National Football League and its teams as the only official professional league.

It was a controversial move that angered some, including the renowned scribe Shirley Povich. In his *Washington Post* column on July 24, 1947, Povich exclaimed that the "'holier than thou' pose . . . that the NFL was looking for, of which this move was it, . . . won't work. The All America [AAFC] can't miss winning recognition as a major league as fully important as the NFL." The legendary writer went on to point out the success of the Browns, both financially and on the field in 1946.

Povich's stand proved both incorrect and on the money at the same time. While the AAFC was not superior and did fold, despite the fact the Browns, 49ers and Colts were absorbed into the NFL, the "holier than thou" pose the NFL made in giving the mecca to Latrobe did not work, although it wasn't for the reasons stated in the column.

Bert Bell's promise of financial help for a facility never came to fruition, so it fell to the city to raise all the money to build the Hall of Fame. The Latrobe committee once traveled to Cleveland in hopes of getting the NFL to give them funds to support the project.

Carl Mattioli is the Latrobe Historical Society, preserving the proud tradition for this historic city. (Courtesy of Tom Aikens.)

The NFL was not the financial power it is today and they contributed nothing to the cause. According to E.K. Myers, a local Latrobe writer who was a member of the city's committee that was in charge of bringing the Hall to the Westmoreland county city, "We were members of the local Jaycees and it was a Jaycee project. At the time, the commission had an ulterior motive, to build a community center of which the Hall of Fame would be a part of it. Although we didn't receive any money from Latrobe Steel, we did get a letter from the company's president, Marcus W. Saxman, supporting the project. We went to Cleveland to get some funds from the league, and ended up at the Browns Stadium where we met with Paul Brown. He was very cordial, but he said 'You boys are too late,' as he had just got a check for $200,000 from the Timken Company to locate the building in Canton. Mr. Brown told us that if we could match that money 'We'd talk then,' but we couldn't match it."

The project seemed to be going nowhere, but it wasn't necessarily because Latrobe couldn't raise the money. According to the head of the Latrobe Historical Society, Carl Mattioli, "the forefathers of Latrobe sat on their rear ends too long. They kept asking where are we going to get the money? The money would have been there, if somebody had only followed through. Nobody followed through though."

Pete Fierle, the information services manager of the Hall of Fame, backs up this notion, stating that, "The Latrobe effort never materialized. They fell flat on their face and when it was resurrected 10 years later, Canton had what they needed to secure the bid."

Myers gave some other potential reasons for the loss of the Pro Football Hall of Fame. He said that while some felt Art Rooney could have pushed harder, others felt the blame might lie with the Latrobe Foundation. "Some members of the Latrobe Foundation thought it would make Latrobe too much of a tourist town and that it would upset the industrial base."

With nothing being accomplished over the next decade, the NFL opened bids once again for the Hall, with Latrobe, Canton, Detroit and Pittsburgh being originally considered. Through this entire process Canton seemed to have not only the most momentum, but also, more importantly, the money.

For the Ohio community, which was home to the National Football League when it was formed there in 1920, it began with an article in the local paper, the *Canton Repository*. The story was a call for the museum to be built in Canton, and it seemed to spur one of the business leaders in the community to come into action. H.H. Timken Jr., chairman of the Timken Roller Bearing Co., called the paper pledging support for the Hall, $250,000 to be exact. While not necessarily a football fan, Timken properly projected that the Hall could change the perception of Canton as an area more known for crime than anything else.

A quarter of a million dollars was a lot for the time, but not enough to fund the project. A community fundraising effort was put in place, netting $378,026—$2 million in today's standards—and that seemed to be enough to get the league to give them the bid.

While Canton was working hard, Latrobe was still stuck in neutral. Community leaders there seemingly could get nothing organized. "Latrobe didn't come up with anything," hall architect Robert Forsythe acknowledged.

The league held its meetings on April 27, 1961, in San Francisco to decide the matter, with Pittsburgh Steelers boss Art Rooney taking the side of the small Western Pennsylvania community. He wasn't the only one, though. The great *New York Times* columnist Arthur Dailey wrote a piece right before the vote proclaiming Latrobe to be the only rightful place to build the sports mecca. By this time Pittsburgh was no longer being considered, so the choices

Art Rooney, Sr., sits down with several Latrobe civic leaders to discuss bringing the Pro Football Hall of Fame to their city. (Courtesy of the Latrobe Historical Society.)

were down to Detroit, Canton and Latrobe. Dailey pointed out that while "The credentials of the Detroit site are so hazy that they are nonexistent" and that "Canton had more valid credentials" than the Motor City, "Latrobe is off in a class by itself." He went on to point out Latrobe's place in pro football history, telling the story of Dr. Brailler. At the end, Dailey made his plea, exclaiming, "As the historical site of the first pro game, Latrobe deserves that Hall of Fame. Anything else would be a rank injustice."

In the end, preparation and money took precedence over birthplace, and Canton was awarded the Hall of Fame by a vote of 13-1, with Rooney as the lone dissenter. He eventually changed his vote to make it unanimous, but bottom line, the mecca of pro football would now be housed in Canton, Ohio.

"We never got to the point to try and raise money, although we had enough to commission an architect," Myers confided. "Timken pulled the rug out from underneath us."

"Latrobe talked, dreamed and bragged while Canton came up with the land," says Bob Carroll, head of the Professional Football Research Association. "Placing the Pro Football Hall of Fame really makes more sense putting it there than Latrobe or even Pittsburgh, because that's where the sport really took its first steps towards becoming a major sport when the Canton Bulldogs signed Jim Thorpe in 1915."

Well if they couldn't have the Hall of Fame, at least they knew they were the birthplace of professional football. Or were they? As legendary radio guru Paul Harvey often said, "and now for the rest of the story."

Western Pennsylvania was the hotbed of the football world back in the last decade of the 19th century. Two of the top teams in the area were located in the heart of the Steel City, the Pittsburgh Athletic Club and the Allegheny Athletic Association. In the 1892 campaign, both clubs had battled to a 6-6 tie on Columbus Day and had a huge rematch scheduled for November 12.

The PAC and the AAA were the Steelers and the Browns of their time, and this contest would mean everything. So much so that the managers of both teams went on an excursion throughout the East and Midwest trying to recruit the players that could bring them not only the local bragging rights, but also the fruits of winning the side bets that were wagered by both teams at the time. The objects of their affections were three players from the Chicago Athletic Association: Knowton Ames, Ben Donnelly, and the best of the trio, William "Pudge" Heffelfinger. Heffelfinger was a three time All-American guard at Yale and an innovator to boot. While the philosophy of the day for an offensive guard was to simply block the man in front of him, Heffelfinger pulled off the line to lead the way for his running back, known simply as "the pulling guard," something that is a staple in today's game.

After leaving Yale, the All-American took a job on the railroad. When the CAA offered to pay his expenses to play for them, Heffelfinger left his job to continue his career on the gridiron. Everything was going fine until Chicago took to the road, defeating Cleveland 35-0, before traveling to New York to take on a team called the Crescents. Before the game was played, New York complained to the officials about the play of Donnelly. "Sport", as he was known, was famous for his cheap play, often hitting an opponent, then telling refs he was being hit, and getting his opponent tossed from the contest after he would inevitably retaliate.

Chicago decided to give in to the Crescents' demands, not only irritating Donnelly, but his teammates Ames and Heffelfinger as well. All three decided to quit the club, which was good news to the two Pittsburgh clubs who were hoping to retain their services. Sometimes when recruiting, it's important to be in the right place at the right time.

George Barbour, the manager of the PAC, had traveled to Chicago, hoping to meet the players and coerce Pudge and Ames into coming back to the Steel City with them. Unfortunately the two did not change their minds and stayed in the Big Apple, intent on going back to Princeton and Yale, their respective alma maters, to coach. By the luck of the draw, the leaders of the AAA just happened to be in New York at the time. While Barbour returned home empty handed, apparently the men of the Allegheny Athletic Club were a little more fortunate. Pudge had been given $500 by the AAA after turning down the original offer of $250, feeling that it wasn't worth that to risk his amateur status. Donnelly got double the expenses while Ames declined the offer, not wanting to put his amateur standing in jeopardy for any price.

The powers that be kept their mouths quiet, probably in hopes of getting better odds on the game. A crowd of 3,000 rabid fans, kept down because of the snow that fell that day, were on hand at Recreation Park and the new Allegheny members, Heffelfinger, Donnelly and Ed Malley (who had played for the Detroit AC and was also given double expenses) were immediately recognized by the PAC. The sight of the so-called ringers infuriated their rivals to the point that they walked off the field, intent on forfeiting the game.

Management from both sides argued back and forth, with the members of the AAA threatening to prove that the PAC was after them, too. Although all were angry, they didn't want the contest to end in a forfeit, so eventually they agreed to call off all bets and play an exhibition game instead. After almost an hour of quarrelling, the game finally began at 3:55 pm. For Allegheny, their recruiting paid off as their new star from Yale picked up a fumble in the first half and rambled 35 yards for the game's only score in a 4-0 victory.

The controversy went on afterward, as claims that AAA had paid the three new members were rampant throughout the crowd. Remember, at the time, professionalism was a dirty word and the sporting community looked on any player that had taken money very unfavorably. Some reports even came out that some members of the Allegheny club had quit so they wouldn't have to play with professionals.

So the deed was done—a player had been paid three years before and $490 more than Brallier had been given by Latrobe. If this did happen, the questions that beg to be answered are: why did the Latrobe QB became known as the first pro player and how did Latrobe get the title of the birthplace of pro football?

Well the answer was simply given two paragraphs earlier: Professionalism in sports was one of the worst things a sportsman could be accused of. Heffelfinger, who was eventually elected to the College Football Hall of Fame, never admitted until the day he died that he had been paid anything. Brallier, who had become a successful Latrobe dentist, proudly admitted he had been paid, the only one from that era ever to make that admission. Because of this, he was recognized as the first pro football player, a distinction that got him a lifetime pass to any NFL game in honor of his accomplishment.

Brallier died in 1960 thinking he was the first professional player, a fact that was disproved when the holy grail of professional football, the AAA expense sheet from the 1892 contest, was found, showing that Heffelfinger was paid $500 for the game and thus was given the moniker of the first paid professional player. Ironically, it was an honor he never wanted.

So, John Brallier must have been the second paid player. Not so fast, though, as the next entry in the expense book, this one from the following game on November 19th, showed Donnelly was paid $250 a game against Washington & Jefferson College. In fact, as further research was done, it was found that Peter Wright was given $50 in 1893 for AAA as was James Van Cleve. Oliver Rafferty was given a full season contract of $50 per game in 1893 while Greensburg gave Lawson Fiscus one the next year at $20 per game. All of the sudden, Brallier became then only the seventh known professional football player, and at a $10 salary, seemed very much underpaid compared to the previous six players.

Unfortunately, this left Latrobe not only without the Pro Football Hall of Fame, but also without its distinction as the birthplace of professional football, a label that now belongs with the city of Pittsburgh. How the mighty had fallen. Would it now be known as the "home of the first man who ever openly admitted to be paid to play the game of football?" Probably not.

This is a city that takes pride in its history and legends and would not take this loss lightly. After all, it fights tooth and nail with Wilmington, Ohio, over which town is "the birthplace of the banana split," to which Mattioli bites back, sharply rebuffing yet another Ohio town's challenge by simply stating "We were the originators of the banana split." Case closed! As far as their now questionable football history, local citizen Tony Novak threatened to sue the NFL in the late '90s, disputing its claim that Heffelfinger was the first pro in an attempt to return their once-proud moniker back to Latrobe. Unfortunately for Novak and the citizens of the Westmoreland county community, a trip to the Hall of Fame in 1999 to review the facts of the situation proved beyond the shadow of a doubt that Pudge Heffelfinger was in fact the first professional football player. Devastated as they were, Latrobe at least can have the birthplace claim substantiated somewhat by the fact that 1897 Latrobe club is still considered the first all-professional team for an entire season.

It may not be everything they used to have, but don't feel badly for them. Latrobe is still the birthplace of Arnold Palmer, a label that no one can take away, unless some football researcher finds a long lost birth certificate linking Palmer to Canton instead. Such would be their luck.

The legacy continues

The Hall of Fame dreams may be in a distant past and the title of "the birthplace of professional football" may still come into question, but the link between Latrobe and the NFL is as strong as it was 110 years ago. Every August the men that represent the Pittsburgh Steelers return to this quaint community to participate in an annual event more commonly known as "summer training camp." It's been an occurrence that has happened for 38 consecutive years now and seemingly will go on at least another 38 more.

For the residents of Latrobe and nearby communities, it's become a family tradition every July and August that has been passed down from generation to generation. In the Finoli family it now has been passed along for the third time.

During the heyday of the Steelers in the 1970s, it was not uncommon for over 10,000 people to fill every nook and cranny of the hillside that overlooks the practice fields. Then, fans were exposed to scrimmages, the Oklahoma Drill (the ultimate tussle of aggressive offensive and defensive lineman going head to head in a death struggle where one would emerge victorious and the other held his head in shame, trying to hide from the coaches) and the lonely existence of the kickers and punters off on the end of the field trying not to be intimidated by the cold stare of veteran punter Bobby Walden. Heck, fans even got to pass the picket line in 1974 when the players were on strike, to see an incredible crop of rookies that included four future hall of famers. There were no vendors, food or drink, just the hot, sweltering sun and 70 or 80 of your heroes trying to make the greatest football team ever assembled.

While they weren't quite as good in the late '80s and early '90s, the tradition continued. Young fans waited at the top of the steps for Greg Lloyd, Barry Foster, Bubby Brister, Rod Woodson, Carnell Lake, Merril Hoge and Dermontti Dawson to stroll down to the field of battle. Afterwards they'd all spend time answering questions and signing autographs, giving kids memories that last a lifetime. It was there young fans learned just what a fine human being

Dawson was, and it was there where D.J. Johnson posed for a picture with the Finoli boys, a picture that hangs proudly on their game room wall to this day.

As the 21st century rolls in and the Pittsburgh Steelers keep their date with the citizens of Westmoreland County, the times are just as special as they ever were. There is a souvenir stand now and a place for kids to play called the NFL Experience (my god, they even have a refreshment stand), but the practice is still the main focal point of the day.

The Finoli boys are nearly grown, but they still remember those exceptional times they spent at Latrobe so many years ago. It's an experience that will be passed on to their younger sister in the next year or two, and one that in the not too distant future they will share with their kids, marking the fourth generation of Finolis to make that special trek to Latrobe; a proud tradition that endures.

Many generations of fans have enjoyed seeing the Steelers at St. Vincent College during the teams' annual training camp. Here Matt Finoli, far left, and his brother Tony Finoli, far right, pose with former Steeler defensive back D.J. Johnson. The Finoli boys have grown a little since, both currently attending the University of Pittsburgh where they not only love the Panthers, but still remain die-hard Steeler fans (Dad would have it no other way).

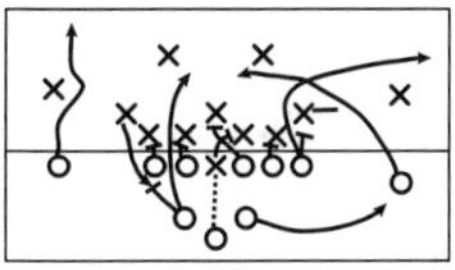

FOUR

Remembering the Steagles

Some 60 years ago, sports meant a morale boost, a break from the hardships and uncertainties of a world at war. In the 1940s, the United States was about to embark on the shores of Europe and Japan to preserve its citizens' freedom. Today's headlines of what athlete was arrested for this, which player was holding out for more money and what person was rumored to be on steroids were replaced by which athletes were entering the service—giving up their families, their way of lives and in some cases their very lives.

After the Japanese attacked Pearl Harbor in 1941 and the country became embroiled in World War II, there were serious discussions on whether or not professional sports would even be allowed to continue. Franklin Delano Roosevelt decided that certain sports were important to the morale of the people who remained here and the soldiers overseas.

The main problem was one of manpower. What was left after the draft was a collection of players too young, too old and too injured to go into the armed services. Baseball suspended many of its minor league systems and moved spring training facilities from the luxurious South to the more frigid Midwest to try and continue the sport. Football, on the other hand, was not the power it is today and the National Football League had to make certain decisions in order to keep the league alive.

By 1943, 376 players with NFL experience had been called to arms. League officials wanted to decrease the size of rosters from 33 to 28 players and then reduce the circuit from 10 to 8 teams in order to solve not only the huge shortage of manpower but to comply with the government mandate to reduce travel by 37 percent in order to conserve energy during the war. The Cleveland Rams were given the go ahead to disband until after the war, which dropped the NFL to nine clubs.

Steeler president Art Rooney came up with a unique idea to bring the circuit to eight without eliminating another team: combine two clubs. Rooney was having discussions with Philadelphia while talking to Cardinals (then of Chicago) president Charley Bidwell, suggesting he merge with the crosstown Bears. Bidwell, incensed, shot back sarcastically "I can't understand why Rooney doesn't merge with the Washington Redskins instead of the Eagles. Hasn't he heard the Redskins are champions?" While the Bears were receptive to talking about a potential merger in these difficult times, Bidwell complained about having two ballparks and the other complications that would evolve. He warmed up to the idea, eventually trying the proposed merger with the Bears.

Ironically, 12 months later, it would be Bidwell that joined forces with Pittsburgh to form one team.

There were hurdles to overcome before a merger could be completed. There was fear that a new combination of the Bears and Cards would be too powerful, so the league decided that the players from both clubs would not be merged into the new team, but set aside as free agents while what was in effect an expansion team of all new players would be put together. The two Chicago clubs were not excited about this new development and decided to remain as individual clubs. Eventually, the league decided to relax the rule, allowing players from both merging teams to be pulled together into one club, although the new configuration would be permitted to have only one vote in league matters instead of two. After the rule was relaxed, Rooney, co-owner Bert Bell and Eagles boss Alex Thompson came to an agreement to join together as one squad. In a meeting in the Windy City on June 19, 1943, the league passed the new merger by a 5-2 vote. Thus came the birth of perhaps the most unique professional team in the proud annals of the Steel City—the Steagles.

When asked why the two clubs chose to merge, Bell simply stated, "Had to do it. Pittsburgh had no backs left and Philadelphia had no lineman. Of the 146 Steelers we had on our active reserve, 132 of them are in the service."

The Steagles would be based in Philadelphia with four of the six home games played at Shibe Park in the city of Brotherly Love, and the remaining two at Forbes Field in the Steel City. Eagles Hall of Fame coach Greasy Neale and the Steelers head man Walt Kiesling, also a Hall of Famer, combined forces as co-head coaches, leading the configuration of two teams with exactly one winning season (the Steelers in 1942) between them in 20 combined NFL seasons. Despite the fact both coaches retained their designation as head coach, it was a combo that didn't get along well. After one particular practice they had a heated argument in front of the team and stormed into the locker room. "They were like two little kids," Steagle Ernie Steele would later recall.

It was a club that, despite its lack of history, did have some notable players on the active roster. Allie Sherman, who backed up starting quarterback Roy Zimmerman, later went on to be an outstanding coach with the New York Giants between 1961-1969, leading them to three straight NFL championship games in his first three seasons (unfortunately losing all three). Hall of Fame receiver Bill Hewitt came out of retirement after four seasons, while two rookies, Al Wistert of Michigan and Bucko Kilroy out of Temple, would go on to have long careers with the Eagles, playing pivotal roles on Philadelphia's first two NFL championship teams in 1948 and 1949.

Wistert, who had the honor of having his number 70 retired by both the University of Michigan and the Eagles, had somewhat of a controversial beginning with the Steagles in his rookie campaign. He demanded a $4,500 salary out of Michigan before he signed, a large amount during that time period, eventually settling for $3,700. Coach Neale told some of the veteran players about his so-called extreme salary request, and Wistert was met with somewhat of a cold shoulder. He went to Hewitt, also a former Wolverine, in hopes he would introduce him to the rest of the team. Hewitt was not enamored with the young rookie and refused to acknowledge him. "I stuck out my hand and introduced myself, and he turns his back on me. I said, 'Well, this is a fine thing.' He won't even talk to me."

Without much winning experience between them, the Steagles took to the gridiron on October 2nd to face the Brooklyn Dodgers in a night game at Shibe Park to begin their inaugural campaign. Night games in both baseball and football had become a more important development during the war. Their original intention was to give more people an opportunity to go to games after work to boost morale. What eventually came from this was an idea that would increase the fan base incredibly, increasing attendance and profits during the next 60 years.

A crowd of 11,131 showed up to see the home team exhibit a powerful, disciplined T-formation that shut out the Brooklyn Dodgers 17-0.

As perfect as they were the first week of the season, they were anything but when they faced the Giants in Shibe Park. The Steagles fumbled 10 times, which remains an NFL record to this day, losing five. And Zimmerman tossed three interceptions, helping to stake New York to an early 14-0 first quarter lead. It was at that point Jack Hinkle, the Steeler running back who had been discharged from the Air Force with ulcers, helped the Pennsylvania club turn things around. Hinkle, who finished with a career-best 571 yards (only one behind the Giants' Bill Paschal for the NFL rushing lead), helped what would turn out to be the NFL's best rushing attack accumulate 191 yards as the Steagles scored three times in the game's final stanza to up their mark to 2-0 with a 28-14 win.

Zimmerman tossed fourth quarter scoring passes of 11 yards to Bob Thurbon and 31 yards to Tom Miller, giving the home team a 21-14 advantage. Ernie Steele ended the scoring when he returned an interception 91 yards late in the game giving the Steagles the exciting come-from-behind victory.

Following their surprising start, the world came crashing down for the squad with two humiliating losses to the Bears and Giants, being outscored 90-35, before meeting up with Bidwell and his Cardinals in the clubs first encounter in Pittsburgh.

It was at that point that the potent Steagle offense became unleashed as the all-Pennsylvania conglomerate crushed the Cards 34-13 in front of 16,351 excited Forbes Field fans. The Steagles broke out to a 21-0 first quarter lead thanks in part to an 86-yard interception return by University of Pittsburgh star Ben Kish, before letting Chicago score 13 unanswered points in the second and sending the two clubs in at the break, 21-13. Zimmerman completed only four passes in the game, but two were scoring tosses to Tony Bova, one for 31 yards and the second for 26 in the fourth quarter, as the home team scored on touchdown marches of 63 and 66 yards to break open what was a close game.

Bova himself was probably the most interesting story in 1943 for the team; his is truly a tale of what wartime sports was about. Completely blind in one eye and partially blind in the other, the St. Francis, PA, alum nevertheless led the Steagles in receptions with 17, five of them going for touchdowns.

The squad kept their momentum going the next week as Zimmerman hit Ernie Steele with a late, 35-yard TD pass to tie the undefeated and defending world champion Washington Redskins 14-14. Unfortunately, the resurgence ended there as the Pittsburgh-Philadelphia club wasted an early 7-0 advantage in a 13-7 upset loss the following contest to the visiting Brooklyn Dodgers.

Scoring only three times in two games, it was time once again to shake the cobwebs of the Steagles T-Formation attack against the Detroit Lions in the second and final game of the season at Forbes Field. Pittsburgh-Philadelphia crushed the Lion defense to the tune of 262 yards on the ground in front of 23,338, who watched the two clubs battle tooth and nail through three quarters with the Pennsylvania squad clinging to a 21-20 lead. After falling behind 27-21 on the first play of the fourth quarter, Zimmerman led the Steagles on a 76-yard scoring drive before giving the club a 35-27 advantage with a quarterback sneak following a Kish interception return to the Lions 7.

The following week saw the Steagles play by far the most impressive game in their short history, crushing the 6-0-1 Redskins 27-14 as their incredible rushing attack tallied 297 yards against the defending champs. For Washington it was a bitter defeat, ending a 17-game undefeated streak over two seasons. The Redskins went 16-0-1 over the course of the streak, the 14-14 tie to the

Steagles being the only blemish, not being defeated since a 14-6 loss to the Giants in the second game of the 1942 campaign. Following the upset loss, Washington dropped its final two games of the season blowing what once seemed like a fairly easy run to the NFL Eastern Division crown.

With Washington losing, the Steagles had a miraculous shot at a piece of the division crown, a championship that would have been stunning considering the Pennsylvania combination was with perhaps two of the worst franchises in the National Football League's first decade. Pittsburgh-Philadelphia would play the Green Bay Packers in Shibe Park in the very important season's finale.

Green Bay was in the midst of a fine season, 6-2-1 at that point, that saw them challenge the powerful Chicago Bears for the Western Division championship. Unfortunately, the Bears had concluded their season a week earlier and with only one loss, the Pack was mathematically eliminated from their quest for the title.

While the Pennsylvania club still had a shot at the postseason and Green Bay was playing for nothing, their great receiver Don Hutson (except for Jerry Rice probably the finest receiver ever to play the game) claimed that this would be his last game. If it was to be his last contest, (which it was not as Hutson hung on for two more seasons) he went out with a bang, scoring two touchdowns and a 25-yard field goal as the Packers ended the Steagles dreams 38-28 before a record 34,294 fans, the most to ever see a game in the City of Brotherly Love. The game was close for a while, tied at 14 in the first quarter after Bova leapt over Hutson for a spectacular 48-yard touchdown.

Hutson's field goal was the only score of the second quarter, before two Packer touchdowns in the second half gave Green Bay what seemed like an insurmountable 31-14 fourth quarter advantage. Unfortunately for the Pack, this Steagle team did not quit, as they always seemed to come up with their best efforts in the fourth quarter. Led by a rushing attack that humbled the Packer defense to the tune of 318 rushing yards, the Steagles mounted a furious fourth quarter comeback, scoring twice and cutting the Green Bay lead to three points, 31-28. Hutson's second score, a 23 yard toss from Irv Comp, stuck a dagger in the improbable Steagle season, giving Green Bay the victory.

As it turned out, a win would have forced a three-way tie for the Eastern Division championship with the Redskins and Giants. It was not to be, though. The season ended and with it the short history of the Pittsburgh-Philadelphia Steagles.

The fact that the majority of the games and the base of operations was in Philadelphia didn't sit right with Steelers co-owner Bert Bell. "I owe it to the fans of Pittsburgh to see that at least a majority of the games are played there next year—that is if we make an agreement with any other club."

At the NFL meetings in mid January of 1944 in Chicago, the split became official. The Steagles were no more. The Philadelphia Eagles went their own way, and the Steelers hooked up with the Cardinals to form one team for the '44 campaign. With the addition to the NFL of a franchise in Boston and the reemergence of the Cleveland Rams, the combo was necessary to give the league an even 10 teams.

Bell got his way, getting three of the team's five home games in Steel City, but the results were far from the previous season as the squad went a miserable 0-10. They were outscored 328-108. The Chicago-Pittsburgh combo, referred to in the media as the Car-Pitts (carpets) due to the fact teams walked all over them, was said by Art Rooney to be the worst club he had ever seen.

Pittsburgh became a separate team once again in 1945 as the war came to an end, but regardless, the Steagles will live as perhaps one of the most interesting squads in the long and storied history of the franchise. In 2003, the Steelers current boss, Dan Rooney, brought back some of the surviving Steagles, a group that included Kilroy, Sherman, Hinkle, Wistart, Steele, Tom Miller, Vic Sears, Ted Doyle and Ray Graves, to celebrate their 60th anniversary at Heinz Field before an exhibition game against the team that made up the other half of the World War II conglomeration, the Eagles.

Speaking at the celebration, Rooney recalled, "The fans really liked it. Their attendance picked up. People were looking for things to do, so it worked out pretty well."

While things "worked out pretty well," and the franchise had a very surprising campaign, the Steagles and the men who played the game during that time meant so much more to a nation in the grips of war; it meant for a couple of hours the citizens of the USA could forget about the horror that was going on with their loved ones an ocean away. Even though it's a contribution that often gets lost in the world of money, drugs and attitudes that sometimes dot the sports sections in the 21st century, it's one that nevertheless should not be forgotten.

Those Steelers who served in World War II

These 33 players were active members of the Pittsburgh Steelers roster and gave up their careers to serve time in the military during World War II.

Dick Bassi	Don Looney
Tom Brown	Vern Martin
Chuck Cherundolo	Coley McDonough
Joe Coomer	Clure Mosher
Russ Cotton	Carl Nery
Milt Crain	John Patrick
Dick Dolly	Stan Pavkov
Bill Dudley	Rocco Pirro
Clark Goff	Mike Rodak
George Gonda	Jack Sanders
Moose Harper	Curt Sandig
Joe Hoague	Andy Tomasic
Art Jones	Ralph Wenzel
Walt Kicefski	Don Williams
George Kiick	John Woudenberg
Joe Lamas	Frank Zoppetti
Hubbard Law	

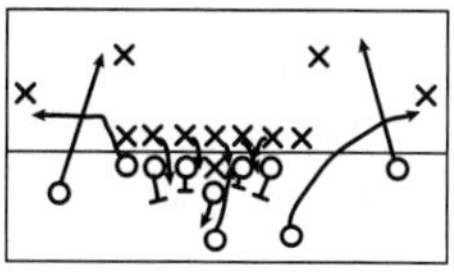

FIVE

The Steelers' First Postseason Game

Ask the average Steeler fan when the first playoff game in team history was and a high majority will respond proudly, the Immaculate Reception game against the Raiders in 1972. Unfortunately, with the success of the '70s, those same fans often don't acknowledge team history before 1972. The answer was actually a forgotten contest 25 years earlier in 1947, when the Pittsburgh Steelers hosted their cross-state rivals from Philadelphia for the Eastern Division crown and the right to face the surprising Chicago Cardinals in the NFL championship.

There was good reason for fans to try and forget; the team stunk. By the mid 1940s the only success was a 7-4 record in 1942 followed by the Steagles in 1943, which finished with a 5-4-1 mark.

In 1944, when the team combined with the Chicago Cardinals, it was winless in 10 affairs and then posted a poor 2-8 mark in the last World War II season of 1945. The team was not only sick of losing on the field, but off, as the club was not on strong financial footing.

Co-owner Bert Bell had been tabbed to replace Elmer Layden as commissioner of the league, so Rooney was on his own again, looking for a way to bring the team back to respectability. Before Bell left, he had been in contact with the former University of Pittsburgh highly successful coach Jock Sutherland to see if he'd be interested in coming to the Steelers. Sutherland had left Pitt in 1939 with a 111-20-12 record, after frequent disputes with administrators who wanted to de-emphasize the football program. Afterwards, he performed a miracle in his only NFL stint by raising the Brooklyn Dodgers from cellar dwellers to second-place finishers in 1940 and 1941, before resigning to enter the service as a lieutenant commander in the Naval Reserve.

The problem with Bell's negotiation was that the Steelers still had a coach, James R. Leonard, who eventually resigned his post, not face to face with Rooney, but in the newspaper. "This is probably the first time an owner has found out that his coach had quit by reading the paper," Leonard chided following a 2-8 record in his only season with Pittsburgh.

Sutherland eventually signed a five-year deal that also included a vice-presidential position with the club. Despite the fact Jock got a "five-figure salary" and some generous perks, reportedly $15,000 with an agreement for 25 percent of the profits from increased attendance and the option to buy Bert Bell's stock in the club (all extreme amounts for the time), Rooney got much more for his investment. "If it hadn't been for the Doctor [Sutherland] I never would have been able to continue in pro football," the Chief later confided. The reaction to the hiring of Jock Sutherland was mind-boggling. Season ticket sales rose from 1,500 in 1945 to 22,000 a year later.

While the town was certainly excited, there were some who doubted whether or not the legendary coach had what it took to bring the Steelers back from the dead. *Washington Post* columnist Shirley Povich wrote that, "Confidentially, other Eastern Division coaches in the National Football League are not at all alarmed by any prospect that the Pittsburgh Steelers will be a title threat following the signing of Jock Sutherland as head coach. Sutherland is an exponent of power football in a league where two touchdowns don't win." The Eastern Division coaches and Povich would horribly underestimate the coaching talent that was Jock Sutherland.

Led by star Bill Dudley, the black and gold finished 5-5-1 in a 1946 campaign where the Steelers stood 5-3-1 with a shot at a piece of the division crown before close, late-season losses to the Giants, 7-0, and the Eagles, 10-7.

The momentum that came from 1946 was threatened by the discontent of Bullet Bill Dudley. There was a standoff between the Steelers' best player and their strong-willed coach. In one corner was Dudley, who led the league in rushing, punt returns and interceptions while also being the top Steeler in punting, kickoff returns, place kicking and passing. Bullet Bill was described as an "independent thinker," feeling at times his opinions were just as good as the coaches, often times openly expressing them. It was an attitude that didn't sit well with Sutherland, the dictatorial coach in the other corner. Jock consistently went on the offensive, knocking down his star back to everyone around in hopes of keeping his ego in check, while forcing Dudley to play even after his star complained his ribs were too banged up.

At the end of his marquee NFL campaign, Dudley had enough of Sutherland's badgering and announced he was quitting. While his official stance was that he was leaving the game at the end of the season because he was small (5' 10," 175 lbs.) and football was too rough, there was no doubt the real reason for Dudley's departure was that the city of Pittsburgh wasn't big enough for the two. Dudley said that if he couldn't be traded he would remain "retired." Rooney reluctantly obliged Dudley by sending him to the Detroit Lions for Bobby Cifers, Paul White and future considerations.

Even though Dudley was much more political about the dispute, Sutherland was once again blunt in his analysis of the situation, stating in the papers that Dudley was bossy and "I know for a fact a few of the boys would not have returned to the squad if Bill had rejoined us this year. When they heard the news that he had signed with the Detroit Lions, one of them remarked. 'Well Detroit got itself another coach.'" Jock further went on to say that Bill begged to return to the Steelers when he heard there were talks with Detroit for a trade but that "I think it is better for all concerned the way things are now."

The Steelers suddenly had a huge hole in their 1947 lineup without the man who was the NFL's Most Valuable Player of 1946. While he certainly didn't have the pedigree of Dudley, Sutherland chose Southern Methodist halfback Johnny Clement to assume the roll of Bullet Bill.

To say Clement didn't have the 1946 NFL MVP's pedigree might be a bit of an understatement. He had only played two prior NFL seasons, one with the Cardinals in 1941 before the war and one in 1946 with the Steelers after he left the military. Certainly there was no reason to believe he could contribute the way Dudley did. Johnny did have some success passing, throwing for 1,035 yards in his first two campaigns, but on the ground he amassed a mere 154 yards for a meager 1.5 per carry average. Despite the less-than-Dudley-like numbers, Sutherland tabbed Clement as his successor, and he did not let him down.

Johnny had what would be his career year—leading the Steelers archaic single-wing attack to the tune of 670 yards rushing, second in the league, and 1,004 yards through the air.

Pittsburgh started the season in a mediocre manner, dropping games to the Rams and Redskins after beating Dudley and the Lions on opening day. They evened their record at 2-2 before facing their cross-state rivals, the Philadelphia Eagles. They proved to be the Steelers' toughest competition, fighting them tooth and nail to see which club would stake claim to its first division title.

Riding the wave of Steve Van Buren's 133 yards on the ground, Philadelphia silenced the large throng of 33,538 fans at Forbes Field, taking a 24-14 lead into the fourth quarter. Clement took over at that point leading the potent Pittsburgh ground attack to 21 unanswered points. The SMU back ran one in from 23 yards, giving the Steelers the lead 28-24 before Steve Lach crashed into the Eagles' goal line for the final tally of the day in an exciting, 35-24 come-from-behind win.

The black and gold used the momentum of the game to ramble off three more wins sending them into a game with the Giants at 6-2. More than 35,000 showed up at Forbes Field to see New York cling to a 7-3 lead going into the game's final quarter. Clement once again led the Steelers to 21 fourth-quarter points, all coming within 1:48, extending Pittsburgh's win streak to six games, and giving them a 7-2 mark, a half game ahead of Philadelphia.

Both Philadelphia and the Steelers lost the following week, setting up a rematch in Philadelphia's Shibe Park for the division lead. Despite the fact they were without four starters, including Clement, they held Van Buren (who would go on to break the NFL's single season rushing mark in 1947 with 1,008 yards) to only 76 yards. The Philly defense was too tough, though, and they stuffed the crippled Steeler offense, holding it to a mere 120 total yards in a 21-0 defeat.

No longer with their destiny in their own hands, Pittsburgh hosted Boston, needing a win and a loss by Philadelphia against the Western Division leaders, the Chicago Cardinals. The Steelers once again played without Clement, but nevertheless led Boston from start to finish for a comfortable 17-7 victory. The Eagles, on the other hand, were thrashed by Chicago 45-21, giving Pittsburgh a half-game lead and at least a share of the division crown (Philadelphia still had a game left against the Green Bay Packers).

With a win, the Eagles would force a one-game playoff for the Eastern Division championship; a loss and the black and gold would come away with the undisputed crown and a spot in the NFL championship game against the Cardinals (who beat the Bears 30-21 on the last day of the season to capture their first Western Division title). Green Bay was having a solid if unspectacular year going 6-4-1, but they would unfortunately be no match for the Eagles. Van Buren scored three times and rushed for 96 yards, eclipsing Beattie Feathers' 13-year-old, NFL single-season rushing mark, to handily defeat Green Bay 28-14.

The win by Philadelphia set up the one-game showdown in Forbes Field (the Steelers won a coin flip in November for the rights to host a playoff game if the two teams tied).

Even before the game between Philadelphia and Green Bay was over, the Steeler players, with a potential opportunity for an NFL championship at hand, were concerned with whether they would receive extra money for the additional game they would have to play if the Eagles defeated the Pack. The team sent two players as spokesmen to management, seeing if they could get the extra money. Center Chuck Cherundolo quickly pointed out that there was no threat for a strike. "Shucks, we're not thinking of striking or anything like that," he said. "We just want to see what we can do about keeping the wolf from the door until the league race is settled." But the fires of controversy had been lit.

Rooney did pay the players for the upcoming playoff game, but Coach Sutherland was very irritated with their actions. The day before the game he exacted his revenge by making the Steelers practice outside in the snowy, unusually cold weather.

With the poor weather, the club tried to save the field as best they could by covering it for most of the week before the contest with a tarp. Odds were that the two clubs would have to play on the Pittsburgh version of "frozen tundra" come game time. Because of this, Sutherland anticipated using sneakers instead of cleats to get what little traction he could from the frozen turf.

The other essential factor in the contest was the left elbow of Clement. Pittsburgh went 1-2 down the stretch without their new star and had he remained healthy during the season, the game against the Eagles might not have been necessary. Clement was to be fitted with a special brace to protect the elbow and expected to play in what was the most important game of his young career. The one thing the brace wasn't expected to do was hamper the SMU alums' passing, as he was right-handed.

Philadelphia came into the contest as a three-point favorite. The injury to Clement as well as the fact that the Eagles were perceived as the dominant team (outscoring their opponents 308-232 while the Steelers were outscored 240-259) was the reason for Philly's role as favorites.

Excitement was at a fever pitch. Scalpers got as much as $40 for a $4 ticket to see the intrastate rivals go at it for the Eastern Division championship. More than 35,000 fans braved the cold in hopes Pittsburgh could continue its surprising season. Unfortunately, the excitement of the week leading up to the contest was more spellbinding than the actual game. The Eagles dominated the tilt from the beginning to the end. With many players injured and sick of dealing with coach Sutherland, the Steelers put on a lethargic show. Louis Effrat of the *New York Times* called it "a contest that was so-one-sided it was almost dull," as Philadelphia thrashed the hometown team 21-0.

The Eagles thoroughly dominated the statistical end of the game, outgaining Pittsburgh 255-154 and getting the first opportunity to score. Quarterback Tommy Thompson, who had a fine day completing 11-18 for 131 yards and two touchdowns, drove the Eagles to the Steeler 24-yard line. After the Pittsburgh defense held, Hall of Fame Philadelphia coach Greasy Neale sent out his field goal unit to try and give his club an early 3-0 lead. Neale instead decided to go for the TD on a fake field goal attempt as backup

QB Allie Sherman took the snap, stood up and overthrew a pass in the end zone to receiver Jack Ferrante.

Pittsburgh dodged the first bullet of the game, but could not even move the ball a yard and had to punt from their own 20. Philadelphia's Pete Pihos broke through the line, blocking Bobby Cifer's punt, giving them the ball on the Steeler 14. The Eagles lost a yard on the first two plays before Thompson opened up the scoring with a strike to Van Buren, giving Philly the early 7-0 advantage.

The Steeler offense made one futile attempt after another to move the ball, but their main offensive threat, Johnny Clement, proved to be just a shell of his former self. Injuries during the season seemed to be taking their toll on the Oklahoma native. He completed only 4 of 17 passes for a meager 52 yards. Thompson, on the other hand, continued to move the Eagle troops by launching a 28-yard toss to Ferrante for a second period score and increasing the Philadelphia lead to 14-0 before the half.

The special teams would prove to be the Steeler's biggest flop. A blocked punt in the first period led to a touchdown. Another special-team's meltdown proved to be a game breaker early in the third quarter. Cifers booted a punt to the Steeler 29-yard line. Philadelphia's Josh Pritchard took the ball and sliced between the Pittsburgh punt coverage, bolting through a wall of defenders at the 40 on the way to a 79-yard touchdown run, effectively rendering the Steelers' Eastern Division championship dreams null and void.

Down by a seemingly insurmountable 21-0 deficit, Clement did not quit trying to lead the black and gold back from the abyss. Late in the third, "Mr. Zero" (as Clement was known) finally got the Pittsburgh offense on track, leading them on a 58-yard drive to the Eagle 9-yard line. The drive stalled there as Clement fumbled while trying a jump pass on fourth down. He recovered the ball, but the Steelers nonetheless were stopped short and turned the ball back over to the potent Philly offense.

Pittsburgh gained one last opportunity in the last quarter to avoid a shutout after recovering a Philadelphia fumble deep in Eagles territory. Unfortunately, they returned the Philly favor, giving the ball right back to the Eagles on a fumble. Philadelphia ended this one-sided affair with a trip to the NFL championship game against the Cardinals where they lost 28-21. The black and gold, however, went away licking their wounds, ending what had been the club's most successful campaign in a disappointing manner.

While the Steelers had been concerned about getting paid for the contest, the Eagles concentrated on winning. Eagles captain Al Wistert said it best when he proclaimed to reporters, "Want to know where the game was won? It was won yesterday in Philadelphia where every man gave a short speech, telling how he thought the game could be won. We knew right then that we wouldn't be beaten."

Despite the humbling defeat, Jock Sutherland, Johnny Clement and the Steelers seemed to be on the right track for the future. Rooney had made the proper choice, picking his coach over the best player the franchise had seen in its short history to that point—Bill Dudley. Sutherland had defied the odds. He made Pittsburgh a power in the NFL in only two short seasons. Clement did the impossible by successfully replacing Dudley and leading the Steelers into their first postseason venture.

For both men, as well as for the franchise as a whole, the dreams and promise of the 1947 season came crashing to an unexpected and tragic halt. Four months after the '47 Eastern Division title tilt, Jock went south on a scouting trip and disappeared. Days later he was found wandering aimlessly. Doctors discovered Sutherland had a malignant brain tumor and operated unsuccessfully to try and save him. Sadly, he died soon after at the age of 59. While it was tragic to lose such a great man, it was also tough for the franchise as a whole. "He won wherever he went," says University of Pittsburgh football historian Alex Kramer. "Had he not died, the Steelers would have probably gotten to the championship game in 1948 and 1949."

Johnny Clement was the direct beneficiary of Sutherland's dispute with Dudley, becoming a star in the National Football League.

However, 1947 was to be the zenith of Mr. Zero's career. Clement lost his job to rookie Ray Evans out of Kansas in 1948. While an early rib injury might have been one of the reasons for Clement's demotion, it wasn't the only one. Author and Professional Football Research Association Executive Director Bob Carroll explains:

"While starting a rookie over a proven star may seem strange, two things should be considered. First, Evans wasn't just another rookie; he was one of the most talented backs in the country in '47 and still is legendary in Kansas. His future looked brighter than Clement's. Moreover, I'm sure the Steeler front office preferred to showcase its exciting new star rather than a familiar veteran. Coach John Michelosen had just taken over for the late Jock Sutherland and was in no position to stand up to the boss (if that's what the boss wanted)."

After his disappointing campaign in 1948, Clement jumped to the All American Football Conference, where he ended his professional football career in Chicago only two years later.

Unable to rebound following the death of Sutherland, the Steelers fell back to the position they had been accustomed to before Jock, the bottom half of the NFL standings. They dropped to 4-8 in 1948. While they did have one winning campaign in 1949, a 6-5-1 mark, it would be 11 seasons before the black and gold became title contenders once again.

We can only imagine how good Pittsburgh could have become had Sutherland not died so unexpectedly. Perhaps the Steeler fans of today would be talking triumphantly about the heyday of the late '40s and '50s instead of the tendency for the Steeler Nation to ignore those teams that represented the franchise proudly in the years prior to Franco's historic catch in 1972.

The forgotten postseason game

Between 1960 and 1969, the National Football League held a game in Miami, Florida between the second place finishers in each division called the Playoff Bowl or the Bert Bell Benefit Bowl. The Playoff Bowl had no relevance to the outcome of the eventual NFL championship and was really only an exhibition contest. The contest, which the great Vince Lombardi once referred to as a "Rinky Dink Game," seemed to be nothing more than the NFL's attempt to divert some of the viewers to watch their contest over the rival American Football League's championship game. Nonetheless in 1962, following a surprising second place 9-5 season by the black and gold, Pittsburgh took on the Western Division's runner-up, the Detroit Lions, winners of the first two Playoff Bowls, in the extravaganza.

On a muggy day at Miami's Orange Bowl 36,284 saw Detroit's Milt Plum throw for 272 yards and one TD in the Lions 17-10 victory; a game where the highlight was probably a fight between the Steelers Hall of Fame running back John Henry Johnson and Detroit's Wayne Walker.

After the NFL and AFL merged in 1969, the Playoff Bowl went the way of the dinosaurs, extinct. Although in their heyday the league and CBS sports promoted the contests as "the playoff game for third place in the NFL," today league officials claim them to be nothing more than exhibition games, therefore excluding them from the NFL's official postseason stats.

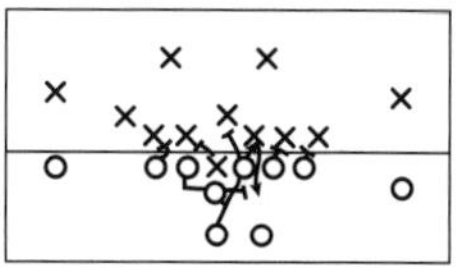

SIX

Giant Killers

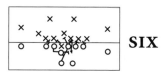

In the 1950s, there were only three things certain in life: death, taxes and the Pittsburgh Steelers mired in mediocrity.

Despite the fact the Steelers had brought on a new coach, Joe Bach, to replace John Michelosen, and even though Bach scrapped the archaic single-wing offense that was responsible for a league-low 183 points in 1951 for the more high-powered T-formation attack, the moves didn't show up in the won-loss column. The Steelers' record stood at 3-6 when they faced the mighty New York Giants on November 30th, 1952.

The Giants were atop the National Football League's eastern division at the time, tied with Cleveland and Philadelphia at 6-3 and were chock full of stars such as Charlie Conerly, Frank Gifford, Emlen Tunnell, Tom Landry, Kyle Rote and Eddie Price. Despite their anemic 3-6 mark, the Steelers were improved over the preceding year. They lost their first four games of the season by a combined 16 points, dropping two of them by a scant one-point margin. There were a few more offensive weapons on this club, but there were still many inquiries about just how good they were. While nobody questioned either Ray Matthews or Elbie Nickel, Lynn Chandnois, a third-year pro from Michigan State, was thought to be lackadaisical by assistant coach Walt Kiesling, and his future with the club was very much in jeopardy. Jim Finks was in his first year as starting quarterback after spending his first three campaigns in Pittsburgh's defensive backfield, and to this point, Finks showed little to suggest that he could be an effective signal caller.

Before the game began most of the so-called football experts and analysts thought this contest was going to be just another win for New York on their way to a season-ending match-up against the Cleveland Browns for the Eastern Division title. Oddsmakers had the Giants as 7-point favorites—a seemingly safe bet. However, the men from Gotham were not at 100 percent going into this game. Conerly, who started the contest, was nursing a bruised shoulder and gave way to Fred Benners at quarterback. The week before, Benners rallied the team for a 14-10 win against the Redskins, leading the Giants to two touchdowns after they fell behind 10-0. Gifford was also out against the Steelers with a pulled hamstring, but New York had a more than capable backup in Rote.

Despite the key injuries, the Giants did get some good news with two members of their powerful offensive line—center John Rapacz and tackle Tom Yelvington—returning to lead New York's potent running attack paced by Price, who was at the top of the NFL rushing charts before the game.

While there were players returning to New York's attack, there were ones leaving Pittsburgh's. Rudy Andabaker and Ed Kissell would be lost to the Steelers not with injuries, but because they had both been drafted into the service the week before the contest. Kissell's loss especially hurt the team. He had already picked off five passes through the team's first nine games.

A less-than-capacity 15,140 fans showed up at snowy Forbes Field this day to see if the Steelers could avoid being embarrassed. So confident was the New York club that coach Steve Owen chose to kickoff to Pittsburgh despite winning the opening coin toss. Owen counted on his remarkable defense to set the tone of the day.

It proved to be a very poor miscalculation when Chandnois took the opening kickoff at his own 9-yard line and didn't stop

Other Steeler Blowouts of Legendary Proportions

By the Steelers		
9/12/99	Pittsburgh 43	Cleveland 0
1/7/79	Pittsburgh 34	Houston 5
12/5/76	Pittsburgh 42	Tampa Bay 0
10/17/76 -12/11/76	Pittsburgh 234	Opponents 28
10/5/75	Pittsburgh 42	Cleveland 6
12/3/72	Pittsburgh 30	Cleveland 0
10/17/54	Pittsburgh 55	Cleveland 27
11/7/48	Pittsburgh 38	Green Bay 7
Against the Steelers		
9/10/89	Cleveland 51	Pittsburgh 0
9/17/89	Cincinnati 41	Pittsburgh 10
11/24/83	Detroit 45	Pittsburgh 3
11/9/69	Chicago 38	Pittsburgh 7
9/29/68	Baltimore 41	Pittsburgh 7
10/29/50	Cleveland 45	Pittsburgh 7
All of 1944	Opponents 328	Pittsburgh 108
11/23/1941	Green Bay 54	Pittsburgh 7
10/15/33	Green Bay 47	Pittsburgh 0

running until he gave the men in black and gold a quick 7-0 lead.

New York failed to tie the score, instead giving the ball back to Pittsburgh on the Giants 47. Eight plays later Chandnois went in from five yards out to up the Steeler lead to 14-0. The star from Michigan State was showing the franchise it had underestimated his ability. Chandnois' incredible performance this day would vault him from being tagged a lackadaisical player to being awarded the Touchdown Club's NFL Player of the Year in 1952.

Confidence now brimming, Finks decided he would share in what had been the Lynn Chandnois show to this point by unleashing an aerial attack that sent the favored Giants reeling.

The Steelers QB launched TD strikes of 21 yards to Nickel and 42 into the arms of Matthews, making the game a laugher as the two teams went into the locker room with the black and gold up by an incredible 28 points.

As impressive as the potent T-formation had been on offense, so was the tough Pittsburgh defense. Not only had they held New York off the board, but they also destroyed their two quarterbacks, sending Conerly out of the game as he reinjured his shoulder and Benners with a torn ligament in his knee. With little else to choose, Owen went into his defensive backfield, pegging future Hall of Fame coach Tom Landry to run his offense and see if he could at least keep this game from becoming more embarrassing.

While the Giants hoped the Steelers would try and run the clock out and take their victory before the game got too out of hand, Bach had other ideas, as did reserve end Dick Hensley. They had a different motivation—retribution. Owen unceremoniously let Hensley go from the New York organization in 1949, and the end had always wanted to get a measure of revenge. Bach gave him the opportunity, putting him in the lineup to begin the second half. It didn't take long for Hensley to live his dream as Finks hit him from 25 yards out to give Pittsburgh an insurmountable 35-0 advantage.

Finally, after so much torture, Landry helped his team find the end zone, although it was done in a very unorthodox way. Landry hit Bill Stribling with a pass. Stribling lateraled it to Joe Scott, who returned the favor by giving it back to Stribling to finally break the ice ending the third quarter 35-7. New York didn't know it at the time, but 15 minutes later, it would long for the day when it was only 35-7.

As bad as the first 45 minutes were, the final-frame deluge the Steelers put on the Giants was worse than anything they could ever imagine, and it would last longer than that final quarter. It started with Finks hitting Hensley with a bomb. The former Giant was knocked off his feet by Tunnell at the 15, but in the 1950s, the rule stated that the defensive player had to be on top of you to be considered down. Hensley got up to complete the 60-yard play for his second touchdown of the day. Revenge smells so sweet.

Soon after, Landry tried a quick kick only to have it blocked by Pittsburgh's Dale Dodrill. The Steelers recovered it at the three-yard line and George Hays took it in for the team's seventh touchdown of the day. Bach emptied his bench, inserting kicker Gary Kerkorian into the game at QB for his first time under center in his career. He replaced Finks, who had one of his best games ever, completing 12 of 24 for 254 yards and four touchdowns. Kerkorian, a Stanford alum who would be the Colts' starting quarterback two years later, wanted to get his full experience at quarterback and chose to go to the air, completing his first NFL touchdown pass to Jack Butler, a man who was more known as the Steelers all-time interception leader with 52 before Mel Blount broke his record years later.

Down 56-7, the Giants were still in a generous mood, giving the Steelers the ball back at the Giants 35 when Hall of Fame defensive lineman Ernie Stautner pounced on a Landry fumble. A few plays later Pittsburgh made the destruction complete when Ed Modzelewski ran it in from four yards out making the final score 63-7.

While the offense took a lot of the credit for the club's 63-point outburst, (which remains a team record 52 years later), the defense were truly the stars of the game. Linebacker Jerry Shipkey led a defensive charge that held the potent Giant ground game to a mere 15 yards as Price, the league's leading runner before the contest, ended the game with only 3 net yards. The defense took a physical toll on their opponents that would last the remainder of what turned out to be a disappointing season for the Giants. Not only did the tough Steeler D knock out Conerly and Betters, but it also put Rote on the shelf with a concussion.

The Pittsburgh defense limited the Giant offense to 172 yards and eight first downs but more importantly forced New York into nine turnovers. Defensive back Claude Hipps turned into the Giants best receiver. He intercepted three passes, leading a Steeler pass defense that picked off an incredible seven New York aerials. (The Giants only threw 15 in the team's other 11 games in 1952.) For Hipps, it was a game of a lifetime. His three picks accounted for not only his entire 1952 total, but 60 percent of his career interceptions.

To say the humiliating defeat derailed New York's eastern division title hopes was an understatement; it totally crushed them. Not only did the physical beating leave them without a quarterback for their next game, but it had to have left them mentally scarred. The loss was the worst the franchise had ever endured, and it came at the hands of a team considered much inferior. While crushed, Owen put a humorous spin on it claiming, "It's a good thing that I am such a great defensive coach. Otherwise the score would have been 100-7."

The momentum the Steelers built followed them the next week to San Francisco. They won yet another one-sided game, this time by a more reasonable 24-7 margin. The beaten-up Giants, on the other hand, were eliminated from the division race with a 27-17 loss to the Redskins. This time there would be no Giants rally.

New York was a winning franchise before it entered the Steel City on that fateful day, posting a 31-7-1 in the previous two years. However, the loss against the Steelers would reverberate. Following that game, the G-men went 4-10, including a catastrophic 62-14 loss to the Browns in a 3-9 1953 campaign.

Unfortunately, the win didn't change the Steelers' fortunes. Pittsburgh lost the final game of the year to the Rams 28-14. The team fell back to the trademark mediocrity that had surrounded them in their 20-year history. They finished the '53 season at 6-6.

While chants of SOS (Same Old Steelers) followed the club for most of the next 20 seasons, for one day the loyal fans of the Pittsburgh Steelers got to hold out their chests proudly as the club put on a performance of a lifetime. For one day they were amid the best the National Football League had to offer—a performance that to this day is among the finest the franchise has ever produced.

SEVEN

Rah Raw

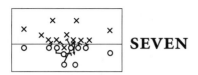

We've been living a lie. All our lives we'd taken comfort in the absolutes that govern any true Steelers fan: Terry Bradshaw's Immaculate Reception pass hit Jack Tatum and Jack Tatum only. The path to championships was paved with a strong ground game and an attacking defense. Iron City Beer only tasted good at the stadium—and only if it was really, really cold and you were really, really hot. One logo was all you truly needed on a helmet. And, unlike those showy and despicable Dallas Cowboys, the Steelers, a team of grit and substance, just didn't have cheerleaders.

However, that comfort zone crumbled while doing research for this book. We came about it quite by accident while searching for one of the many obscure facts that are found between the covers of *Steel City Gridirons.* Curse you, Google. Damn you, Yahoo. It seemed the Steelers did have cheerleaders at one time—the cleverly named Steelerettes, who rooted on the team from 1961 to '69.

We weren't sure which hurt more, the fact that our smugness in having a pompom-free zone was shattered or that we hadn't known about the existence of the Steelerettes. Just to top it off, our wives both knew the Steelers had once had cheerleaders. It prompted a trip to the statue of Art Rooney to ask, "Why, Chief, why?" The old Irishman offered no answer—it's a statue, after all.

But a little more research revealed some answers. The Steelerettes were the NFL's first cheerleading squad. Already some of the hurt was gone, as we took solace in the groundbreaking efforts of the Steelers. (Another hallmark of a Steelers' fan is the ability to recover quickly from disappointment.) Soon disappointment gave way to intrigue. The squad was the idea of William V. Day, who much like Kordell Stewart three decades later, had the slash mentality (although it's not known whether he was any more accurate than Kordell in hitting an open receiver). Day was the Steelers' entertainment coordinator while also serving as a vice president for Robert Morris Junior College, the precursor to Robert Morris University.

At the time, the small junior college lacked a football team (it could also be argued that the Rooneys could make the same claim), and the student body had all but adopted the Steelers as their own. Day thought dressing up some of the Robert Morris coeds would add to school spirit, and maybe even inspire the fans at Pitt Stadium to cheer for the home Steelers. In the spring of '61, Day posted notices for tryouts. The young women were judged on appearance, poise, personality, coordination and gymnastic ability. They also had to have some football knowledge and were required to pass a football exam that tested their ability to identify key Steelers. Being that there were few players that qualified for that litmus test, if you knew quarterback Bobby Layne, defensive lineman Big Daddy Lipscomb and coach Buddy Parker, you were in. Points were probably deducted for being able to ID any other Steelers from the '61 roster. The young women couldn't neglect their school studies either. Day required them to carry at least a 2.0 average. And, for Rooney to sign off on this experiment, there was another rule for the Steelerettes—no fraternization with the players. That would be cause for dismissal, he said. (Being that the women were volunteers, he couldn't fine them or anything.)

The squad was launched in time for the '61 season, with the eight women selected showing the right stuff. Or, more accurately, not showing much at all. Their uniforms seemed to be from the

June Cleaver collection—gold jumpers that went below the knees with long sleeved black shirts underneath. The only thing less revealing is a presidential candidate during a debate. And to finish the ensemble, they wore gold hardhats. Okay, the hardhats were kind'a hot.

Unfortunately, the hardhats would disappear by '63, about the same time the Steelerettes would be immortalized in film because of their signature human pyramid. The squad made it into one of the NFL's blooper films, as the cameras captured their on-field pyramid collapse—much like the Steelers of that decade.

Slowly the uniforms became less matronly and the women were accepted into the fold. In 1966, Rooney softened the no-fraternization policy and invited the women to the team's annual Kickoff dinner held at the Pittsburgh Hilton. The Steelerettes also began to appear at other events around town, from Duquesne University basketball games to an Andy Williams/Henry Mancini concert at the Civic Arena—they appeared on stage as the crooners belted out "Watching All The Girls Go By."

But three years later it would be the Steelerettes who would go by. A 1-13 Steelers squad made it tough to find much to cheer about. Moving to the ultra-modern Three Rivers Stadium meant logistical changes for the Steelers. Somehow incorporating the Steelerettes didn't make the list. There was talk about Robert Morris starting its own team, complete with cheerleaders, making the Steelerettes mere football footnotes, but ones with cherished memories. The women who donned the hardhats and cheered try to get together for lunches and even had a reunion at Heinz Field a few years ago.

There's also a charming Web site (www.steelerettes.com) that a former member, Diane Feazell Rossini, has put together to chronicle their existence, complete with year-by-year breakdowns of the squads. She also lets us know where the Steelerettes are now: She serves as chief deputy treasurer of Fayette County; Patricia Tanner is managing director of Calliope, the Pittsburgh Folk Music Society.

Tanner recalls her time as a Steelerette, cheering from '65-'67. "It was one of those highlights that you remember in your life. I remember getting off the bus in my uniform and walking up that big hill to Pitt Stadium. For an 18-year-old to be recognized and have people come up to you and ask for your autograph, it's something you just don't forget."

Unfortunately, the squad has been forgotten, or at least not recognized as being the pioneers they were. The shame of it is that the Steelerettes had bad timing. They got a raw deal, in fact. They missed out on the wave that they should have initiated when the Dallas Cowboy Cheerleaders gained notoriety via calendars, posters and other merchandise directed toward pubescent boys and testosterone-laden football fans. But then again, it wouldn't have fit the blue-collar image of the Steelers.

Perhaps more disappointing, they missed out on cheering for a winning team. Had they hung on a few more years, the Steelerettes might have been in highlight films for celebrating touchdowns rather than picking themselves up from a pyramid gone wrong. And we could have accepted the concept of Steelers cheerleaders, just as long as we never find out that Bradshaw's pass really hit off of Frenchy Fuqua.

EIGHT

Huddle Diplomacy

1969

It was a contentious peace, one struck three years earlier. Representatives from two rival leagues, the established National Football League and the upstart American Football League, were in two different suites of a New York hotel. Bitter rivals since the AFL's arrival on the scene in 1960, the two factions were there to put the final touches on a merger that would finally bring peace and stability to professional football.

In one room was the old guard, the representatives from the 16 NFL franchises, the hardliners. After all, many of them thought, *we* invented the professional game. *We* nurtured it and brought it to the nation's consciousness. *We* should dictate the terms of this peace.

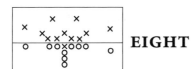

In another room sat "The Foolish Club," the name given to the 10 AFL owners by Chet Soda, the one-time owner of the Oakland franchise. The AFL was the flashier league, where flea flickers, reverses and half-back options lured many fans away from the NFL's three-yards-and-a-cloud-of-dust mentality. And the AFL was not necessarily the inferior league as many had thought. A few months earlier its New York Jets had shocked the football world by defeating the heavily favored NFL champion Baltimore Colts in Super Bowl III, a team many considered to be perhaps the best team in league history. Make no mistake about it, the AFL minions felt, we belong at the table and we will get our due.

Down the street in NFL commissioner Pete Rozelle's 410 Park Avenue office in Manhattan, yet simultaneously in the middle of all of this, were the Pittsburgh Steelers' owner Art Rooney, Sr., and his son Dan, who was being groomed to take the reins. Inter-league play was scheduled to start in 1970, yet at these meetings in New York in May of 1969, the two leagues were far from reaching an accord as to how to structure the new combined league that would be grouped into two conferences—the National Football Conference and the American Football Conference. Rozelle wanted an even split of two, 13-team conferences, meaning three former NFL franchises would have to move to play in the conference made up of the former rival AFL teams. The hardliners wanted to keep it 16-10. AFL commissioner Al Davis—the former Raider coach and managing general partner—wanted no part of that. For Davis, a merger meant the leagues needed to be viewed as equals, although there were some difficult economics to iron out. But along with rational, dollars-and-cents issues were emotional issues, and in this case, pissiness ruled the day. Hard feelings festered in both hotel suites.

And so, removed from yet enveloped by the tension in the hotel, Rozelle turned to the Rooneys and asked them to move their Steelers to the new AFC. He reasoned that if the owners of one of the league's oldest franchises would make the move, it would be an easier sell. "I told my dad I was dead set against it," recalls Dan Rooney, now chairman of the Steelers. "I wasn't ready to forgive."

The roots of the skirmish dated back to 1958, when a young, rich Texan named Lamar Hunt tried to get in the NFL "club" by purchasing the dying Chicago Cardinals franchise with the expressed desire to move the team to Dallas. When those efforts were rebuffed, Hunt took the "fine-I'll-start-my-own-league" approach, and he put out feelers to other entrepreneurs. Among those who answered Hunt's call to huddle up were hotel magnate Barron Hilton, oilman Bud Adams and auto executive Ralph Williams.

Eight American Football League teams were organized and put in major markets, including New York, Boston, Los Angeles, Houston, Dallas, Buffalo, Denver and Minneapolis.

The NFL attempted to diffuse the situation by offering to do its own expansion in Dallas and Houston, hoping that Hunt and Adams would jump from the fledgling AFL ship and join the established league. After all, NFL officials reasoned, they would be crazy to launch their own league if we gave them the chance to join our club. They get a franchise and the whole untidy AFL goes away, much like the old All-American Football League did in the late '40s. No one gets hurt, and we get new teams in growing markets. Although the Minneapolis group would jump ship, Hunt and Adams stayed with their league, and "The Foolish Club" was born. (The NFL did put a franchise in Dallas, seemingly just to piss off Hunt.) The first shot had been fired.

The second shot, and the one that opened up a talent bidding war, was returned by the AFL. The Los Angeles Rams drafted and signed Billy Cannon from LSU, even though the 1959 Heisman Trophy winner still had a bowl game left to play. (Rozelle was the Ram's GM at the time.) After that game, Adam's Houston Oilers signed Cannon to an AFL contract, which was later upheld by a judge. Score one for the new guys, who weren't so foolish after all.

Despite some shaky seasons and severe growing pains that included franchise relocations and ownership changes, the AFL won its share of talent battles, and, even in those cases when it didn't win, drove up the prices for players. To keep an edge in the bidding battles, the NFL launched "Operation Hand Holding," (yes, they really named it) in which team representatives would pretty much baby sit draftees, often moving them from hotel to hotel to keep AFL reps from contacting them. Dirty tricks played out on both sides.

In 1962, both leagues drafted strong-armed quarterback Roman Gabriel, projected universally by scouts as being a can't-miss, franchise-type quarterback. Dallas owner Hunt wanted Gabriel to join the AFL. Gabriel had also been selected by the Los Angeles Rams of the NFL, who immediately put him in the draftee protection plan. Hunt finally reached who he thought was Gabriel on the phone and laid out the details of the contract he was offering the North Carolina State QB. Hunt was told, "No thank you, I plan on signing with the Rams." Years later Hunt would learn that he wasn't actually talking to Gabriel. On the other end of the phone was the Rams' new GM Elroy Hirsch, who was about to sign Gabriel to a contract.

But three years later, two things turned the tide for the AFL. First, its New York Jets franchise signed Alabama quarterback (and former Beaver Falls star) Joe Namath to a record-breaking $437,000 contract. Immediately, he became the darling of the Big Apple. The biggest media city had professional football's most glamorous new star—and he played in the AFL, white shoes flair and all.

Secondly, and more importantly, the AFL gained financial strength. Its wide-open brand of football and the Namath signing led NBC to pony up a five-year, $36 million television contract for the right to broadcast its games. The AFL wasn't going away and would have to be dealt with by the NFL if costs were to be kept in line.

That same year, secret talks began between representatives of the two leagues. Leading the charge for the NFL was Baltimore Colts owner Carroll Rosenbloom; the AFL was represented by Buffalo Bills owner Wilson. The two leagues were managing to co-exist while the talks about a possible merger went on behind the scenes. But once again, hostilities escalated when, in 1966, the NFL made a grab for an existing AFL player—something that had been previously off-limits. The Bills' soccer-style kicker Pete Gogolak played out his option with the club and then signed with the NFL's New York Giants. The status quo was disrupted. The AFL forced out commissioner Joe Foss, the former governor of South Dakota, a genial man who gave credibility to the new league upon its launch, but not a lot of fight in the head-to-head battles with the NFL. His replacement, Davis, was then, as he is now, a true maverick with a serious hard-on for the NFL. Davis set his sights on NFL veterans, using the Gogalok signing as justification for breaking the gentlemen's agreement not to raid the rosters of the rival league.

Although they would never play for the rival league, NFL stars like San Francisco 49er QB John Brodie, Dallas Cowboys tight end Mike Ditka and Gabriel signed huge AFL contracts.

Offers to players now included bonuses in the six-figure range (Gabriel reportedly was offered a $100,000 signing bonus to jump to the Raiders), stock options and travel getaways. Yet despite all the clamoring, Rozelle was able to broker a merger, announced in June 1966. Among its key points were a common draft to begin in 1967 and a long-awaited game pitting the NFL champion against the AFL champion that same year. And in 1970, interleague play would begin.

There were still a lot of details to work out. For 30 hours plus, talks among the 26 vested parties yielded little progress. Rozelle knew he had Rosenbloom, since the Colts' owner was an early agent in brokering an agreement with the other league. There were rumors that the Washington Redskins might be willing to move, but the team's fiery coach and part-owner Vince Lombardi, in his Lombardi-like way, called those rumors bullshit, effectively ending any trial balloon there.

Conversely, the Cleveland Browns' owner Art Modell was said to be warming to the idea. Originally, Modell was among the hardliners opposing any NFL franchise moving to the newly created AFC. He said such a move would be "emasculating," but with talk of establishing a pool of cash to entice a NFL franchise to make a move, Modell would be interested in listening. The problem was he was in the hospital, being treated for a bleeding ulcer.

That's when Rozelle began some huddle diplomacy with the Rooneys as key change agents. Despite their two teams' bitter rivalry, Modell held the Rooneys in high regard—and vice versa. If Rozelle could get the Rooneys to side with him, the chance of Modell coming along increased. It also made sense for the new conference to have the historic regional Pittsburgh-Cleveland rivalry in place.

"God, we argued it out," Dan Rooney remembers. "My father was taking the position to consider it, but I convinced him, and finally he said, 'Okay, we won't do it.'" For the younger Rooney, a lot of the debate centered on economics. Many of the AFL stadiums couldn't compare with those of their NFL brethren in one key area—capacity. Fewer fans in the stadium meant fewer dollars to the visiting teams. It was a losing proposition at the gate.

But Rozelle was ever the salesman. He suggested that the three take a break and grab some dinner and a few drinks before rejoining the other owners. "So we're back in Rozelle's office, and he hands me this piece of paper that's about an inch wide and about ¾-inch deep," Dan Rooney recalls. "And my father says, 'What's that?'

"And Rozelle says, 'Gentlemen, this is your new division in the AFC.' And I look at this small piece of paper and it says PITTSBURGH, CLEVELAND, CINCINNATI and HOUSTON, and all of a sudden, I'm really beginning to like this."

It was a shrewd set-up—professional football's version of The Great Compromise. Rozelle retained the regional Pittsburgh-Cleveland rivalry and added another piece to it with Paul Brown's young Cincy team. Houston had been an early AFL powerhouse and played in the Astrodome, one of the largest-capacity stadiums in the league. Cleveland also could squeeze in the fans—72,000, in fact. And Cincinnati, like Pittsburgh, would soon be moving into a state of the art (for the time, people) stadium.

"I looked at that slip of paper, and I knew it was the right thing for us to do," Rooney says. He contacted Modell at the hospital and let him know that the Steelers were ready to move if the Browns were. Modell was in.

Rozelle dispatched Rooney to spread the word to the other franchise representatives. He called the different factions together and laid out the division groupings devised in Rozelle's office. The AFC's Division I would feature the Steelers, Browns, Bengals and Oilers. Division II would bring the NFL's Colts to join the Boston Patriots, Buffalo Bills, Miami Dolphins and New York Jets of the AFL. Division III grouped AFL teams the Denver Broncos, Kansas City Chiefs, Oakland Raiders and San Diego Chargers. It's all set, Rooney told the league power brokers. But there was at least one more uprising to deal with, albeit a short one.

"I'll never forget it," Rooney says. "There's Al Davis, who stands up and says, 'Those divisions are not set.' I think he might have been testing me, but I wasn't going to back down, and I said, 'Listen, Al, these are set and if you think that they aren't then we're out of here and this whole thing collapses.' And then Lombardi tears into him.

"Finally, Sid Gillman (coach of the San Diego Chargers), stood up and said, 'Our division is set.' That calmed it down."

The owners voted unanimously for the shift and the set-up of divisions in the AFC. However, it would take a few more months for them to agree on how to divide the NFC's divisions. The owners also agreed on paying the Steelers, Browns and Colts $3 million in guarantees to make up potential losses at the gate.

Rooney had one more sales job to do. He called his new coach, Chuck Noll, to make sure that he was okay with the decision. Noll was familiar with some of the AFL teams and welcomed the challenge of competing in a new conference. Rooney also called player representative Roy Jefferson, who also was quickly on board for the move. His last call was to *Pittsburgh Press* sports editor Pat Livingston to give him the scoop. "He said to me, 'Rooney, you went for the money, didn't you?'" he laughs. "I told him to look at the division and the rivalries it set up—both old and new. And (until realignment in 2001) those rivalries really held up.

"I always say Rozelle is a genius," Rooney continues.

And he proved to be a shrewd judge of who to get in his huddle.

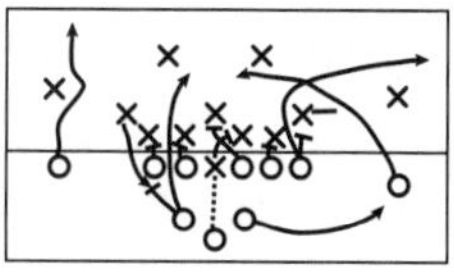

NINE

The NFL's Greatest Mystery: The Immaculate Reception

It was the great mystery of American sports history. Did he or didn't he? The moment was filled with suspense and intrigue and there was no Zabruder film for this episode to decipher what the outcome should have been. Ask the fans of the Steeler Nation and they will tell you there was no way their man touched the ball, while the patrons out by the bay will argue just the opposite. Yes, the Immaculate Reception, a play that gave the Steelers a 13-7 victory over the hated Oakland Raiders in a 1972 first round playoff two days before Christmas, is still hotly disputed 32 years later.

Three months earlier this match-up seemed very unlikely. While the Raiders had been a perennial power in the American Football Conference, representing the old AFL in Super Bowl II, Pittsburgh had been the doormat of the NFL throughout most of their 40-year history, going a combined 12-30 over the previous three seasons. Several astute drafts included a clutch decision by head coach Chuck Noll to take a running back from Happy Valley by the name of Franco Harris over Robert Newhouse, a short, stocky cannonball out of Houston. Harris seemed to be the missing link, helping transform the black and gold from laughingstock to powerhouse for the 1972 campaign, a season that began with the Steelers shocking the silver and black 34-28 at Three Rivers Stadium on opening day.

Franco went on to become only the fifth rookie in NFL history to rush for 1,000 yards in a season, compiling 1,055 yards for an AFC-high 5.6 per carry average and an NFL record six consecutive 100-yard games which tied the great Jim Brown's mark. Harris teamed up with the flamboyant John "Frenchy" Fuqua, he of the clear platform shoes which housed goldfish, to form an outstanding rushing duo that combined to gain more than 180 yards per game at a mind-boggling 5.1 yards per carry. Little did anyone know that the combination would be remembered for their contribution to that bizarre playoff ending.

Pittsburgh came through 1972 winning 11 of their 14 games and capturing the first division title in the team's history with the Central Division crown while Oakland took the West with a 10-3-1 mark. Both clubs returned to the confluence of the Monongahela, Allegheny and Ohio Rivers to face each other in what would turn out to be the first of several classic postseason match-ups in the 1970s.

While most people remember what is quite possibly the greatest play in National Football League history, the remaining 59 minutes and 38 seconds was perhaps one of the league's most forgettable playoff affairs, save the dramatic ending.

Pittsburgh's fabulous Steel Curtain was devastating, thwarting the mad bomber Daryl Lamonica time and time again, allowing the Raider quarterback to complete only 6 of 18 passes for 45 yards with interceptions by Andy Russell, and Jack Ham. The Oakland stop troops were equal to the task, chasing the Steelers quarterback Terry Bradshaw from one end of the field to the other and forcing him into tossing an interception of his own.

After Russell's first quarter pick-off, the black and gold had the first opportunity of the game to score, but the Raider defense held tough and kicker Roy Gerela's 52-yard field goal attempt fell short, keeping the game scoreless. Despite the failed opportunity, the Pittsburgh front defensive line wore Lamonica like a glove and kept the Oakland offense from executing their famous long bomb strategy with the incredible amount of pressure they put on him.

The black and gold once again put themselves in a scoring position as Bradshaw hit receiver Ron Shanklin twice and Pittsburgh moved to the Oakland 31, where it had the ball on a fourth and two. Instead of going for a 38-yard field goal, Noll decided to go for the first down. A sign of things to come happened as the Raiders hard-hitting defensive back Jack Tatum shot through the hole created by the Pittsburgh offensive line and knocked Fuqua back, giving the Raiders the ball and keeping the young Steelers off the board once again. Had the Emperor gone for the seemingly easy three pointer (Gerela was 8 of 12 in 1972 from that range), the dramatic final play would not have been necessary. Both teams went into the locker room after 30 minutes with the score remaining as it had begun, a 0-0 tie.

After misfiring twice in the first half on solid drives, the Steelers began the third quarter with their most impressive drive, an 11-play, 67-yard possession on the strength of short passes underneath the strong Oakland secondary. Bradshaw hit Harris out of the backfield before connecting with Shanklin inside the Raider 30. Pittsburgh made it down to the 11 before the drive finally stalled and Gerela put the first points of the game on the board with an 18-yard field goal.

All day the Pittsburgh defense kept the potent Raider offense in check with poor field position, thanks partly to the booming leg of veteran punter Bobby Walden who launched shots of 59 yards and 62, the two longest punts in AFC postseason history at the time. Oakland, who penetrated no further than the Pittsburgh 44-yard line until their last drive of the day, was stalled once again on their first possession of the second half turning the ball over to the black and gold.

With both offenses failing Lamonica tossed his second interception of the game in the third quarter. Oakland head coach John Madden finally went to his bench, picking his third-year quarterback, Ken Stabler. "The Snake," as he was known, studied under the legendary Paul "Bear" Bryant at Alabama. But despite that pedigree the Steel Curtain treated the young signal caller as rudely as they had Lamonica, who came in the game weakened by the flu.

With Pittsburgh in Oakland territory once again at the 32,

Bradshaw, who had tried to pick on Nehemiah Wilson all day, went to the well once too often and was picked off by Wilson as the Raider defensive back stepped in front of Shanklin at the 22, stopping yet another Pittsburgh scoring chance. Dominating the opportunities in the game, the Steelers only had a 3-0 lead to show for it and three points most certainly would not be enough to give Pittsburgh their first postseason victory ever.

This was a day for defense, and the Pittsburgh stop troops came to save the day once again as Stabler lost the ball and defensive back Mike Wagner dove on it at the Oakland 35, setting up Gerela's second three pointer of the day, giving the black and gold a 6-0 advantage with the game clock winding to an end.

Throughout his career, Stabler earned a reputation of never giving up, leading his team to victory from the jaws of defeat. Unfortunately for Pittsburgh, on this day he would show that attribute. Stabler hit tight end Raymond Chester for a first down, then running back Pete Banazak took a pass for another as Oakland, for really the first time in the game, began to drive on an impenetrable black and gold defense that had given up only 21 points in the last 21 quarters it had played. A pass to Hall of Fame receiver Fred Biletnikoff gave the Raiders the ball at the Pittsburgh 43, their deepest drive of the contest. There were under two minutes left in the game and the Steelers were giving up yardage grudgingly, knowing Oakland needed a touchdown to win. With the ball at the 30, rookie defensive end Craig Hanneman and linebacker Jack Ham broke into the Oakland backfield to chase Stabler. The Alabama alum broke to his left and took off down the sideline, ran past L.C. Greenwood at the 20, cut inside Wagner at the five and dove into the end zone at the 1:13 mark of the 4th, giving them a 7-6 advantage.

All the missed opportunities now haunted the Steelers. Had Noll not gone for it on fourth down earlier in the game, had the club more conservatively run the ball in the second half instead of trying to force a pass to Shanklin resulting in the Wilson interception, the game would be over and the Stabler scramble would be meaningless. Ah, but "what ifs" are what make special moments possible. Had Pittsburgh played safely on those two drives the most memorable moment in team history would not have occurred, and this contest would have been little more than a snoozer. There was more than a minute left, and the Steelers were running out of opportunities. After a screen pass to Harris took the ball to the 30, the Pittsburgh drive appeared thwarted at the 40 when Tatum knocked the ball away from tight end John McMakin, giving the black and gold a 4th and 10 with only 22 seconds remaining. Once again the Steelers would not go for the safe play, with Noll calling a post pattern to little-used receiver Barry Pearson. The Oakland front line would not allow that to happen. The Raiders put incredible pressure on the young Louisiana quarterback. Tony Cline and defensive end Horace Jones chased Bradshaw, trying to end this last-gasp Steelers' drive. As Bradshaw stopped at the 29 trying to elude the rush, Jones fortunately ran by him, allowing Terry to toss the ball down the field toward what he thought was an open Frenchy Fuqua. As he threw the ball, Cline got to him too late and what happened afterwards is subject to whomever's opinion you choose to believe.

From a technical standpoint, the ball hit off a two-headed monster formed by Tatum and Fuqua at the Oakland 34-yard line, bouncing up about eight yards into the waiting arms of the day's savior, Franco, who rambled the remaining 42 yards into the end zone for what appeared to be the miraculous winning score with only five seconds left.

There was no holding, no pass interference, so why you may ask was this play called into question? The answer is simply that in 1972, there was a rule that an offensive player could not catch a pass that hit off of another offensive player without first touching a defensive player. In today's game that rule doesn't exist, so this game would have ended without incident. But this play wasn't today, so throughout the past three decades it is the most argued ending in NFL history. Let's start by saying also in 1972, there weren't 10 million cameras to follow every nook and cranny of a contest, so it's tough to tell from the two lasting views of the play if the ball hit off of Tatum or Fuqua before Franco's famous catch. The NBC view, even in ultra-slow motion, shows little as to where the ball hit. The NFL Films version only gives a good view of Harris' hustling play, which is the most overlooked part of the whole proceedings.

Franco was supposed to be a blocker on the play, protecting against a blitz by the linebacker, but when it didn't happen, Harris decided to go out as a safety valve.

". . . I went downfield in case he [Bradshaw] needed me as an outlet receiver. I was always taught to go to the ball, so when he threw it, that's what I did," Harris, the game's hero, would recall. Pittsburgh fans remember Franco as making a hustling play; Oakland's star linebacker Phil Villipiano remembers differently, saying that Harris was lucky to be in position, claiming he was just lazy and jogging down the field when the ball surprisingly came into his hands. Villipiano also claimed he was about to tackle Harris when McMakin gave him "the biggest clip ever," hitting him on the back of the legs.

While Tatum to this day swears that the ball hit off of Fuqua's helmet—"I touched the man, but not the ball," is his claim—Fuqua from the outset would never say one way or another whether or not he hit the ball last. Immediately after the contest, Frenchy stated emphatically, "No comment. I'll tell you [the reporters] after the Super Bowl. I'm not chopping down any cherry trees, but no comment." He never actually made a statement afterward, claiming in a recent interview with the *Post-Gazette's* Chuck Finder that "Something like that you want to keep immaculate for all-time." Fuqua remains in the Steeler record book with the highest single-game rushing total (218 versus the Eagles in a 1970 game). He remains a fan favorite and is a colorful interview, despite his no-comment stance on the Immaculate Reception. And perhaps the reason for the no-comment posture originated from Tatum whacking Fuqua into another time zone during the play, thus distorting any memories. No matter, we love a good mystery.

If any fan thinks this was purely a Pittsburgh versus Oakland controversy, think again. So controversial was the play that Pittsburgh columnist Bob Smizik wrote this in a column later in the week: "The fingers balk at typing such a line, but it must come. I DO NOT BELIEVE THAT OAKLAND'S JACK TATUM TOUCHED THE BALL ON FRANCO HARRIS' MIRACLE TOUCHDOWN RUN SATURDAY." Smizik went on to surmise that the ball probably banged off Frenchy's shoulder pads, giving it enough force to pop back to Harris.

As bizarre as the actual play was, the circus that happened right after took the proceedings to a new level. The story changes depending upon whom you talk to. Following the game Madden said, "If the officials really knew what happened, they'd have called it right away. They called upstairs to Art McNally, NFL supervisor of officials, and he said it was a touchdown. He better have seen the replay. He better not have made the decision on his own."

What actually happened was referee Fred Swerington, the same ref who was involved in the controversial pass interference call against the Cowboys in Super Bowl XIII, consulted with his crew, one of whom was back judge Adrian Burk, who signaled touchdown, and claimed he called up to McNally to inform him that two members of his crew said Tatum touched the ball. McNally told him to go with the call. According to the toothless legend of Raider lore, executive Al LoCasale, the refs were concerned with how many security people there were to escort the crew out if they didn't call a touchdown and that's what the phone call was about. This was an explanation that was supported by Madden directly following the contest when he said that he thought the decision was made more toward "self preservation," claiming that he knew the referees were afraid someone would have been "killed" if they changed the call.

There is also the claim that this was the first time instant replay was used despite the fact there was no rule for instant replay then. That story is fueled by an announcement made in the press box that the officials were consulting the tape, a claim NFL officials deny.

Whatever happened, the Steelers won their first playoff game in a manner which NFL Films claims to be the No.1 moment in NFL history. It also remains the league's most controversial mystery, one that no matter how much time passes by, never comes any closer to being solved.

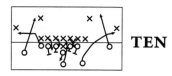

TEN

A Picture-Perfect Draft

"They beat the hell out of us."

That was Steelers head coach Chuck Noll's assessment of his team's 33-14 playoff loss to the Oakland Raiders that marked the end of the 1973 campaign. "We're too good a team to be losing."

But if the 1973 season had revealed anything to Pittsburgh management, coaches, players and fans it would be this: The Steelers may have been a good team, but they were not yet a great team. Oh sure they made their second straight playoff appearance—a first for the long-suffering franchise—but the team's 10-4 record and wild-card berth were both misleading.

There were a lot of creampuffs on the schedule, and, as expected, the Steelers won those games. The team was 6-0 against teams with losing records and had the benefit of two games against the 1-13 Houston Oilers, the worst team in the league. However, against teams with winning records, the Steelers were 4-4, losing their last three games against above-.500 squads.

Their biggest problem was an inconsistent offense. It lacked the firepower to match its stifling defense. Opposing quarterbacks completed only 45.7 percent of *their* passing attempts against the Steeler D. But on offense, the Steelers' quarterback crew of Terry Bradshaw, Terry Hanratty and Joe Gilliam connected with only 45.3 percent of their passing attempts—the worst mark of any playoff team. For much of '73, the defense was able to pick up the slack for the offense. But against the Raiders neither side of the ball was effective.

Although the team would be criticized for vanilla play calling, much of the season-long offensive woes could be traced to a series of debilitating injuries. Quarterback Terry Bradshaw, running back John "Frenchy" Fuqua, wide receiver Frank Lewis, tackle Gordon Gravelle and guard Jim Clack all missed significant amounts of time with injury. But great teams find a way to overcome. Great teams have depth at key positions, and more than anything else, that lack of depth led to a first-round playoff exit. For the Steelers to join the NFL's elite, help would have to come through the annual NFL Draft.

The pre-Noll draft years were lean, very lean. Then, the words "good" and "draft" were rarely used together in Pittsburgh unless, of course, you were talking about a beer poured at a local tavern. For some football aficionados, the types who sit in rapture as Chris Berman, Mel Kiper and company host the spectacle that has become NFL Draft Day, a draft class can be like a work of art, with each piece adding to the landscape. A dab of speed for the receiving corps here, a bold stroke of toughness for the backfield there, and a picture-perfect season is the result. If the draft is art, through much of their history, the Steelers' body of work had resembled a Velvet Elvis collection.

How bad was it? Consider that this was the team that could have picked Jim Brown, perhaps the greatest football player of all time. It did select another Hall of Famer, quarterback Len Dawson, in that year's draft—and then promptly cut him. Linebacker Dick Butkus? Pass. Instead of Butkus, the player who would define the middle linebacker position in his era, the Steelers chose defensive ends Jim Kelly and Ben McGee. (Who, you're probably asking? Exactly.)

Even when the team made what would seem to be good personnel decisions, they rarely worked out. For example, although the Steelers didn't actually draft him, they signed Johnny Unitas, a fixture on every list of the league's all-time-great quarterbacks. In Steeler fashion, he too, was cut. As a result, Pittsburgh fans would never be treated to this play-by-play call: "Unitas drops back to pass. Wait, it's a draw to Jim Brown. He's breaking free for the Steeler touchdown!" Double yoi indeed.

Then there was the team's "historic" 1963 draft. The Steelers had no picks in the first *seven* rounds, having traded them all away to pick up a gaggle of veterans who were either past their prime or longed one day to even have a prime. Two years later, they traded their first, third, fourth, fifth and sixth choices again for little in return. On the bright side, however, they made few really bad picks in those years' drafts.

But the arrival of Noll marked a seismic shift in the Steelers' fortunes. This would be a different Steelers team, one that had an actual personnel strategy: build through the draft.

The Steelers' tradition of piecing together a roster made mostly from other teams' cast-offs was a thing of the past. Selecting from the college ranks now meant something—particularly that there would be no more Kellys or McGees. Instead, an unmatched era of draft day success was on its way, thanks to a more systematic and collaborative approach. Noll's scouts would actually have a say in the draft, something that had not happened in the team's history. In fairness, though, it's also how it worked throughout the league at the time. Scouts would turn over their reports to the teams' front office staff and then head back out on the road to start the process all over again. There was little interaction.

Noll changed this. He wanted to know more than what was in the reports. He actually talked directly to the scouts and *welcomed* their input. This would lead to a landmark first pick of the Noll era—a defensive end from tiny North Texas State named Joe Greene, who would anchor the Steelers' defense for more than a decade.

And never discount the specter of luck, either. After 37 miserable years, the law of averages finally applied to the Steelers. There were hints, starting on Jan. 9, 1970. That day, representatives from the Steelers and the Chicago Bears met in New Orleans' Fairmont Hotel for a coin flip that would determine which team would have the first pick in the draft that year (each team finished the 1969 season with a dismal 1-13 record).

In a most un-Steelerlike twist of fate, Pittsburgh won the toss and the right to choose the consensus first overall pick, a rifle-armed quarterback from Louisiana Tech named Terry Bradshaw.

Noll's first four drafts brought players who would have key roles in the dynasty that would rule football for the decade of the'70s: Bradshaw, Greene, L.C. Greenwood, Mel Blount, Jack Ham and Franco Harris. Clearly, momentum was building.

Yet even with the shrewd drafts that Noll had under his belt, nothing could have pointed to the success that the 1974 draft would bring. "It's the best draft ever," says Bill Walsh, the former San Francisco 49ers coach, general manager, undisputed football genius and architect of the West Coast offense. Another GM, John Butler, who orchestrated the Buffalo Bills team to an unprecedented four straight Super Bowls, adds, "It's phenomenal, absolutely phenomenal, to have that great collection come out of one class."

It's not hyperbole either. Any way we look at it, this is *the* greatest NFL team draft of all time: Twenty-eight Super Bowl rings, if you count the free agents (more on that later). Twenty-nine Pro Bowl appearances. And most impressive of all, four Hall of Famers. Most entire drafts didn't yield four Hall of Famers. To further put it in perspective, no other team has drafted more than two players who would later go on to enshrinement in Canton in a single year. The Steelers doubled that.

Velvet Elvis had left the building. The Steelers painted the draft picture that all teams strive to copy.

But it's unlikely this masterpiece will ever be duplicated. The football world has changed dramatically in those 30 years, particularly as it relates to the player draft. First, there are fewer rounds and more teams. In 1974, 26 teams went through 17 rounds looking to build for the future. Today, 32 franchises sort through only seven rounds.

And there are no sleepers today. Prospective pros show up at the scouting combines to show off their athletic abilities for all teams. Athletes from even the smallest colleges go through a series of workouts and interviews they hope will enhance their chances of being selected in the draft. There was no such animal in 1974.

Now on draft day, each team stocks its "war room" with file upon file on each of the players in the draft. How much can that linebacker from Marshall University bench press? What was the 40-yard-dash time for that wide receiver from Alcorn State? That running back from Vanderbilt looks a little pudgy.

Drafting a dynasty

Although 1974 gets the attention as the greatest draft in NFL history—and rightfully so—nonetheless there have been some other memorable drafts for the Steelers that led to their unparalleled success in the '70s. Noll's first draft in 1969 brought defensive linemen Joe Greene and L.C. Greenwood, along with guard Jon Kolb. The following year the Steelers drafted two Hall of Famers—quarterback Terry Bradshaw and cornerback Mel Blount.

In 1971, two other key pieces to the Super Bowl puzzle were added—linebacker Jack Ham, another Hall of Famer, and safety Mike Wagner. The following year brought running back Franco Harris, the leading rusher in team history and another player enshrined in Canton.

After 1974 the Steelers didn't have a true impact draft for years. For one thing, their success translated into later draft picks. And the rest of the league caught up with them in terms of finding players from the black colleges.

What's his body-fat analysis say? That defensive back from Mount Union, what's his vertical leap? The answers are at the fingertips for members of the franchise's personnel team.

Much of that info comes from scouting services whose staffs scour the country to collect all the vitals on players, potential players and anyone who just happens to look good in pads and a helmet. In 1974, the fledgling BLESTO scouting service was the only game in town. The Steelers were one of a handful of teams that BLESTO counted as members. (The BLESTO acronym comes from Bears, Lions, Eagles, Steelers Talent Organization.) Today, all 32 teams receive BLESTO reports. And, of course, there was no "SportsCenter," where highlights of even Division III teams will show up during ESPN's coverage of all things football.

In addition to the then-novel draft service, the Steelers also had a bit of a secret weapon—Bill Nunn, only the sixth African American to be a full-time NFL scout. His specialty was working the black colleges—an untapped goldmine at the time. Nunn had the best contacts of all the small number of scouts working that circuit. For more than two decades he had selected the black college all-star team for the *Pittsburgh Courier*, the nation's most influential African American newspaper.

It was Nunn who found Greenwood at Arkansas AM&N and defensive tackle Ernie Holmes at Texas Southern. As the 1974 draft approached, Nunn found another black college gem—wide receiver John Stallworth—who soon became a favorite of Noll's, too. And that's where the drama of the January 29-30, 1974, draft began.

There was a split in the draft room. The Steelers were in dire need of some offense, especially at wide receiver. One of the starting wideouts, Frank Lewis, had missed six games because of a broken sternum and leg injuries. In his absence, the Steelers' receiving core was exposed, and their only remaining legitimate threat, Ron Shanklin, drew double and even triple coverage. Noll, thanks to a glowing report from Nunn, wanted to address that need by choosing Stallworth with the team's first-round pick, the 21st pick overall. Other scouts pointed to another wide receiver, Lynn Swann from USC. An All-American and team captain, Swann had made his mark as a big-play receiver. He was a key weapon on the school's 1972 national championship team, and his talents were widely showcased on national television, including two Rose Bowl games. Stallworth, on the other hand, wasn't on a lot of radar screens. That anonymity can be traced on some level to Nunn.

At the time, teams shared film of college prospects. Nunn conveniently held on to the only existing film of Stallworth's 11-catch performance against Tennessee State so that other teams' scouts wouldn't see it. And for those scouts who knew something about Stallworth, the lanky wide receiver's 4.7-second time in the 40-yard dash eliminated him from early round consideration. Nunn saw something, though. He faked an illness and stayed behind after other scouts left to re-time Stallworth, who would run a faster 40 for his private audience. Nunn made sure that time was kept a secret.

Like Stallworth, Swann didn't exactly impress with his workout time, either. Despite his college credentials, his 4.65 was ordinary at best. BLESTO re-timed him at 4.58 seconds in his final run for the Steelers. It was a precursor to Swann's NFL career: he wasn't very speedy until there was something riding on it. Races didn't mean a lot to Swann. He thrived on competition. When it came time to get open on a big play, his adrenaline pushed him for that extra burst.

With the 21st pick, the Steelers chose Swann. The teams' scouts had convinced Noll, who did have the final say on draft picks, that Stallworth would last past the first round. In selecting Swann, the Steelers started a theme that would repeat itself throughout this draft. On paper, this draft class wouldn't seem to be anything special. But on the field, once the huddle broke, these guys could play. No stopwatch could measure a player's hunger to compete.

While the first round offered a tough choice, the second round brought the biggest gamble. In the weeks leading up to the draft, a scout was making his case for another sleeper pick. Besides a persuasive argument, this scout had something else going for him—the name Rooney. Tim Rooney, one of owner Art Rooney, Sr.'s five sons, had raved about an undersized linebacker from Kent State University. Rooney was impressed with film of Jack Lambert. But the clincher came when his brother, Art, Jr., visited Ohio to watch practice. The day Art, Jr., arrived on campus the field was too wet for the team to practice on it. Instead, the team worked out on a gravel parking lot. And there was Lambert diving to make tackles and pulling cinders from his bloody body. Great desire, productivity and determination, Rooney noted with astonishment. But 195 pounds for an NFL linebacker? Conventional wisdom said that Lambert was 20 pounds too light for the position. (Wide receivers and even some kickers weigh 195 pounds today). But the Steelers lacked depth at linebacker and would need to select one in the draft. The more prudent choice, and one argued for by many scouts, would have been Matt Blair, a prototypical linebacker and an All-American from Iowa State who, unlike Lambert, had played against major-college talent. But the cinders, argued the Rooneys, were a clear sign that Lambert deserved a more serious look.

Adding to the deliberation was the Steelers trade with the Raiders for Tom Keating, which cost them a third-round pick in the 1974 draft. Whether they chose Stallworth, Lambert or Blair with the draft's 46th pick, they would have to wait another 36 picks for their next selection. Once again Nunn told Noll that Stallworth would still be on the board later, should the team opt not to pick him in the second round. This time, however, he wasn't as sure. After all, other scouts *had* seen Stallworth, many even projecting a move to the defensive backfield. In fact, a few months earlier, Stallworth had played defensive back in that year's Senior Bowl, which turned out to be a break for the Steelers. Teams didn't get a look at him at wide receiver, and Stallworth made no impact as a defensive back because it was a new position for him. For the Steelers, Lambert was the pick, a "cinder-ella" story, to be sure, of a linebacker who would embody the very toughness for which the Steeler dynasty would be known.

An excruciating two hours passed before the first of the Steelers' fourth-round selections (they had another thanks to a September trade with the Patriots). With the 82nd pick, much to the relief of the coaching staff, Stallworth was still available. And the Steelers didn't hesitate this time. The gamble had paid off. Despite playing much of his career, ironically enough, in Swann's shadow, Stallworth would retire as the franchise leader in receptions.

With their second pick in the round, No. 100 overall, they chose Jimmy Allen, a defensive back from UCLA to shore up their special teams, more so than the secondary. Allen had four solid years for the Steelers before moving on to the Detroit Lions.

Lambert and Stallworth had been the scouts' sleeper picks. But for the fifth round, Noll had a sleeper of his own. When Clack and Gravelle went down, it became increasingly clear that the Steelers needed additional depth on their offensive line. Noll, himself a former NFL lineman, liked what he saw in Wisconsin center Mike Webster. Once again, it surely didn't show up on paper. Webster barely broke the 200-pound mark and could have been clocked with a calendar rather than a stopwatch with his 5.3 time in the 40. But the film didn't lie. Noll reviewed footage from the East-West Shrine Bowl. Despite being outweighed by nearly a hundred pounds, Webster manhandled the defensive tackle he lined up against in that college all-star game. For 14 years Webster would do the same in the NFL once he added nearly 30 pounds of muscle—not bad for a guy picked 125th in the draft.

In five rounds, the Steelers had drafted four future Hall of Famers, but they weren't through yet, even

Not even Noll was infallible

The Steelers also had some bad draft picks in the Noll years, particularly with their first-round selections; the team would drift to mediocrity and below in the '80s.

It started with Baylor running back Greg Hawthorne, who was the top choice in 1979. He was given the "best athlete available" label, but ended up as a special teamer at best. The BAA label also applied to Arizona State quarterback Mark Malone, selected first in the following year's draft. Although he quarterbacked them to an AFC championship game appearance in 1984, Malone's biggest accomplishment came as a wide receiver, as he hauled a 90-yard touchdown reception, a team record that has been tied but never beaten.

The downward spiral continued with defensive lineman Keith Gary in 1981. He wasn't the BAA, just a B-U-S-T. So was Walter Ambercrombie, the following year's pick and perhaps the softest running back in team history.

The streak seemed to end in 1983 with the selection of Gabe Rivera, a hardnosed defensive tackle from Texas Tech dubbed "Señor Sack." Rivera's NFL career was cut short by a tragic auto accident that left him a paraplegic during his first season.

In 1985, Daryl Sims, a Wisconsin defensive end, made fans long for Keith Gary. A year later, guard John Reinstra from Temple sent fans to temple to pray for better draft picks. Defensive end Aaron Jones ('88), running back Tim Worley ('89) and defensive end Huey Richardson ('91) were the final first-round flops picked by Noll. Bill Cowher took over as coach for the 1992 season.

as the draft ended. Once again, Nunn's network would pay off. His friend, Willie Jeffries, a coach at South Carolina State, called to talk about one of his players that had not been drafted—a hard-hitting, if undersized, linebacker named Donnie Shell. Shell, another black college phenom, came to Pittsburgh for a free-agent tryout and impressed the coaching staff. They signed him and moved him to safety, where he would make five Pro Bowls and retire as the franchise's all-time interception leader. He also could end up as the fifth member of the 1974 rookie crop to be inducted in Canton (that's another chapter in this book).

Another piece to the Steelers' puzzle came via free agency. The team needed a tight end. Randy Grossman, largely unheralded in his four years at Temple University, showed enough in a tryout to be signed. He, like Shell, would earn four Super Bowl rings.

The 1974 draft was the high-water mark of Noll's tenure. Without the contributions of that draft class, it's difficult to say if the Steelers would have won one Super Bowl let alone four. The rookies had an early head start, thanks to a players' strike that kept most of the veterans out of training camp for a few weeks. During that time, Swann, Stallworth and Webster learned the offense, working out with backup quarterback Joe Gilliam, one of the few non-rookies to report to camp on time. Lambert also made good use of the extra time in camp and worked his way into the starting lineup.

When the Steelers and Raiders met later that season in the AFC championship game, the rookie class would help the team get revenge for the previous year's playoff rout. Lambert led a defense that held the Raiders' running game to 29 yards. Swann caught a touchdown pass that broke a 10-10 tie and propelled the Steelers to a 24-13 victory and a Super Bowl date with the Minnesota Vikings two weeks later. Again, the defense would dominate, as the Steelers captured their first Vince Lombardi Trophy with a 16-6 pasting of the Vikings. This time, it was the Steelers who "beat the hell out of" their opponents. The Steelers were not just good, not just great, but super.

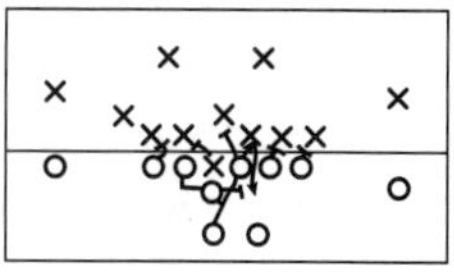

ELEVEN

The White Stuff

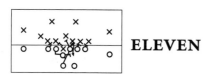

"Hero" is one of one of the most overused words in sports. It's tossed about cavalierly and has become almost an announcer's game-summary cliche: when the starting quarterback goes down and the rookie backup who hasn't taken a meaningful snap the entire season takes over and leads the team to an improbable victory; when the defensive end jars the ball loose from the opposing running back with a crushing hit and his teammate—out of position on the play—falls on the ball and preserves the victory; when the place kicker who hasn't hit from outside of 45 yards since anyone can remember, lines up on a frozen field with the wind gusting in his face and splits the uprights as the clock expires.

All are likely to get the hero tag. All are great football stories. All are great athletic accomplishments and are inspirational outside of football. The life lessons: always be prepared to give your best when called on; make sure to show up since sometimes being in the right place at the right time can make the difference; and you never know what you can accomplish until you try. Great axioms, but are the players and their actions heroic? No.

Such is it with one of the great moments in Pittsburgh Steelers' history, one that has gained legendary status over the years. It's Jan. 12,1975, Super Bowl IX, the team's first-ever championship game appearance, and defensive end Dwight White gets out of his hospital bed to lead the team to victory over the Minnesota Vikings. Down 20 pounds because of his illness and listed as doubtful for the game, White plays all but the last few downs when the game is far out of reach. And it's White's sack of Vikings quarterback Fran Tarkenton that opens the scoring—just to add a dash of Hollywood.

"It's a good story," White says, adding that it's one he's told countless times over the years. Though his hair is now dotted to match his surname, his eyes gleam with youth as he relates what has become his signature football tale. As any good storyteller does, he provides a little background.

"It was a real knockdown, draining season," he begins. "I seem to think it was the coldest winter I could remember. It seems like every practice it was like 8 degrees and just nasty, and that really takes a toll on your resistance. By the time we got to New Orleans [for the Super Bowl] I had been fighting this nagging cold for months, and going from 10 degrees in Pittsburgh to hot and 80 percent humidity in New Orleans just brought it to a head."

In those early stages of the Super Bowl, it was common for the league to take a week off after the respective conference championship games to create marketing and viewership buzz before the game. It also allowed the players to mix some fun with the preparation for the game.

"Joe Greene, L.C. Greenwood and I were having dinner in the French Quarter early in the week and I was getting sicker and sicker," White recalls. "It got to the point where I just couldn't breathe. I was literally bent over gasping for air. Joe picked me up and carried me to a cab and got me to the hospital."

At the hospital, the diagnosis wasn't good: pleurisy and viral pneumonia. White was immediately admitted. For those without medical degrees, pleurisy is a rather unpleasant little malady, where the lungs' two layers are inflamed and rub together with each breath, causing almost stabbing pain. Or there's White's diagnosis. "It just hurts like hell no matter what you do." Combined with pneumonia, he says, "I was one sick puppy. When it comes to getting sick, you can't do much better than that."

But then again White was always somewhat of an over-achiever. He grew up in the projects of Dallas, one of 10 kids. A tight end in high school, he attended East Texas State University where he was selected by the Steelers in the fourth round of the 1971 NFL draft. At the time, the Steelers were among the pioneers of finding and signing athletes from smaller, mostly black colleges. White worked his way into the starting lineup in his rookie season and was named to his first Pro Bowl in 1973. His edge had always been his hard work and ability to outwork his opponent.

But in the days leading up to that first Super Bowl, it was all he could do to breathe. "I was on this ventilator or respirator thing to help me breathe, and I lost 20 pounds during those five days I was in the hospital. I was really weak."

White checked himself out of the hospital the Thursday before the Super Bowl and tried to practice. Bad idea. He found himself back there on Friday. But he was determined to give it one more try. He checked out a second time the night before the game.

"I woke up the next morning and went to the pre-game meal like everything was normal, you know, let's get ready and go," he says. The coaching staff and the other players seemed to be humoring him, he thought. "They figured there was no way I was going to be in any shape to play in that game. I don't think they expected me to make it through the warm-ups."

Head coach Chuck Noll was chief among the doubters. He instructed Greene to go over and "work out" White to see if he was game-ready after his hospital stay. "Joe whacked me with a couple of really good shots... really good shots, but I took it and I was okay to go." You have to figure, if you can get the snot knocked out of you by Joe Greene and be ready to line up for more, you can handle pretty much anything the other team's offensive line can throw at you.

But one thing that White wasn't ready for or didn't appreciate was the mothering he got from his teammates. "It was getting annoying real quick to keep hearing, 'Are you okay?' all the time," he says. "It was like they were asking me that in the huddle after every play. Every play: 'Are you okay?' I said, 'Can we just play the damn game already. I'm fine, just get away from me and let me catch my breath. You're cutting off my air."

It was a tough game, very physical and dominated by the two defenses—particularly the Steelers. White was a mainstay in disrupting the Vikings' attack, and he surprised everyone by playing all but a few meaningless series at the end. But there was that one play that would live in Steeler lore.

Late in the second quarter, on second down from their own 10, Vikings quarterback Tarkenton and running back Dave Osborn mishandled the hand-off on a running play, resulting in a fumble. Tarkenton scrambled to cover the ball a yard deep in the end zone to prevent a Steelers touchdown and was tagged by White for a safety and a 2-0 Steelers' lead. Ironically, he wasn't the one given credit at first. "If you look at a lot of the pictures, they show (middle linebacker Jack) Lambert standing over Tarkenton, but if you look at the record book, it's my name that's there. I scored that safety."

That score opened the floodgates for the Steelers' defense, which harassed Tarkenton for the remainder of the game. The Steel Curtain set Super Bowl records for fewest rushing yards allowed (18) and total yards (119). The offensive charge was led by running back Franco Harris, who would be named the game's MVP, and his 158 rushing yards. The Steelers won 16-6 in a game that was nowhere near as close as the score would suggest.

And White had gone from a hospital sickbed to world champion. A remarkable story, to be sure. But put the hero question to White and he'll very quickly downplay the notion. "Hero? Hell, I was a football player," he says. "I was doing what I was supposed to do, what I was programmed to do, and that's to play football. There's nothing heroic about it."

In fact, part of his motivation might even be somewhat selfish. Keep in mind the Steelers' record of futility up until the '70s. In 40-plus years they had only rarely sniffed the championship game, let alone played in a Super Bowl. Their first real playoff experience was in the 1972 season, beating the Oakland Raiders on the miracle Immaculate Reception before losing to the Miami Dolphins in the AFC championship game. The following year, the Raiders eliminated the Steelers in the first round. This was not exactly a team with a championship pedigree.

"Who knew if we ever going to have this chance again?" White says, explaining his determination to play in the first Super Bowl game. "This was my lifetime dream. To miss it would be unacceptable. No way in hell. Uh-uh. You cannot tell someone who competes on this level, 'I'm sorry, but you can't play.' That wasn't going to fly for me."

Maybe it was adrenaline that carried White through that day, along with that passion for playing football. When it was over and his teammates were celebrating what would be the first of four championships in a decade of excellence unmatched by any other franchise, he had little left to give.

"I went to this little diner across the street from the hotel and had a cheeseburger with sportswriter Vito Stellino and his son. Then I crashed. I got back to Pittsburgh and spent eight more days in the hospital."

White looks back fondly on that Super Bowl for a number of reasons. "It was our first championship, the first time the Steelers had ever won anything," he says. "It also meant a lot having to go through what I did to get there. It was very motivational."

But not heroic.

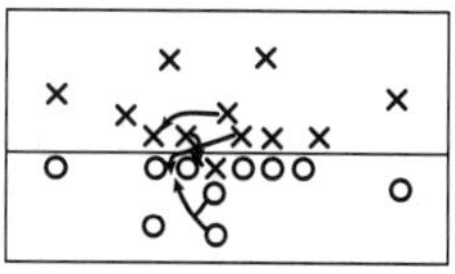

TWELVE

The Defense Never Rests

It happens every decade or so. Some defense steps up, plays at such a high level and becomes so dominant that the comparisons begin. In 1985, the Chicago Bears and their 46 defense crushed everything in their way. In 2000, it was the Baltimore Ravens, led by an intense middle linebacker Ray Lewis, who battered and bruised their opponents en route to a Super Bowl victory. Most recently, the Tampa Bay Buccaneers entered the discussion via a dismantling of the powerful offense of the Oakland Raiders in Super Bowl XXXVII.

The teams those defensive stalwarts are compared to is the Pittsburgh Steelers. Although each of those teams had remarkable, even record-setting years, they didn't match the decade-long excellence and four Super Bowl wins that the Steelers of the '70s produced. And in 1976, despite—or maybe because of—a rough start, the Steelers defensive 11 laid claim to being the best ever.

The Steelers were coming off back-to-back Super Bowl wins. The smart money said a third was in their grasp. Not since the Green Bay Packers of a decade earlier had any team pulled off a three-peat. The Steelers, so dominant in dispatching the class of the National Football Conference, the Minnesota Vikings and Dallas Cowboys, in successive Super Bowls, were all but anointed to be champs again. On paper nobody matched up to them.

On the turf, however, it was a different story. Early on there were signs that a championship would not be that expected cakewalk. The season started with a grudge match against the hated Oakland Raiders in Oakland. Just nine months before, the two teams met on the frozen turf of Three Rivers Stadium with a trip to the Super Bowl on the line—just as they had done the year before. The Steelers and Raiders were the top teams in the conference, and the Steelers were having their way with Oakland.

In the 1976 season opener, it looked to be more of the same. Thanks to an alert Franco Harris lateral to John Stallworth, who scrambled the final 47 yards for a touchdown, the Steelers broke open a tight game. Add a Harris 3-yard touchdown run, and the Steelers had a 28-14 lead. A 14-point lead late in the fourth should have signaled game over.

But Oakland had Ken Stabler, a quarterback with a knack for comebacks. He found his trusty tight end Dave Casper for completions of 21 and 25. Another sure-handed receiver, Fred Biletnikoff, hauled in a pass for 18. Running back Pete Banazak, whom the Steelers had held mostly in check for three and a half quarters, slammed up the middle for 11. Stabler wrapped up the drive by finding Casper alone in the end zone for a touchdown. With 2:56 remaining, the Steelers' lead was down to 7.

But the offense couldn't run out the clock. Two running plays were stuffed by the Raiders' defense. On third down, the Steelers chose to pass instead of keeping the ball on the ground. Instead of running more clock or forcing the Raiders to call a timeout, Bradshaw's pass to John Stallworth was batted away, and the Steelers were forced to punt.

Former Steeler Warren Bankston knifed in to block the punt. The Raiders recovered the ball on the Steelers 29 and set up for a tying touchdown. The Steelers forced three straight Stabler incompletions, but on fourth down, the Oakland signal caller found the speedy Cliff Branch who knifed through the Steelers' secondary, down to the 2. On the next play, Stabler kept it himself and plowed in behind the Oakland line for a tying touchdown.

With a little over a minute left, it seemed this showdown of the AFC titans was headed to overtime. But Steelers' quarterback Terry Bradshaw wanted to press the issue during regulation. It turned out to be a bad decision when he was picked off by the Raiders and returned to the Steelers' 12. Two runs later, Oakland kicker Fred Steinfort booted the game-winning field goal, with 18 seconds left.

The Steel Curtain defense had blown a huge lead, but the game had a more lasting impression on both the Raiders and the Steelers. For the Raiders, the win brought confidence. If the road to the Super Bowl were to indeed run through the Steelers, the Raiders knew they could beat their rivals. For the Steelers, letting this one slip away brought the team into a bit of a funk.

The next week against division rival Cleveland, the Steelers sleepwalked through the first half. Two Brian Sipe touchdown passes had the Browns up 14-0, before a game-changing punt block by Jack Ham paced a 31-14 comeback. The defense and ground game brought the Steelers back in the game. Bradshaw had an off day, completing only 7 of 23 passes for 77 yards. An unproductive passing game was a cause for alarm, particularly if the team would get behind. They didn't seem to have the firepower to mount a comeback.

In game three, questions about the offense continued. The Steelers turned the ball over six times in the first half—all on fumbles. The New England Patriots capitalized on the turnovers and turned a 20-9 deficit into a 30-27 lead, thanks to two long touchdown passes—a 38-yarder to Russ Francis and a 58-yarder to Darryl Stingley. The Steelers moved down the field to attempt to tie the game, but some crucial penalties cost them field position. Roy Gerela's 48-yard field goal attempt fell short as time expired.

The following week saw more heartache against the Vikings. Once again, the offense committed six turnovers, four of them Bradshaw interceptions. This time, however, the defense kept the Steelers in the game and led to the game's opening touchdown. A Jack Lambert interception set up the Steelers' lone score, a 1-yard pass to tight end Bennie Cunningham. However, the offense was unable to cash in on three other Vikings turnovers in a 17-6 loss.

It got worse in week five, a rematch with the Browns in Cleveland. What seemed to be a positive quickly turned negative: The Steelers blocked a Don Cockcroft field goal attempt, but the Browns recovered when the ball crossed the line of scrimmage. The Browns continued the drive and scored a touchdown that turned out to be the difference in their 18-16 victory over the Steelers. But the Steelers lost more than the game. They also lost their quarterback to back and neck injuries when the Browns' Joe Turkey Jones dumped Bradshaw onto the turf helmet-first.

As Bradshaw lie on the grass at Municipal Stadium, it became apparent that the Steelers' slim hope of making the playoffs, let alone winning a third straight championship, would rest on two things: their ability to run the ball and, more importantly, the Steel Curtain.

The Steelers had built their two Super Bowl champs on the strength of their defense. "We were a very powerful, very intimidating bunch," says defensive lineman Dwight White. "There may have been players as good, but nowhere were there as many on one team. And we knew it."

The Steel Curtain was a mix of players with different skills and different styles. There was the physical, with Mean Joe Greene, the anchor of the line and arguably the greatest player in franchise history. Greene redefined the defensive tackle position, often forcing opposing offensive coordinators to create blocking schemes to slow him down. The problem for opposing linemen was that opened opportunities for other members of the front four. That was the finesse part of the defense.

On one end was the speedy L.C. Greenwood, who retired as the franchise's all-time sacks leader. Another physical member of the front four was often overlooked. Tackle Ernie "Fats" Holmes was the only of the four to not appear in a Pro Bowl. Holmes relied on the power game as one of the strongest players on the team. For White, 1976 would be a challenging season. He was injured in the preseason and sprained his knee against Cleveland, sidelining him for five games. John Banaszak filled in admirably, as the front four didn't miss a step. It was their job to occupy the offensive line and allow the team's linebackers to make plays.

And what a linebacking core it was. It also featured a blend of styles, starting in the middle with Lambert, perhaps the most intense and vocal on-field leader. "Once I walked on the field, it was my field," the Hall of Famer would say. He had the season of his career, being named the NFL's Defensive Player of the Year by both the AP and UPI. Lambert used emotion and intimidation to fuel his efforts.

On the outside, Ham took a different approach. He was the thinking-man's linebacker. Schooled at Penn State's "Linebacker U," Ham was a master of technique. He was as skilled covering tight ends or receivers out of the backfield as he was stuffing the run or sacking the quarterback.

On the other side, Andy Russell and Loren Toews split time. Russell was a six-time All-Pro playing in his last season with the team. He was a link to the bad teams of the pre-Chuck Noll years. Even as his career was winding down, Russell was still well schooled in the finer points of playing linebacker. He passed that along to Toews, a willing student with great speed and mobility.

The defensive backfield had its stars, too. It started with Mel Blount at corner, arguably the greatest to ever play the position. Blount played a physical brand of football, jamming wide receivers at the line to effectively shut them down. So dominant was Blount that the league changed the rules so that defenders could only hit receivers within five yards of the line of scrimmage. It was often referred to as "The Blount Rule." At the other corner was J.T. Thomas, a ferocious hitter, who had a lot of passes thrown his direction because teams tried to avoid throwing to Blount's side. Thomas, however, was a shutdown corner in his own right. He also had a knack for the big play.

So did the Steelers' safeties. Glen Edwards had already proved his mettle in Super Bowl play, coming up with key interceptions against Dallas and forcing a Minnesota turnover with a crushing hit. His counterpart, Mike Wagner, called the coverage for the defensive squad, and like Edwards was named to the AFC Pro Bowl squad. Backups Donnie Shell, also known for his hard hitting, and Jimmy Allen provided depth.

How good was this defensive unit? When the NFL named its all-time team in 1994, it included Greene, Blount and Lambert.

All had stellar careers, but for the squad as a whole, 1976 was the best they played collectively.

Sitting at 1-4 with their starting quarterback out and the offense shaky at best, it was time for the defense to take over. "Defense is a matter of imposing your will on them," White says. "And that's what we did." It began with a must-win game against division rival Cincinnati. Hell, at 1-4, *every* game became a must-win affair. The Bengals were the Steelers' toughest division opponent. Led by crafty quarterback Ken Anderson, the Bengals were a legitimate threat to the Steelers' AFC Central crown—even before the Steelers' miserable start.

With Bradshaw unable to play, the team turned to rookie quarterback Mike Kruczek to handle the offense. His instructions: Don't do anything stupid, hand the ball off to Harris and Rocky Bleier, and get out of the way. We don't expect you to win games; we just expect you not to lose them.

Then the Steel Curtain took over. The Bengals managed only a pair of field goals as the defense dominated in a 23-6 Pittsburgh victory. The Steelers allowed only 171 yards to a fairly explosive offense and repeatedly harassed Anderson, sacking him five times and intercepting him twice.

The following week against the New York Giants, the defense was even sharper. The Steel Curtain completely shut down the G-Men, allowing only 151 yards in posting a dominant 27-0 shutout. Thomas' interception and 38-yard return sparked the offense. Kruczek was efficient, completing 12 of 19 passes, while the running gamed chewed up the Giants for 230 yards. Things were beginning to gel.

The Steel Curtain was on a roll. They beat up their opponents. They stuffed the run and then unleashed a relentless pass rush against opposing quarterbacks. Should they get the pass off, their receivers had to work against the very physical, punishing secondary. The onslaught would continue in week eight. For the first time in 42 years, the Steelers posted consecutive shutouts. This time the victims were the San Diego Chargers. The Steelers pummeled the rebuilding Bolts, 23-0. San Diego managed only seven first downs and were stymied to the tune of 134 net yards—a season low for the Steelers. The offense received a boost as well, with Bradshaw coming back to play. But the way the defense was playing, the offense didn't have to do much.

But against Kansas City the following week, the offense broke loose for 451 yards, including 330 on the ground. That effort was overshadowed, however, when the Steel Curtain pitched its third consecutive shutout and forced six turnovers. The Steelers thumped the Chiefs 45-0.

Next on the schedule were the Miami Dolphins. The Dolphins, the last team before the Steelers to earn a Lombardi Trophy, had fallen on hard times. But it was a team that was always dangerous with wily quarterback Bob Griese. The Dolphins did manage to halt the Steelers' scoreless streak, thanks to a long field goal by Garo Yepremian. But that was all they could muster in a 14-3 loss. Once again Bradshaw was injured, forcing

Kruczek to come in relief. Once again, he minimized mistakes in guiding the Steelers to victory.

Kruczek started the next week in division match-up against a dangerous Houston Oilers team that was better than its record indicated. The Oilers were the first team in 22 quarters to reach the end zone against the Steel Curtain, but it wasn't nearly enough. The Steelers battered Oilers' QB John Hadl and intercepted him twice in the 32-16 win. That set the stage for a showdown against Cincinnati the next week that would all but determine the winner of the division.

"Going into that game," White recalls, "we told the offense just get us one touchdown, and we'll do the rest." Coming into the contest at Riverfront Stadium, the Steelers trailed the hometown Bengals by two games, but knew that their earlier win against the team provided an important tie breaker, should both squads finish with identical records. The Steelers caught a break with the weather, too. Forecasts called for heavy snow. That would, in essence, ground Cincy's passing game, the strength of the team. The game would be predicated on defense and running the ball. And the Steelers were superior in both those areas.

But the Bengals were no slouches defensively. Through the first half, they matched the intensity of the Steel Curtain. The only score in the first 30 minutes was a 40-yard Chris Bahr field goal, giving the Bengals a 3-0 half time lead. But in the second half, as the snow squalls hit, the Steel Curtain really clamped down. The Bengals twice made it into black-and-gold territory only to be turned away with nothing to show for the effort. Kruczek quarterbacked a ground game that churned out 225 yards and, as requested, gave the defense the touchdown it needed on a 4-yard Harris run in the third quarter. As White predicted, that touchdown held up. And the Steel Curtain began a new scoreless streak. "That game was huge," White recalls. "If we lose, we don't make the playoffs."

Even with the victory, the Steelers had no room for error. They still trailed the Bengals by a game with two remaining on the schedule. But the Steelers had an easier row to hoe. Week 13 brought the hapless Tampa Bay Buccaneers, a first-year expansion team that might have been the worst team in NFL history. The Bengals, on the other hand, had to travel to Oakland to play a team that had only one loss. That match-up on the coast quickly became a must-win for Cincinnati, as the Steelers crushed the Bucs 42-0. Kruczek and Bradshaw split duties behind center. Bradshaw tossed two TD passes to Swann. Once again, the defense was impenetrable, holding Buccaneer quarterbacks to 11 net passing yards.

Cincinnati didn't fare as well against the Raiders, dropping a 35-20 decision. The Steelers and Bengals were both 9-4, but two of the Cincy losses came against Pittsburgh. Just to make matters a little more complicated, the Cleveland Browns quietly posted a 9-4 record as well. Conceivably, all three teams could have finished at 10-4. The important word would once again be "tie breaker." The Steelers held their destiny in their own hands: they would win the division with a victory against the last place Houston Oilers on the basis of a sweep in their season series against Cincinnati and the fact they outscored Cleveland in the two games the club split during the campaign.

Order was restored on the final regular season weekend as the Steelers blasted Houston 21-0 Saturday in the Astrodome to complete a remarkable comeback and render the two games the following day for the Bengals and Browns useless. The team that started 1-4 closed with nine straight wins and their third straight division crown. Once again the defense keyed the victory. Blount's interception return set up the only score the Steelers would need. Harris and Bleier each rushed for more than 100 yards, and each eclipsed 1,000 yards—only the second time in league history that two backs from the same team accomplished that feat. The Steelers were ready for the playoffs. They entered the postseason with an 11-quarter scoreless streak. The Bengals, despite a 10-4 record, didn't even make the playoffs. New England, at 11-3, secured the wild card spot, losing the division title to Baltimore because of tiebreakers. New England would travel to Oakland in the first round. The Steelers drew the Colts in Baltimore. But it really didn't matter whom or where they played, the Steelers were firing on all cylinders.

To even make the playoffs was a remarkable achievement. The numbers for the Steel Curtain during that nine-game winning streak were downright scary—five shutouts, two games where they allowed just a field goal and another where they allowed only six points. The combined score of those last nine games was 234-28. And the team didn't exactly face a bunch of lightweights. Their opponents carried a winning percentage of .538. Eight members of the Steel Curtain were named to the AFC Pro Bowl squad: defensive backs Thomas and Blount; safeties Edwards and Wagner; linebackers Ham and Lambert and defensive linemen Greene and Greenwood.

"I think it was the best defense ever," Steelers chairman Dan Rooney says almost 30 years later. "I don't know another that was even close to that accomplishment. With the offense banged up pretty good, with Bradshaw out, what they did on defense was absolutely amazing. It will never be repeated."

The offense did chip in, though, thanks to a rushing attack that controlled the clock and kept the defense off the field. However, there was a lack of balance that would soon spell disaster. Consider that Lynn Swann led all receivers with just 28 catches. Today, albeit in a different age of football where teams pass much more often, Hines Ward catches 28 passes in three games. Steelers quarterbacks tossed only 10 TD passes. For the Steelers to advance far in the playoffs, the formula was clear: get a lead and run the ball.

The Steelers came to Baltimore brimming with confidence. On the game's third play, Bradshaw read the Colt's double coverage on Swann and instead hit receiver Frank Lewis with a 76-yard scoring strike. A Gerela field goal upped the Steelers' lead to 9-0. The Colts stormed back with a long drive capped by a 17-yard scoring strike from quarterback Bert Jones to receiver Roger Carr to cut the lead to 9-7. But the Steelers took control in the second quarter. Reggie Harrison, subbing for an injured Rocky Bleier, who left the game after only one carry, went in from the 1-yard line to finish a 68-drive. On their next possession, the Steelers moved 54 yards, culminating in a Bradshaw TD pass to Swann from 29 yards. Bradshaw had the best day of his career, hitting 14 of 18 passes for 264 yards and three touchdowns. He was relieved by Kruczek, who was his usual efficient self, as he hit on 5 of 6 passes.

Curiously though, despite a big lead and already thin at running back because of the loss of Bleier, Noll opted to keep Harris in the game. He and the Steelers were cruising, with the star back rushing for 132 yards early in the third quarter. The gamble turned out to be a bad decision. Harris was injured. The Steel Curtain clamped down on the Colts for a convincing 40-14 victory. But it was a costly one. Both Harris and Bleier would be unavailable for the championship game against the

Raiders, who avenged their only loss of the year with a last-second win over New England 24-21.

Memories of the opener came back to haunt the Steelers. Without their two 1,000-yard backs, the worst scenario would be for Oakland to score quickly and force the Steelers to play catch up. Unfortunately, that's exactly what happened. The Raiders took advantage of Steeler miscues—a partially blocked punt and an interception returned to the 1 to grab a 10-0 lead. The Steelers appeared to get back in the game, scoring on a Reggie Harrison 3-yard run. But the Raiders scored a backbreaking touchdown with 19 seconds left in the half. From the Steeler 4, Stabler faked a handoff and found the former Steeler Bankston, who once again haunted his old team by taking a touchdown pass that completely changed the momentum of the game.

The Raiders took away the Steelers' ground game in the second half, forcing the Steelers to pass, something the offense was not designed to do. Bradshaw finished the game, going 14 of 35 for 176 yards and an interception and didn't get the team into the end zone again. On offense, the Raiders did something that other teams had not been able to do against the Steel Curtain—they ran the ball for 157 yards. Stabler did just enough through the air, hitting key short passes set up by the success of the running game, to control the clock. Although the Steel Curtain played well, they couldn't overcome those 10 points scored off Steeler mistakes. Oakland ended Pittsburgh's championship reign with a 24-7 win.

In the Super Bowl, Oakland crushed Minnesota 32-14 to capture its first NFL championship. Ironically, the Raiders' 1976 season—arguably one of the greatest in NFL history—and 16-1 record often gets overshadowed by the team it beat in the AFC championship game. That has a lot to do with the record-setting Steel Curtain that came as close to perfection as any defense had in NFL history. For the Steelers, there's a certain irony, as well.

"This may have been our most dominant team," Rooney says. "But in the end, we didn't win it all. Still, give me that defense and I like our chances against anybody."

THIRTEEN

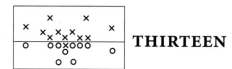

Reflections On Joe Gilliam, Pittsburgh's Pioneer Quarterback

Dave looks back at a career and life that were over too soon.

Sitting high above the gargantuan Three Rivers Stadium scoreboard in the south end zone on a sparkling September day in 1974, I had the thrill of seeing the magnificent 54-yard TD bomb from the arm of the new starting Pittsburgh Steeler quarterback "Jefferson Street" Joe Gilliam into the hands of a rookie wide receiver from USC by the name of Lynn Swann. The touchdown gave the Steelers a 10-0 lead over the visiting Baltimore Colts, en route to a 30-0 annihilation in the first game of what would turn out to be Pittsburgh's inaugural Super Bowl season.

More than just the victory, it was a delight to see the success of the former 11th round pick, who had taken over the starting reigns at QB from the more heralded first choice overall in 1970 out of Louisiana Tech, Terry Bradshaw.

Gilliam had come to Pittsburgh in 1972 after a sparkling career at Tennessee State, where he threw for 5,879 yards and 65 touchdowns, leading the Tigers to a 21-1 mark over his junior and senior campaigns. In his senior season, Jefferson Street Joe made the NFL scouts stand up and take notice with a 384-yard, 5-touchdown (he ran for two of them) performance in a 41-35 upset over Eddie Robinson and Grambling, snapping their 11-game win streak.

The strong-armed signal caller led his club to their fourth consecutive Grantland Rice Bowl appearance, where Gilliam helped Tennessee State recover from a 16-6 half time deficit to beat McNeese State 26-23 with three, second half scoring tosses. With his effort, Joe was named to the second team of the Associated Press Little All-American Team (for non-division I schools) and on the first team of the *Pittsburgh Courier* squad for the second consecutive season, an All-American team comprised of the 51 predominately black colleges around the nation.

Joe was also given another honor as he was chosen to play for legendary coach Paul "Bear" Bryant in the Coaches All-American game when Heisman Trophy winner Pat Sullivan pulled out at the last minute. Bryant seemed more than happy to have Gilliam join his forces, throwing many superlatives towards the Tennessee State star. "I haven't seen Gilliam throw under pressure, but he has one of the quickest releases I have seen. He can get rid of the football. . . BOOM, and it's gone. And he can run a 4.5 in the 40. That's moving."

After limited playing time in his rookie campaign, Jefferson Street Joe got his first real opportunity to showcase his abilities in 1973. With Pittsburgh up 14-9 against the Washington Redskins, Terry Hanratty went down with sore ribs, causing Steeler coach Chuck Noll to turn to his second-year pro. Despite the fact he threw two interceptions, Gilliam tossed a beautiful 46-yard scoring strike to Barry Pearson, the first TD pass of his career, giving Pittsburgh a 21-9 lead en route to a 21-16 victory.

His next chance came three weeks later when the black and gold went up to the shores of Lake Erie to visit their nemesis, the Cleveland Browns. Bradshaw was still down with a broken collarbone and Hanratty was injured early in the first quarter with a sprained wrist, prompting Noll once again to call on Gilliam. While it wasn't the best game of his career, Joe showed what he was made of, completing 12 of 29 passes for 197 yards and a touchdown in the hostile environment of Cleveland's Municipal Stadium. He paced the Steelers to a 16-14 fourth quarter lead. Greg Pruitt put the Browns up 21-16 with only a minute left to play. But Gilliam remained cool and led the club down to the Browns' 15, where the drive finally stalled, ending the game on the wrong end of a 21-16 score.

Despite the loss, Noll was duly impressed and named the young 22-year old signal caller to start against the defending world champion Miami Dolphins in Florida the next week in front of the nation on *Monday Night Football.* In football terms, it would be one of Jefferson Street Joe's lowest points as he went 0 for 7 with three interceptions as Miami went out to a 30-3 first half lead. Bradshaw returned and made the game close, 30-26, but for all intents and purposes, Joe would have to wait for the next season to get another shot at starting.

The 1974 preseason was certainly an odd one. The NFL was in the midst of its first labor stoppage and what the football fans of the Steel City were privileged to observe was a collection of impressive draft picks that is considered among the greatest class in the annals of professional football (Hall of Famers Swann, Jack Lambert, Mike Webster and John Stallworth all were drafted in '74), who all got extensive opportunities to play in the preseason while the veterans hit the picket line. What the Steeler Nation would also get was a chance to see the emergence of a third-year quarterback who would set the city on its ear. With Bradshaw on strike, Joe Gilliam decided to cross the line in order to get his opportunity to take controls of the team. Gilliam didn't disappoint as he completed 74 of 124 passes for 1175 yards and 11 TDs while leading the club to a perfect 6-0 record. With his performance, Joe lived his dream as he wrestled away the starting quarterback job from Bradshaw; the sky seemed to be the limit.

What wasn't necessarily in the cards at the time was the way some in the predominantly white city of Pittsburgh would react. After being named the starting quarterback over Bradshaw, who was suffering from a sore arm, Joe began to receive hate mail and the talk shows were not always complimentary of the decision to start him. "I thought if you played well, you got to play," Gilliam would later say. "I guess I didn't understand the significance of being a black quarterback at the time."

Despite the controversy, Joe had a spectacular opening day showing the critics that the color of a man's skin does not determine how successful he can be. It was an outstanding performance, but unfortunately at my age then, I really didn't understand the greatness of the moment any more than Gilliam did when he took the field on September

15th, 1974. As Marlin Briscoe and James Harris did before him, the Tennessee State alum was to be a pioneer, becoming an African American starting QB in the NFL; in fact, Jefferson Street Joe was to be the first ever to start a National Football League contest on opening day (James Harris started for the Buffalo Bills of the AFL on the opening day of the 1969 season).

To me, he was an exciting player who had just thrown for 151 yards in the second quarter, leading the club on a tremendous 13 play, 99-yard drive that culminated with the most gorgeous pass I have ever seen, even to this day, his famous 54-yard toss to Swann.

It wasn't until later on that week when the family's *Sports Illustrated* arrived adorned with my new hero on the cover and the headline, "Pittsburgh's new Black Quarterback" that I was to truly understand the importance of what I had just seen. I asked my dad why Gilliam's race would be such a big story. It was at that time he told me the in-depth stories of Jackie Robinson, Roberto Clemente and Larry Doby. Although baseball players, each had a hand at tearing down the walls of racism that American sports had built during the first part of the century.

Despite the fact the nation was more tolerant in 1974 than in Robinson's historical rookie season of 1947, racism was still rampant and Gilliam had the pressure of trying to break the stereotype that African Americans did not have what it took to become great NFL quarterbacks.

Gilliam's story became even better the following week as he threw for the second highest total in Pittsburgh history, 348 yards, in a 35-35 tie against the Denver Broncos.

Unfortunately for the young gunslinger from Charleston, WV, the Denver game was the high point. Each successive game brought with it a more difficult performance. Papers started to take polls on who the starting quarterback should be. Even though the Steelers were 4-1-1 at the time, head coach Chuck Noll replaced Gilliam with Bradshaw, the former incumbent, after a poor 5 for 18 performance by Jefferson Street Joe in a 20-16 victory against the hated Cleveland Browns. Bradshaw certainly was not the polished quarterback he was later on in his career, and it certainly created controversy taking the starting job from Gilliam. Little did we all know at that point that heroin and cocaine had begun to take over Joe's life.

Former teammate Dwight White says that while he doesn't excuse Gilliam from his behavior, the situation was mishandled. "They knew they had a high-strung kid on their hands but they basically caved on this one." Did getting benched start that downward spiral? To White it did, and he thought the Steelers needed to accept some responsibility for how Gilliam's life turned out.

As the story goes, Bradshaw went on to become the second youngest quarterback to ever start a Super Bowl, was inducted into the Hall of Fame and secured a lucrative broadcasting career after his days in Pittsburgh were over. Conversely, Gilliam was let loose following the 1975 campaign, despite the success of his short tenure in the Steel City. Even though Terry was certainly talented, Joe might have been even more, once prompting Bradshaw to admit that if not for the drugs Gilliam put into his system, it might have been him at the controls in the Super Bowls and not the future Hall of Famer.

After he was cut from the Steelers, Gilliam tried to hook on with the New Orleans Saints when the club picked him up off waivers. It would be a short, tumultuous stay in the Crescent City as Joe was arrested less than a week later when he was pulled over going 85 mph in the borrowed car of running back Rocky Thompson. The officer who approached the young signal caller found cocaine, and a .380 automatic pistol under a towel. Gilliam disappeared for a few days following the incident, reappearing at the Saints training camp three days later with the club fining him $750.

Not long afterwards, New Orleans parted ways with the troubled quarterback, leaving Gilliam to wonder whether he had blown his last chance in the NFL. "I don't know whether anybody will give me a second chance now. . . I don't have any hard feelings, [but] I set the house on fire in practice and I'm waived the next day."

Eventually, Gilliam was given 60 days of community service for the incident, but that wouldn't be the end of the situation. Not long afterwards he was arrested outside the house of a drug dealer for possession of heroin with the intent to sell. The judge was not so lenient after Gilliam violated his parole and sentenced him to 45 days in the penitentiary.

Jefferson Street Joe eventually was committed to a drug rehabilitation facility in Virginia and was transferred to a similar one in New Orleans in early

1977 with the intent of the club giving the down-on-his-luck former star another opportunity to stick in the NFL. While Gilliam stayed sober, he had a tough time consistently making practices as the nausea and headaches that accompanied his withdrawal from heroin proved to be too much to overcome. He was ultimately cut once again by the Saints in what would prove to be his last chance to crack an NFL roster.

There would be other opportunities for the Tennessee State product to turn his life around. In 1978 he signed to play with the minor league Pittsburgh Wolf Pak. Fans who once tortured Gilliam turned out to support him as 8,000 people jammed into Valley Memorial Field to see him lead the Pak to a 3-0 victory. Joe's homecoming was short. A dispute with the coaching staff led to his departure from the team with whispers that he was back on drugs. "We thought it was just a matter of time before he would be back in the NFL," says Wolf Pak executive director R.J. Baker. "Then things deteriorated. I think he got back on the junk. His weight slipped from 187 to just over 170. He started skipping practices and arguing with the coaching staff."

While his former club, the Steelers, were in the midst of winning their record fourth Super Bowl championship in 1979, Jefferson Street Joe was leading the Baltimore Eagles to the Atlantic Football Conference title against the Pittsburgh Colts. Despite the championship, 1979 would be a very painful and controversial season for Gilliam. He jumped ship in the minors from Baltimore to Birmingham, causing the Eagles to consider legal action. Joe eventually returned to Baltimore, where he was the victim of a savage, drug-related beating that sent the 28-year-old quarterback to the trauma unit of University Hospital.

Gilliam would make one last splash into the pro ranks, with the USFL's Washington Federals in 1983. The highlight was when he started a game on April 11th in a 22-21 loss to Arizona where the former Steeler threw for 203 yards and two touchdowns.

There were many chances over the years that would eventually get blown by the addiction. So many times, Joe tried to become sober and we heard the inevitable feel-good TV reports that led us to hope that he finally would turn the corner. Somehow Gilliam always slipped back into the grasp of his addiction. He told tales of living on the streets of Nashville in a cardboard box under a bridge in the mid 1990s, the "Ritz-Carlton" as he would refer to it, and pawned his two Super Bowl rings to survive.

As the 20th century came to an end, Joe seemed to have finally solved his problems, going sober for a reported three years. He got to meet with his teammates at the scene of his greatest moments, Three Rivers Stadium, in the final contest ever at the legendary facility. For him it seemed to be his step back into a normal life. Joe Willie Gillie finally seemed to have a bright future as well as the love of his family and his former teammates.

Gilliam's father, Joe, Sr., had gotten back the cherished Super Bowl rings that his son pawned and was waiting for the right moment to return them to Joe, Jr. Unfortunately, he would not be afforded that opportunity. On Christmas Day 2000, Gilliam was watching a game between Tennessee and Dallas, when he reportedly suffered a heart attack and passed away. Later, we sadly learned that it turned out the addiction had reared its ugly head again. The final cause of death was listed as an "accidental cocaine intoxication."

One of the greatest tragedies in the Steeler Nation over the past 30 years was the fact that Gilliam was not given the chance to see a career blossom that could have been one of the most spectacular in NFL history. I still have the *Sports Illustrated* celebrating one of the greatest moments in his short NFL career on the wall in my TV room, reminding me daily of all the talent he had and what a bright future was facing him. . . and just how quickly drug addiction took it all away.

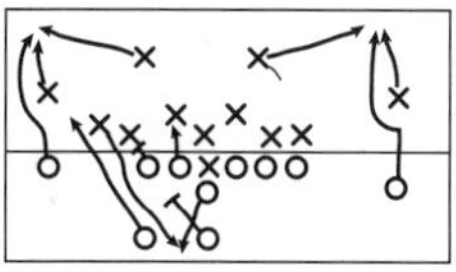

FOURTEEN

Defending The Honor Of The Steeler Nation: The Maulers' Home Opener

It wasn't about welcoming the newest member of the Pittsburgh sports fraternity to the city, seeing the reigning Heisman Trophy winner or even just showing their love for the sport of football. No, 53,771 people came to Three Rivers Stadium on this frigid, snowy March day in 1984 as soldiers defending their nation, the Steeler Nation. The enemy was an expatriate who committed the most vile of sins against these citizens—the first of which was not being Terry Bradshaw. Perhaps even worse was that this enemy left our fair city on his own terms before he was properly flogged and banished by the powers that be. It ended up being a game not remembered for its play on the field, but for the embarrassing moments in the stands that showed the worst side of the Steeler Nation.

The cretin who committed this act of treason was Cliff Stoudt, the former Pittsburgh quarterback. Stoudt was a star quarterback with Youngstown State before being selected by the Steelers on the 5th round of the 1977 draft. He held the most popular position in the Steel City sports world, that of backup Steeler quarterback, the man who fans screamed to be inserted into the game for the poor soul who had the unfortunate task of being the starter. In fact, Stoudt stood around with clipboard in hand long enough to not only win two Super Bowl championships without ever taking a snap in a regular season game, but also earn his NFL pension.

Finally, in 1983, Stoudt got his opportunity to start for the black and gold when Hall of Fame legend Terry Bradshaw injured his elbow. Stoudt showed he could play the game early on, leading Pittsburgh to a 9-2 start. However, Cliff soon learned why the least popular position in Steel City sports was being the starting Steelers quarterback. Stoudt fell apart, contributing to the club's three-game losing streak while completing only 40.9 percent of his passes in the latter part of the season. Bradshaw came back for a miraculous start against the Jets in the next-to-last regular season game, leading the club to a 34-7 Central Division-clinching victory before reinjuring his arm. It would be the last NFL game Bradshaw would play in; it also served to show the Steeler Nation that the kid from YSU was no Bradshaw.

What had begun as a magical season ended with the Steelers possessing the second-worst pass offense in the National Football League. The abuse Stoudt took was of legendary status, abuse he did not want to endure anymore. If he thought the actions of the Steeler Nation could be no worse, he was in for a rude awakening when he returned a few months later.

The United States Football League (USFL) provided players with an out they did not have in previous seasons. Stoudt signed a contract with the Birmingham Stallions for the 1984 campaign. The Stallions' third opponent of the season was the expansion Pittsburgh Maulers. The third game of the season also proved to be the home opener of the Maulers, right at the scene of Stoudt's torment only four months before, Three Rivers Stadium.

Edward DeBartolo had purchased the franchise in hopes of exploiting Pittsburgh's all-consuming love of the sport of football. Unfortunately, the team showed the Steel City a taste of what the Steelers gave them before Chuck Noll came to town—a losing, pathetic, yet almost comical, brand of football.

Start with the name, the Maulers, or as some people referred to it as, the Mallers, in reference to DeBartolo's shopping mall empire, a name that didn't exactly instill fear. Only 4,000 season tickets were sold until the club made the bold move of signing Heisman Trophy winner Mike Rozier of Nebraska to a $3.1 million contract for three years, a very generous amount for the time. It was a masterstroke financially as the fans and media woke up and took notice. The team's season ticket base shot up to 20,000 and excitement was at a fever pitch when it was announced the first home game would be against Stoudt and the Birmingham Stallions. On the first day individual game seats went on sale, 5,000 people bought tickets for the opener.

Unfortunately for general manager George Heddleston and coach Joe Pendry, the Maulers may have had a Heisman Trophy running back, but they forgot the rule that a running back needs a strong offensive line in front of him to actually be successful. Add to the mix a quarterback who seemed to have his most success throwing interceptions, an offensive line that Glen Carano could sue for nonsupport, and a defense that took the phrase "Swiss cheese" to a new level.

While their first two games were close, 7-3 against Oklahoma and 27-24 to the defending USFL champion Michigan Panthers, they were nonetheless losses with two incredibly inept offensive performances. Regardless of their 0-2 record, the people of Pittsburgh were gobbling up opening-day tickets like there was no tomorrow. By the time the dust settled, the Steel City football fans had given the USFL its first-ever sellout—all 60,000 seats sold. The fans were coming to defend the proud honor of the Steeler Nation.

Both the Birmingham and Pittsburgh teams were astute enough to realize why the game was sold out, and both seemed to understand that Cliff Stoudt might be in danger. There were three former Steelers that stood on the Birmingham sideline that day, head coach Rollie Dotsch, wide receiver Jim Smith and Stoudt. In a news conference before the game Dotsch made the statement that "Don't stand too close to Rollie, Smith or Stoudt on the sideline because one hand grenade will get you all." What he didn't understand was that the Steeler posse did not want him or Smith; it was Cliff they were looking for.

Dotsch feared things being thrown at them; Mauler president Paul Martha feared that if the former Steeler assistant didn't shut up, the fans would truly take him up on his suggestions. "If no one mentions security there won't be a problem," he said. "But if they mention it and the media brings attention to it, we'll have problems."

Martha and the team took it seriously. Fifty security guards and 15 policemen were at the game, six more than for a Steeler contest. Stoudt was diplomatic, claiming he'd rather get the treatment as an opposing quarterback than as the Steeler starter. He went on further to say that he had no hostilities against the Steeler fans and considered them the best in football. Twenty-four hours after his statements, Cliff might have had a different opinion.

The day of the game finally came on March 11th, 1984. The soldiers of the Steeler Nation smartly camouflaged themselves in the purple and orange colors of the Pittsburgh Maulers so they wouldn't be recognized. Nature was on their side for this conflict; it was a very cold, snowy March day with temperatures hovering in the 20s, so the soldiers would have an extra of weapon at their disposal, snow balls—soon to be icy snow balls—to mix in with their arsenal of beer bottles.

The citizens of the nation gathered for their pregame ritual of tailgating in the parking lot, so the beer could have its proper effect for their mental state. They were ready; no Cliff Stoudt would defeat them on this day.

The fans gathered into the house that had been the scene of so many great Steeler moments. Stoudt was introduced and the onslaught began. Snowballs and beer cans and bottles littered the field. The fans knew they would have to try and stop the insurgent because the Maulers were certainly having trouble doing it themselves.

Mauler quarterback Glen Carano, who stated earlier in the week that he wanted to succeed so the fans wouldn't turn on him, tossed a first quarter interception into the hands of Birmingham free safety Chuck Clanton, who returned the pick 53 yards for the first score of the day. The Stallions soon made it 10-0 before the supposed savior of the new franchise, Mike Rozier, lost a fumble late in the first quarter as Joe Cribbs soon after took it in from four yards out to give the Stallions a commanding 16-0 lead. Rather than kick the extra point, Dotsch decided to go for two. Stoudt rolled into the end zone to increase the lead to 18 points and the ire of the Maulers. . . we mean Steelers nation.

The fans turned up their pressure on the former Steeler quarterback, continuing the onslaught of snowballs and beer containers as well as several signs. A local radio station WEEP, passed out about 15,000 signs that read WEEP for Stoudt; there were many more that weren't exactly G-rated. Many went up, even one as tall as the Jumbotron scoreboard comparing Cliff Stoudt to a part of the male anatomy that security guards confiscated very quickly.

While the abuse got to Stoudt (he completed on 2 of 16 passes for the day for a meager 29 yards), the team and the fans alike had forgotten about Cribbs. The former Bills All-Pro running back rambled for 191 yards, keeping the game from being a close affair. Stoudt did get his revenge, though, running through the porous Mauler defense for a 10-yard touchdown run in the third quarter that put his team up 24-6. It was the third quarter when the fears almost turned to reality as the snowballs became ice and the Steeler Nation began pelting the field with everything from beer containers to oranges. It became so bad that Stoudt pleaded with the officials to pull the teams off the field. The officials, not wanting to further incite the crowd, refused to do it.

When the contest finally came to an end, Birmingham had won a convincing 30-18 victory in a game where the score was hardly indicative of how one-sided the contest was. After the game, a triumphant Cliff Stoudt smashed a snowball into the side of his own head, proclaiming that he never had so much fun completing only two passes.

Following the ugly affair, Stoudt went on to have a fine season, completing 57.9 percent of his passes for 3,121 yards and 26 touchdowns. Better yet he tossed only seven interceptions while leading his club to the semi-finals before they lost 20-10 to the eventual USFL champion Philadelphia Stars. The Maulers, on the other hand, imploded. They won 3 of 18 games that season, Rozier ran for only 792 yards and Joe Pendry lost his job in midseason. Eventually, DeBartolo decided to cut his losses and ended his USFL venture after only one season, prompting Martha to state at the press conference announcing the team demise, "I'd like to apologize to one person in particular, the man who won the 'name the team' contest and won a lifetime pass."

For the Steeler Nation, it wasn't exactly their proudest day as they gave themselves and the city a black eye in a performance before a national audience that was so embarrassing it was only exceeded by the humiliating one the Maulers exhibited on the turf of Three Rivers Stadium. Luckily, despite the fact Carano had a bad season, he didn't have to endure the same abuse that Stoudt did the year before. Nobody really cared how bad the Maulers were. Nobody cared about the team at all. They only seemed to care that one day, March 11th, 1984, when they came en masse to protect the honor of their city and their favorite team against a man who in the end remained classy and proved to be above their humiliating taunts.

Other professional football teams

Current teams

The Pittsburgh Colts, founded in 1979, have been one of the most successful semi-pro franchises in the North American Football League.

The Pittsburgh Tornadoes, also a semi-pro team, played from 2003-2004 and were 5-6-1 in two seasons.

The Pittsburgh Passion, a women's professional team, came into being in 2003 with a 2-6 record and in their second season finished 6-2 in second place in the Mid-Atlantic Division.

Extinct clubs

The Pittsburgh Gladiators: The gone but not forgotten Arena Football League franchise for the city of Pittsburgh. In their four-season existence between 1987 and 1990.

The team eventually moved to Tampa Bay in 1991 and turned into the Tampa Bay Storm, the five-time Arena Bowl Champions.

- The Pittsburgh Wolf Pak
- The Pittsburgh Ironmen
- The Pittsburgh Cubs
- The Bloomfield Rams
- The Duquesne Ironmen
- The Pittsburgh Valley Ironmen

And let us not forget a classic name among Western Pennsylvania Minor League teams: The Latrobe Zimbos circa 1946-1950.

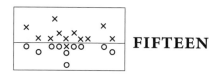

FIFTEEN

The House of Thrills

Dave bears witness to the passing of an era.

On February 11th, 2001, 31 years of memories came crashing down as Three Rivers Stadium was imploded to make room for Heinz Field.

February 11th, 2001 was a cold, memorable day in the 'burgh—one where 31 years of memories came crashing down in a matter of seconds. It was the day when the grand lady of the Steelers, Three Rivers Stadium, was imploded to make way for progress in the name of Heinz Field.

I could have watched the event from the warmth of my house; after all it was only 12 degrees outside, eight below zero when you take into effect the phenomenon known as the wind chill factor. I wanted to be there though, with her when she stood for her final moments, to honor every cherished memory I encountered within her walls, both tragic and joyous during her magical 31-year run.

Three Rivers Stadium was all I knew as a sports fan. I was too young to take in a game at Forbes Field before it was torn down in 1970. I remember my father had no regrets back then about losing the sports palace of his youth. He claimed it had outlived its usefulness, "It smelled like urine and the seats were too uncomfortable."

Years later he remembers Forbes Field differently, fondly, almost sorry that it became extinct. It seems like the same sequence the sports fans of Pittsburgh went through in the late '90s desperate to build new parks for the Pirates and Steelers and get rid of that pre-fab, cookie-cutter, outdated stadium. It was only at the end when they realized what my father had already discovered about his field of dreams, Forbes Field: It's not the structure that makes a place special, it's the memories you encounter on the way. And make no mistake, Three Rivers created more memories than any sports fan has a right to enjoy.

The Steelers shared the structure with the Pirates, as they had done for several years at Forbes Field. The difference back then was they were playing in the Bucs' place; at Three Rivers, it was almost the reverse. Yes, the Pirates won nine division titles and two world championships in their new park, but it wasn't a baseball stadium and everyone knew it. This facility was built for football. It was the place the Steeler Nation was born.

There is no better honor in Pittsburgh than to be part of the Steeler Nation, but in 1970 it was just a collection of survivors with no concept of the special ride they were about to take. Most of what they shared were war stories of bad years gone by, "the joke of the league" as the Steelers were known back then. They were coming off a 1-13 season, the first under a new coach, a man who had played for the hated Cleveland Browns, Chuck Noll.

The Steelers were going to take their sorry act to a new facility as the new decade began, the first they could really call their own. Plans had been under way for quite a few years to build this multipurpose stadium. At first, it was to be constructed on top of a bridge crossing the Allegheny River. Then it was supposed to be a sloped stadium on the North Side with an opening so fans could see the beautiful skyline of the Steel City (a novel approach that was done for PNC Park and Heinz Field three decades later). Finally, it was built in almost a perfect circle, at the point where the three rivers of Pittsburgh met, hence the name.

Things did not come easily at first for this magnificent new sports beacon of the city. Nobody properly prepared the area for the incredible traffic jams that ensued. It was late being done, so the Bucs couldn't move in until midseason of their 1970 campaign. When it finally opened, there was mud and muck everywhere. Last but not least, a bond the city took in to finance the new building still hadn't been significantly reduced when they finally paid it off to build the new parks three decades later.

But what problems there were would pale in comparison to the joy that lay ahead. The Bucs went on to win their first title of any kind since Maz rounded the bases against the Yankees 10 years earlier. They reached the pinnacle a season later, defeating the powerful Baltimore Orioles for the World Championship in 1971, a series where Pittsburgh showed off its tremendous new facility in the first night World Series game ever. For the Steelers, the championship express was not too far behind.

Names like Bradshaw, Greene, Harris, White, Holmes, Ham, Greenwood and Blount were replacing those of Nix, Calland, Mingo and Hillebrand. Three Rivers slowly became a house of horrors for the opposition, and the club rewarded the Steeler faithful with their first outright division championship in the team's 40-year history.

I was there in 1972 when the black and gold faced their first postseason opponent since 1947, the rival Oakland Raiders. Unfortunately, when 50,000 people were going nuts as Franco Harris took the Immaculate Reception into the end zone for a game-winning touchdown, we were walking down the corridor, convinced the contest was over after Raider QB Kenny Stabler sliced through the Pittsburgh defense to give Oakland a 7-6 lead only moments before.

The next week in the AFC championship against the Miami Dolphins we stayed put, although I still have nightmares of some bumbling punter named Larry Seiple running down the field on a fake punt to help keep the Dolphins undefeated, thwarting the Steelers Super Bowl hopes with a 21-17 Miami victory. I also remember only 24 hours later when the greatest baseball player I had ever seen before or since, right there in the confines of Three Rivers Stadium, died tragically as the plane Roberto Clemente was in went down in the Atlantic.

As the '70s went on, the Steeler Nation became legendary. Factions of the group broke off to cheer for their personal heroes. Franco's Italian Army with its lieutenant Frank Sinatra, Jack Ham's *Dobre Shunka* (Polish for great ham) group, Gerela's Gorilla's, Kolb's Kowboys, the list goes on and on.

There was a bond within the ranks, one that knew of the fans' responsibilities before every game. Blow your vocal cords out and make the game a difficult hell for those who stupidly came to try and defeat Pittsburgh in their house. With an enclosed stadium those chants of "HERE WE GO STEELERS, HERE WE GO" would reverberate for miles. You felt the stadium rock so much there were fears it might explode any minute. Add to the mix the legendary twirling gold towels that broadcaster Myron Cope introduced to the throng, (a/k/a the Terrible Towel, an accessory that no true Steeler fans would ever think to be without) and you could see why having a trip to Pittsburgh on your NFL schedule was generally not met with glee.

Not many opponents lived to fight another day after they exited Three Rivers Stadium. Between the preseason, regular season and postseason from 1970 through 2000, 255 opponents came in to the Steel City and only 73 escaped victorious.

After the Miami loss in 1972, the Pittsburgh Steelers would lose no more home playoff games during that dominating decade. Three AFC championship wins, including a biting, bitter cold day in January of 1976 when the field resembled a hockey rink, highlighted a seven-game playoff win streak. It was that day when I sat above the scoreboard that my distaste for hot drinks proved an unwise choice. I had gotten my pre-game ritual of two hot dogs and a coke and placed the coke by my feet. The wind swirls within Three Rivers were legendary and within minutes my drink was frozen solid. It was forgotten two hours later as the Steelers emerged with a hard fought, albeit sloppy, 16-10 win against the hated Raiders for their second consecutive trip to the Super Bowl.

With the end of the seventies came the end of championships for both the Pirates and Steelers, but nonetheless the memories at the old ballpark kept coming. The '80s were mixed with both joy and bitterness when I think of Three Rivers. The joy came in the fact that I was able to take my new, beautiful bride there and with the help of a mother of a collegiate friend, secure Steeler season tickets for myself and my family. I also had the honor of taking my infant sons Tony and Matthew there in the late 1980s, stretching the Finoli generation list to see games at the House of Thrills to three.

The bitterness came not with the mounting losses that both clubs would suffer in the less that memorable decade, but on a Monday night against the Broncos in 1986, September 15th to be exact. My Uncle Vinny, along with my father, first introduced me to the Steeler Nation and the joy of Pittsburgh Steeler football in 1970 when they took me to my first game, a 28-9 thrashing of the hated Browns on November 29. It was with Uncle Vinny I was able to see all the special moments in the '70s as we went to the games via his season tickets for so many years. He helped me so much not only to appreciate football, but in all aspects of my life, helping to teach the importance of family, a lesson I carry with me to this day. It was that night on September 15, 1986, that Uncle Vinny had a massive heart attack as he entered those hallowed halls that he enjoyed for so many years to see his beloved Steelers take on the Broncos. A few hours later he passed away. For 14 years following his death, in the many times I passed through those gates, I always thought of him, with sadness at first, before eventually thinking of all the happy moments the family had enjoyed in this Pittsburgh mecca.

As the grand old lady of the Steelers entered her third decade, a resurgence of Pittsburgh Steeler football was about to begin. New coach Bill Cowher came aboard, returning the winning tradition within Three Rivers and bringing three more AFC championship tilts. Although they only emerged victorious once, it was a win for the ages, 20-16 against the Indianapolis Colts. It was a moment I had feared I would never get the opportunity to experience again and when I did, it brought back a flood of memories from the early '70s, when Three Rivers Stadium was considered an architectural marvel instead of the outdated white elephant it had become.

I understood why there was a need for a new baseball stadium, embracing that idea wholeheartedly, and I also realized why, in the high-finance world of the NFL, the Steelers needed their own new facility to create more revenue and allow them to compete in the league. But as the '90s came to an end I couldn't help feel a sadness that the black and gold were going to leave the only place they had ever enjoyed success.

Decade number four approached, and the 2000 campaign would be the last the Pittsburgh Steelers would ever play in the House of Thrills. On December 16, 2000, the memories would come to an end as the black and gold played their final contest in the legendary facility.

My mother-in-law, Viv Pansino, whom I enjoyed games with during the last 15 years of Three Rivers existence, unfortunately came up sick that last day. Instead I entered Three Rivers for my final time with my wife, her friend Mary Pianko and Chris Fletcher, my close friend from our Duquesne University days and the co-author of this book.

Pittsburgh was in the midst of a mediocre 9-7 campaign that year, but they didn't disappoint the large throng that day crushing the Washington Redskins 24-3. They played a memorable game that afternoon, but I don't remember a lot of it as instead I chose to reminisce about all our experiences at the House of Thrills.

When Kordell Stewart took a knee to end the affair, 31 years of memories came flashing before my eyes. All the classic Steelers, those from the current team and those stars and Hall of Famers from days gone by, entered the field following the contest to say goodbye to the place that had meant so much to their lives. When it all came to an end, the members of the black and gold took a victory lap, giving them an opportunity to shake hands and thank the proud members of the Steeler Nation that had stood steadfast behind them throughout the good times and the bad.

And now all that was left was a shelled out stadium, standing in the cold waiting for its ultimate doom. I woke up at 4:00 am that fateful day, dragging my two boys and my neighbor Mark Richard to see the end of a legend. We got a prime parking space at the top of a downtown parking garage, with a perfect view to see the implosion.

While the boys slept a while longer, Mark and I talked for three hours about the special times we had spent within the facility's borders. We looked at PNC Park and marveled at its beauty, much the same as my father looked at Three Rivers Stadium when it was being built in 1970.

Finally the moment of truth came to pass. 8:00. The explosions went off, one after another, in rapid motion. For a second, 25,000 loyal fans who had braved the frigid weather, held their breath as the grand old lady stood up defiantly instead of tumbling over. Finally she came plummeting down in a domino effect, 31 years of memories reduced to rubble. Only the post signifying Gate D withstood the blast, a post that remains to this day as a kind of memorial to the old lady outside of Heinz Field.

Fans cheered loudly at first and then sadness came over the throng (as Fletcher tells it, "especially the poor ones who sat at the edge of the river directly across from the stadium and had a toxic dust cloud blown in their faces"). We immediately got in our cars and followed a long line of mourners who entered a funeral procession across the Fort Duquesne Bridge, not only to see the damage that had been done, but to say our final farewells.

I collected all my souvenirs, a piece of rubble, a couple of stadium seats and a huge chunk of turf that a construction worker kindly gave to my college roommate Bill Ranier. But in the final analysis, it isn't the tangible souvenirs I will always treasure of Three Rivers Stadium, but the memories, fine memories that will always make this facility my field of dreams.

Finoli's personal top five football games from Three Rivers

1/14/96: Pittsburgh 20 Indianapolis 16. The Steelers finally reached the Super Bowl for the first time in 16 years as Jim Harbaugh's last-second pass fell to the turf harmlessly in the end zone, allowing the Steelers to escape with their fifth AFC championship.

1/4/76: Pittsburgh 16 Oakland 10. I believe it was the coldest I ever was in my life, but it was all worth it when the Steelers won the AFC title. If you look at the Sports Illustrated cover from that game you can see a tiny blue spec above the scoreboard. That was me in my first SI cover.

12/23/72: Pittsburgh 13 Oakland 7. This game would rate much higher if I wasn't on the ramp leaving gate C when I heard the roar of the crowd. We had thought Gerela had won it with a field goal, before another who had followed us out with a transistor radio told us of the unbelievable play. Since the game was blacked out as they all were back then, I never saw the play until a day later when the rebroadcast came on.

11/26/76: Pitt 24 Penn State 7. My Uncle Paul got us to the game as the first quarter ended, but that was no problem as we only missed a Penn State score. Not only was it the first time Pitt had beaten the Lions in the Paterno era, but it was the marquee win in their national championship season and one of the finest performances a tail back named Tony Dorsett ever put on.

12/15/85: Pittsburgh 30 Buffalo 24. Why does this meaningless game at the end of a disappointing 7-9 campaign make my list? From an aesthetic standpoint, Pittsburgh came back from a 21-0 disadvantage to win, though that's not why it ends up here. Bill Ranier and I had overindulged a tad that afternoon, trying to forget our sorrows of a football season gone bad. After the game we decided we would go and buy the first Christmas tree that my pregnant wife Viv and I would enjoy as husband and wife. Bill and I thought we bought a winner. When we got home Viv busted out laughing, as in retrospect, it resembled more of the kind Charlie Brown would have chosen.

Fletcher's personal top five football games from Three Rivers

12/23/72: Pittsburgh 13 Oakland 7. I really didn't see a lot of the play, as it was heading away from our seats. But for an 11-year-old who had just ignited a lifelong love of the gridiron, it gets no better than this. It also provided a great life lesson: Never give up.

9/4/83: Denver 14 Pittsburgh 10. This selection has little to do with the game. A few days before, I had been down at the stadium buying tickets for an upcoming Pirates game. I ran into Art Rooney, Sr. in the parking lot and struck up a conversation. When he found out I was a student at his alma mater, Duquesne University, the chief invited me into his office, handed me a pair of tickets to the game and introduced me to the staff. "Say hello to Chris Fletcher," he said. "He's a Duquesne man and is going to be a great writer one day." I think about that day each time I pass the Art Rooney statue outside of Heinz Field.

9/3/81: Duquesne 27 CMU 10. For some reason, Duquesne and CMU were chosen to kickoff the NCAA football season in a locally televised game.

11/14/94: Pittsburgh 23 Buffalo 10. It was the first—and last—time I would watch a game from the confines of the Allegheny Club. On the plus side, we were spared from the torrential rain that fell for almost all of the game. On the negative side, being behind the glass of the Allegheny Club made the sterile Three Rivers Stadium even more sterile. You're very removed from the game. The Steelers laid a serious pasting on the Bills that night. And as with any Steelers' Monday Night Football appearance, the fans tailgated for several hours up to game time. There were more than a few drunks, including the two who decided it would take too long to wait through the pedestrian traffic jam going across the Fort Duquesne Bridge. They decided to swim the Allegheny instead and were fished out by the River Patrol. It seems the river cops had done this before.

12/16/00: Pittsburgh 24 Washington 3. The final game at Three Rivers Stadium allowed me to re-experience my love of football. Again, it wasn't the game that stood out for me. It was the closing ceremonies when the great names of the past came back for a final Steel Curtain call. I realized how lucky I had been to be a rabid fan during a decade of excellence.

Exposition Park may be more famous as the home of the Pittsburgh Pirates at the end of the 19th century but it also played host to many great club football games, especially between the Allegheny Athletic Association and the Pittsburgh Athletic Club, the Steelers and Browns of their era. The park sat on what is now the parking lot between Heinz Field and PNC Park. The approximate spot where home plate stood is marked in the parking lot thanks to the local chapter of The Society of American Baseball Research. (Courtesy of the Carnegie Museum.)

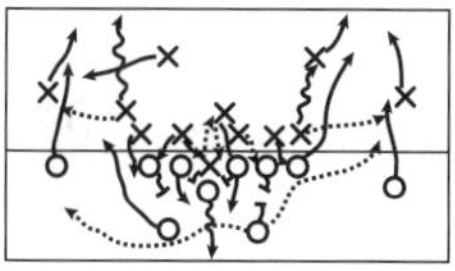

SIXTEEN

The Feel-Good Football Story of 2004

The year 1996 was a watershed year for sports agents everywhere. Long considered the sharks of the professional sporting food chain, they became humanized—a kinder, gentler predator, if you will. That year they went Hollywood, thanks to the release of the movie *Jerry Maguire*. No PR exec could have done a better industry makeover.

For the eight of you who never saw the feel-good movie of that summer, Tom Cruise was cast as a sports agent whose epiphany, called the "Mission Statement," upset the apple cart in a big way. In the Mission Statement, Jerry describes how agents should have fewer clients, with the goal of delivering more personal care at the expense of greater earnings for the firm. Jerry circulates his epiphany throughout the agency, promptly becomes an outcast and is stripped of all his clients, save one, Rod Tidwell (played by the curiously short Cuba Gooding Jr.). Jerry leaves his mega sports agency, opens up his own shop, complete with one client, and with the help of a wonderful woman (Renee Zellweger), overcomes his doubt and succeeds by focusing on the ideals contained in the Mission Statement.

Critics were mixed in their reviews (although it brought Gooding Jr. an Oscar). Agents, however, rejoiced. They were glamorous, thanks to box-office king Cruise. *Tom &$@&!!! Cruise was one of us!* Soon, true-life agents had an epiphany of their own: This Jerry Maguire goodwill could be exploited—for profit. They began lining up, claiming to be the real-life Jerry Maguire. Show me the money, indeed. Super agents Drew Rosenhaus and Leigh Steinberg *both* have it in their bios—"served as the inspiration for the character Jerry Maguire." Now that's good acting.

Although *Jerry Maguire* filmmaker and writer Cameron Crowe couldn't pick him out of a lineup, there is a sports agent who had already adopted the Mission Statement manifesto long before Cruise and company would hit the red carpet at the movie's premiere. Only this agent's version is communicated through a series of Joe-isms: "You can't be ethical and honest some of the time" is one. "I will never represent someone I don't believe in as a player and a person" is another. They're called Joe-isms because they come from Joe Linta, the president of Branford, Connecticut-based JL Sports. Linta, a native of Freedom, PA, has more than a little Maguire in him. Since founding his company in 1994, Linta has created a boutique agency that tries to differentiate itself by providing increased personal service.

When training camp concluded in summer 2004, there were 35 players represented by Linta's company playing in the National Football League. Many, like New York Giant Pat Crummey, an undrafted center out of Youngtown State University, may not be in the league if it weren't for Linta's team's contacts and hard work. And then there is the case of Khiawatha Downey, a prospect that no agent or team would represent after he was diagnosed with multiple sclerosis. That story should be made into a movie.

Freedom, a tiny town of about 1,700 in Beaver County, is about as far away from Hollywood as you can get—although it's populated by more than its fair share of characters.

But football was Joe's game, first at Freedom High School (class of 1978) and then in the college ranks at Yale, where he played defensive end for a Bulldogs squad that won three straight Ivy League titles. After graduation, Linta went to work for Prudential Securities, but he kept close to the program, serving as the defensive coordinator for Yale's freshman team for seven years. But when the freshman team was eliminated in 1991, he found himself out of football for the first time.

That's when a friend suggested he combine his two loves—finance and football. While still working at the securities company, Linta got certified and became a sports agent. In his first year, he signed five clients. "It's about relationships," he says, adding that he was confident that once he got to meet prospective clients and their families, he would show himself to be ready to be that athlete's representative. And besides being a good presenter with a solid financial background, it didn't hurt to have friends.

Linta played high school football with Jimbo Covert, who went on to have a very solid career as an NFL lineman, including winning a championship with the Chicago Bears. Covert helped introduce Linta to some aspiring linemen, including a very big catch—Will Shields, the Outland Trophy winner from Nebraska and now an eight-time Pro Bowl guard for the Kansas City Chiefs.

That Linta would do well with lineman is not surprising. It's the position he played and coached. And it's also a matter of preparation. "I watch a lot of film, so I can do a pretty good job of determining a guy's ability to play the line," he says. "I'd say I could watch about 10 plays and get an idea if he's really a prospect or not.

"If I don't think the ability is there," he continues, "I'll tell him. You have to be honest with people."

Grant Wiley had been positioned by the partisan media covering West Virginia University as a can't-miss prospect. He had a successful college career with the Mountaineers and expected to have similar success in the NFL. After viewing the film, Linta advised him not to get his hopes up—an assessment that turned out to be correct on draft day.

Besides good technique, the other thing Linta looks for is character. "The guys I have are like family, they stay at my house," he says. "It's simple; you tend to do more for people you like. I sign people I like."

One of his clients, Steelers backup center Chukky Okabi, offers this read on why he signed with JL Sports. "Instead of talking about money, he talked about football," he says. "He became the measuring stick for every agent out there."

Linta figures his ability to do that analytical and character scan of potential clients helps differentiate him in a very competitive field. First, by giving an assessment that includes areas to improve, he hopes to set a foundation built upon trust. "You can't blow smoke," he says, noting that it would come back to haunt him. Second, it helps him mine the college ranks at all levels to find those athletes that somehow fall between the cracks of the scouting and draft services. Look at the roster of JL Sports clients and you'll find them coming from colleges like Southern Connecticut State, Catawba and Wisconsin-Lacrosse.

"Probably 75 percent of the time is spent recruiting," he says. "Doing the deals isn't nearly as time-consuming as signing up players." That means lots of scouting trips, including a family vacation to Montana that included side recruiting trips to the University of Montana in Missoula and Montana State University in Bozeman. It was a similar recruiting trip that brought Linta to Indiana University of Pennsylvania.

Khiawatha Downey was a highly prized recruit out of North Carolina who ultimately chose to attend the University of Pittsburgh. He started 10 games for Pitt at left guard in 1999 and moved to right tackle the following season. That year started off with nagging injuries which Downey fought through to return to the starting lineup for the final seven games of the campaign. It was after Pitt's 37-29 loss at the Insight.com Bowl that Downey underwent a series of tests. He had been suffering from persistent stingers—neck and shoulder injuries that can cause pain or numbness in the extremities.

The results of the test pointed to multiple sclerosis, an incurable disorder that in its worst form leaves those who suffer from it unable to walk or even communicate. As could be expected, Downey nosedived into depression. He turned to marijuana, and twice tested positive for the drug. Pitt coach Walt Harris booted him off the team in the spring of 2001, a move that Linta says showed a complete lack of understanding.

"Had it been me getting that kind of news, I think I would have done worse than have a few joints," he says. "Clearly Walt Harris was completely ignorant of what was going on with this kid. He heard 'MS' and never took the time to find out what it really

Change agent

Joe Linta and JL Sports have caused some controversy in the sports agent industry with a pricing structure that is half of what many other agents charge. Typically, agents get 3 percent of the contract that they're able to negotiate for their clients. JL Sports charges 1.5 percent for established players.

The Yale-educated Linta believes that he earns his commission more for creating a player's initial contract than he does for any follow-up contract. "I believe a player earns a contract, not an agent," he says. And those percentage points add up. Consider this: In the case of Will Shields, whose six-year deal with the Kansas City Chiefs is worth $26.2 million, the difference in commission rates adds up to $393,000 over the life of the contract.

His stable of 35 NFL clients accounts for less than 2 percent of the league's personnel. That client list could bill more under the typical structure, but Linta likes his boutique agency as it is.

"I wouldn't say that I'm rich, but I don't have to look at a lot of price tags," Linta says. "My family and I have everything we need. I love what I do. I have the world by the balls. What's better than that?"

meant. I think that Pitt figured he [Downey] wouldn't be able to play, so they used the marijuana as an excuse to get that scholarship back."

It wouldn't be the first time that what Linta calls "ignorance" would follow Downey. Lesions on the brain and spine are present in millions of MS victims, many of whom continue to function normally on a daily basis. Although there is no cure, medical treatments have advanced to the point where it's not the same long-term diagnosis it was 20 years ago. Sadly, though, the public's knowledge and the removal of the stigma of the disease have not yet caught up.

For Downey, that stigma meant that no Division I schools wanted him to play football. He ended up at tiny Division II

Indiana University of Pennsylvania. His coach there understood some of what Downey was going through. Frank Cignetti had been let go from West Virginia University as he was battling cancer and following his recovery, got back into coaching at the small college in Indiana. Downey took medication to keep his condition under control, but there were side effects. Weekly injections of Avonex left him weak and brought on severe headaches and nausea. Yet he was still playing football—and at an extremely high level.

IUP is also where Downey met Linta. "I have an affinity for guys from the area," says the agent. "I watched him on tape and watched him play and we struck up a conversation and hit it off.

"I brought him up here, and the way he treated my wife and my kids," he continues, "just pointed to the fact that he was a great, great guy. I was rooting for him, and I thought, 'I may never make a dime off of this guy, but I just want him to succeed.'"

So did his coach. Cignetti called Downey a top prospect for the NFL, comparing him favorably to two former IUP players he coached that had reached the pros—Chris Villarrial and Leander Jordan. Sports draft guru Mel Kiper Jr. had Downey ranked as the 13th best offensive lineman for the upcoming 2004 NFL draft. A 6-foot-4 1/8 lineman, weighing 332 pounds, with good hands and feet should have been off the board by the fourth round at the latest. But that didn't take into account "the ignorance."

"We wouldn't touch him." That was the message Linta received about signing Downey from an NFL executive shortly before the draft. That exec was not alone. "They would see the letters MS and they immediately would get the image of Jerry's Kids," Linta lamented. "It's not like that at all. It was caught early enough that he probably won't have any symptoms until much later in life—if at all. But that didn't seem to matter much."

Hearing similar "we wouldn't touch him" assessments of Downey, Linta became proactive in selling his client's abilities. First, he turned to Dr. Rock Heyman, a neurologist at the University of Pittsburgh Medical Center, who has treated thousands of cases of MS. He had been treating Downey and helped regulate his medical regimen so that side effects were becoming increasingly negligible. Dr. Heyman wrote a letter of support that Linta sent to all 32 NFL teams. It read, in part, "regarding the issue as to whether his medical condition would place him at significant risk for playing professional football, I do not believe this to be the case. Multiple Sclerosis is a disease that has not been shown to be aggravated or caused by trauma."

The letter had little effect, even as Linta was beginning to make Downey a cause celebre. Numerous sports columnists had picked up the story in advance of the draft. But Linta's sources saw little movement or interest by pro teams. That caused the agent to take an aggressive next step. He faxed a waiver document to all 32 teams that would essentially release teams from all liability associated with MS should they draft his client. Ironically, ESPN's sports news magazine show *Outside the Lines* featured a story on Downey that would air only hours before the network would broadcast coverage of the draft's second day. That day and its seven rounds passed without the young lineman being selected.

If he were to make an NFL roster, it would have to be through the free agent route. It's not unusual, however, for Linta to place undrafted clients. "Having watched the films, I knew he could play in the NFL," he says. "Getting someone to move past the MS thing was an incredible challenge."

For two weeks, Linta worked the phones, and through a friendship with one of the franchise's regional scouts, he was able to arrange an audition with the San Francisco 49ers. Downey impressed the 49er officials with his workouts, although questions remained about the level of competition he had faced in college and a general lack of conditioning (which not being drafted had something to do with). Still, the team tendered an offer—$230,000, the rookie minimum, should Downey make the team—and invited him to participate in the team's off-season programs.

"I knew that if someone would give him the chance he would show them he could play in the NFL," Linta says. "I never doubted that."

But the Hollywood ending wasn't to be—at least not yet. A week into training camp, Downey twisted his knee in an awkward way and tore his MCL. It was a season-ending injury, but not necessarily a career-ending one. Linta reached an injury settlement with the 49ers, and the team left the door open for Downey's return after rehabbing his knee.

"The worst case is that he spends a season playing in NFL Europe," Linta says. "Or maybe he'll be back and signed to the practice squad."

In either case, Linta looks back on the effort. "I never worked harder for a player, but when you believe in someone, that's what you do."

That sounds like the cornerstone for a mission statement.

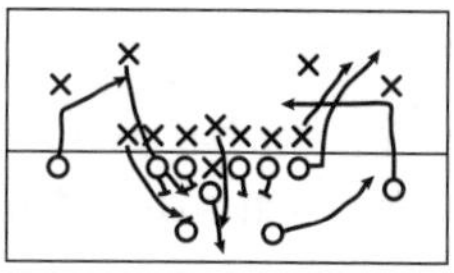

SEVENTEEN

Shoe-In

When the Steelers arrived in New Orleans for Super Bowl IX in 1975, off in the background they could see the new, state-of-the-art Louisiana Superdome. This striking, all-purpose stadium was designed to rival Houston's Astrodome and was built to host football spectaculars like the NCAA's Sugar Bowl and the occasional NFL Super Bowl. At least that was the plan for Super Bowl IX. The problem was it just wasn't finished yet, thanks to a series of construction delays.

Instead of the luxuries of the climate-controlled Superdome, the Steelers and Minnesota Vikings would play a short distance away in rundown, open-aired Tulane Stadium. Its surface was especially worn down, as the first generation of artificial turf had reached the end of its useful life. But for a team that had waited 42 years to even make it to the championship game, the field didn't matter in the grand scheme of things. They were in New Orleans to win a championship.

Besides the many fans making the trek to follow their team into the French Quarter, the Steelers found another familiarity in New Orleans—Pittsburgh-style weather.

Walking the turf at Tulane Stadium, Steelers' equipment manager Tony Parisi knew that if the surface got wet, footing would be treacherous. He also knew a thing or two about playing in slippery conditions. Parisi grew up in Niagara Falls, Ontario, and before joining the Steelers, he had a 16-year career in professional hockey, closing out his career as a goaltender/equipment manager for the Pittsburgh Hornets of the International Hockey League. Add some rain to this field, he thought, and it would be just like playing on ice.

"I called up the Weather Bureau and asked for a long-range forecast," Parisi told *The Sporting News*. "They told me there was a good chance there would be a lot of rain before Sunday." It was then that Parisi placed another important call, this time to a shoe company in Montreal. He had read about a new rain shoe it had developed for use on artificial turf. Although the shoes weren't yet available on the market, the company sent 75 pairs to a fellow Canadian in time for the big game.

At kickoff time, the weather forecasters turned out to be right, and 80,997 fans struggled to stay warm in Tulane Stadium. Down on the field, players struggled to find their footing, as Parisi predicted. Both offenses sputtered in the first quarter; the Steelers managed four first downs, the Vikings one. The Steelers gained 64 yards on the ground, the Vikings none. And the Steelers passed for 15 yards, the Vikings 20.

Twice the Steelers made it into field-range, with kicker Roy Gerela missing from 37 yards out the first time and not even getting off a kick the second time because of a botched snap. The Vikings had a chance to get on the board early in the second quarter after recovering a fumble deep in Steelers territory, but Fred Cox's field goal attempt went wide. The weather contributed to the only score of the first half when Viking running back Dave Osborn couldn't handle a pitch from quarterback Fran Tarkenton, who fell on the ball and was tackled in the end zone for a safety and a 2-0 Steelers lead.

In the locker room at half time, Parisi suggested changing shoes. "I don't tell the players what to wear," Parisi explained to *The Sporting News*. "I only suggest and if they like the suggestion, fine." Running back Franco Harris and quarterback Terry Bradshaw were among those who decided to take the suggestion and make the switch to lace up the new shoes. Both players would make major contributions in the second half.

The Steelers' running game punished the Vikings throughout the remainder of the game. Harris ended the game with then Super Bowl records for rushing attempts (34) and rushing yards (158). Bradshaw led an efficient offense that controlled the game, but the Vikings had crawled back into the game after blocking a punt to narrow the score to 9-6.

However, the Steeler quarterback kept his footing on the slippery turf during a roll-out and fired a scoring strike to tight end Larry Brown for the clinching touchdown in the Steelers' 16-6 victory. The Vikings, on the other hand, never were able to get their footing. They set Super Bowl records for futility—gaining only 17 yards on the ground and 112 through the air.

The Steelers' first Super Bowl appearance was a memorable one, and long-suffering owner Art Rooney, Sr. held high the Vince Lombardi trophy in an emotional locker room. They may have been a Cinderella story, one of only six teams to win in their first Super Bowl appearance. But thanks in no small part to their equipment manager, they were a shoe-in.

Agony of the feet

Besides his notable footwork for Super Bowl IX, equipment manager Tony Parisi had another long-lasting effect on the Steelers ground game. It was Parisi who developed a special insert for the shoes that helped Rocky Bleier to run without pain. Bleier had been wounded in Vietnam, and doctors told him that he would have difficulty walking let alone playing football. Bleier's hard work and determination brought him back to the game. Parisi helped make that historic run a little more comfortable.

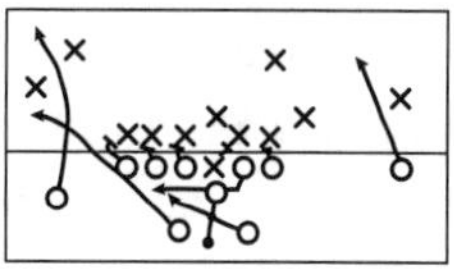

EIGHTEEN

Redecorating the Hall—with Steelers

Wherein Chris makes a few perfectly reasonable suggestions.

With the enormous popularity of the National Football League, there's a strain on those stewards of football history to keep up. While the folks in Canton, Ohio, who run the Professional Football Hall of Fame have recently overseen a major redo, you have to guess that within a few years the building that looks like a giant juicer will need an addition.

Here's a thought for the space planners: create a wing dedicated to the Pittsburgh Steelers. With 16 players who spent a significant amount of time wearing the black and gold, 4 players with some service and 3 front office types, I can envision a nicely appointed room dedicated to all things Steelers. And while they're measuring the dimensions of this new wing, the planners should include some extra space for Steelers that aren't yet in the Hall, but deserve to be.

Unfortunately, it seems, for some of these Steelers greats it will be just as hard to sell their induction as it will be for the Hall to build a wing for the franchise. These former Steelers have a major drawback—black and gold envy.

Says Steelers chairman Dan Rooney, "Unfortunately, having so many players in Canton from those teams of the '70s has worked against L.C. [defensive end L.C. Greenwood] and [safety Donnie] Shell. There's a bit of a backlash that they're facing. Look at how long it took for (wide receivers Lynn) Swann and (John) Stallworth to get in."

After years of the Steelers' wide receivers splitting votes amongst the nominating committee, Swann's induction came in 2001, where he used the occasion to openly lobby for Stallworth's induction. The following year, Stallworth received the call to don the prized yellow blazer and joined his former receiving corps teammate in Canton. The two had always been joined in Steelers' lore. They were both members of the historic 1974 draft class (see "A Picture-Perfect Draft," Chapter 10) and formed the best receiving tandem of the '70s. Already that draft class has produced a record four Hall of Famers. That number should be five, says Rooney, once again pointing to Shell.

Shell is among nine Steelers, we believe, that could have a case made for induction into Canton. Some are sure bets once they reach eligibility. Others have been finalists in the past, but not garnered the necessary number of votes. Still others have been overlooked. Consider the credentials of:

Rod Woodson

The only thing holding back Woodson is eligibility. Retiring after the 2003 season, Woodson won't be eligible for the Hall until 2008. He is without question, however, a first-ballot Hall of Famer.

Woodson was named to the league's 75 year all-time, all-star squad and was one of the NFL's greatest defensive backs. In a 17-year career, Woodson intercepted 71 passes (third all-time) and scored 12 defensive touchdowns (first all-time).

The Steelers have always taken the view that it was better to be rid of a player a season too early than a season too late. However, this is one personnel decision the team has to regret. Woodson suffered a serious injury, tearing his ACL in the first game of the 1995 season. Although he amazingly made it back to play in the Super Bowl for the Steelers that year and played well in 1996, the team had questions about his ability for the future. They shouldn't have. Woodson would go on to have more productive years, including playing for the Super Bowl champion Baltimore Ravens in 2000 and the AFC champion Oakland Raiders in 2002. Quite simply, Woodson made any defense better.

Although he's sure to be remembered primarily as a Steeler on his induction day, it would have been great to have had his career be only in black and gold. Still, he spent ten years with the team and ranks beside Mel Blount as the best corner in franchise history.

Gary Anderson

Like his former teammate Woodson, Gary Anderson has a couple of drawbacks for getting into Canton. The biggest is that he won't retire. Twice, the record-setting placekicker has been lured out of retirement to help teams who lost their kickers either late in the preseason or in the midst of a season. And in both those instances, Anderson filled in without missing a beat. But perhaps the biggest obstacle to Anderson's enshrinement is history: not counting George Blanda, who was also a terrific quarterback, there is currently only one pure kicker in the Hall (take 10 points if you knew it was Jan Stenerud).

That should change when Anderson eventually becomes eligible. He holds NFL records with 2,346 points and 521 field goals in 650 attempts. He spent 13 seasons with the Steelers and holds many of the franchise's kicking records.

Dermontti Dawson

The Steelers have a strong tradition at center, which Dawson continued. Taking over for Hall of Famer Mike Webster, Dawson spent 13 years anchoring the line until his retirement in 2000. It should be only a matter of time—perhaps in his second or third year of eligibility—before Dawson's bust appears in Canton.

Dawson was named to seven Pro Bowls and was arguably the best center of his time. He was a powerful run blocker—one of only a few at this position who could pull and lead a run to the outside—and a terrific pass protector as well.

L.C. Greenwood

A member of the Steelers' famed front four, Greenwood retired as the franchise's all-time sacks leader with 73.5. In 13 years with the team, he was named to 6 Pro Bowls. Where teammate Joe Greene would overwhelm opponents with power, Greenwood relied on his speed and a knack for being in the right place at the right time as his 14 fumble recoveries attest. At 6'6" and with long arms, Greenwood also had a knack for batting away quarterbacks' passes. And he was at his best in big games. In the Steelers' first Super Bowl appearance, he swatted away three Fran Tarkenton passes and harassed the Minnesota quarterback all day. The following year he sacked Dallas QB Roger Staubach three times. Greenwood has been close to induction, being named as a finalist four times, most recently in 2002.

Donnie Shell

He was the safety who hit like a linebacker. In fact, says Rooney, "No safety ever hit harder than Donnie did." Shell first made his mark on special teams, but settled into the secondary. He retired with 51 interceptions, the third most in franchise history and tops among safeties in NFL history. He was named to five Pro Bowls in his 14 years with the team. Shell was an undrafted free agent and part of the historic rookie class of 1974. Should Shell make it to Canton, it would only add to the Steelers' record: No other class has more than two. Shell was a finalist in 2002.

Kevin Greene

Although he only spent three seasons with the Steelers, they were memorable ones as he led the team in sacks each of those years. Greene finished his 14-year career with 157 sacks, third most in NFL history. A ferocious pass rusher from the linebacker position, Greene says he wasn't blessed with the natural talent that many NFL stars have. Instead, he notes, he made his mark by studying, particularly as a rookie with the then Los Angeles Rams in 1985. "Some of those old, crusty guys who played for the Rams... brought me into the film room and showed me how to work the projector, and watch the film and know what to look for." Prior to the 2004 season, the Steelers brought Greene back to help coach their linebackers. That same year was Greene's first to be eligible for the Hall, and his stats match-up well with linebackers already in Canton.

Gene "Big Daddy" Lipscomb

This defensive tackle, who played two years for the Steelers in the early '60s, should have gotten in on the strength of this quote alone, describing his philosophy for playing the line: "I just wrap my arms around the whole backfield and peel 'em one by one until I get to the ball carrier. Him I keep." Lipscomb made his mark with the Los Angeles Rams, who signed him straight from the sandlots, and the Baltimore Colts. Big Daddy was the first of the truly big men of the league, topping 300 pounds and standing 6'6". He was a feared defender. His weapon was the head slap—now outlawed—where he would hit opponents on the ear hole of their helmets. Twice he was named MVP of the Pro Bowl and was a two-time finalist for Canton.

Jack Butler

When he retired, this Steelers defensive back held the franchise record for interceptions with 52, a figure he achieved remarkably enough during an era where most teams ran the ball. Known for his coverage abilities, Butler spent eight years in black and gold and was named to four Pro Bowls. Despite being among the best defensive backs of his generation, Butler has yet to be a Hall of Fame finalist.

Andy Russell

For 12 years, Russell was an elite linebacker for the Steelers, bridging the SOS years (Same Old Steelers) to the first two Super Bowl squads. Although overshadowed by Hall of Famers Jack Ham and Jack Lambert, Russell was a star in his own right. He was named to seven Pro Bowl squads, and was equally adept at pass coverage as he was on the blitz. Russell, like Butler, has not been a finalist in Hall of Fame voting.

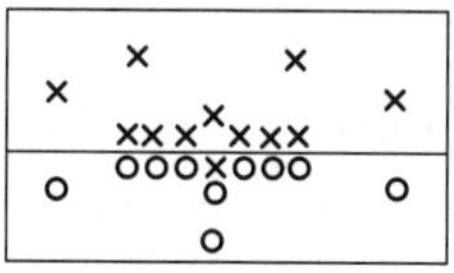

NINETEEN

The Ultimate List: the 20 Greatest Pittsburgh Steelers

It's like going to the Playboy mansion and having Hugh Heffner ask which girl you want to dance with next; you realize there's a decision to be made and its tough, but you know it can never be a bad one. That's what picking the top twenty Steelers of all-time is like, so many Hall of Fame talents, so difficult trying to slot them into a position, but you know no matter whom you choose, the decision is good.

Obviously a huge percentage of the list is comprised of the Hall of Fame members of the 1970 dynasty teams, but the franchise has been around for 71 years and there is a potpourri of great players from eras outside of the greatest decade in the annals of Steel City football that deserve the honor, too.

Trying to fit 80 back ends into 20 seats is a daunting task, but it was a challenge we were truly ready for. And now, in reverse order, the ultimate list.

20. Jack Butler

Defensive Back (1951-1959). 4 Pro Bowls (with the Steelers); 1st Team All-Pro (with the Steelers) 1956-1959.

The St. Bonaventure product held the all-time Steeler record for career interceptions with 52 before Mel Blount eventually broke it. Butler also spent some time at wide out where he caught seven career passes for 102 yards and four touchdowns. After his career, he became well known for his use of computers for college player scouting.

19. Hines Ward

Wide Receiver (1998-). 3 Pro Bowls.

Ward could eventually become the greatest receiver in the history of this legendary franchise. He is not just the only Steeler ever to eclipse the 100 catch barrier (112 in 2002), but has averaged 100 catches per year between 2001-2003, breaking the 1,000 yard barrier each time. Add to the mix he gives 150 percent every play and is also a devastating blocker and you can see clearly why a top 10 finish in this list a few years down the road is not an impossibility.

18. Andy Russell

Linebacker (1963, 1966-1976). 7 Pro Bowls; 1st Team All-Pro 1967, 1970, 1972-1975.

The three men that made up the greatest core of linebackers on one team in NFL history were Jack Ham, Jack Lambert and Andy Russell. While being the only member of the group not enshrined in Canton, Russell nevertheless had a career that should be considered very seriously for such an honor. He is the one link between the bad Steeler teams of the 1960s and those of the championship days in the '70s. Might Russell have made the Hall if not being overshadowed by his wildly successful mates at linebacker? Perhaps, but whether or not he was overlooked by the men who make such decisions, he is one of the greatest ever to don the black and gold.

17. Bullet Bill Dudley

Running Back, Defensive Back (1942, 1945-1946). Pro Bowls (N/A); 1st Team All-Pro 1942, 1946.

His career spanned only three seasons in Pittsburgh, but they were three campaigns that were not only the best of his nine year Hall of Fame career, but perhaps the finest three seasons a Steeler turned in until the heydays of the 1970s. Dudley was a smallish man, 176 pounds, but a devastating runner, leading the NFL in rushing in 1942 and 1946. In 1946, he not only led the NFL in rushing, but also in punt returns and interceptions. He was named as a first team All-Pro (an honor he also won in 1942) and won the league's Most Valuable Player Award. Unfortunately, Bullet Bill was as well known in Steeler lore for his legendary tiff with coach Jock Sutherland that got him sent to the Motor City in 1947 as he was for his play on the field.

16. John Henry Johnson

Running Back, Defensive Back (1960-1965). 3 Pro Bowls.

John Henry Johnson was drafted by the Steelers in the second round of 1953, but chose to go to Canada rather than play with the rag tag group that represented the Steel City in that era. He was a freight train run amok when he was on the field, with a running style that could only be described as a tank running through a row of trees. Instead of running around defenders, he would trample them. He started his NFL career in the famous "Million Dollar Backfield" with the 49ers before moving to Detroit. Johnson returned to Pittsburgh in 1960 and promptly became the first Steeler ever to rush for 1,000, which he did in 1962 and 1964. From 1960 to 1964, he finished in the top ten in both carries and rushing for the league. John was selected as a second team All-Pro in 1962. When he retired, he was the fourth all-time leading rusher in the NFL. While overlooked for years by Hall of Fame electors, Johnson was enshrined in 1987.

15. L.C. Greenwood

Defensive End (1969-1981). 6 Pro Bowls; 1st Team All-Pro 1973-1975, 1978-1979.

Like Russell, L.C. Greenwood is still waiting enshrinement in Canton, overshadowed by several great Steeler defensive players during that era. Year after year, he is nominated and year after year, others go before him. Drafted 10th in 1969 out of little Arkansas-Pine Bluff, Greenwood was a prime example of the kind of talent the Pittsburgh scouts would mine out of small colleges, talent that was the cornerstone for the Steeler machine in the 1970s. While Jason Gildon may have eclipsed his all-time team sack record of 73.5 in 2003, Greenwood held the distinction for 22 years over the rest of the Hall of Fame mates. He truly had a career that deserves a selection to pro football's hallowed hall.

14. Donnie Shell

Defensive Back (1974-1980). 5 Pro Bowls; 1st Team All-Pro 1979-1980, 1982.

While he was part of the most phenomenal rookie class in NFL history in 1974, Shell was not part of the legendary Steeler draft that season. Instead, he was a free agent pick out of South Carolina

State. Shell picked off 51 passes in his pro football career, more than any other strong safety in league history. Shell amazed football fans not with his incredible penchant for interceptions, but with his devastating hits on opposing receivers. His legendary crushing of Earl Campbell on *Monday Night Football* in 1978 is still considered one of the greatest hits in league history, especially considering the fact that Shell was a dwarf when compared to the Hall of Fame back. Add Shell to the list of Russell and Greenwood when talking about Steelers who are unjustly ignored for Hall of Fame consideration.

13. Lynn Swann
Wide Receiver (1974-1982). 3 Pro Bowls; 1st Team All-Pro 1977-1978.

Swann was the first-round selection of the team in the famous 1974 draft. His name was befitting of the most acrobatic Steeler wide receiver, as his graceful catches adorned many a highlight reel. Swann led the league in punt returns his rookie year and led the NFL in TD catches with 11 the following year. His four-catch, 161-yard performance in Super Bowl X is still among the greatest games a wide receiver has ever played. Each catch he made that day was spectacular as his performance earned him the game's MVP award. Playing in a run-oriented offense kept his numbers down until 1978, when the club opened up the offense a bit. Despite that he was still the most-feared deep threat in the league. His ability to go through the middle to catch balls where hard-hitting defensive back were waiting with forearms outstretched helped keep his career short. After his retirement, he became a successful broadcaster with ABC. His long Hall of Fame wait ended in 2001 when he finally entered the doors of Canton.

12. John Stallworth
Wide Receiver (1974-1987). 3 Pro Bowls; 1st Team All-Pro 1979, 1984.

When Lynn Swann was elected to the Pro Football Hall of Fame in 2001, he pleaded for the electorate to also bring in the other member of the greatest wide receiver duo in Steeler history—John Stallworth. Stallworth also came to Pittsburgh in the 1974 draft, but he came in under the shadow of Swann, a shadow he would live under for most of his pro career. John was the steady sure receiver to Swann's big play capabilities. The Alabama A&M product broke loose in 1979, breaking the 1,000-yard barrier while having a phenomenal Super Bowl of his own, snagging three catchers against the Rams in Super Bowl XIV for 121 yards and a TD. Stallworth went over 1,000 yards on three occasions, including 1984 when he caught 80 catches for 1,395 yards and a career-high 11 TDs. The 1,395 yards was a team record for 13 years until Yancy Thigpen broke it by three yards in 1997. By the time he finished, he was no longer under Swann's shadow, he was the greatest Steeler receiver ever to play the game. His 537 catches, 8,723 yards and twenty-five 100-yard games are all Steeler records today. Fortunately, the Hall of Fame electorate listened to Swann's plea as Stallworth was given pro football's highest honor in 2002.

11. Dermontti Dawson

Center (1988-2000). 7 Pro Bowls; 1st Team All-Pro 1993, 1995-1997.

Dermontti Dawson continued the proud legacy of playing center for the Pittsburgh Steelers that started with Ray Mansfield and continued with the great Mike Webster. Drafted in the second round in 1988, Dawson had a sparkling career that included his selection to the NFL's all-1990s team. Injuries cut short his career in 1999 and 2000, but nonetheless, Dawson started 175 consecutive games, second in team history behind Webster. A deserving end to the Dermontti Dawson story would be enshrinement in the Hall of Fame for one of the greatest centers to ever grace the gridiron.

10. Mike Webster

Center (1974-1990). 9 Pro Bowls; 1st Team All-Pro 1978, 1979, 1980-1983, 1987.

Yet another jewel of the 1974 draft, Mike Webster was probably the least known of the four Hall of Fame picks the Steelers made that year. By the time he was done 17 years later, he was among the best players ever. Webby was a workout nut and perhaps the most technically gifted lineman ever to play in NFL history. After his career, Webster suffered through homelessness, bouts of drug addiction and mental afflictions that may have been caused by a brain injury he suffered from all the hard hits he took over the years. He was eventually elected to the Hall of Fame in 1997, but tragically died two years later of an apparent heart attack. He was honored in 2000 by being placed on the All-Time NFL team as the league's greatest center.

9. Jerome Bettis

Running Back (1996-2004). 3 Pro Bowls; 1st Team All-Pro 1996, 1997.

The team pulled off one of the most lopsided deals in NFL history when they obtained Bettis in 1996 from the Rams for a second round pick in 1996 and fourth round pick in 1997. (The 1996 pick was Ernie Conwell, a tight end who's caught 172 passes with the Rams and Saints. The Rams ended up giving away the 1997 pick.) Bettis has become one of the most prolific runners in the history of the National Football League, passing both Eric Dickerson and Tony Dorsett in 2004 to rank fourth all-time in rushing. He finished third in the NFL in rushing in 1996 and 1997. Beyond being wildly successful on the field, Bettis has also been one of the best ambassadors for the team off the gridiron, and was awarded the 2001 Walter Payton NFL Man of the Year for his contributions to the community. A bust awaits him in Canton when his playing days are over.

8. Ernie Stautner

Defensive Tackle (1950-1963). 9 Pro Bowls; 1st Team All-Pro 1955-1959, 1961.

Ask what is the only number the Steelers ever retired (read more about that in Chapter 20) and the answer is No. 70, in honor of the great Ernie Stautner. Before the heyday of the franchise in the 1970s, Stautner was regarded as the greatest Steeler through their first four decades of existence. Considered too small for professional football when he was drafted out of Boston College in 1950, the native of Germany proved the critics wrong with attitude and determination. Stautner's incredible effort eventually earned him pro football's highest honor, being selected to the Hall of Fame in 1969. He later went on to a successful coaching career, spending 23 years with Tom Landry and the Dallas Cowboys before stints as a head coach with the Frankfurt Galaxy in NFL Europe and the Dallas Texans in the Arena Football League, where he was coach of the year in 1990.

7. Terry Bradshaw

Quarterback (1969-1983). 3 Pro Bowls; 1st Team All-Pro 1978-1979.

The luck of a coin flip with the Chicago Bears brought the Louisiana native to the Steelers as the first overall pick in the 1969 draft. While eventually ending up as one of the game's greats, Terry was not an immediate hit in the Steel City as he struggled through several tough seasons fighting unsuccessfully with the opposing teams, fans and media alike. Through 1974, Bradshaw tossed 48 touchdown passes and 81 interceptions; in 1975 that all changed. Things finally clicked as the Louisiana Tech alum lived up to his incredible promise when he was second team All-Pro while leading the team to a second consecutive Super Bowl title. It was in the postseason when Brad was at his best, tossing for 300 yards on three occasions including Super Bowls XIII and XIV when he was named MVP each time. His best season was in 1978 when he capturing the NFL's MVP award, only the second Steeler in history (Bill Dudley was the other) to be given such a prestigious honor. An elbow injury ended Bradshaw's career prematurely, but not before he made one last dramatic appearance tossing two touchdowns against the Jets in 1983 and leading the team to the postseason in his last NFL game. After his career, Bradshaw was elected to the Hall of Fame in 1989, began an extremely successful broadcasting career for CBS and Fox, and finally ended his long standing dispute with the Steel City as he was welcomed back with open arms by the Steeler Nation in 2003.

6. Franco Harris

Running Back (1972-1983). 9 Pro Bowls; 1st Team All-Pro 1972, 1975-1977.

He was the missing piece to the Steeler offense when he was selected in the first round out of Penn State in 1972. Franco almost never became a Steeler as Coach Chuck Noll wanted Robert Newhouse instead. It was fortuitous for the team that the coach didn't go with his first choice. Harris broke in with a bang. He captured the Offensive Rookie of the Year award with 1,055 yards and a 5.6 per carry average and helped the team to their first Division crown ever. He also made his mark in NFL history by catching the Immaculate Reception, the play that saw Pittsburgh beat Oakland on the last play of the game in the first round of the playoffs, 13-7. While Harris had his critics for his running style, running out of bounds instead of being hit when it looked like the play was over, he was one of the greatest running backs in the history of the league. He gained 1,000 yards eight times, including 1974 when he not only finished fifth in the NFL in rushing, but rambled for a Super Bowl-record 158 yards in Super Bowl IX. That earned him designation as the game's MVP. With Harris only a few yards away from breaking Jim Brown's all-time rushing yard record in 1984, Franco made one of the few mistakes of his career by holding out for more money, a move that saw Pittsburgh instead release him. He went to Seattle and ended his career there in 1984, never able to set the all-time record. Regardless, he was elected to Canton in 1990 and was also one of the greatest Steelers ever outside the field of play.

5. Jack Lambert

Linebacker (1974-1984). 9 Pro Bowls; 1st Team All-Pro 1975-1983.

The Steeler defense in the 1970s was considered the best ever produced in the annals of the NFL. It was a defense that had an attitude for destruction, and that attitude that was brought to a new level when they selected linebacker Jack Lambert out of Kent State in the second round of the memorable 1974 draft. "Count Dracula with cleats" as he was called (because of the menacing look he gave minus his front teeth) was a star in the league the minute he stepped on the football field and never looked back. Lambert was named the NFL's Defensive Rookie of the Year in 1974 and Defensive MVP in 1976 and 1983. Ironically, one of the meanest men to put on a pro football uniform was eventually felled in 1984 by a toe injury, an injury so severe it necessitated his retirement following the '84 campaign. Lambert joined Bradshaw in the Hall of Fame's class of 1990 and was named to the NFL's 75th anniversary team in 1994.

4. Rod Woodson

Defensive Back (1987-1996). 7 Pro Bowls; 1st Team All-Pro 1989-1990, 1993-1994.

His career in the NFL began with a lengthy holdout where the Purdue alum threatened to pursue a track career instead of playing football if the Steelers could not meet his needs. Luckily, the team met his needs, and he returned his first interception 45 yards for a touchdown. It was something he would repeat time and time again throughout his career as he has picked off 71 passes, third most in league history, while scoring an NFL all-time best 12 touchdowns off interceptions. Woodson was continually one of the best in the league throughout his tenure in Pittsburgh, and was awarded 1993 NFL Defensive MVP. In 1994 he was chosen to the NFL's 75th anniversary team. Woodson unfortunately tore his anterior cruciate ligament in the 1995 opener and missed the entire season. In true Woodson form, he came back heroically to play in Super Bowl XXX. After the 1996 season the Steelers gambled that his career was about over; they were wrong. Woodson went on to play successfully through the 2003 season with the 49ers, Ravens and Raiders. Now that his career is over, he is a certainty to be enshrined in the Hall of Fame.

3. Jack Ham

Linebacker (1971-1982). 8 Pro Bowls; 1st Team All-Pro 1973-1979.

Jack Ham was a consensus All-American for Joe Paterno in the early 1970s. Remarkably every team in the NFL passed on him, even the Steelers, who took Frank Lewis instead, with Pittsburgh picking him up in the second round, the 34th player overall. Ham didn't disappoint, becoming the only linebacker in the era to make eight consecutive pro bowl appearances and winning the NFL's Defensive MVP award in 1975, an honor he shared with Mel Blount.

Jack was more than just a great linebacker; he was among the greatest ever to take the field. Always in place, always making the big play, he was the quintessential thinking man's linebacker. There was no better man at his position in an era of great linebackers.

An injury forced Ham to miss Super Bowl XIV. Had he not, perhaps the Ram's magical ride that day would have been curtailed and the game could have been a rout. Injuries eventually ended his career two years later, but the honors for Jack kept coming in. He was selected to the Pro Football Hall of Fame in 1988 and made not only the NFL's 75th anniversary team, but the all-time team selected by the powers that be in Canton in 2000. Today Jack is a successful analyst for both the NFL and his beloved Penn State Nittany Lions.

2. Mel Blount

Defensive Back (1971-1983). 5 Pro Bowls; 1st Team All-Pro 1975-1977, 1981.

There are not many athletes in professional sports today that can make the claim that they changed the way the game is played; Mel Blount is one of those special players. Coming out of Southern University in the third round of the 1970 draft, Blount became so good at keeping the best receivers the NFL had to offer away from the ball that league officials eventually created a rule to combat him by not allowing contact of a receiver by a defensive back after five yards. His best season came in 1975 when he led the league in interceptions, sharing the NFL's Defensive MVP with teammate Jack Ham. After his career was over, Blount was elected to the Hall of Fame in 1989 and was chosen to the NFL's 75th anniversary team in 1994.

1. Joe Greene

Defensive Tackle (1969-1981).
10 Pro Bowls; 1st Team All-Pro 1969-1979.

He is the foundation upon which the Dynasty of the 1970s was built. Mean Joe Greene was the first draft pick of the Chuck Noll era and turned out to be, at least in our humble opinion, the greatest player ever to don the black and gold. His aggressive, winning attitude was the basis for the Steel Curtain defense that is considered one of the best ever to grace the gridiron. Joe was an impact player from the outset and the unabashed leader of the club. Named Defensive Rookie of the Year in 1969 and the NFL's Defensive MVP in 1972 and 1974, Greene was a dominant figure in the league and was at his best in his first Super Bowl appearance, Super Bowl IX, when the North Texas State alum ripped through the vaunted Vikings offensive line time and time again. The honors flowed for Mean Joe following his retirement: first of the Dynasty to receive his immortality in the hall of Canton in 1987, selected to the league's 75th anniversary club in 1994 and to the All-Time NFL team in 2000, and number 14 on the *Sporting News*' all-time top 100 players in NFL history. He returned to the organization in 2004 in an administrative capacity as a special assistant of player personnel. Without Joe Greene on the field, there might have never been four super bowl championships.

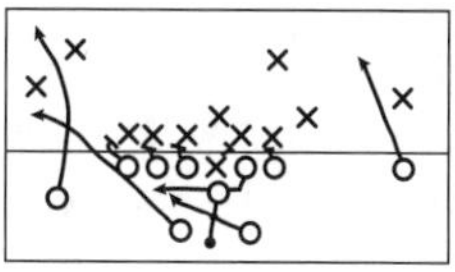

TWENTY

The Numbers Game

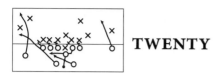

Chris calculates and ciphers in a uniform manner.

Football is a numbers game. How fast a player runs the 40 will often determine his position in the draft. A running back who averages less than 4.0 yards per carry won't be carrying the pigskin for long. Game-breaking receivers are measured in yards after the catch. And then there is that mystical formula for determining a quarterback's passer rating. Warning: do not try this unless you're quite accomplished in your gazintas (you know, three gazinta nine, three times, etc.)

Behind the scenes, it's a numbers game in a different sense, particularly if you're the equipment manager. It's the equipment manager who assigns each player a number that most often will stick with him for his entire stay with the team. The National Football League in its infinite wisdom—and control—first issued rules for assigning numbers in 1973. Remember, this is a league that actually has a paid staffer go to each game to ensure that uniforms are worn to league specification. That untucked shirt will cost you, rookie. And when it comes to uniform numbers, it's all very orderly, thanks to the suits in New York: 1-9, quarterbacks and kickers; 10-19, quarterbacks, receivers, and kickers; 20-49, running backs and defensive backs; 50-59, centers and linebackers; 60-79, defensive linemen and offensive linemen; 80-89, receivers and tight ends; 90-99, defensive linemen and linebackers.

One area where the league shows some flexibility is its granting the right to its franchises to retire the numbers of former players at each team's discretion. It's the highest honor a team can bestow to a former star, saying that no one will ever wear that number again. Yet despite having a rich history, the Steelers have only retired one number. And they do a pretty good job of keeping that one a secret. Award yourself 20 points if you knew the No. 70 jersey worn by defensive lineman Ernie Stautner is the only "official" retired number. That happened in 1969, the year of Stautner's induction in Canton. Even now, there's little ink or notice given to that lone retired number.

It's something that a certified uniform junkie like me would notice. Like any good fan, I knew every player's number. Even those reserves that more or less served as bodies for practice. And unfortunately, I still remember them, and I can't help but feel that some more useful area of my brain isn't functioning because of that jersey retention. Even now, I gaze upon the roster at the end of training camp, updating my file of useless information. And that's when the pattern emerges, and I call Steelers equipment manager Rodgers Freyvogel to get the scoop on the lack of retired numbers. Hey, writing a book can come in handy sometimes.

He says that, unofficially, there are a number of numbers that just don't get assigned. It's a tradition that was started by his predecessor, Tony Parisi, and is continued today. "I don't give out the numbers 12, 32, 47, 52, 58, 59 or 75," Freyvogel explains. Any diehard black and gold follower has the corresponding players who wore those numbers in the glory days tattooed in his or her collective football unconscious—Terry Bradshaw, Franco Harris, Mel Blount, Mike Webster, Jack Lambert, Jack Ham and Joe Greene, respectively. All of them are Hall of Famers. More recent inductees, like John Stallworth and Lynn

Swann, still have their numbers in play. Antwaan Randle El currently wears Stallworth's 82. Matt Kranchick wears Swann's 88.

"I try to give each player a number they can keep for the entire time they're here," says Freyvogel. "And I wouldn't ever take a number away from a player just because someone who wore it before goes into the Hall. It wouldn't be right to take 82 away from Randle El. That's *his* number." Given the numbers restriction imposed by the league, sometimes it's like a puzzle for Freyvogel. Sometimes the pieces don't always fit. He recalls Todd Seabaugh, a third-round draft pick in 1983, who because the league didn't expand the available numbers for linebackers, had to wear the No. 59 jersey. Seabaugh had a rather uneventful career as a Steelers linebacker. He played one season for the team and then, because of back problems, was out of the league. Not exactly a great homage as the last Steeler to wear the sacred 59, but such sacrilege is a rarity.

"Luckily, we've been able to keep the other numbers out of circulation," says the team's equipment manager. But that begs the obvious question: If you're not going to give out the numbers, why not just retire them? "You'll have to ask Mr. Rooney [chairman Dan Rooney]," Freyvogel explains. "I think the league asked him not to do it." Unlikely. Most teams do retire numbers.

Taking Freyvogel's advice, I ask Dan Rooney why no more numbers are retired. "Because we wouldn't have any numbers left," he says. "We've had so many great players throughout the years, it would become very difficult. I don't think that many teams can claim as many as we've had."

There are some franchises, however, that operate similarly to Pittsburgh when it comes to not retiring jerseys—the Oakland Raiders and Dallas Cowboys also pass on the tradition. (The Baltimore Ravens, Houston Texans, Carolina Panthers and Jacksonville Jaguars haven't been around long enough to have a tradition). Like the Steelers, the Buffalo Bills and Washington Redskins both have retired only one jersey (Jim Kelly and Sammy Baugh, respectively). But the Redskins and Cowboys have incorporated Rings of Honor into their stadiums, where past players' names and numbers are displayed and honored on concrete facades. The Bills have a Wall of Honor. Other teams, including those who do retire jersey numbers, have established these rings—even Detroit is considering adding one to its fairly new Ford Field (hold all jokes about it being a very short ring).

"I don't like to copy others," Rooney says as the conversation turns to creating a similar display for the Steelers. "And again, we have so many great players. I went down to Washington and saw all the Redskins names [in their Ring of Honor] and there were so many names, you lose the impact. This is a franchise that has seen a lot of great players—particularly in the '70s."

Perhaps that's the problem. Maybe fans aren't meant to be reminded of dynasties anymore. Frankly, it's impossible to think that the Steelers—or any other team for that matter—will ever enjoy such a period of prolonged excellence as the franchise had in the 1970s. Eight straight playoff appearances. Four Super Bowl victories. In this era of player movement, it's best not to get attached to your athletes or their numbers. How many Kordell Stewart jerseys still occupy the bargain racks at sporting goods stores? Although for the league, it's not a bad thing. After all, it forces the diehard fans to go out and buy new jerseys every couple of years or so—just to stay current.

But for me, current isn't always good if tradition is forced to sit on the bench. I would love to see a Ring of Honor in Heinz Field. Yes, the team has done a nice job in remembering its great players throughout the Coca Cola Great Hall. The entrance to the space is marked by huge action portraits of Steelers' greats like Bradshaw, Greene, Swann, John Henry Johnson, Dwight White and Ernie Holmes. Step inside and you'll find faux lockers of others like Bryan Hinkle and Stallworth. There are also trophies from Steelers' league MVPs.

But it's not the constant reminder that a Ring of Honor would provide. (Note to Mr. Rooney: Sponsors would pay heavily to be associated with such a display in the stands. The King's Jewelers' Ring of Honor has a nicely commercial name to it. Just send my 20 percent commission.) I'd like to be able to gaze up from my seat on a day when the breaks are beating the boys and remember the intensity of Jack Lambert or the laser passes from Terry Bradshaw. I'd relish the pre-game ceremonies where Franco Harris is presented to the crowd one more time as his name and number are unveiled on the concrete of the pavilion. My Ring of Fame would be small. It would include Greene,

Harris, Ham, Lambert and Blount as an initial class. Each year I would allow another player to be added. Eventually Bradshaw, Rod Woodson, Swann and Stallworth would make their way to the Ring. Think of the great debates that would ensue. Think of the sale of new throwback jerseys each year.

Football may be America's No.1 sport, moving baseball back a notch or two. But baseball does a much better job of remembering and celebrating its past. Football does get it right occasionally. (How else could you explain the music from NFL Films now being available on a CD?) Following the last game at Three Rivers Stadium, the team brought back some of the great players in franchise history for a farewell to the building where they made NFL history. I remember feeling like I was a teenager again as players like Andy Russell, Blount and Dwight White strolled along the turf one last time. At that moment I didn't care that there would be no Super Bowl for the current Steelers. I had my dynasty one more time.

When I mentioned all of this to Dwight White, the former lineman didn't share my romanticism. "Retiring numbers isn't important," he said to me. "Players come and go. We each had our time, but it's in the past. Who cares what numbers we wore?"

But I can't help but play my own numbers game. I remember growing up at a time when all the great quarterbacks wore No. 12—Bradshaw, Joe Namath, Bob Griese, John Brodie—and the great running backs wore No. 32—Jim Brown, Franco and O.J. It was a time before NFL games were played on Thursday nights, before the league had its own cable channel, before there were two hours of pre-game coverage and nightly shows that dissect the pro ranks into such minutia. Don't get me wrong, I watch all of those things. But there's something I remember fondly about watching the *weekly* highlight shows hosted by Pat Summerall and Tom Brookshier. In those pre-ESPN days, it was the only way to see the other games or even those Steelers home games that were blacked out. I remember discovering that the San Diego Chargers had a defensive back named Chris Fletcher. (He wore No. 44, by the way.) So maybe my fascination with numbers dates back to the NFL of my youth. Is that such a bad thing?

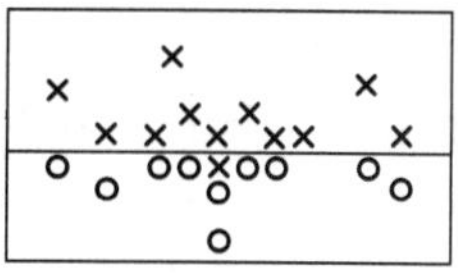

TWENTY ONE

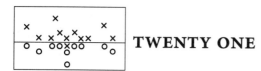

Get back—Then Get Going

We're living in an age of specialization in professional football. Rosters are filled with players who are one-dimensional, like the pass-rushing specialist, the third-down cover man or even the place kicker who does nothing but kickoff. Coaching has become specialized as well. Each position has a member of the coaching staff dedicated to it, from tight ends to quarterbacks.

It takes a village to raise a child and apparently to coach a football team. There are inventive titles like the quality control coach, which a few teams have. All teams, however, have a coach with an interesting title—the get-back coach.

The get-back coach is a relatively new addition to coaching staffs around the league, although you'll never find it as an official title on someone's resume. The get-back coach is the one on the sidelines who tells the players and coaches to "get back" and stay off of the field so that the team isn't charged a penalty. For the Steelers, the man with that unofficial title is Anthony Griggs, or A.G., as he's commonly known. Officially, and when the game is over, Griggs serves as the team's director of player development. In that role, you'll never hear Griggs say, "get back." Then his role is to make the players push forward and achieve goals away from the football field.

"I'm the best damn get-back coach in the league," Griggs smiles. "People don't know a lot about us, but we're pretty important. And I'm the best. I even went to Hawaii because of it." (Okay, a little exaggeration: Griggs was on the sideline when head coach Bill Cowher coached the AFC squad at the Pro Bowl in Honolulu. He served as the get-back coach that day.)

There are important nuances to the role. You can't be polite, prefacing your conversations with niceties like "please" or "would you mind. . . " Instead it's: "Move!" "Backup!" "Get off the white!" Or the ever popular "Get back!"

Should players begin to creep onto the field, the referees may throw a flag for unsportsmanlike conduct, a 15-yard penalty. Actually, what the refs should be calling is the "I tripped over your big feet while I was running backwards following the play and fell on my ass in front of 50,000 people and millions of viewers at home" penalty. But unsportsmanlike conduct is much more concise, if a little vague. Even Griggs isn't sure of the exact wording and subsection of the thick and stately NFL rulebook that gave rise to clubs designating someone on the sidelines to keep the team off the field.

Griggs has a routine of talking to the officials before the game, exchanging pleasantries and filling the men in stripes with confidence that the Steelers' sideline will be under control. "I make sure to tell them, 'Hey, you don't have anything to worry about with me here. You can just concentrate on the game.'"

Then, Griggs makes his way over to a few potential wanderers to let them know that they need to be particularly careful on this given Sunday. "I'll say something like, 'Man, you better be careful. I just talked to that official over there and he's really tough about enforcing the rule." The message is then passed from player to player. It's a subtle way of engaging lieutenants in the campaign to keep players off the field, but you have to be crafty in delivering the message. Such is the life of the get-back coach.

It's training, he says, that starts from the moment a player joins the organization. "I begin early, so that it comes to a point where they just hear my voice and they move back," Griggs explains.

"They're like Pavlov's dogs. I talk. They move."

It gets a little more difficult in the first preseason games with rosters expanded far beyond the typical 53. There can be as many as 80, in fact. "And our starters like to line up right there against the sideline when they're done playing for the night, so there are a lot more bodies to try to keep track of," he says.

In one of those preseason games, the Steelers were flagged for an unsportsmanlike conduct penalty, as an official took a tumble. "I looked around and saw there weren't any players tangled up there," he says, "so I was able to breathe a little easier." The culprit who drew the penalty was assistant head coach/offensive line coach Russ Grimm, who apparently didn't see the official coming and consequently didn't get back.

Dealing with the coaching staff, particularly head coach Bill Cowher, offers a different kind of challenge. The emotional Cowher has a reputation of making his way onto the field. There Griggs has to use a little tact. "He's [Cowher] into the game and talking to coaches up in the box, to the quarterback on the receiver, yelling to the players or screaming to the refs—there's a lot going on there, so for me to go up to him and say 'get back' he's going to look at me like, 'Do I know you?' 'Who are you?'" So Cowher gets a different treatment, a softer approach. It's an "I need you to move back a little," as opposed to something more forceful.

But it's all in the challenge that comes from being a get-back coach. Not everyone can do it, nor would everyone want to. But Griggs loves it. He keeps a sense of humor about the role. "This game is about entertainment," he says. "It's something I talk to the refs about, even during the game. Isn't this entertaining? Man, how could you not be having a great time?"

The other six days of the week you'll find a much more serious A.G., moving through the Steelers' facilities on the South Side. He introduces players to new fields rather than keep them off of them. Griggs works with them on continuing education, helping them to finish college degrees that were not completed before entering the NFL. He provides career development advice and sets up internships to get players work experience that will help once their playing days are over. And he provides financial and business education that will help them in budgeting and in ensuring there is money left when they hang up the cleats.

"This is a high-performance business," he says of the NFL. "You're out there going the fastest you can go, like one of those top-fuel dragsters that hits 300 miles per hour. But whatever's in your tank is going to burn quickly. Are you ready?"

Griggs wished the player development position existed when he played in the NFL. Drafted in the fourth round by the Philadelphia Eagles in 1982, he spent seven seasons as a linebacker with the Eagles and the Cleveland Browns. When he was released by the Browns in '89, he had his communications degree from Villanova to fall back on, but not a strategy of his post-NFL life. He got into coaching, working part-time with the Falcons in strengthing and condition and splitting time with an Atlanta athletic club.

Then Griggs took part in a seminar sponsored by the NFL that looked to help place minorities, especially players and ex-players, in management positions in professional sports.

It opened his eyes to the possibilities and gave him the desire to become a change agent in ensuring that players left the league ready to tackle life outside of the gridiron. In 1991, the league officially launched its Player Development Program, with most teams devoting a full-time employee to the cause. Griggs joined the Steelers that same year.

"I try to get them to think about their other interests outside of football," he says. "What else inspires you? What do you think about when you're not here?" From there, Griggs sets up meetings and internships to provide players with experience in a professional setting.

Griggs cites two examples of former players that have been incredibly successful—Roger Staubach and Fran Tarkenton. The two former quarterbacks hold interests in businesses worth millions of dollars. "They knew how to connect with people and how to build relationships," he says. "And that's why I try to use them as examples. Meet people and exchange information."

Financial education is another key service Griggs provides to the players. He introduces them to principles of retirement planning and investing. Each player receives a financial management playbook during his rookie symposium. Griggs strives to make that information a little more digestible.

And he's also there to provide assistance to players and their families on all areas from lifestyle changes to relationships. Talking about a player's education, future job prospects, money management and personal family relationships requires developing a high level of trust. It's something of which Griggs is acutely aware. "You need to be patient," he says in developing those relationships with the players.

It also presents some challenges. First-round draft picks are virtually guaranteed a position on the Steelers. The same could be said of the second rounders. But, Griggs says, it's the guys who came in the later rounds who probably need some of his help the most. Do they have a degree to fall back on? Are they carefully saving some of their upfront money?

Unfortunately, those players on the bubble are the ones who sometimes are harder to get through to, he says. "They're primarily focused on 'I have to make this team.' They're not thinking about anything else but now." And even then, he notes, the athletes tend to go through a progression. First-rounders think about being contributors. Contributors think about being starters. Starters think about being stars.

It makes it imperative to get to know the players as people before highlighting some of the services the league has set up to help its athletes. Griggs hopes to have developed enough of a reputation in his 13 years with the Steelers that players know what he can do. Occasionally there are a few surprises. "Ben Roethlisberger came in the other day and said, 'A.G., I want to finish my degree, what do we need to do?"

For a first-round pick with a six-year deal worth more than $22 million to make an unsolicited decision to finish his college education sends a sign that Griggs' messages got home.

"That's when it's really gratifying," he says. "I think they know what I'm all about, and sometimes you have only a small window here. Let's do something with it."

For Griggs that window closed as he left the Steelers to pursue other opportunities after the 2004 season. Nevertheless, his mark was made. The get-back coach had his players going forward.

Section III:

Panthers on the prowl: the legends of Pitt Football

There perhaps has never been a greater coach in the history of football in the Steel City than Hall of Famer Jock Sutherland. After a highly successful career as both a player and coach at the University of Pittsburgh, Sutherland led the hapless Steelers to their first playoff spot in 1947. (Courtesy of the University of Pittsburgh.)

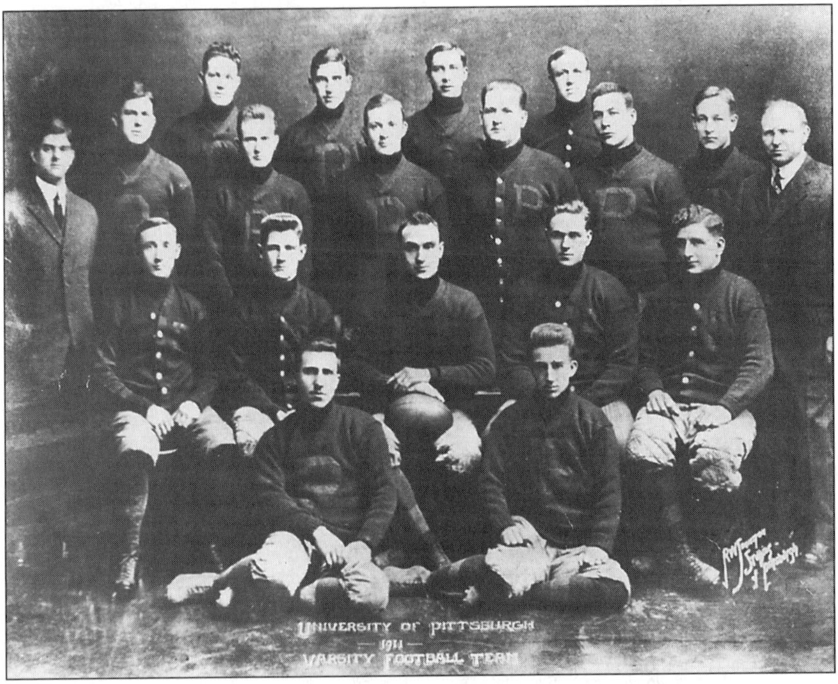

In 1911, Pitt was in the midst of embarking on one of their most impressive decades, but had a small roadblock this season finishing a mere 4-3-1. (Courtesy of the University of Pittsburgh.)

TWENTY TWO

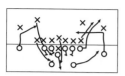

Match-ups of Mythological Proportions

Pitt versus Fordham

In mythology, Sisyphus was condemned to roll a huge boulder up a hill, a burden that inevitably and repeatedly rolled back down again, throughout eternity. It was his punishment for telling about one of Zeus' secret love affairs. It was a task filled with nothing but frustration, never reaching his ultimate goal. It was the same feeling that the offensive units of the University of Pittsburgh and Fordham University must have felt almost 70 years ago as they battled tooth and nail on the football field, going 180 minutes without ever scoring a point. Up and down the gridiron each team went only to be turned away. It became a legendary three-game run that brought to mind Sisyphus' fate.

Coming into 1935, Pitt had boasted a tradition of mythical proportion in college football history, winning a share of six national championships in 1915, 1916, 1918, 1929, 1931 and 1934. They had been led over the years by two Hall of Fame coaches—Pop Warner and Jock Sutherland—and were coming off a fine 1934 campaign, where they finished 8-1, capturing a piece of the national championship by being awarded the top spot in the Park H. Davis Ratings.

Fordham, on the other a hand, a small, private Jesuit college located in the heart of New York City, was trying to bring its program up to the level of Pitt and had hired one of the members of Notre Dame's celebrated four horseman, Jim Crowley, to lead the way. While they may not have been on the Panthers' level, the Rams certainly did have fine tradition on the gridiron, and they did possess a secret weapon on the sideline—a great coaching collective. "Fordham did have a great tradition back then," says Pitt historian Alex Kramer. "They had the former four horseman as head coach [Jim Crowley], and the line coach, Frank Leahy, went on to become the very successful head coach of Notre Dame."

The two schools had never met on the field of battle before that first contest, November 2nd, 1935, but within 36 months they would form a bond that remains strong to this day in the annals of college football history. "Fordham, Duke, who they had some great games with in the '30s, '40s and '50s, Penn State and WVU are probably the most celebrated series in the [University of Pittsburgh's] program's history," Kramer notes.

Coming into the contest, the only thing each school had in common was four wins and one loss, each coming to Indiana schools, the Rams losing to Purdue 20-0, and the Panthers falling to the Irish of Notre Dame 9-6. Pitt, though, was coming off a much more impressive win, beating their Keystone State rivals Penn State 9-0, while Fordham shut out Lebanon Valley College 15-0. Pitt, the defending national champions, were going into the game as the prohibitive 2½-1 favorites, despite the fact they were on the road playing the contest in the Polo Grounds, more famous as the home of baseball's New York Giants.

Thirty-eight thousand fans were on hand to see the first of three contests, a game where Fordham stuffed the vaunted Pitt attack, holding the Panthers to only 73 total yards in the affair. Although the Rams looked like the better team on the field that day, their offense was not world-beaters, either, amassing only 178 yards.

Saying the game was a defensive battle was an understatement; the offenses were nowhere to be found. Seven times the Panthers broke the midfield stripe, while the Rams only penetrated on five occasions. Of those twelve times each club made it into enemy territory, only twice each were they able to take the ball inside the 40 yard line. Pitt's biggest drive of the day was only 23 yards with Fordham amassing drives of no more than 37 yards. The futility had begun.

Fordham had the first, and best, opportunities to break the deadlock with two plays in the first half. The first, a long pass from Andy Palau to Joe Maniaci to the Pitt 18, was called out of bounds by the referee and the second came at the hands of a poor Panther punt in the second quarter. The Rams had pushed Pitt back deep in their own territory winning the battle of field position with some outstanding punts. Panther punter Nick Kliskey hit a ball from his six-yard line, giving Fordham the ball at the Pitt 28. The Panther defense rose to the occasion, stopping Fordham at the 20. Palau missed a 28-yard field goal attempt off to the side, keeping the game a scoreless affair.

The Rams had another chance when they returned a punt 60 yards to the Pitt 30, only to have the play called back when Lou Shedlosky stepped out of bounds 40 yards earlier at his own 30. Pitt made their only scoring effort of the day in the third quarter when they drove to the Ram 27 yard line, turning the ball over on downs four plays later.

With the game winding down in the final period, Pitt blocked a Palau punt, giving them the ball in Fordham territory at the 41. The good fortune for the Panthers would not last. The passing game for Pitt was not exactly the forte on that November day, hitting only one of nine aerials. Backup quarterback Arnold Greene tried to go through the air one last time giving up the ball instead as the Rams' Ed Franco intercepted the ill-fated pass at the Rams 38.

There were only seven minutes left when Fordham took over and came up with their most impressive drive of the game. The stands were going wild as Palau led the Rams on a meticulous 37-yard drive taking the ball to the Pitt 25 with time running out. On a fourth down and 2, Crowley and Palau decided to win the game with a 33-yard field goal. Fortunately for the Panthers, the kick came up woefully short and the favored Panthers escaped with a 0-0 tie. For Fordham, it was a moral victory that they used as a springboard into the national limelight. Nonetheless it was a frustrating offensive contest, each team trying to roll the boulder up the hill, only to have it roll down time and time again.

Pittsburgh would be prohibitive favorites no more the

following year as they entered the 1936 contest with a 4-1 mark, still stinging from a 7-0 upset loss to crosstown rivals Duquesne University only two games earlier. The angry Panther squad crushed Notre Dame the following week 26-7 and rode into this game on the heels of the most talented sophomore running back in the land, Marshall Goldberg.

Fordham was undefeated to that point in '36 and would travel no more. All nine of the Rams' remaining regular-season contests would be played in the friendly confines of New York City. Fordham's defense displayed against Pitt the previous season proved to be no fluke, giving up only 19 points in four games, defeating such schools as SMU and St. Mary's of California in the process.

With the Rams now a national power, New York was filled with excitement as 19,000 more fans than the previous year showed up at the Polo Grounds to see if Crowley and his boys could make a run to the national championship with an impressive victory.

The first half was completely a wash, with neither team getting a serious chance to break the scoreless hex that had overtaken the series. One of the other cogs in the great Panther rushing attack of the 1930's, Bobby LaRue, thought he had finally ended the jinx. LaRue took the opening kickoff in the second quarter, and raced into the clear at the 50, only to be yanked down by Palau out of the blue. Years later Bobby would recall that moment as his chance to make All-American with the New York press on hand. "I threw the guy a fake, a nice hip fake that by all rights he was supposed to take," he remembered, "but he didn't. He was too dumb."

Palau was the only man LaRue had left to beat on his way to a touchdown. As clutch of a tackle as it was, it would be overshadowed by a defensive stand Fordham would embark on late in the third quarter. Goldberg, LaRue and Frankie Patrick ran roughshod through the formerly impenetrable Rams defensive wall, gaining 46 of the team's 52 yards on the drive to that point. With the ball at Fordham's 13, LaRue and Goldberg ripped through to the 4 yard line, the deepest drive by far either team had embarked on in two years. Confident he could get the first, Sutherland went on fourth down sending LaRue into the middle of the Rams defensive line. Bobby shot in and Alex Wojciechowicz played the part of a brick wall sending LaRue backwards, ending

Before Tony Dorsett, Marshall Goldberg was considered the greatest Panther running back ever and the most famous member of the Dream Backfield in the 1930s. (Photo appears to be of a mural on a concrete or stucco covered wall. Courtesy of the University of Pittsburgh.)

the threat to the delight of the 57,000 rabid Fordham fans.

Pitt would get one last chance late in the game when Bob McClure was inserted into the game at quarterback late in the contest. McClure noticed Crowley had stacked the line, giving no respect for a pass. McClure pitched to Johnny Wood, who launched a long pass. The receiver had broken wide open as McClure had hoped, only to have the ball tip over his fingers. Just as the Panthers appeared to finally carry their burden to the top of the mountain, it came rolling back again. Sutherland, who was not a fan of the passing game, immediately pulled McClure from the game for his decision.

Despite the fact Fordham had no serious scoring threats, losing the ball on downs at the Panther 27 in the fourth quarter in their deepest venture into Pitt territory, they did have some accomplishments against the tough Pittsburgh defense rushing for 160 yards. What success they were having early on was largely thanks to speedy Frank Mautte, who exited the game in the second quarter with an injury.

The Rams ended the scoreless contest as only one of two eastern schools that were undefeated (Georgetown was the other). They eventually went 1-1-1 to end the season, losing to NYU 7-6 on the final game of the campaign. Their 5-1-2 mark in 1936 got them a No. 15 ranking at the end of the year in the first ever Associated Press poll.

Pittsburgh on the other end licked their wounds from a second disappointing scoreless tie and crushed their final three opponents, Penn State, Nebraska and Carnegie Tech by a combined 84-27 margin, getting a No. 3 spot in the final poll and a bid to play Washington in the granddaddy of all bowl games, the Rose Bowl. Pitt pounded the Huskies 21-0 in Pasadena and won a piece of the school's seventh national championship in the process.

Game No. 3 in 1937 was the most anticipated of the affairs. Pitt had one of their best squads ever, an extremely high-powered, bruising offensive attack led by Goldberg, Patrick, Curly Stebbins, Dick Cassiano, John Chickerneo and John Michelosen. Fordham had the legendary seven blocks of granite defense that numbered Alex Wojciechowicz, Ed Franco, John Druze, Al Barbartsky, Marty Petroskas, Mike Kochal and Harry Jacunski among its ranks. Future NFL Hall of Fame coach Vince Lombardi was also a member of that memorable defense.

It would be the irresistible force against the immovable object match-up. Could Pitt's powerful running attack finally roll the boulder up the hill and toss it over the other side or would the staunch Ram defense toss it right back down as it had so many times over the last two games? While the experts of the day couldn't imagine a third consecutive scoreless tie, the question the sporting world asked was: which defense would break their unscored-upon streak? Both teams seemed to have momentum on their side. Fordham had crushed its first two opponents of the year, Franklin and Marshall and Waynesburg, flexing its muscle 66-0 and 48-0, respectively. Pitt's stop troops were the Rams equal as their defense was also perfect in the first three games of 1937, beating Ohio Wesleyan, 59-0, West Virginia, 20-0 and getting revenge over cross-town rival Duquesne, 6-0.

The Panthers, for the third year in a row, entered the contest as the favorite, once again almost 2-1. This game, however, would have two differences: First, Pitt actually played like the much better team. And second, there were many scoring opportunities. But like Sisyphus, their burden seemed eternal as they never could quite make it up the hill as the only thing that remained the same was the score, the unbelievable score of 0-0, a final score that was helped along by the game's most influential player, Curly Stebbins. However, Stebbins was not remembered for his impressive runs, but for the fact he fumbled five times in the game. Two days earlier, Curly had his hand fractured in practice as a teammate stepped on it and he had trouble holding on to the ball. A player in today's game would sit out the contest with a broken hand, but in 1937, much to the chagrin of the Panther faithful, such an injury was viewed as little more than a scratch.

Pitt started the game by knifing through the seven blocks of granite for 37 yards on four carries. Crowley moved Franco to left tackle at that point, plugging the gaping hole that the Pitt backs had been rambling through.

As impressive as the Panthers had been, it was Fordham who got the first opportunity of the day to break the 10-quarter drought. The Rams recovered a Pitt fumble at the Panther 23. The staunch Pittsburgh defensive wall shut down the Fordham offense allowing their opponents only six more yards. Crowley sent Johnny Druze on for a 25-yard field goal attempt. But Druze could not get the rock up the hill, missing the field goal and the score remained once again, as it always had been in the series, 0-0.

A funny thing happened as the first half was coming to an end. It looked like Sisyphus finally was going to get that boulder over the top of the mountain. Stebbins, who was not enjoying his best day, took a Ram punt and shot up field 35 yards to the Fordham 40 yard line. It was at that point he inexplicably cut inside, where he was tackled. According to accounts of the game, had Curly stayed to the sidelines, he had an armada of blockers that could have escorted him into the end zone. But that only would add to the myth of the three-game series.

Fifty-three thousand stunned Polo Ground patrons watched as Pitt marched down the field to the Fordham 5. The futility streak seemed to be finally over on the next play when Goldberg shot in for a touchdown to give Pitt an apparent 6-0 lead. The hands of fate were not kind on this day as tackle Tony Matisi was called for holding and the play was brought back, the score nullified, the rock still not at the summit. Time ran out in the half before the Panthers had a chance to make up for Matisi's error. After 10 quarters in this series, neither team had scored.

Stebbins kept the goat tag on in the third period, fumbling the ball at his own 28, where Jacunski pounced on it. The Rams then made their deepest penetration to that point at the Pitt 10 yard line. For three years, they were able to run with some success against the Panther defense, then all of the sudden Fordham unbelievably tried to throw three passes when they seemed like they could finally break the ice in this scoreless series. Three incomplete tosses later, Druze lined up for an 18-yard field goal that once again threatened to break the scoreless tie. The hands of fate again intervened, this time in the form of a Panther defender who got a hand on the kick and kept the Rams off the scoreboard. Yet again the frustration continued.

Now it was Goldberg's turn to take the mantle of goat from the head of Curly Stebbins. After a first down run, the Pitt All-American halfback put the ball on the turf that Druze recovered on the Panther 8 yard line. A score now seemed inevitable. How many times could these teams get a golden scoring chance without converting? The answer for the Rams apparently was three. A 15-yard holding penalty (holding was 15 yards in the 1930's instead of 10 as it is today) later, Druze missed his third field goal attempt of the game, this time from 30 yards out.

The Panthers took over at this point and were bending the impenetrable Ram defensive wall. Pitt had out-rushed Fordham 165-87, and took the ball 35 yards down field to their opponents' 35 where Frankie Patrick punted the ball deep in Ram territory. Pittsburgh's defense shut down the Fordham offense getting the ball back at the Rams 31. Pitt took it to the 15 when Bill Daddio tried to finally end the scoreless hell with a 23-yard field goal. A kick that went wide right remarkably still left this series scoreless with time running out in the game.

Stebbins would have one last chance to remove his goat horns and be a hero when he correctly read the Fordham offense, stepping in front of an errant Ram pass. There was nothing but clear field ahead for Curly as Pitt seemed destined to break the ice and win the game. There was only one problem though; Stebbins forgot to hang onto the ball—the rock rolled down the hill once more—and the game ended once again without a single point.

As classic as the series was, the 1937 game had to be the most frustrating for the Pitt faithful. They had outgained Fordham 195-114, limiting the Ram offense to a mere four first downs. "It was very frustrating for Pitt," Kramer says, summing up the series. "But one must remember that Fordham was a power and had a superb defense."

As they walked off the field, Crowley leaned over to Sutherland and told him, "I would have rather been beaten 27-20 than have this happen again." Crowley would get his wish in 1938, as the two teams finally left the auspices of New York City for the friendly confines of Pitt Stadium, where 75,857 saw the cork come off the offenses with the Panthers scoring three touchdowns in the fourth quarter to erase a Ram 7-3 lead and giving Pitt a dramatic 24-13 victory.

For the time being though, Fordham had frustrated a more talented Pitt team for the third consecutive season. While some experts felt the tie would derail the Panthers national championship aspirations, Sutherland and his boys went about their business, crushing their next six opponents, a line up that included the likes of Wisconsin, Notre Dame, Penn State, Nebraska, Carnegie Tech and Duke, on their way to an undefeated 9-0-1 mark. Despite the tie, they landed atop the Associated Press final poll, giving the school its eighth national championship in one of the greatest seasons in the history of the university.

The Rams, on the other hand, were finally one of the premiere teams in the land. They held their next five teams to only 16 points on their way to an unblemished 7-0-1 record, outscoring the opposition for the season 182-16. For their efforts they finished the campaign third in the final AP poll.

Pitt's program went in the tank a couple of years later after the powers that be de-emphasized football and chased Sutherland out of Oakland (a subject that is covered more in depth in chapter 28). Fordham's team went the way of the dinosaur. The university dropped its program after a dismal 1-7-1 mark in 1954. Nevertheless, these two teams will always be linked in history by their three scoreless contests in three consecutive seasons, a Sisyphean feat that will likely never be duplicated again.

The Beast of the East: Pitt versus Penn State

A generation of Western Pennsylvania college football fans are cheated in the new millennium without one of the greatest rivalry games in the history of the sport: the annual tussle for the title "Beast of the East"—Pitt versus Penn State. Whether or not it was Nittany Lions' coach Joe Paterno's bitterness over an eastern football league not being formed in the '80s for his refusal to play the University of Pittsburgh now that they are in separate conferences (which is the rumor that has always been thrown around), these teams have not met since the 2000 campaign when Pitt ended the series with a dominating 12-0 victory at Three Rivers Stadium. They originally put a halt to the game after a 57-13 destruction of the Panthers in 1992 and then played four contests between 1997-2000 before ending the rivalry for the foreseeable future.

On the other end, the game had begun to lose its luster in the early '90s with Pitt slipping down the major college football ladder under the leadership of Paul Hackett. In the '70s and '80s it was a battle of two top ten programs, a match-up that was not just anticipated in the Keystone State, but everywhere in the college football nation. Not only were local bragging right up for grabs, but the contest also had national championship implications. Penn State won their national crowns in 1982 and 1986, while Pitt took the title in 1976 and 1980, when they were named champions by the *New York Times* computer rankings (a system that helped determine the BCS combatants for the current national championship games until it was discontinued in the BCS calculations this past year).

Dave Remembers

Growing up in Greensburg, PA, about 35 miles outside of the Steel City, you were surrounded by Penn State and Notre Dame fans. I always assumed the love of the Nittany Lions was fueled by the fact that the blue and white were among the best programs in the land in the late '60s and early '70s, while the University of Pittsburgh was a laughing stock, lucky to win three contests a season. The lure of Notre Dame came from the fact that Greensburg was a predominately Catholic city and for some reason a school that was located half a nation away in Indiana always had to be the school of choice for many Catholics who loved the sport. Despite the fact I, too, was Catholic, I never equated religious affiliation with a school I wanted to root for. I always felt you cheered for the team that was either close to your home or one that you actually attended. Win or lose you stayed with them and even though Pitt was an embarrassment in the early '70s, I had fallen in love with the sport and the University of Pittsburgh was the local team, so I hopped on their bandwagon and hoped they could find a way not only to compete again, but to beat those hated Lions of State College.

Every time Penn State would beat Pitt, which they did every season between 1970 and 1975, the first six seasons I followed the sport, I would endure weeks of abuse from the local blue and white faithful who enjoyed every moment of those victories with equal intensity to my disappointment in losing those classic tussles.

The worst was in 1975 when the improved Panthers looked like they finally would climb the hill and beat the Lions for the first time since 1965 (when they defeated Penn State 30-27). Pitt had one of the best and most accurate place kickers in NCAA history, Carson Long. Long, who finished his collegiate career as the highest scoring kicker in the annals of the sport the following season, missed on an extra point and three field goals that included two in the fourth quarter from 30 and 40 yards, the last on the final play of the game. The inopportune misses snatched defeat from what would have been a great victory, allowing the men from State College to escape with a 7-6 win.

With the teams now seemingly on even terms, Pitt finally got over the hump in 1976, destroying the Nittany Lions 24-7 at Three Rivers Stadium. In 1979, Pitt beat them on their own turf 29-14. They would repeat the process a year later at Beaver Stadium, nipping Penn State 14-9. It was a win that was especially gratifying for me as it was my first trip to Mount Nit. There was never such joy in being at a facility with 80,000 blue and white faithful so quiet that you could hear a pin drop on the soft Nittany Lion turf. It gave me bragging rights for 24 consecutive months, which for Pitt fans at the time was a nirvana unequaled in many a decade.

Twenty years later, I would have them once again, this time after the 12-0 victory in 2000. As it turned out, I would have the bragging rights in perpetuity, as the clubs will not meet in the foreseeable future. While I enjoy getting on my comrades who are fans of the blue and white that we won the final game, I would gladly give up those taunts to have this game played once again.

It's a shame that the generation growing up today will never really have the opportunity to enjoy this match-up year in and year out and it really has taken some of the luster off the sport in the Pennsylvania. Despite the fact Penn State versus Michigan State and Pittsburgh against West Virginia (their other legendary rival) are fine contests, it's a disappointing way to end a season. In my mind, Pitt versus Penn State is the only way a campaign should conclude, a battle for the Beast of the East, a title that the University of Pittsburgh holds, frozen in time, hopefully not for eternity.

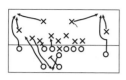

TWENTY THREE

The Greatest Day in Pittsburgh Collegiate Football History

In 1936, the 14th ranked Duquesne Dukes went 8-2 defeating Mississippi State 13-12 in the Orange Bowl. (Courtesy of Duquesne Athletics.)

Until its untimely demise in 2000, college football fans in Western Pennsylvania would point to the yearly clash between the University of Pittsburgh and Penn State University as the unquestioned high-water mark of any college football season. After all, their battles became legendary in the 1970s and '80s, often resulting in top ten finishes and on four occasions between 1976 and 1986 at least a share of the national championship was claimed (Pitt in 1976 and 1980 (the New York Times Poll), and Penn State in 1982 and 1986).

As much anticipated as those games were, in the 1930s and early '40s the college football fans of the Steel City didn't need to travel two hours to find a rival, they just needed to go down Forbes and Fifth avenues as the Duquesne University Dukes provided Pitt with a level of competition that was the equal of any Pitt-Penn State match-up. In fact, so successful were the two schools that they gave the city of Pittsburgh a New Year's Day to remember in 1937 when they both participated in a major bowl.

Pittsburgh had traditionally been one of the most powerful collegiate football programs at the time, winning six national championships, including three under their great coach, Jock Sutherland, in the previous seven seasons leading up to the 1936 campaign. Despite the fact they were a small school of only 1,300 students, Duquesne also had a fine football history, including a 10-1 season in 1933 (the only loss coming to Pitt 7-0), when they outscored their opponents 206-33 including a dominant 33-7 win over Miami in the Palm Festival on New Year's Day. But they were not of national championship caliber coming off a solid if unspectacular 6-3 season in 1935.

John "Clipper" Smith took over the reins of the Dukes in 1936 and led them to three shutout wins to begin the season over Waynesburg, Rice and Geneva, outscoring their three adversaries by a 61-0 margin. Pitt also got off to an unblemished start spanking Ohio Wesleyan, West Virginia and Ohio State to the tune of a 93-0 advantage going into their fourth

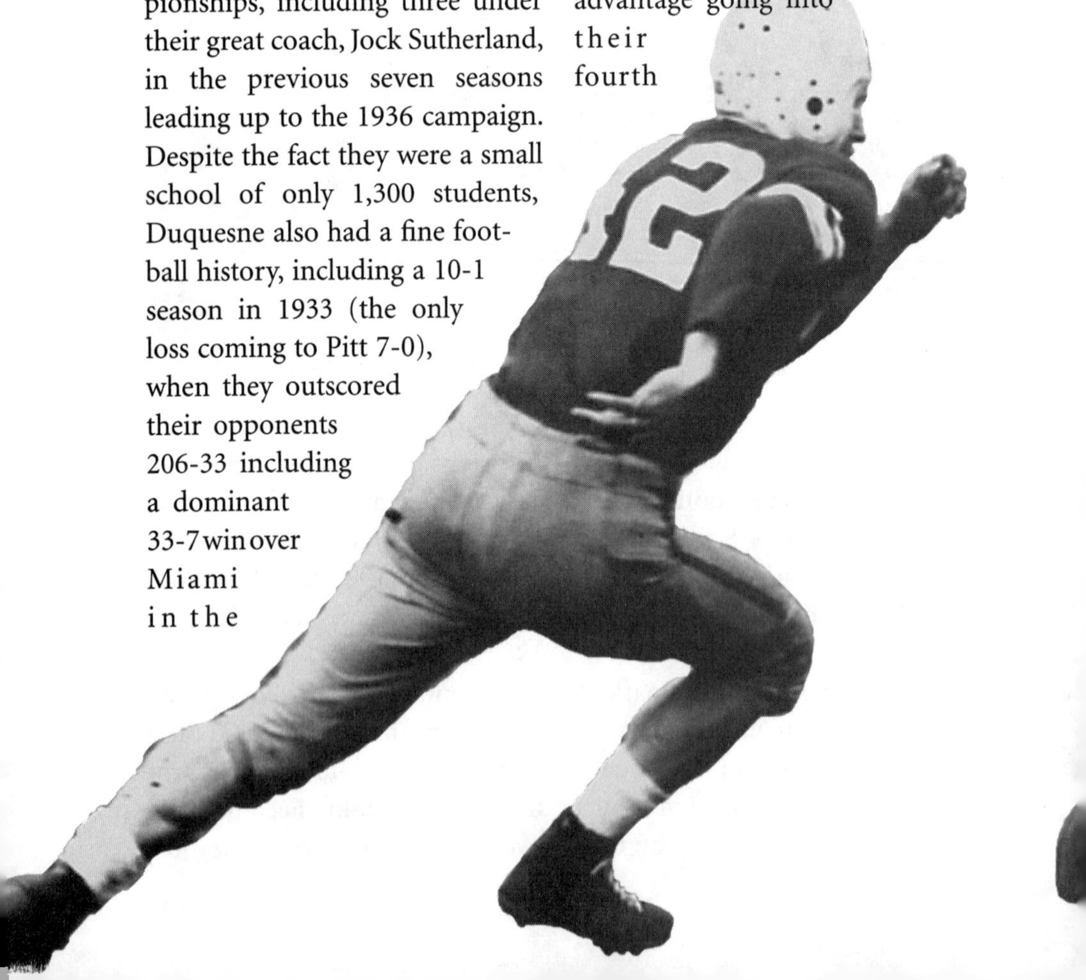

game of the season against their Steel City rivals from the Bluff.

The Dukes had faced Pitt three times before, never scoring a point, but were coming into this game with an air of confidence, a confidence that was most likely there a few years before when they also came into games against their rival in 1932 and 1933 undefeated (especially in '33 when they were 8-0), only to be stopped in their tracks by the mighty Panthers 33-0 and 7-0.

Wanting to keep his players minds off anything else but football, Clipper took his squad out of town right before the contest, bringing them back the day of the game and heading straight to Pitt Stadium, where a disappointing crowd of only 20,000 fans braved the cold, rainy Pittsburgh weather to see the match-up of the two local titans.

Smith had done a good job early on in his inaugural season at Duquesne, so the powers that be wanted to lock him up for another season, giving him a gift the day before the big game against Pitt, a contract for the 1937 season as both coach and athletic director. The Dukes' coach would be well worth the price as he marched his

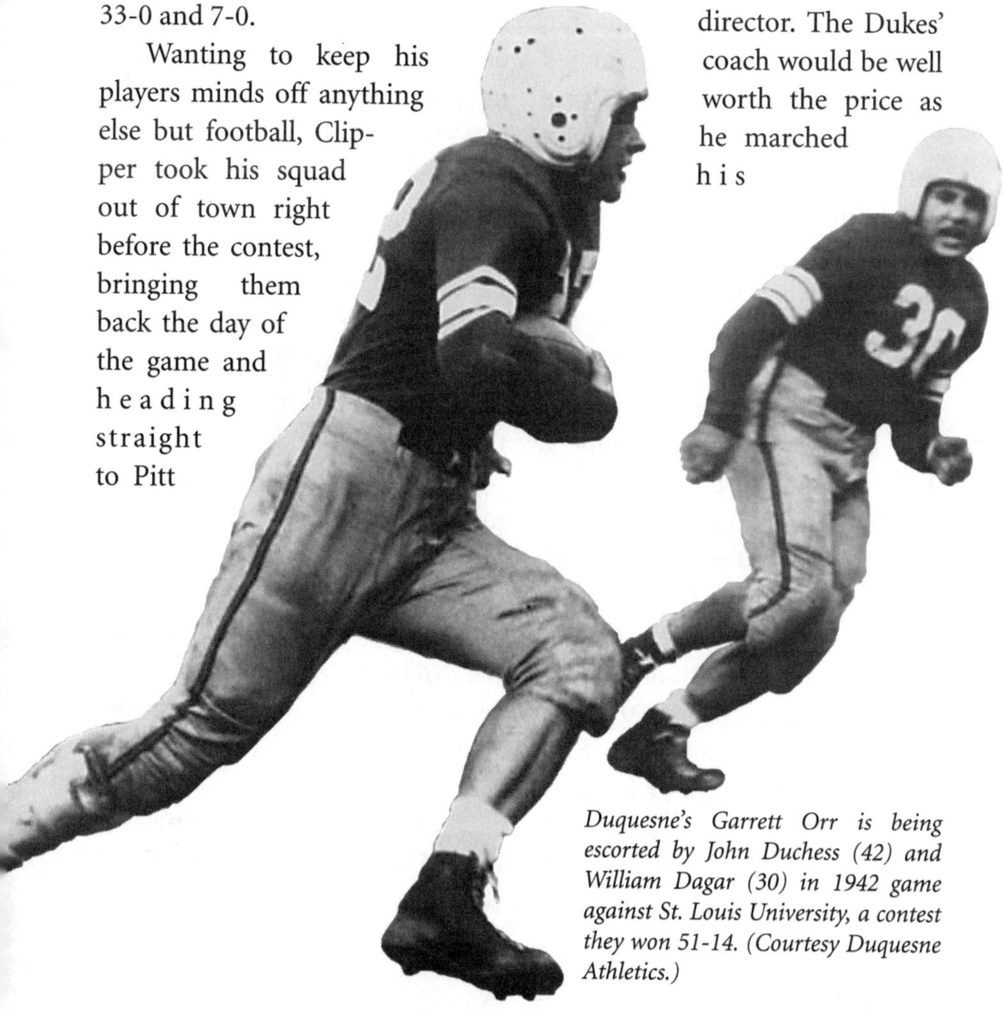

Duquesne's Garrett Orr is being escorted by John Duchess (42) and William Dagar (30) in 1942 game against St. Louis University, a contest they won 51-14. (Courtesy Duquesne Athletics.)

undermanned squad onto the field and came away with not only the first score Duquesne ever had in the series between the two schools, but the first victory in a shocking 7-0 win.

After a scoreless first period, where Pitt had the best opportunity taking the ball to the Duquesne 14 before turning it over on downs, the Dukes put the first points on the scoreboard as a substitute junior running back by the name of George Matsik ran through the vaunted yet stunned Panther defense on a 72-yard jaunt to score what still today might be the most important touchdown in Duquesne football history, giving the underdogs a 7-0 lead at the half.

Forced to play from an unusual position, behind, Sutherland scrapped his mighty running attack led by Marshall Goldberg, Bill Stapulus, Bobby LaRue, Frankie Patrick, Harold Stebbins, John Chickerneo and quarterback and future Steeler and Panther boss John Michelosen, to try and defeat the Dukes through the air. It was a strategy that bit the Panthers back time and time again. After not throwing at all against Ohio State the previous week, Pitt launched fifteen passes with almost as many finding Duquesne defensive hands, three, as they did Panther receivers, four.

Pittsburgh had many opportunities, but one mistake after another kept them off the board. They reached the Dukes' three-yard line after picking up a fumble at the 28, but returned the favor by fumbling the ball back to Duquesne. Sutherland's crew made two more deep treks into Duke territory, but interceptions each time cost Pitt a chance to tie the contest as Duquesne dodged one bullet after another, preserving the incredible surprising win.

While the Dukes' upset victory resonated all over the country, they were unable to overtake the Panthers in the Associated Press poll as Pitt dropped to ninth, while the Dukes managed to only climb to eleventh. Despite that fact, the students of the small Catholic school took to the streets of Pittsburgh honking their horns in a wild celebration. They then took off to the Oakland in search of disgruntled Panther fans. While they lined up on either end of the street taking verbal shots at each other, the police took to the middle to make sure violence didn't erupt.

For Duquesne, the win turned out to be the highlight of their season, as they couldn't keep the momentum going, losing their next two games to West Virginia Wesleyan and Detroit before shutting out Washington (MO), Carnegie Tech and Marquette to end the season 7-2. Pitt, on the other hand, learned from their loss and not only crushed Notre Dame the next week 26-0, but also punished Penn State, Nebraska and Carnegie Tech on their way to a 7-1-1 mark (the only other blemish being a 0-0 tie against Fordham, the second of the three consecutive scoreless affairs against the New York school).

With the solid seasons turned in by both schools, the city of Pittsburgh boasted two teams in the Associated Press' inaugural poll at the end of the regular season, both hopefully vying for bids to major bowls. Pitt had moved up from ninth, where it stood after the disappointing loss to the Dukes, to third behind Minnesota and LSU, while Duquesne rebounded after its two defeats to rise to 14th.

The lofty spot in the polls had the Panthers in contention for a spot in the top bowl of the day, the Rose Bowl, against the best team in the west, Washington, with the Dukes hoping for a return to Miami and a place in the Orange Bowl.

Pitt had made three other unsuccessful trips to Pasadena in the past and were no sure shot to face the Huskies come New Year's Day. The top team in the nation, the Minnesota Golden Gophers, would have been the obvious choice, but Big 10 rules at that time prohibited their teams from playing in a postseason game, so they were out of the picture. It came down to who Washington would select to be its opponent (back then the western champs chose the opposing team) for the Rose Bowl—an eastern team in the University of Pittsburgh, Yale or the Naval Academy. Or would they go south and pick the Tigers of LSU or the fourth-ranked Alabama Crimson Tide?

From the east, Yale, although there were rumors the Eli's were being considered, really didn't look like they had much a chance. They were ranked 12th in the country and had an agreement with Princeton and Harvard not to accept any postseason bid, an agreement that is still binding in the Ivy League today. If an eastern team was to go to Pasadena over the Panthers, Navy looked to be more of a possibility than Yale. Although they lost three games and were ranked 18th, Navy defeated Notre Dame and Army and had the tradition of facing Washington in a past Rose Bowl, a classic 14-14 tie in 1926. The thought was also that since Puget Sound was the part-time home of the American fleet as well as the University of Washington, it would result in a larger, more profitable turnout.

While the Panthers may have been one of the front runners in the east, some of the Husky players felt Washington athletic director Ray Eckmann would choose between the two highly ranked, undefeated teams from the south—Alabama and LSU. The Tigers were considered a more powerful team as well as the highest-ranked club that was eligible for a postseason bid. Alabama, although ranked below LSU and Pitt, had the very vocal support of their governor, who made a plea to Eckmann and the Tournament of Roses committee to bring the Crimson Tide out west for the nation's premiere Bowl game.

In the end, Eckmann made the announcement, giving the bid to the Panthers because of their tough schedule and strong finish, a bid that Pitt AD Don Harrison gladly accepted. The Washington AD further claimed that the Panthers, in fact, were the front-runners with no other team involved. He also said that Sutherland and his Pittsburgh squad would give the Rose Bowl a team that represented "the best of eastern football." It was a choice that was met with enthusiasm by the Husky players, as there was a rumor that the team voted unanimously to play Pitt over the rest of the contenders.

With so many outstanding teams for Eckmann to choose from, the selection of the Panthers was certain to create controversy. Alabama coach Frank Thomas said, "I am surprised by the choice. Alabama didn't expect to be picked, but I believe Louisiana State had the right to expect the nomination. I saw Louisiana State conquer Tulane and if Pittsburgh is better than Louisiana State, it would have to be world beaters."

The legendary Pittsburgh sportswriter Al Abrams shot back at the Panthers' critics claiming, "Pitt was beaten once and tied once—so what." Abrams went on further to point out that the Panthers' 7-1-1 record was the same as Washington's, which was selected to represent the West Coast, and that "The Panthers' tough schedule and convincing triumphs over Notre Dame, Ohio State and Nebraska certainly entitled the Sutherland eleven to the consideration they received in the matter."

While the selection of Pitt to the Rose Bowl was one laced with controversy, the choice of Duquesne to the Orange Bowl was greeted with much more acceptance. The Dukes, who turned down three other post-season bids, were to represent the north in the Miami extravaganza while rumors were rampant that it would either be 16th ranked TCU or No. 17 Tennessee to stand in for the south, but each had one regular-season game left before a bid could be extended. Texas Christian went on to defeat Santa Clara in the season finale and then accepted a bid to the Cotton Bowl instead, while the Volunteers tied Mississippi and stayed home for the holidays, declining the Orange Bowl bid.

Still looking for an opponent to face John "Clipper" Smith and his Dukes, the Orange Bowl committee went to Starkville, MS, to invite the Bulldogs of Mississippi State. The Bulldogs were 7-2-1 under coach Ralph Sasse, losing only to the jilted Rose Bowl clubs, LSU and Alabama, and would provide Smith's crew a very tough game.

For Pitt, the Rose Bowl wasn't just about proving they belonged; it was also about erasing the bad memories of the first three trips to Pasadena to play in the Granddaddy of all Bowl games. In 1928, they lost a close one to Stanford, 7-6, before being thrashed by Southern California, 47-14 and 35-0, in 1930 and 1933 respectively. Sutherland worked the club hard, but was satisfied they were ready to go when they left the Steel City by train for the West Coast.

"We had our best practice of the season today," the Hall of Fame coach said. "The boys are putting out. Their spirit is great. I won't make any predictions. I am satisfied. I know we are going to try our best." While Sutherland was not making predictions, the so-called experts weren't either, claiming the contest too close to call.

Washington was certainly a formidable opponent, losing only to the top-ranked Gophers of Minnesota in the season opener 14-7 and tying Stanford 14-14. The Huskies finished the season fifth-ranked with an identical record as Pitt, 7-1-1. What may have given the Panthers a small advantage was the fact that one of the Washington fullbacks, Al Cruver, cracked three ribs in practice and would be out for the contest. The other was the youth of the Huskies. Washington started four sophomores in the backfield; quarterback Chuck Newton and running backs Jimmy Johnston,

Merle Miller and Jimmy Cain. The quartet may have been young, but they were fast and potent.

There were two stories making the rounds in the week leading up to the game. The first was the hot rumor in Los Angeles that the Panthers were planning to add some wrinkles in the passing game to surprise Washington. It was a tactic that worked horribly in their only loss of the season against Duquesne, and one that many Panther fans had hoped would not reappear in Pasadena. The other story was the Panthers' refusal to wear white shirts for the game. Washington being the home team was to wear its purple shirts, and it was hoped Pitt would don the white jerseys. Instead, they wore a very similar shade to Washington with their blue shirts. "We'll wear blue. It's all we've got. We left our white jerseys at home," Sutherland proclaimed.

While there were hot stories and head games in California, rumors were alive and well 3,000 miles away in Miami, too. Despite signing a contract extension earlier in the season, Smith leaving Duquesne was the hot topic. The report stated that three schools had given Clipper offers, including one from the powerful Big 10. Even though Smith did not deny the story, stating instead that he was too busy preparing for the game to comment, he did keep his commitment to stay on the Bluff the following season.

Smith's Dukes went into the game a 7-5 favorite, but he was not injury free as his star runner, Boyd Brumbaugh, was doubtful for the game, suffering from a bout of tonsillitis. Mississippi State also was missing an important piece of their club with star back Victor Dixon out of the contest with appendicitis.

It was a warm day in Miami as a very disappointing crowd of 12,000 showed up in what turned out to be the classic game of New Year's Day 1937. Smith and the Duquesne faithful got a very good New Year's Day surprise as Brumbaugh recovered from his illness and was ready to go against Mississippi State. Brumbaugh not only played in the game but proved to be its star by the time the final gun went off.

The Bulldogs went on top early with halfback Ike Pickle scoring on an eight-yard run. Charley Armstrong missed the extra point, but MSU had a 6-0 advantage at the end of the first quarter. Brumbaugh got the Dukes on the board in the second, bolting over from a yard out and then tacking on the extra point for a 7-6 lead.

Armstrong was not done, though, hitting another touchdown pass to put Mississippi State on top at the half 12-7. Pickle missed the extra point, a miss that would be costly for the Bulldogs later on. Unfortunately for the Dukes, the pre-game prediction of Clipper Smith seemed to be coming true. Smith said he would be lucky if they could hold the powerful Bulldogs to only one or two scores and that it didn't look like they had much of a chance as "the weather and everything else seem to be to Missisippi State's advantage."

Luckily, the Dukes' defense stiffened as both clubs came up scoreless in the third quarter, with MSU only 15 minutes away from pulling off the mild upset. Just as in the huge win against Pitt, the game came down to one big play, one that turned out to be in favor of Duquesne. Brumbaugh went back at his 25-yard line after a Mississippi State punt and launched a 45 yard pass to Ernest Hefferle. Hefferle took the ball the final 30 yards, giving Duquesne a precarious 13-12 lead. The defense continued to ward off the Bulldog attack as it intercepted four of MSU's 23 passes, preserving what was and still is today, the Dukes' most important victory in the history of the school's football program, a program that can proudly boast to be the 1937 Orange Bowl champions.

With one title to their credit for the day, Steel City college football fans turned their attention to Pasadena to see if Pittsburgh could enjoy an unprecedented sweep on this special New Year's Day. Attendance was not an issue at the Rose Bowl, as a sellout crowd of 87,196 jammed the famed stadium to see if Eckmann had indeed chosen the right team to play his Pacific Coast Conference champions. If you're a fan of college football, you'd agree the Washington athletic director did do a good job. If you're a staunch supporter of the Huskies, you had reason to be upset.

Angered by the lack of respect they got and the fact that Pitt wanted to get the Rose Bowl monkey off their backs, Sutherland and his troops came into the game taking no prisoners. Reports of a more aggressive passing attack were just a smoke screen as was their star running back Marshall Goldberg. Sutherland had Goldberg as nothing more than a decoy, instead using the fleet-footed Bobby LaRue and bone-crunching fullback Frankie Patrick to rip through the vaunted Washington defensive line to the tune of 248 yards.

The final score of the game, 21-0, was probably not indicative of the total dominance the Panthers had in this contest. As impressive as LaRue and Patrick were offensively, All-Americans Bill Daddio and Averell Daniell were on the defensive side smashing through the staunch Husky offensive wall time and time again, limiting their once prolific offensive attack to a mere 48 yards on the ground, minus 4 in the second half.

Pittsburgh opened the scoring in the first quarter with the only tally of the half as Patrick and LaRue ripped through the Huskies defensive line on a 55-yard drive, with Patrick scoring the touchdown after two tries from the five yard line, giving Pitt a 7-0 lead that would last until the third quarter. It was at that point the Washington offense got an opportunity to tie things up. Goldberg lost a fumble on his own 33, where the Huskies took over to try and change the momentum. Unfortunately, the Washington momentum took a quick hiatus when Byron Haines threw a first down pass right into the waiting arms of Pitt's Don Hensley at the 25, giving Sutherland and his boys the ball right back. The contest, for all intents and purposes, was about to be over.

LaRue immediately broke loose for 43 yards, before Patrick rambled in from 13 yards out a couple of plays later to give the men from the Steel City a comfortable 14-0 lead. The Huskies were not done, though. They mounted their first real offensive threat of the game.

Forsaking a running attack that was going nowhere, three passes (the last from Haines to Ed Nowogroski) took the ball from their 22 to the Pitt 47. Elmer Logg caught a pass at the Panther 36 before Haines ran it to the 30. For Washington, the drive was about to end abruptly. Haines tried a lateral, which Daddio snatched instead, rambling 71 yards with the interception to put the nail in Washington's coffin, 21-0.

A thoroughly humiliated Husky team threw in the towel at that point as only luck and the clock kept this contest from being a more convincing blowout. Pitt lost the ball on downs at the Washington one-yard line late in the game, before going deep into Husky territory once again on the heels of a 30-yard pass as time expired.

The coach of the Pacific Coast Conference champions, Jimmy Phelan, was stunned at his team's humbling defeat, blaming the press for incensing the Panthers with their pre-game reporting. *Los Angeles Times* reporter Braves Dyer put it into perspective, though, telling Phelan that it wasn't the reporters, it was the fact that, "... you picked a team that couldn't afford to lose in the Rose Bowl again. That, to me, was far more important than the psychological prodding given the Panthers by some of our scribes. When it is a case of life and death, a Panther is no animal to pick on."

The big day for Pittsburgh collegiate football not only ended with two stunning victories, but was the catalyst for bigger things ahead. With the win for the Panthers came not only retribution from their critics, as LSU was humbled by Santa Clara in the Sugar Bowl 21-14, but an unexpected gift when Pittsburgh was awarded a piece of their seventh national championship, taking the crown in the *Illustrated Football Annual* and *The Football Thesaurus*. It was also a springboard to a back-to-back championship as the Panthers were recognized by the Associated Press and several other polls as the kings of 1937.

For Duquesne, the Orange Bowl victory ushered in the golden era of the University's football program. The Dukes had big success under Buff Donelli, who replaced Smith in 1939 and led them to undefeated campaigns in his first season, 8-0-1, and 8-0 in 1941. Both years, Duquesne finished in the top ten as they were 10th in 1939 and 8th in 1941.

Regardless of the good fortune the teams would enjoy in the near future, it was on this day, January 1, 1937, that the city as a whole could celebrate its lofty place in the college football world. James Long of the *Pittsburgh Sun Telegraph* put it best when he proclaimed that it made "Pittsburgh the most prominent spot on the entire football map." Quite simply, this was truly without question the greatest day in Pittsburgh collegiate football history.

TWENTY FOUR

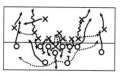

Bobby Grier, Reluctant Pioneer

Jackie Robinson was a true pioneer in sports. His trials and tribulations led to opportunities afforded to other African Americans to play on fields they were never permitted on in the past. While his life and career are celebrated today, deservedly so, there are many other, lesser-known athletes who fought their own battles on the baseball diamonds, gridirons, hockey rinks and basketball courts and helped pave the way for sports to be a place where any man or women could participate, regardless of race. Bobby Grier, a halfback and defensive back on the 1955 University of Pittsburgh football team, was one of those special combatants.

Robinson was well suited for his spot in history as a pioneer for racial equality. After all, he was an All-American football player at UCLA who had come under prejudice in the armed forces during World War II, when he was ordered to go to the back of the bus and refused. They tried to court martial him and he stood up for his rights and won. And then, of course, came his historic debut in the majors in 1947 and the Hall of Fame career that ensued despite numerous threats and taunts.

Grier, on the other hand, had little exposure to the spotlight he was about to be thrust under in the 1956 Sugar Bowl.

He came to Pitt from a storied high school program in Massillon, Ohio, where Grier fondly remembers, "We had a great program where we won a couple of state championships. I think they may have won four or five in a row back then." Several colleges in Ohio, including Miami (OH) recruited him. Robinson's alma mater at UCLA also went after the halfback as well as the University of Pittsburgh. Grier eventually chose to continue his football career in the Steel City and was part of a resurgence to the national spotlight under coach John Michelosen his senior season.

The Massillon native felt the 1955 Panther squad had the ability to compete for a national championship, although the shy Grier sheepishly admits he wished he had the opportunity to contribute more. "I think if I had gotten the ball more, we might have had a better offense," he says. "I could have contributed more, but I only ran the ball five or six times a game.

"I thought the best game of my career at Pitt was the game against California in the season opener," he recalls. "I had quite a few yards that game." Quite a performance indeed. Grier, who was known for his hard-hitting style of running, plunged in from one yard out to tie the game at seven in the second quarter, then rumbled on a 33-yard jaunt late in the last quarter of a contest that was played on an oppressive, 92-degree day in the Steel City to cap a 20 point fourth period in the impressive 27-7 victory.

Despite disappointing losses to Oklahoma, Navy and Miami (FL), it was a good season for a university that had only seen three winning seasons since 1940. For their efforts, the team was rewarded with a bid to the Sugar Bowl in the segregated South, New Orleans to be exact. The campaign was also a fine one for Grier, although he was not prepared for the problems that were to lie ahead. "I didn't encounter many racial problems during the regular season, but you have to remember most of the games were played up north," he explains.

By 1955, restrictions on race in sports had been loosened quite a bit, but make no mistake about it, African American athletes still faced prejudice and injustice in many corners of this country, quite a few of them in the South. There were still limitations on where blacks could eat, sleep and even exist. Sweeping civil rights laws were still about a decade away, so situations such as the one Grier would find himself in for the Sugar Bowl in New Orleans, although deplorable, were not all that uncommon.

As common as they might have been, they still caught the Wexford resident off guard. Not long after the University of Pittsburgh accepted a spot to play Georgia Tech, Georgia Governor Marvin Griffin called on Tech to refuse the Sugar Bowl bid unless Pitt did not play Grier. While for most of the 20th century to that point it was not uncommon for a southern team to refuse to play an integrated one, this was the mid 1950s and the world was starting to change. Well, most of the world, that is, except for Griffin. The governor seemed in a time warp, stuck in the Civil War when he uttered the statement "The South stands at Armageddon. The battle is joined. We cannot make the slightest concession in this dark and lamentable hour of struggle. There is no more difference in compromising integrity of race on the playing field than in doing so in the classrooms."

When Pitt accepted the bid, they did so on the condition that there would be no problem with Grier playing, and there would be no segregation of the African Americans that came to see the game.

Through it all, the fullback was suprised by Governor Griffin's pleas. "I was shocked, everybody was shocked," he says. "The school was behind me, though. My teammates were behind me, and everybody here was behind me."

There was no precedent for this. No team from the deep south had ever played an integrated squad, but the students at Georgia Tech were fully behind the team in its quest to play Pitt. Fifteen hundred students at Tech held a violent demonstration in support of the team going to the bowl game. Signs against Griffin reading, "To Hell With Griffin," "Impeach Griffin" and "Griffin Sits On His Brains" were everywhere, although the protest strangely turned into a panty raid before it was all over. Students from the University of Georgia also protested in support of the brethren state school. While denouncing the students' actions, the board at Georgia Tech did vote to accept the bid, going against the Governor's cause. The school's president, Dr. Blake Van Leer, threatened to quit if the board reached any other decision. Van Leer was greeted by the school's faculty with a standing ovation when he announced the vote.

The players for the Yellow Jackets had also voted to play in the game, and according to Grier acted very professionally. "Georgia Tech had no problems with me, they were here to play ball," he says. "Even when they tackled me, they picked me up."

Georgia Tech was coached by the legendary Bobby Dodd, who, according to one of his assistants, John Robert Bell, "always preached that we honored your play and not your color. (Pitt) had our honor and respect. As long as you were a good citizen, you had our respect."

Despite the fact Grier didn't encounter the constant racial taunting that Robinson had endured before and Hank Aaron did afterwards, there were still some restrictions on where he was allowed to go in segregated New Orleans. There was a Louisiana law that prohibited whites and blacks from sleeping and eating in the same places. The team had to stay at Tulane University instead of a fine downtown New Orleans Hotel like the St. Charles, where the Yellow Jackets were housed. While claiming beforehand that he would attend the dinner with the team at the annual Sugar Bowl party located in the St. Charles, and that he would leave before the dancing began, saying in a classy manner "I wasn't aware that a dance would be held. But it doesn't make much of a difference, a friend of mine from Pittsburgh is giving a small party for me in town," Grier in reality was not permitted to attend the party at all, instead going to a function at nearby Dilliard University for the whole evening.

There was the fear of the unknown as the game began. How would the primarily southern fans react to Grier and the scores of African Americans that came to support him? Would the team get a fair shake from the officials amid all the controversies? Both questions would be answered and answered fairly quickly.

On the plus end, there seemed to be little disruptions among the fans. "The crowd was fine. Pitt had made the stipulation that they would accept the bid, only if blacks could sit anywhere in Tulane Stadium that they wanted to. It was nice, there were quite a few of them who made the trip from Pennsylvania." Grier remembers. On the negative side,

Pitt's first African American football player

While Bobby Grier is remembered for breaking the color barrier in the Sugar Bowl, he was not the first African American to play football at the University of Pittsburgh. That honor goes to Jimmy Joe Robinson.

Robinson was a game-breaking halfback who lettered at the university in 1945, 1947 and 1948, leading the team in rushing in '45 with 273 yards and in receiving, nabbing 11 passes for 160 yards.

Even though he is acknowledged as a pioneer at Pitt, Robinson is more known as the Reverend Jimmy Joe Robinson of the Bidwell Street Presbyterian Church in Pittsburgh. In 1968, Reverend Johnson saved the North Side from being destroyed during the riots following the assassination of Martin Luther King. He did this by keeping the youth of the area off the streets, doing other things.

Robinson and his wife Betty dedicated their lives to those children they saved and started the Manchester Youth Development Center. At a recent dinner to honor the two, Steeler great Franco Harris made the observation, "Your presence is testimony to the love and respect we all feel for Betty and Jimmy Joe Robinson. My first day there, seeing what their dream was all about, it really makes you see that people can have a big impact on people's lives."

While Jimmy Joe's efforts on the field were certainly important it was his deft handling of the tough situation in 1968 and the love and support he brought to the children of the area that will always make the good Reverend a Steel City Hero.

a controversy involving the Panther pioneer reared its head early in the contest, a controversy that eventually cost the club the game.

Halfback Lou Cimarolli of Pitt fumbled the ball at the Panther 32-yard line in the first quarter, setting up a play that is still talked about almost a half a century later. Dodd wanted to go for the jugular immediately after the Pitt miscue. Yellow Jacket quarterback Wade Mitchell dropped back after a play fake, launching a pass into the end zone in the direction of receiver Don Ellis. Ellis was being covered by none other that Bobby Grier, who unfortunately slipped in front of the Tech end. Luckily for the Panthers, the ball flew over Ellis' head and Pitt was seemingly out of danger; that is until the flag of official Frank Lowery came tumbling down. Would it be offensive interference as Grier was lying on the turf? Unfortunately not. Lowery had incredibly called pass interference on Grier, giving Georgia Tech the ball at the one-yard line. After a Pitt offside call, Mitchell took the ball in for the touchdown, then tacked on the extra point, giving Tech the only points of the game.

While many remember the officiating crew as an all-southern squad, author Marty Mule in his book *Sugar Bowl: The First Fifty Years* points out that it was a split crew, only part southern, and was approved by the powers that be at the University of Pittsburgh. Regardless, it only takes one official to throw a flag and in this case a seemingly very erroneous one at that.

To this day it's a call the mild-mannered Bobby Grier still can't believe. "I was playing defensive halfback at the time," he says. "I felt a push on my back, and I fell down. The Georgia Tech receiver jumped for the ball and the pass went about three feet over his head and I was called for pass interference." There were immediate charges of racism, a charge that the Pitt defensive back concurs might have been the reason. "I think it was racially motivated, but it's hard to tell."

Ellis disagreed, claiming "I got behind him. Then when I turned around to look for the pass, he shoved me in the stomach knocking me off-stride. It was a fine pass and I think I could have caught it."

Looking at the frame-by-frame clip of the play, it appears Ellis may have been remembering a different encounter with Bobby, as it shows clearly, at least at the end, to back Grier's claim. While it's unclear whether or not Ellis pushed Bobby in the back, it does show both players turning around to the ball with Grier losing his footing and falling to the turf, seemingly never putting a hand on the Yellow Jackets' receiver.

After the controversy, Pitt took control of the game, knocking at the Georgia Tech end zone time and time again, only to be turned away. As time in the first half was running out, the Panthers went on a 79-yard drive to the one, where quarterback Corny Salvaterra was stopped on fourth down, rushing the play too quickly when he thought the clock was about to run out (the game clock was kept on the field as the scoreboard one was malfunctioning, causing Salvaterra to be confused as to how much time was left).

In the third quarter Grier got a bid of revenge, ripping off a 26-yard run only to have the drive stalled by an interception. A fumble cost them a score at the Yellow Jacket seven later in the quarter. Then as time ran out in the contest, the Panthers were at the five, still confused as to how much time remained in the game.

Overall, Pitt dominated every aspect of the Sugar Bowl, outgaining Tech 311-142. The only stat they didn't dominate in was the final score, a disheartening 7-0 defeat; a loss that didn't stick well with the team following the game. Afterwards, a tearful Bobby Grier asked the question in the locker room to the reporters, "I didn't push that man. I was in front of him, how could I have pushed him?" As for Lowery, Bobby said "After that game I believe that official never officiated another game again."

Despite the sideshow that was the 1956 Sugar Bowl, Bobby Grier ended up having a fine life, joining the Air Force for 11 years where he became a captain, delving in missiles and radar before returning to Wexford, his home today, working for U.S. Steel, then taking a position as an administrator at Allegheny Community College.

As for the aftermath of the memorable contest, what effects did Grier playing as the first African American in the southern located Sugar Bowl have? At first, not good ones.

After the game, the Louisiana State legislature set out to initiate a ban on white Louisiana State colleges from playing schools that were integrated. It was a ban that so irritated the University of Pittsburgh they refused to play in any future Sugar Bowls as long as such laws existed. It was a stance that cost the third-ranked 1963 Pitt Panthers a bowl bid as they turned down the opportunity to return to New Orleans. Furthermore the Sugar Bowl was hesitant to invite any more northern teams. Over the next decade, only teams from the primarily southern Atlantic Coast Conference, Southeastern Conference and Southwestern Conference were invited to play in the Crescent City.

The immediate good that came out of it, though, was found at the campus of Pitt's 1956 Sugar Bowl opponent, Georgia Tech. In 1961, the southern school brought their first African American student into their fold.

Whether or not any instantaneous good came out of Bobby Grier's appearance in New Orleans is inconsequential. By him playing, as well as any other African American athlete who broke the various color barriers during that time, he made it easier for those who followed to be treated more fairly not only on the fields of play but on the streets of the country. Grier may have been a reluctant pioneer in the world of college football, but his efforts in the game, no matter how unfortunate they were, are still remembered proudly by the university who stood by him so strongly.

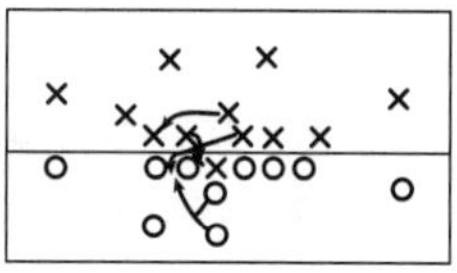

TWENTY FIVE

An Irish Feast

One of the first things coach Johnny Majors did in coming to the University of Pittsburgh was to stake his claim in the courtship of one Anthony Drew Dorsett. Majors began wooing Dorsett on the very day the coach arrived in Pittsburgh fresh from his stint at Iowa State, where he had done a pretty fair reclamation project on a Cyclones team that had a history of not having a history in football. He faced a similar task at the University of Pittsburgh in 1973. If Majors was going to duplicate his Iowa State success at his new venue, the key would be to attract the locals that southwestern Pennsylvania turned out each year. And Dorsett was the prettiest one at the dance.

Though small at 5'11" and weighing all of 157 pounds, Dorsett nonetheless had a long line of suitors wooing him. A phenom and All-American at Hopewell High, he was contacted by representatives from 68 schools. His speed and elusiveness had marked him as a possible elite running back, the kind that a program could rebuild around.

Despite joining a team that just came off a woeful 1-10 season, Majors had a couple of distinct advantages in the effort to land Dorsett. First, Majors was a pretty fair running back in his day—finishing second in the Heisman Trophy balloting in 1956 to Notre Dame's golden boy Paul Hornung—and he could speak the sweet language of tailbacks to Dorsett. But an even greater advantage was having Dorsett in his backyard. Majors pressed that advantage over cookies and pies. Ten times Majors made the trip from Oakland to Dorsett's home in Aliquippa for meetings with the family, often accompanied by treats and soft drinks. He even sent in assistant coach Jackie Sherrill with a secret weapon—a homemade rhubarb pie baked by Sherrill's 70-year-old mother from Biloxi, Mississippi.

It was a sweet calculation. The chance for Dorsett to play in front of his family and friends was too good to pass up. Majors' courtship effort was successful. By the time he reported to campus in Oakland, the young running back "bulked up" to 170 pounds, mostly through working in the weight room. And as much as Dorsett feasted on rhubarb pie during his four years at Pitt there was something else he ate up—the Fighting Irish of Notre Dame. In four games against Notre Dame, Dorsett wracked up more yardage than you can shake a shillelagh at.

In his first year, Majors was beginning to have an impact, as was his star freshman running back. Heading into November's showdown with Notre Dame, Pitt sported a 5-2-1 record, with Dorsett the key reason for the turnaround. In eight games, the exciting 19-year-old had rushed for 1,139 yards. However, the Panthers were about to face a nationally ranked Irish team that had the nation's No.1 rated defense. It also had the mystique that Pitt lacked. Notre Dame was *the* storied school in college football. Wake up the echoes and all that jazz. (Or as they would say at Pitt Stadium, n 'at.) Pitt was, well, Pitt. It was hard to hail to Pitt when its glory days were back in the days of the single wing.

None of that mattered to Dorsett. He would not be intimidated. "Notre Dame had the big-name advantage, but it didn't scare me, and it didn't scare Pitt," he told *Sports Illustrated*. Nor would he be stopped on this cold and snowy day at Pitt Stadium, at least not by the Irish. Dorsett carried the ball 29 times for 209 yards. Not even the great Irish killers of the distant past like Glenn Davis or the recent past like Anthony Davis could match those numbers. Dorsett did just about everything that day, except get in the end zone. The

Panthers' lone touchdown came on a 1-yard Dave Janesek run. In a bend-but-don't-break performance, the Irish defense twice thwarted Pitt drives deep in Notre Dame territory—once at the 21 and once at the 34—and picked off quarterback Bill Daniels three times. Notre Dame also had a strong goal line stand, as they held the Panthers out of the end zone for four downs from the Irish 7. Pitt moved into that position after Dorsett ripped off a 65-yard run. But once he got the team near the goal line, he was forgotten. Instead of riding Dorsett into the end zone, there was some curious play calling. Twice Daniels tried to run the ball in on quarterback keepers. Twice he was thrown back. Two passes fell harmlessly to the turf, as the Irish took over possession at their own 5 and essentially ran out the clock for a 31-10 victory.

Pitt had out-rushed and out-passed a superior opponent, but still ended up on the losing side of the score. Dorsett's performance wasn't enough. He drew praises from Notre Dame coach Ara Parseghian. "He's a super football player and I'm very impressed," he said. "He's definitely someone to watch."

So was Pitt's football program. Major's rebuilding effort was well under way, but it was apparent that one player does not a team make. Dorsett's second game against Notre Dame was more of a team effort. Pitt continued to improve and entered the November 1974 game in South Bend with a record of 7-2 and had attracted the attention of more than a few bowl game organizers. The Irish were 7-1 and perhaps looking ahead to a bowl game of its own—an Orange Bowl bid against Alabama on New Year's night that it had accepted earlier in the week.

The stage was set for a Pitt upset. The only thing missing was a healthy Dorsett. The week before, against Temple, the running back sprained his ankle. To make matters worse, Notre Dame Stadium was a mess. Snow and rain had made the footing poor. With his ankle taped and tender, Dorsett wasn't much of a factor. He rushed for only 61 yards, one of the lowest totals of his college career.

But this was a Pitt "team." It held tough. Notre Dame scored on its opening possession as quarterback Tom Clements—a local boy who chose South Bend over Oakland—tossed a 3-yard touchdown pass. The Irish threatened to blow open the game on a 90-yard drive that began on their own 1-yard line. The 19-play, 9-and-a-half-minute drive ended when the

Panthers recovered a fumble at their 9.

Pitt somehow stayed in the game, even with Dorsett being ineffective on the day. To make matters worse, Daniels was injured on a trick play. The Panthers' quarterback went out for a halfback pass from Dorsett and was crushed on the play. He left with torn ligaments in his knee. His backup, Bob Medwid, led the team on a touchdown drive, taking the ball in himself from the 1 before the half ended. The score stayed 7-7 until late in the third when Carson Long booted a then-school-record 52-yard field goal. Pitt led 10-7.

But Touchdown Jesus was not to be denied. Clements led the Irish on a 55-yard drive and ran the ball in from the 3 for a 14-10 Notre Dame lead with just under 3 minutes remaining.

The Panthers came storming back, but fell just short. Two passes in the end zone were batted away, and Notre Dame held on. But Majors and Dorsett knew the gap between the teams was closing.

In Dorsett's junior year, the gap closed completely. Notre Dame had to play the game at Pitt Stadium without quarterback Joe Montana. The Ringgold native fractured his finger and could only watch from the sidelines. Notre Dame came in with a very un-Notre Dame-like 7-2 record. Pitt was 6-3. Although the 56,480 on hand had to brave a little cold and wind, the game conditions were perfect, and the stadium's artificial surface offered a fast track. No one was faster than Dorsett, who served up a record-setting performance.

On Pitt's first possession, Dorsett zipped for 14 yards. A few plays later, he ran through the left side of the Irish line for 57 yards, setting up quarterback Matt Cavanaugh's touchdown run and a 7-0 Pitt lead.

Notre Dame came back with a field goal and a fumble recovery on the ensuing kickoff. Four plays later, the Irish's substitute quarterback Rick Slager plunged in from about a foot out to give his team a short-lived 10-7 lead. The Panthers' near goal line stand fired up the team, particularly Dorsett. When Pitt got the ball back, he started the drive off with a nifty 9-yard run and then on the next play dashed 71 yards for his first-ever touchdown against Notre Dame. At the time his stat line read four carries for 151 yards.

The two teams traded field goals, and Pitt got the ball back before the end of the half. This time Dorsett would attack through the air. He hauled in a Cavanaugh pass and darted through the Irish secondary for a 49-yard touchdown reception. In the first half, Dorsett had put up numbers that most backs couldn't do in an entire game.

In the third quarter, Notre Dame threatened to make a game of it. For most of the quarter, they finally contained Pitt's running game. Then Slager tossed a 10-yard touchdown pass to pull the Irish within 7 at 27-20.

But the fourth quarter belonged to Dorsett. Pitt marched 80 yards on a drive that included Dorsett runs of 18, 18 and 16 yards as he made would-be tacklers miss on his way to the 1. Another Cavanaugh sneak made the score 34-20. Notre Dame never threatened again. Pitt's ground game ran out the clock, including a final 9-yard run that brought Dorsett's totals to a gaudy 303 yards on 23 carries. Add in another 71 yards through the air, and it was a record-setting day. No back had ever piled up that kind of yardage against Notre Dame. And he more than made up for the previous year's disappointment. Pitt was headed to the Sun Bowl, and Notre Dame was left to ponder: how do we stop this guy?

Before the last of the Dorsett games against Notre Dame, the Irish pulled out all the stops to get its team fired up for stopping Pitt's back, who had decimated them the previous year. This year, the game would open the season for both teams. At a pep rally before the student body, Notre Dame brought out "The Golden Boy" to stir up emotions. Twenty years removed from his Heisman Trophy season and serving as the voice of the Irish in broadcasting their games, Hornung told the crowd he would "jump out of the press box if number 33 of Pittsburgh gained 200 yards" against the Irish the next day. Perhaps Hornung would have cursed the stringent academic requirements of his alma mater on the way down, foreshadowing the stir he caused in the 2003 season.

But on this day in 1976, Hornung didn't exactly set the bar real high. It seemed that he was expecting Dorsett to top the century mark. But we draw the line at 200, his comments seemed to suggest. Not exactly the best way to fire up a team, as it turned out.

Notre Dame knew it had a battle on its hands. It enlisted the South Bend groundskeepers to help keep Dorsett in check by letting the grass grow to slow down the track for the fleet Pitt running back. Walking the field the day before the game, Majors said he had been in "Iowa cornfields that were shorter than this." Groundskeepers claimed to have cut the grass only the day before.

Taking advantage of that home (corn)field advantage, the game started well for Notre Dame. The Irish took the opening kickoff and went 86 yards in 11 plays to take a 7-0 lead. However, that would be their only trip to the end zone for the day.

On Dorsett's first carry of the game, he didn't let grass, defensive linemen, linebackers or safeties slow him down. He bolted for 61 yards, breaking a simple dive play to the outside and through the Irish secondary. Five plays later, he took a pitch and ran it into the end zone to tie the game at 7. By his eighth carry, Dorsett had wracked up 110 yards. Leg cramps forced him out of the game for a while. (He attributed the cramping to a pair of elbow pads he wore across his knees that had cut off circulation and so he cut the pads off.)

Pitt wouldn't need much more from its Heisman Trophy-winning back. The Panthers' defense stifled Notre Dame's offense. The Irish lost their first season opener in 13 years, as Pitt pasted them 31-10. Hornung would be spared from taking a header. Dorsett finished with *only* 181 yards, mostly because he sat out the Panther's final two offensive series. The victory over the Irish served notice that the transformation was complete. Pitt went from 1-10 and the basement of the East to a national championship in four years. Along the way, Dorsett set a mark that would last for more than 20 years. In four games against Notre Dame, he ran for 754 yards. No other back rushed for more yards against Notre Dame. No back had rushed for more yards against *any* team. Dorsett left Pitt as the leading rusher in NCAA history. And he won the Heisman that had eluded his coach. Both he and Majors got to the big dance, and they left as royalty.

TWENTY SIX

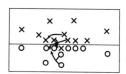

Which Were Better: the 1976 or the 1980 Panthers?

Panther championships won: 1976 versus 1980
1976: 12-0-0
Consensus national champions Lambert Trophy winners Sugar Bowl champions
1980: 11-1-0
New York Times national champions Ranked no. 2 by the coaches and writers Lambert Trophy winners Gator Bowl champions

Perhaps the worst move in the history of collegiate football at the University of Pittsburgh was the administration's decision to part ways with Jock Sutherland after the 1939 season. It took 35 years before the program could claw its way back up the chart and become the national power that it had been under Sutherland and his predecessor, Hall of Fame coach Pop Warner.

Once Johnny Majors had rebuilt the Panther fortunes, culminating in the university's ninth national championship in 1976, Pitt enjoyed a six-year run as one of the nation's elite programs. That run came to a grinding halt a season after Majors' replacement, Jackie Sherrill, signed the most lucrative contract ever given a college coach, leaving for Texas A&M following the successful 1981 campaign that was Pitt's third consecutive 11-1 season.

Between 1976 and 1982, the Panthers were usually among the nation's top-ten football programs; each year producing a powerful club that often times was competing for a national title. There were two teams in particular that stood above the rest, the 1976 national championship team and the squad four years later in 1980; two teams that are not just considered the best among their eras, but perhaps two of the most potent squads ever produced by the university. To take it one step further, the 1976 and 1980 University of Pittsburgh Panthers can certainly take their places among the best collegiate football teams nationwide ever to take the gridiron.

The debate over who was better has always made for a lively argument among the Panther faithful. There is no consensus, and perhaps there never will be. Ask several different Pitt fans at any given time and you're bound to get several different answers and reasons, even among two of the most knowledgeable Panthers fans around. Alex Kramer, the former administrative assistant to several Pitt coaches between 1977 and 1995 and the unmatched Pitt football historian, says it's the 1976 team. Kramer, who knows more about Pitt football than any man ever to grace this fine city, says if those teams played each other "Tony Dorsett would be the difference."

There is the other camp that believes a great defense would beat a great offense and the 1980 Panther stop troops would have disabled the Dorsett express. Joe Huber has been among the most knowledgeable Pittsburgh sports fans for most of his life. The jewel in his eye has always been University of Pittsburgh football, though. Huber is better known to fans of the popular Pittsburgh sports talk shows over the past 20 plus years as "The Titleman." The Titleman quite simply says that the 1980 club was "the greatest team I've ever seen in college football." And so the great debate begins.

To evaluate the two championship teams, they will be dissected and compared by unit and then by intangibles. Finally, thanks to the magic of the computer and the expertise of "Action Football" by Dave Koch Sports, one of the most statistically accurate computer football games on the market, the two clubs will face off against one another to find out which is truly the best Pitt football team in the modern era.

Quarterbacks

Analysis: Robert Haygood was the starting quarterback for Pitt as they started their national championship campaign in 1976. He helped guide the Panthers to a big win at South Bend versus Notre Dame and had started the following game at Georgia Tech. Haygood went down for the year in the second quarter of that contest with torn ligaments in his knee. Enter the understudy Matt Cavanaugh.

Haygood was a one-dimensional QB, a very effective runner who was limited in his passing abilities; Cavanaugh changed all that. He gave the offense a more rounded look with his accurate arm. This fact was never more evident than in the game against Duke when the Blue Devils stacked the line to stop the potent Pitt rushing attack. Cavanaugh made Duke pay for not respecting his arm by setting a school record by tossing five touchdown passes in a 44-31 win. With Matt in the lineup, the defense now had to respect the pass, which opened up the Panthers' running lanes. What Cavanaugh never gets credit for is the fact that he was also a very effective running quarterback who gained 124 yards in a 24-16 win against West Virginia.

While Tom Yewcic gave a gutsy effort in relief of Cavanaugh after the junior broke his fibula against Louisville, he succeeded more because the injury happened at an opportune time, as the three opponents he started against ended up with a combined 10-23 record. What Yewcic did effectively was hand the ball off to Tony Dorsett, throwing only 34 passes in his stint as a starter.

Cavanaugh returned with three games left in the campaign, and led Pitt the rest of the way, capping off the undefeated season with an MVP performance in the Sugar Bowl. Despite the fact nobody knows for sure whether or not the Panthers would have won the national championship with Haygood at quarterback, having Cavanaugh at the helm certainly made them a much more effective team.

Even though Matt Cavanaugh gave Pitt a decent passing attack, they were still primarily a running offense. In 1980, the Panthers did things a little differently. Sophomore Danny Marino gave Pitt something the team never had in its history to that point, a devastating quick-strike offense. He not only became the greatest signal caller ever to grace the University of Pittsburgh, but perhaps that of the NFL. In 1980, though, he was a very talented 19-year-old sophomore who showed brilliance, but also had a penchant for interceptions. It was interceptions that inevitably helped cost the club a shot at the national championship as he tossed three in the team's only loss of the season, a 36-22 defeat at the hands of Florida State.

The following week against West Virginia, Marino hurt his knee, so coach Jackie Sherrill went calling for an old friend to come in and save the day, Rick Trocano. As a freshman in 1977, Trocano rescued what looked to be a very disappointing season after Cavanaugh went down in the opening game. He started the next season and was at the helm for the first part of his junior year, until a freshman phenom by the name of Marino took over. Danny set the all-time NCAA freshman passing efficiency mark of 133.4 while leading Pitt to a top 10 finish and a spot in the Fiesta Bowl.

Sherrill moved Trocano to safety in 1980, to make room full time for Marino. That experiment was tossed out the window as the coach tabbed the senior to fill in for the future hall of famer after the knee injury. Trocano took most of the snaps the rest of the way, finishing his career at Pitt as the all-time leading passer with 4,219 yards, a mark that Marino would eclipse a year later.

Advantage: 1980—Cavanaugh was good, but Marino was one of the best ever. The tandem of Marino and Trocano, who were the two most productive passers in the school's history after the 1981 campaign, combined to give the Panthers the fifth most prolific passing offense in the nation with 268.4 yards per game, a school record.

Running Backs

Analysis: "Tony Dorsett was simply the greatest running back ever to play the college game," Kramer points out emphatically. It's a statement that pretty much shows the reason the 1976 Panthers had such a devastating offense and were national championship contenders.

The season began with Dorsett taking the Panthers first offensive snap of 1976, 61 yards for a score against Notre Dame, and ended with him running for a Sugar Bowl-record 202 yards in the 27-3 annihilation of the Georgia Bulldogs for the national championship. In between, the fleet-footed Aliquippa native ran for an NCAA-record 1,948 yards, becoming the first runner in NCAA history to eclipse 6,000 for a career with 6,082. He led the nation in scoring with 134 points while setting the all-time career NCAA marks with 356 points and 59 touchdowns (along with breaking or tying 10 other career NCAA records). And, of course, he captured the 1976 Heisman Trophy along with just about every other award and honor there was to be given—the greatest running back to ever play the college game indeed.

While Dorsett pretty much was the bulk of the Panthers 290.7 rushing yards per game, good enough for seventh in the nation, there was also a talented runner at full back by the name of Elliott Walker. Walker finished the year with 348 yards, following it up with 972 yards in 1977. By the time they were both finished with their careers, Dorsett and Walker did in career rushing yards what Marino and Trocano did in passing, finished 1-2 on the all-time Pitt career list. Rounding out the unit was Bobby Hutton, a tough, physical back who didn't see many opportunities with Dorsett and Walker in the backfield, rushing for 172 yards on 51 carries.

After Dorsett and Walker left the school in 1976 and 1977, the Panthers were left with a relatively small backfield that Sherrill had to run out of a split formation. It was one of the main reasons for Pitt's insufficient running game in 1978, a problem that the Panther head coach wanted to rectify going into the 1979 campaign. Sherrill did that and more when he reached into the junior college ranks and pulled out a bruising, 230-pound fullback, Randy McMillan. The legend of the "Big Mac Attack" had now begun at Pitt.

Although the prolific passing attack that the Panthers employed in 1980 prohibited McMillan and the running game from showing what they potentially could do, he still finished with 633 yards and 9 touchdowns, leading an effective—if unspectacular—ground game that helped the team finish eighth in the nation in scoring with 31.2 points per game.

Joe McCall was a scat back who rambled for 453 yards, while the cannonball Wayne DiBartola and the speedy Rooster Jones and Artrell Hawkins chipped in for 160, 154 and 123 yards, respectively.

Advantage: 1976—Offensive line coach Joe Moore said that McMillan could have rushed for 1,500 yards if they tried to run the ball. They didn't and he didn't. The backs in 1980 were a collection of solid if unspectacular runners, while Dorsett was not only one of the greatest to lace up the cleats in the NCAA, but also in the NFL as he carved out a Hall of Fame career with the Dallas Cowboys. Add to the mix that their fullback was the second leading rusher in Pitt history and fourth on the all-time scoring list by the time he was done and you can see why '76 had such a significant advantage in this category.

Wide Receivers

Analysis: According to Alex Kramer, "Gordon Jones was yesterday's Larry Fitzgerald." Jones was a sophomore receiver who despite the fact he didn't exactly have his best year ever in 1976, nonetheless gave the Panther offense its quick-strike capability. While he only caught 18 balls in 1976, several were of the spectacular variety as he pulled in a 51-yard TD toss against Georgia Tech, two spectacular touchdown catches versus Duke, a 53-yard catch in the Penn State victory when the Panthers were down 7-0, and a clutch 59-yard second quarter touchdown reception in the Sugar Bowl to give Pitt a 14-0 lead. By the time Jones had completed his collegiate career, he was a first team All-American (1978) and held the all-time school record for receptions with 133, TD catches, 21; and receiving yards, 2,230.

Having Jones on the team would lead people to believe that he was the go-to guy for Matt Cavanaugh, something that was absolutely incorrect. Tight end Jim Corbett was far and away the team's leading receiver, pulling in 33 catches for 528 yards and two scores. He was one of the best receiving tight ends in the nation, being named to the Associated Press' second team All-American list.

Taylor was a quick receiver and a devastating down-field blocker. He had the ability for the big game, scoring two touchdowns against Duke, including a 66-yard TD reception. He also caught four balls for 72 yards in the Sugar Bowl. Willie led the team in yards per reception with a 17.7 average.

Like the 1976 club, in '80 a tight end led the way as Benjy Pryor, the only high school All-American in the vaunted 1977 recruiting class, caught 43 balls for 538 yards. Pryor might have had more catches, but the unquestioned leader of the receiving corps had to be freshman Dwight Collins. Collins was a track star at Beaver Falls High School and made the transition to collegiate football in a big way, catching 30 catches for a school record of 827 yards (a 27.6-yard-per-catch average) and 10 touchdowns. Collins was the lone bright spot on an otherwise miserable evening at Florida State, breaking the Pitt single-game record for receiving yards with 183. Collins eventually would tie Jones with 133 career receptions, becoming the all-time leader in receiving yards with 2,264. Willie Collier was the other flanker, catching 32 balls for 537 yards.

Advantage: 1980—Jones was certainly one of the school's best receivers, and Corbett was one of the top tight ends in the land, but they were the only threats in the 1976 Panther arsenal.

The 1980 crew had more depth at flanker with Collins, Collier and Julius Dawkins. While Corbett was the superior receiver, Pryor was a better blocker and had a fine group of tight ends to back him up in Mike Dombrowski and John Brown. Even the running backs were more a part of the passing game, catching 54 balls compared to the 1976 output of 10.

Whether or not the superiority of the '80 receivers over '76 was because of Pitt's dependence on the run that year will never really be known. What is known is that the'80s group seemed very well rounded, allowing Marino and Trocano several targets who put up some pretty good numbers.

Offensive Line

Analysis: It's true that the biggest part of the success of the running game in 1976 was Tony Dorsett, but even the greatest runners in the world can't be successful without a solid offensive line in front of them.

Tom Brzoza was the anchor of the squad, being named second team All-American by both the UPI and AP. While being a devastating blocker on the line, he was equally as effective downfield.

John Hanhauser was the big man of the group and a first team All-East selection, being dubbed the "USS Hanhauser" by center John Pelusi.

Pelusi was the tough center. He was also named first team All-East as well as honorable mention All-American by UPI. He was also selected as the player of the week from *Sports Illustrated* following an outstanding performance against Penn State, where he helped Dorsett rip through the Nittany Lion defense to the tune of 224 yards.

As good as the '76 squad was, the 1980 group was legendary, sporting not just All-Americans, but All-Pro players. Every member of the starting line went on to play in the NFL with Mark May, who won the Outland Trophy, emblematic of the best collegiate lineman in the nation, and Russ Grimm and Jimbo Covert leading the way.

So big was this crew that man for man, they were bigger than the offensive line of the Super Bowl XIV Champion Pittsburgh Steelers. This line was so good that there were times Marino's uniform would not be dirty. "There were games when I never hit the ground," Marino remembers. "That's incredible."

Advantage: 1980—The 1976 crew took a backseat to no one, except the 1980 offensive line. The '80 group may have had the most talent ever to be assembled by one offensive line in NCAA history. "That group led by Grimm, May and Jimbo, were incredible, the best ever," Titleman claimed.

May and Grimm, taken in the first and third rounds by the Redskins in 1981, were two vital members of the Hogs, Washington's phenomenal offensive line that helped the club win several

Outland Trophy winner Mark May has become a successful college football analyst with ESPN. Recently May was given the highest honor a college football player could achieve being elected to the College Football Hall of Fame in 2005. (Courtesy of the University of Pittsburgh.)

Super Bowls. Covert went in the first round of the 1983 draft to the Bears and had a great nine-year career in the Windy City that also included a Super Bowl victory.

Defensive Line

Analysis: When comparing these two squads, you are inevitably crossed with a defensive line that was very underrated in the 1976 line and one that is hailed as being among the best ever in NCAA history with the 1980 team.

"The 1976 defense was a very tough one and could have handled the 1980 offense," Kramer proclaims, while Huber counters "the '76 defense didn't have the talent of the phenomenal defense in 1980. They were murderers' row with Green, Jackson, Meisner, Boyarsky and Neill."

They may not have been murderers' row, but Cecil Johnson, Ed Wilamowski, Al Romano, Don Parrish and Randy Holloway took a backseat to nobody. Johnson was All-East, Parrish was second team All-East and honorable mention All-American while Holloway, who was also All-East and honorable mention All-American, led the team with 18 sacks. Romano was the unabashed leader of this crew. He was a unanimous first team All-American, finishing the '76 campaign with 10 sacks and 128 tackles, second on the team, a phenomenal amount for a middle guard. Romano, still considered one of the greatest defensive linemen in the history of the school, finished the season as runner-up in the Outland Trophy voting.

This group led the Panthers to the fourth-best rushing defense in the country, giving up only 113 yards per game.

The 1980 unit stands among the best ever to play the game. They were aggressive, devastating and wonderful to watch. Hugh Green, who led the team with 17 sacks, was a unanimous All-American and probably the finest defensive end in collegiate football history. In a recent survey by the *College Football News*, he was rated as the fifth greatest player, regardless of position, in college football history. By the time he was a sophomore, he had already been chosen to the all-time Pitt team and by the time it was all over, he had won the Maxwell, Walter Camp and Lombardi Awards and finished second to South Carolina's George Rodgers in the Heisman Trophy voting. Titleman makes the observation that before he was injured with the Tampa Bay Buccaneers "Green was every bit as good as Lawrence Taylor (in the NFL)."

Ricky Jackson led the team in tackles with 137, finishing behind Green in sacks with 12. While Green did most of his damage with speed, Jackson did his with a mean attitude and aggressiveness.

Meisner, Neill and Boyarsky all enjoyed NFL careers and completely stuffed the middle of the line for opposing offenses. They helped the Panthers concoct the No.1 rushing defense in the nation, giving up only 65.3 yards per game, as well as the top overall defense, surrendering 205.5 yards per game.

Advantage: 1980—While the difference is not as much as most people would believe, the 1980 Pitt Panther defensive line was so good, it could have been one of the best in the NFL in 1980.

Linebackers

Analysis: Jim Cramer and Arnie Weatherington were as solid a group of linebackers as there were in the country. Cramer was honorable mention All-East and got a nod on the Football News honorable mention All-American team. Cramer led the team in tackles with 136 and made one of four Panther interceptions in the Sugar Bowl.

Weatherington was a player with an attitude; he wanted to rip apart anybody who had the ball. Like Cramer, Arnie was also an Honorable All-East player and got an interception against Georgia in the Sugar Bowl.

Sal Sunseri, who led the team with five interceptions, and Steve Fedell were solid linebackers on the 1980 Panthers, but too many running backs never made it

While not as well known as teammate Hugh Green during his Pitt days, Ricky Jackson went on to a much more renowned professional career enjoying a 16-year all pro career with New Orleans and San Francisco. (Courtesy of the University of Pittsburgh.)

through the mammoth defensive line for them to pile up many stats.

Advantage: 1976—By a very slight margin.

Defensive Backs

Analysis: The strength of the Pitt Panther defense in 1976 was their aggressive unit of defensive backs. The crew was the youngest on the Pitt team, not a senior among them, and they combined to achieve some pretty impressive numbers. Opponents completed on 35.5 percent of their passes against this bunch, best in the country, while intercepting an NCAA-high 24 passes.

Bob Jury led the way with nine picks; good for second in the nation while being named third team All-American. Jeff Delaney was next with an NCAA-seventh-best total of seven. JC Wilson and Leroy Felder, a third team All-East, rounded out this crew.

Carlton Williamson, Tom Flynn, Terry White and Lynn Thomas formed a solid nucleus in 1980. Williamson, who according to Kramer, "was one of the heaviest recruited players in that memorable 1977 freshman class," was the best of the group. Flynn was an outstanding freshman, while Thomas tied with Sunseri for the team lead in interceptions with five.

Advantage: 1976—The 1980 crew might have had a little more talent, but the numbers the '76 unit put up were phenomenal and speak for themselves. Perhaps the 1980 DB's were never put to the test much because of the dominant defensive line, but the 1976 crew made the most of their opportunities, making games a nightmare for opposing quarterbacks.

Special Teams

Analysis: There was no better kicking duo in America in 1976 than Carson Long and Larry Swider. Long was a second team All-American who was 11th in the nation in scoring with 90 points (tops for kickers), while setting the all-time NCAA record for points scored by a kicker in a career with 256. He was perfect on all 42 extra point attempts while hitting on 16 of his 23 field goal attempts. Larry Swider, the future Pittsburgh Mauler, was fifth in the country in punting with a 44.8 average, including a 77-yard bomb.

David Hepler was no Larry Swider in 1980 with a mere 37.6 per kick average. Trout had a strong leg and was solid if unspectacular missing three of his 42 extra point attempts and going 15 for 20 in field goals for 71 points.

Advantage: 1976—Alex Kramer said it best when he stated, "If the two teams met, Swider's punting and Long's kicking would definitely give the '76 team an edge, especially in a close game."

Turnovers

Advantage: 1976—this was truly the 1980 team's Achilles heel. It cost them an undisputed national championship as they gave up eight turnovers alone against Florida State, their lone loss of the season. Conversely, 1976 used their defensive backfield as a big advantage helping them to a +17 turnover rate for the season.

Strength of schedule

Advantage: 1980—This is the one big criticism of the 1976 national champions, their opponents were only 63-69-2 with a .478 winning percentage. The 1980 Panthers played a much tougher schedule, as their opponents had a 75-59-3 record, a .558 winning percentage.

Coaches

Advantage: No one—Pitt was blessed to have two of the greatest coaches in the modern era leading its program in Johnny Majors and Jackie Sherrill. When Majors came in, Pitt football was a joke. But in four short years he built it into a national champion.

After Majors left for his alma mater Tennessee, Sherrill took over the now powerful program and kept it clicking, going 50-9-1 with four top-ten finishes in five years.

Talent level

Advantage: 1980—This is not to insinuate that the 1980 club was a better college football team than the 1976 version, but when comparing how many of each team played in the NFL, the numbers are staggering. Twenty-six men from the 1980 team went into the NFL while only 16 made from the '76 club. Here are some other intriguing comparisons: six first-round picks from the 1980 team compared to two for 1976. Thirteen were chosen in the first three rounds compared five from the national champions. Twenty-nine members of the 1980 Panthers were selected in the NFL draft (30 if we include Sam Clancy, the great Pitt basketball player who went to Seattle in the 12th round in 1982 and had a successful career in the NFL and USFL) with 18 members from the '76 club picked. The chart on pages 250-252 that shows how many of these players went on to

Jackie Sherrill took over the Panthers after Johnny Majors departed for Tennessee in 1977. Sherrill had one of the most successful runs in school history leading Pitt to a 33-3 mark between 1979 and 1981. (Courtesy of the University of Pittsburgh.).

enjoy careers in the NFL, the best way to see which club truly had the most talent.

And now, finally, we will use the magic of the computer to see which team may have truly been the greatest Pitt team in the modern era.

Predictions

Alex Kramer: 1976—"The 1976 defense would have had an advantage over the 1980 offense while Tony Dorsett would have found a way to score on the 1980 defense in a low-scoring affair."

Joe "Titleman" Huber: 1980—"I don't think 1976 had the talent of the '80 club. I think the 1980 defense was a shutdown defense and would have shut down the 1976 offense. The '80 D was truly incredible."

The *Sporting News*: 1980—In 1988, the *Sporting News* wrote a book chronicling what its editors felt were the 25 greatest teams of all time. They ranked the 1980 Panthers No.12 (the top club not to win a national championship) and the 1976 club No. 17.

The Outcome

While there is no denying the 1980 Pitt Panthers had more talent, they certainly were very charitable with the turnovers. The other factor in the contest was the

1976 Panther defense proved to be underrated and did make a huge difference.

The game was played 100 times on the computer with the '76 team continually coming up the winner by an average of 19-10.

The University of Pittsburgh Modern Era Championship

While this was a dominant victory for the 1976 club, remember there is no way a computer can measure the heart of a club, no way it can predict how a great player like Danny Marino would react in such a contest, perhaps not tossing four costly interceptions.

Also recall that a computer, especially in the college game, can't properly measure strength of schedule. Were the 1976 stats inflated because they played inferior teams? What we do know is that these two teams are among the greatest the school ever produced. If they ever did really play, the loyal Pitt fans would be on the edge of their seats in what would most likely be a classic affair, especially Alex Kramer and Joe "Titleman" Huber, who would finally be able to prove their argument as to who is the best Pitt team of the modern era.

Which was the greatest Pitt team of all time?

There is no greater expert on the history of football at the University of Pittsburgh than historian Alex Kramer. Here are his all-time top 10 Panther teams.

1. 1976: Tony Dorsett was the greatest back of all-time.
2. 1980
3. 1937
4. 1929
5. 1932
6. 1934
7. 1910: Joe Thompson's team was unbeaten and unscored upon.
8. 1916
9. 1955
10. 1963

Which is the best Pitt football team of the modern era? Here are Joe "Titleman" Huber's top five modern-era Pitt football teams.

1. 1980
2. 1976
3. 1979: Danny Marino's first year. "I thought the kid threw like Bradshaw."
4. 1981
5. 1977

And, the Titleman's most underrated squad:

1987: "The 1987 club had everything but a QB. Not to take anything away from Sal Genilla, but if we had a quarterback with better passing abilities, this team would have played on New Year's Day.

Pitt players in the NFL			
1976 Name	Teams In NFL	Years In NFL	Round Drafted
Matt Cavanaugh	New England San Francisco Philadelphia NY Giants	1978-1982 1983-1985 1986-1989 1990-1992	2
Jim Corbett	Cincinnati	1977-1981	7
Jeff Delaney	LA Rams Detroit Tampa Bay Baltimore	1980 1981 1981 1982-1983	7
Tony Dorsett	Dallas Denver	1977-1987 1988-1989	1
Jo Jo Heath	Cincinnati Philadelphia NY Jets	1980 1981 1987	6
Randy Holloway	Minnesota St. Louis	1978-1984 1984	1
Cecil Johnson	Tampa Bay	1977-1985	N/A
Gordon Jones	Tampa Bay LA Raiders	1979-1982 1983-1984	2
Bob Jury	San Francisco	1978	3
David Logan	Tampa Bay Green Bay	1979-1986 1987	12
Carson Long	Buffalo	1977	11
Don Parrish	Kansas City	1978	N/A
Larry Swider	Detroit St. Louis Tama Bay	1979 1980 1981-1982	7
Willie Taylor	Green Bay	1978	9
Elliott Walker	San Francisco	1978	6
J.C. Wilson	Houston	1978-1983	8

1980 Name	Teams in NFL	Years in NFL	Round Drafted
Emil Boures	Pittsburgh Cleveland	1982-1986 1987	7
Jerry Boyarsky	New Orleans Cincinnati Buffalo Green Bay	1981 1982-1985 1986 1986-1987	5
Dwight Collins	Minnesota	1984	6
Jimbo Covert	Chicago	1983-1991	1
Julius Dawkins	Buffalo	1983-1984	12
Rob Fada	Chicago Kansas City	1983-1984 1985	9
Tommy Flynn	Green Bay NY Giants	1984-1986 1986-1989	5
Hugh Green	Tampa Bay Miami	1981-1985 1985-1991	1
Russ Grimm	Washington	1981-1991	3
Rickey Jackson	New Orleans San Francisco	1981-1994, 1996 1995	2
Rich Kraynak	Philadelphia Atlanta Indianapolis	1983-1986 1987 1989-1991	N/A
Tim Lewis	Green Bay	1983-1986	1
Bill Maas	Kansas City Green Bay	1984-1992 1993	1
Dan Marino	Miami	1983-1999	1
Mark May	Washington San Diego Phoenix	1981-1990 1991 1992-1993	1

1980 Name	Teams in NFL	Years in NFL	Round Drafted
Randy McMillan	Baltimore/ Indianapolis	1981-1986	1
Greg Meisner	LA Rams Kansas City	1981-1988 1989-1990	3
Bill Neill	NY Giants Green Bay	1981-1983 1984	5
Dave Puzzuoli	Cleveland Indianapolis	1983-1987 1989	6
Ron Sams	Green Bay Minnesota NY Jets	1983 1984 1986	6
Jim Sweeney	NY Jets Seattle Pittsburgh	1984-1994 1995 1996-1999	2
Lynn Thomas	San Francisco	1981-1982	5
Rick Trocano	Cleveland	1981-1983	11
David Trout	Pittsburgh	1981, 1987	N/A
Al Wenglikowski	Buffalo	1984, 1987	10
Carlton Williamson	San Francisco	1981-1988	3

TWENTY SEVEN

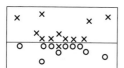

A Prelude to Excellence

For the alumni it's exciting. For the coaching staff it's an excuse to celebrate or drown your sorrows. For a collegiate football program it may be good press, but it's only a beginning and casts absolutely no guarantees for a team's future success. That's just about the worth of the ratings from the many men and companies that analyze collegiate recruiting classes.

They see high school talent, and they can recognize the parameters that may differentiate the football tools one player has from another. But these kids are raw, often times playing against competition that makes it difficult to truly judge their future success. It's the training and development at the college level that will truly determine whether or not the findings by the recruiting experts will actually come to fruition. The recruiting services do the best possible job they can, but rating recruiting classes is a very inexact science. If it were a sure thing, Notre Dame and Penn State would be top five programs every year, and West Virginia would never have a winning record.

Perhaps the best example of the process is the class Jackie Sherrill and his staff put together in 1977 for the University of Pittsburgh. In retrospect, it was among the greatest collections of collegiate talent ever put together in one freshman class, a collection that even went one step further by providing the National Football League with several outstanding players, including four All-Pros. But at the time it would have been hard to judge. It appeared only to be a decent class that had exactly one All-American in it ranks, tight end Benjy Pryor from Valley High School, a first-team Parade All-American and considered the best prospect in this football rich state. "Pryor was a Parade All-American, but Bill Neill, Greg Meisner, Jerry Boyarsky, Ricky Jackson and Hugh Green were not heavily recruited by anyone," Pitt football historian Alex Kramer remembers.

There has never been a more dominant player in the history of football at the University of Pittsburgh than No. 99 Hugh Green. Green was the most celebrated defensive player of his time finishing second in the 1980 Heisman Trophy race.

(Courtesy of the University of Pittsburgh.)

Imagine Hugh Green, one of the greatest collegiate defensive players ever to don the gridiron, not being heavily recruited. As tough as that is to fathom, it's true. In fact, our vote for MVP of this class is running back Rooster Jones, even though Jones turned out to be only a mediocre running back at best. Why MVP? Without Jones, Green would never have become a Panther.

Kramer explains. "Rooster Jones was being heavily recruited," he says. "The Pitt coaches were watching film of him at the time. Jones' high school, in Pascagoula, Mississippi, was taking on a team from Natchez. Instead of noticing Jones, they saw a 6-2, 210 pound defensive player, who was the heart of the defense dominating the game. That player was Hugh Green." Luckily for the university, Sherrill was not only able to land Rooster Jones, but also the impressive defensive lineman that caught their eyes in the film. Green became a three-time consensus All-American, had his No. 99 retired by the university, won the Maxwell, Walter Camp and Lombardi Awards while finishing second in the Heisman race (the closest a defensive player had ever come to winning the prestigious award at the time), was elected to the College Football Hall of Fame, and was recently rated as the fifth all-time best collegiate player in NCAA history by the *College Football News*. Those would all be good enough reasons why Jones was the most important commodity in this class.

Actually, despite the fact Jones never quite lived up to his promise and couldn't be an MVP on his own merit, in 1977 he was considered among the best running backs in the land. Rooster was quick, running a 4.4 40 yard dash, and had gained 1,895 yards his senior year at Pascagoula, scoring 28 times. Jones had been named by the experts as a "can't-miss prospect," one of eight that would be a part of the Panther class. Again, the list of the eight can't-miss prospects showed how rating recruits is such an inexact process. On the list were:

WR-Mike Christ
QB-Lindsay Delaney
HB-Artrell Hawkins
HB-Ray Charles "Rooster" Jones
TE-Benjy Pryor
OT-Wayne "Skip" Sylvester
QB-Rick Trocano
DB-Carlton Williamson

Out of this group, the recruiting honchos hit 37.5 percent on their can't-miss recruits. Williamson, whom Kramer describes as "not only being a good player, but a good man," became a four-year letterman whom coach Foge Fazio felt was the defense's "unsung hero," intercepting three passes his senior year. Carlton was drafted third by the 49ers and carved out a successful eight-year career in the city by the bay. Trocano became the man who saved Pitt twice: once during the 1977 campaign as a freshman when Matt Cavanaugh broke his arm and his more experienced replacements Tom Yewcic and Wayne Adams could not pick up the slack, and again in 1980 when sophomore phenom Dan Marino succumbed to a knee injury. Trocano had been switched to safety in the off-season and returned to quarterback to help lead the Panthers to a No. 2 ranking. By the time he was done at Pitt, he was the all-time leader in passing yards. Trocano was drafted by the Steelers and spent three years in the NFL, ironically with their rivals, the Cleveland Browns

While not making it in the NFL, Pitt's top recruit, Benjy Pryor, did have a good run at the university. He led the team in catches his senior year with 47, and finished fourth on the all-time receiving yards list with 1,267. The rest of the group unfortunately proved the prognosticators wrong as they were "can-miss prospects." Christ moved to safety and did letter in 1979 and 1980; Delaney lettered in 1977 and 1978, but never came close to living up to his promise. Hawkins and Jones started at various points and time, gaining 474 and 1,248 yards in their four year careers, respectively, hardly the stuff legends are made of. And then there was Sylvester, who never cracked the starting offensive line, finally lettering his senior season.

Despite the fact the so-called "cream of the crop" didn't meet expectations, the average part of this group ended up being everything the "can't-miss group" wasn't. Here is a list of the "other" members of the 1977 recruiting class that made it such a special group:

DT-Jerry Boyarsky
DE-Hugh Green
LB-Russ Grimm
DE-Ricky Jackson
OL-Mark May
OT/DT-Bill Neill
DE-Greg Meisner
DB-Lynn Thomas
K-Dave Trout
HB-Terry White

This was a group that didn't just make NFL scouts salivate, but were vital cogs on the legendary Panther defense and the incredible offensive line that were among the greatest units not only to play for the school, but in the annals of NCAA football.

May and Grimm were the key players on the memorable offensive line and not only became top-notch college lineman (Grimm won three letters while May won four, became a first-team All-American, and won the Outland Award as the nation's top interior lineman) but both became important members of the Hogs, the Washington Redskins offensive line that helped them become Super Bowl Champions in the 1980s. During their time in Washington, Grimm became a five-time All-Pro between 1982 and 1986, with May finally attaining the honor in 1989.

Green's collegiate exploits were illustrated earlier in the chapter; his NFL career began with a bang also. He was an All-Pro in 1982 and 1983 before injuries cut short his career. Jackson, who played second fiddle to Green at Pitt, was the maestro in the NFL, becoming an All-Pro five times in his illustrious, 15-year professional career.

Boyarsky, Meisner and Neill were the other important members of the impenetrable defensive front wall that stuffed the middle of many potent collegiate running games. They helped the Panthers lead the nation in rushing defense in 1980. In the pros, they played a combined 21 years, doing the same things for many an NFL team.

White and Thomas became two very important members of the Pitt defensive backfield, swiping five and four passes respectively in the memorable 1980 season. While White never made it to the pros, Thomas played with Williamson on the 1981 world champion 49ers.

Although it's easy to forget the place kicker, David Trout was certainly a great find for Sherrill, leading the club with 71 points his senior campaign. The strong-legged kicker spent time in the USFL as well as playing in the NFL with the Pittsburgh Steelers.

Kramer thinks we should never get too excited about initial ratings by the experts after a class is signed. "You can't tell how good a recruiting class is until after two years," he maintains, adding there are two other reasons this recruiting class was so successful. First, they received strong instruction from the coaching staff. And more importantly, to Kramer, "Jackie Sherrill, was good at putting players where they could excel."

Taking a look at the latter point first, the prime example would be Grimm. Grimm was a 215-pound defensive back at Southmoreland High School where he was named conference MVP because of his phenomenal exploits at the position. He was also a basketball star at the school, scoring 41 points in a game his senior season—not exactly the credentials for a future All-Pro center. But Grimm worked hard, and soon he became one of the best centers in the nation.

But Grimm wasn't the only player that Sherrill moved to a new position to better take advantage of his talent. Other notable changes included shifting Neill and Meisner from offensive line and defensive end, respectively, to the interior defense. He also moved White and Williamson, who played halfback and quarterback coming out of high school, to the defensive backfield. The two turned into extremely capable defensive backs by the time they were done at Pitt. Another great example of this ability of Sherrill's was Jimbo Covert in 1978. Covert, from nearby Freedom High School in Beaver County, was a defensive lineman of note who hurt his shoulder his freshman year. Sherrill moved him to offensive line, a move that brought Covert such success that he was elected to the College Football Hall of Fame in 2004.

Tutelage from the coaching staff was something they also got at Pitt in spades. Sherrill was very well known for having outstanding assistant coaches at his disposal. In 1977, the crew included his assistant head coach Jimmy Johnson, the same Jimmy Johnson who went on to win the national championship at Miami and two Super Bowl crowns with the Cowboys; strength and conditioning coach Dave Wannstedt, recent head man of the Miami Dolphins and now Pitt head coach; offensive back coach Joe Moore, who eventually became one of the greatest collegiate offensive line coaches in the history of the game with Pitt and Notre Dame; and Foge Fazio, a great defensive coordinator both in college and the NFL, who also headed the Pitt program after Sherrill left. Other coaches of note in Sherrill's tenure at the University included Ron Dickerson, who went on to be the head coach at Temple; Bob Davie, future Notre Dame head man; and Kirk Ferentz, who is currently leading the University of Iowa back to national prominence.

Yes, it may be tough to properly judge a recruiting class before it hits the campus, but in 1977, Sherrill had everything in place to make this one the greatest freshman class in the history of the university's vaunted program.

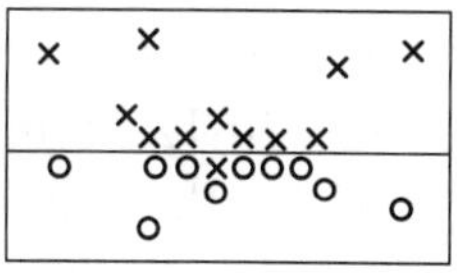

TWENTY EIGHT

Tug of War: Academics Versus Athletics at Pitt

For many NCAA Division I-AA athletic programs it is the ultimate struggle, academics versus athletics. One somehow is sacrificed for the ultimate success of the other. At some schools like Stanford, Notre Dame and Penn State they exist peacefully and successfully but make no mistake, these are generally the exception to the rule. At the University of Pittsburgh throughout the years, the struggle has been constant and bitter. There were times that the football program may have been taking too many liberties with the NCAA and university and needed to be pulled in a bit, but many other times they were not out of control at all. The administration for one reason or another was just hell-bent in not only knocking them down a few pegs, but humiliating them while trying to prove a point: that they could succeed without sacrificing their academic standards. It was a point they were never able to prove. Former NCAA kingpin Walter Byars once concluded, "I've never seen a school that appears to be as embarrassed by winning as Pitt."

Former Duquesne football coach Greg Gattuso coached a very successful team, albeit not at the Division I level, at a school that prides itself on having top student-athletes. He made the observation that to flourish "... everybody has to be part of the success. From the coaches to the administration, who has committed to us not only financially but with their support. With all this, we have gotten great kids to play here throughout the years."

It is that support that the administration at Pitt has given the program throughout its most successful seasons, yet it has also ripped it away when the powers that be wanted to wrestle back complete control. It was these types of incendiary battles, when the administration pulled the plug on their support that destroyed the two golden eras of football at Pitt, eras when the team won a combined nine national championships.

In the early part of the 20th century, the Panthers were among the best in the land. If they were not winning national championships, then they were among a small handful of schools competing for one. John Bain "Jock" Sutherland was the finest coach ever to be employed by the university and the successor to the wildly successful Pop Warner. Sutherland was 111-20-12 in his 15 years with the Panthers and continued the powerful tradition Warner had built, winning shares of five national titles.

Jock defeated teams the way Vince Lombardi did with the Green Bay Packers in the 1960s: by playing basic physical football—no gadgets—just beating opposing teams into submission. His defenses shut out an unbelievable 55 percent of their opponents in Sutherland's tenure (79 shutouts). On offense, Sutherland's running game, built upon a powerful single-wing attack, trampled opposing defenses.

Like any successful coach, Sutherland wasn't without his critics. Most of the volleys other schools would throw his way were claims that his players were professionals. They were charges that in a way were right on the button; Pitt did partake in the paying of players to play at the University of Pittsburgh. The practice had gone on since Jock took over in 1924 and by the time the '30s rolled around, players were receiving $650 a year plus tuition and books. The money was to go for room and board. But in the depression days, housing was relatively cheap and this provided the Panthers' players with a substantial amount of extra money. By 1933, the payout was reduced to $400 before being raised to $480 a year later to give the players a little extra spending money.

In 1937, Jock had his most successful team during his tenure at the university. Unfortunately, it was also the beginning of the end of the first golden era of Pitt Football. Many Big 10 teams, as well as Notre Dame, were sick of getting beaten by the Panthers' "subsidized" players. They had decided that it wasn't in their best interest to play Pitt any more. Pitt football historian Alex Kramer had a different take on it, claiming that the schools coming down against the Panthers weren't exactly saints themselves. "The hypocritical schools in the Big 10 were condemning Pitt for professionalism," he says. "They were incorrect."

Was it professionalism for a player to be given cash for room and board, especially since the school was making a nice profit on their services? Perhaps the $650 was over the top. It was enough money in those times for the players not only to go to school, but to maintain their new families. Several of the Panthers were able to get married with the financial support the university was giving them. The team had been dubbed the "Married Men's Team," and other schools criticized the University of Pittsburgh, claiming they were getting their incredible manpower—many of whom were All-Americans—by paying for them. It was a criticism that did not sit well with University of Pittsburgh Chancellor John Bowman, who banned married men from participating in varsity sports. But still the charges kept coming from the Panthers' opponents, and Bowman became very sensitive to them, especially when the press jumped on the bandwagon.

Athletic Director Don Harrison and Coach Sutherland had a very rocky, yet successful, relationship. That relationship came to an ugly head after the Rose Bowl victory in 1937. The two got into a very heated argument over how much spending money was to be given to the players in Pasadena. Someone had to go, and that person became Harrison when he resigned his position.

Jock had won another battle. But Bowman was sick of seeing the school always bending over backwards to the wishes of the coach. Instead of giving Harrison's position to Sutherland, he turned it over to one of Jock's former players, Jimmy Hagan. Reform was about to rear its ugly head. First, Jock was forbidden from doing newspaper columns, radio appearances and endorsements. Then came one of the hardest cuts of all—the $480 his players were getting for room and board would now have to be earned by working two hours a day. This new policy was called the Hagan Plan. It was perceived that most of the other schools in the nation were subsidizing their players' room and board by making them work, so by instituting this at Pitt, it would lessen the taunts of professionalism.

Not having the various outlets to subsidize his salary, and with his players now having to earn their keep, Sutherland was given a couple more shots by the administration as the club enjoyed their national championship season of 1937. Although Jock was promised more control of the teams' schedule after Harrison left, that promise that wasn't kept. "Sutherland was not consulted about the schedule and it made him feel very unwelcome," Kramer says.

The other and more substantial thorn in the side of the coach had to do with the bid to the 1938 Rose Bowl. California had a fine 1937 campaign and had indicated they were only interested in playing a team of good academic quality—a shot at Pitt. Still, the Panthers had the best team in the nation and were given the bid to play the Golden Bears. The players voted 16-15 to turn the bid down. Two stories went around as to why they had turned down an opportunity to defend their Rose Bowl crown. One was that they wanted $200 a piece to play in Pasadena, a price the school would not approve. And the other was in protest of the poor way their coach had been treated by the administration. The turning down of the Rose Bowl bid was a complete surprise to Jock, as Hagan never told him they got the bid in the first place. It was yet another huge slap in the face.

Bowman wasn't done wreaking his vengeance on Sutherland. He ended the Hagan plan in 1938, instead coming up with his own initiative called Code Bowman. Code Bowman was the straw that broke the camel's back. Under this new plan, a student athlete not only had to work for his room and board, but his tuition and books. Bowman also cut a game off the schedule and ruled that if a player did not move up with his class, he was not eligible to play varsity sports.

Code Bowman crushed the team. Many players dropped out. While the Panthers had a formidable starting team, they no longer had any depth. This cost them dearly in games—especially against Carnegie Tech, a 20-10 loss, when star back Marshall Goldberg was injured.

There was an option that Pitt would de-emphasize the program and the schedule with this new initiative, but Bowman was convinced they could succeed under this format and kept the aggressive slate playing the best teams in the nation. Sutherland was not convinced. He thought the combination of Code Bowman and a tough national schedule was a recipe for disaster and resigned under protest following the '38 season. Sutherland later confided, "It was alright with me if they wanted to de-emphasize the team, but not unless they de-emphasized the schedule, too."

The students were devastated, even threatening to strike, but Bowman and his administration had their way; they got rid of the popular coach whom they considered too powerful. Bowman named Charles Bowser to replace him, saying simply that he believed the team would continue to win its share of games. As it turned out, Sutherland was on the money, and Bowman was completely wrong.

Code Bowman was by far one of the toughest academic policies in the nation for a collegiate sports program. The results were very predictable. Following a 5-4 mark in 1939, the Panthers suffered their first losing season in 1940 since a 3-6 record in 1912. Worse yet, they only enjoyed three winning seasons in the next 15 years. Code Bowman may have been a big win for the administration, but it devastated a proud football program, one that may have needed a little retooling such as the Hagan Plan, but didn't need such distressing changes.

One of Sutherland's star pupil's, former quarterback John Michelosen, came aboard in 1955 to try and right the ship that had fallen horribly off course. Michelosen recharged the program by taking it to the Sugar Bowl his first season before going to the Gator Bowl in 1956. While his teams lost to Georgia Tech in both affairs, it gave the Panthers a return to national prominence, being ranked 11th and 12th in the polls respectively during his first two seasons. It was the school's first venture in the national polls since Sutherland's last season in 1938.

Unlike Warner and Sutherland before him, Michelosen was not able to maintain the school's newfound winning ways, producing only three plus .500 teams over the next six campaigns. All that turned around in 1963, when the ex-Panther QB led Pitt to a No. 3 ranking and a magical 9-1 season.

It looked like the University of Pittsburgh was about to embark on another golden era. But Chancellor David Litchfield would soon put an end to those hopes. In a move that certainly would have made Bowman proud, Litchfield decided to turn the screws to the football program, raising the academic standards by instituting a requirement that made students take two years of a foreign language.

The new standard reduced the Pitt program to a level it had never seen, not even after Code Bowman. "For a kid out of Youngstown, English was a foreign language," says long-time ESPN analyst and Pittsburgh icon Beano Cook. "In the '60s you didn't get F. Scott Fitzgerald out of Johnstown."

The football team promptly posted a combined 16-56 mark between 1966 and 1972, a record that included four embarrassing one-win seasons, the worst of which was a 1-10 mark in '72. At that point, the program had sunk to depths that prompted Chancellor Wesley Posvar to either give up the ship or relax the athletic standards a bit to help reconstruct what was once the most powerful program in the land. He chose the latter and brought Johnny Majors on board to lead the Panthers back to the status of an elite program. Majors had come from Iowa State, where he had taken a program that was on life support and led it to its first two bowl games in the school's history (1971 and 1972). He brought energy and enthusiasm to the moribund University of Pittsburgh football team and showed remarkable progress in only one season.

In this new football regime at Pitt, Majors had everything he needed to needed to win: the support of a fine athletic director in Cas Myslinski and Chancellor Posvar. With the academic noose taken from around the program's neck, Johnny recruited one of the greatest freshman classes in the history of the university. The 69 prospects that he brought in turned out to be the nucleus of his 1976 national championship squad. Players like Al Romano, Don Parrish, Jim Corbett and a small tailback from Aliquippa who would prove to be one of the greatest backs in the history of the game, Tony Dorsett.

Once the players arrived, the second golden era of Pitt football began in earnest. Dividends paid off immediately as the 1-10 Panthers won six games in 1973 and received their first Bowl bid in 17 years to play Arizona State in the Fiesta Bowl. Three years later, they became undefeated national champions, winning their first title since Sutherland left in haste almost four decades before.

Majors was now a very hot commodity and answered when his alma mater Tennessee came calling soon after the 1977 Sugar Bowl win against Georgia. Not wanting to destroy a good thing, Myslinski and Posvar turned to Majors' former assistant head coach Jackie Sherrill, who had left before the 1976 season to take his first tour of duty as a head coach at Washington State.

Sherrill proved to be the right choice, and the University gave him complete control of the program. "It seemed like when Jackie was there he did what he wanted to do—how you traveled, what time you practiced, what time you left for the game, who was on the airplane, who you recruited," former Sherrill assistant and Panther head coach Foge Fazio remembered in an interview by *Pittsburgh Post-Gazette* columnist Bob Smizik.

With this control, Jackie rewarded the school with the best program in the land, finishing a three-year run between 1979-1981 with a sparkling 33-3 mark and earning three top-ten finishes and a New York Times National Championship in 1980. In 1981, Pitt looked to be on the way to another undefeated campaign when they ran into a Nittany Lion buzz saw at Pitt Stadium that saw them surrender 48 unanswered points in a humiliating 48-14 defeat. The Panthers received a bid to the Sugar Bowl where they played and defeated the Georgia Bulldogs on Dan Marino's memorable, last-second TD toss to tight end John Brown. In the future, Pitt should never accept a bid to the Sugar Bowl to face Georgia. Once again, following a sweet win, they lost an outstanding head coach.

Less than a month after the victory, Texas A&M threw at Sherrill the richest coaching contract ever given to that point in college football history—an offer of 10 years, $2.5 million per year. At the University of Pittsburgh he only made $60,000 as a base salary, so who could blame a man for taking a job that would pay him four times more? Well, not many could, but there was seemingly something more at work here than just leaving for a better paying job.

Although Kramer, who was Sherrill's administrative assistant, asserts that his former boss was happy at Pitt and left simply to take a much better offer, there were reports Sherrill was not happy with some things the administration was beginning to do. The reports in a column by Smizik, shortly after he left, said that Jackie was becoming irritated because he did not have more of a say in the scheduling. He also didn't like that travel plans were done without his consent. The story further went on to say that on two occasions before the Sugar Bowl, Sherrill met with Pitt officials, the first time in New Orleans with Myslinski and Vice Chancellor Jack Freeman, and the second time in the locker room after the bowl game with Posvar. On both occasions the head coach was told this wasn't the time or place for discussing the matter. Both times Sherrill was reportedly furious. Eventually, the administration claimed they gave him everything he wanted, including control over the program, and was set to announce that he was named the associate athletic director. According to Smizik, though, it may have been too little too late, as A&M made their generous offer and Sherrill was off to College Station, Texas.

Unlike the Sutherland snafu, academics didn't play as much a part in the subsequent downfall of the program (although new coach Foge Fazio had much tougher recruiting restrictions academically than his predecessors). Instead, it was an issue of administrative control that sent ripples through the program. Fazio, a lifetime Pitt man who was a better human being than a defensive coordinator (of which he was the best in the land), was the universal choice to succeed Sherrill. Nobody could criticize the school, even with 20-20 hindsight. Most observers thought he was the right man at the time to take over. Well, most, except for Myslinski. Fazio was reportedly not the man the Pitt AD wanted. He was the one Vice Chancellor Freeman wanted. Make that Freeman and another member of the administration, Vice Chancellor Ed Bozik. Bozik and Freeman took control of the athletic department from Myslinski, eventually forcing the man who had resurrected the Pitt football program into a powerhouse into "retirement" before the much-anticipated 1982 campaign. It was a retirement that seemed to be not of his own choosing. Thus began the rule of Ed Bozik in the athletic department, a man who had no experience running an athletic department. While he brought the school into the Big East and had some nationally ranked basketball teams, his inexperience helped turn the second golden era of Pitt football into rubble.

As for Freeman and Bozik's first big decision, they should have listened to the more experienced Myslinski. Foge was a fine football mind, but there were whispers that he was not a disciplinarian. As a coordinator under the tough taskmaster Sherrill, he could concentrate on the defensive *X*s and *O*s and all was well. But in college football, as a head coach, discipline is essential. The players are young men who still have a lot of maturing to do. Fazio seemingly did not run a tight, disciplined ship, which perhaps cost the team a shot at a national title in his first season. The team was unanimously considered the best club in the nation before the 1982 campaign. Reported conflicts among the players served as a distraction and helped cause the Panthers to lose as many games in one season as they did in the prior three years.

Fazio's second season was his best. He led an undermanned squad to an 8-3-1 mark before the dam burst, sending the club to a low point of 3-7-1 in 1985. Exit Fazio. Enter Mike Gottfried.

Gottfried, who is now a very successful college football analyst for ESPN, was a good *X*s and *O*s man leading the team to a 26-17 mark, with two successive wins against the rival Nittany Lions—and he brought the program back to a spot in the top 20. While a fine football mind, he proved not to be the most politically astute man in the world when it came to the university's administration. This should have come as no surprise to the Panthers' brain trust. Gottfried reportedly had a history of discord with the administration in his previous job at Kansas.

The University of Pittsburgh was once again tightening the noose of academic reform on the football team, and Gottfried was not thrilled. The coach was very focused and intent on winning. The fact that Pitt's athletic academic requirements were higher than the NCAA's reportedly led the Panther coach to feel this was giving him a big disadvantage. He fought the administration on academic problems with Darnell Dickerson, a very talented quarterback from Detroit, and another QB, Gary Clayton. He lost both times.

Gottfried's embattled tenure ended after four years, amidst criticism from some of his ex-players. Some were irritated, claiming that he would constantly compare the program to Notre Dame, Miami or Penn State, rather than make them proud to be from the University of Pittsburgh. Linebacker

Nelson Walker contended that he felt the team was Notre Dame in a Pitt uniform.

The final straw came in the locker room after a loss to Penn State in 1989. An angered Gottfried reportedly had a very terse speech afterward, prompting Posvar to let him go and promote Paul Hackett to interim head coach. The administration went on a nationwide search that was nationwide in name only—passing over names like Dave Wannstedt and Barry Alvarez to give the job to the man whom they wanted all along, Paul Hackett. It was the move that, in essence, killed the program.

Hackett was a fine offensive mind, but he turned out to be among the least successful head coaches ever to stroll the sideline for the University of Pittsburgh. The administration wanted to restore academic integrity to the football program—an area in which Hackett did excel. But it came at a cost. He dismissed nine starters from the successful 1989 team before 1990. Hackett's problem, however, was that he couldn't win on the field. His teams sported a record of 12-20-1. Some felt he not only was bad at recruiting, but hated doing it. "You could see a huge difference in the recruits Paul Hackett brought into the athletic office compared to the ones that came in before," says a former employee in the athletic office who did not wish to be named. "Under Johnny Majors in the '70s, you looked at them and knew they were football players, under Hackett you looked and saw pre-med majors."

A telltale sign of what kind of recruits he was getting comes by looking at which schools Pitt was directly recruiting against. In the '70s, the players the Panthers were getting came against the likes of Notre Dame and Penn State. In the '90s it read more like a roster of MAC schools (a lower-end conference in Division I football at the time) and upper-end Division II schools.

Despite the fact academics seemed to be on the rise, the program was not only embroiled in allegations of recruiting violations but also of improprieties of organizational funds within the Golden Panthers. Finally, the unsuccessful Bozik administration (unsuccessful at least with the football program) came to an end in 1991. Cook once made the statement that having Bozik run an athletic program was like "having two terms of (Herbert) Hoover."

The administration brought back Majors to try and bring the

magic back to Pitt. The facilities were now poor and Johnny could not revive the program as he had done 20 years earlier.

Hope came in 1996 when Chancellor Mark Nordenberg tabbed Steve Pederson to lead the university athletically into the 21st century. He brought Walt Harris on board to direct the football program and was a leading force in transforming the facilities at the University of Pittsburgh from among the worst to ranking at the top in the country with the construction of the Peterson Center, the UPMC Southside practice facility and Heinz Field (the latter two shared with the Steelers). While still not back among the nation's elite, Pitt has improved and has earned five bowl-game appearances since 1997.

Academically, there are still several questions. An NCAA survey of graduation rates among Division I football programs in 2003 showed Pitt to be last out of 117 Division I programs in the nation at 16 percent, far below the national average of 54 percent. There are several factors in the rating that make one question the numbers. First, the survey took into account the 1996 freshman class, Majors' last recruiting class. Also, it does not include transfers (they are considered as players who do not graduate, therefore going against the rating), and 14 out of the 19 players who began at Pitt in 1996 transferred out when Majors left. Of the five remaining players, three graduated within the six-year timeframe that is acceptable in the survey.

Even with all this, Pitt still falls far behind some of the top schools such as Boston College (95 percent), Notre Dame (92 percent), Penn State (86 percent), and Northwestern (81 percent), all of which have enjoyed some success over the years in their football programs.

What makes those programs more able to succeed academically as well as athletically?

Former Duquesne coach Gattuso feels that at Penn State, where he played as an undergraduate, it was all because of the efforts of coach Joe Paterno. "Some people talk about academics and others truly believe in it," Gattuso says. "Joe Paterno believes in academics more than anything. It is more important for him to graduate players than it is for them to go to the pros. I'm a prime example of this. I was a starter who wasn't as interested in studying. Joe made me take my studies seriously. If it wasn't for him, I wouldn't have graduated."

At Northwestern University, where there is a reputation for high academic excellence, there has been a resurgence in football, beginning in 1995, that has seen the school not only be invited to four of the university's five bowl games in its history in the past nine seasons but also win three Big 10 titles (1995, 1996 and 2000). On top of their success on the field, Northwestern maintains a sparkling graduation rate within their football program. Justin Sheridan, director of football operations for the Wildcats, believes success both academically and athletically starts with what players the school recruits. "It's a tough question—how to maintain success in academics and on the football field—but it all starts with the fact we recruit great kids here. There's no magic way to do it, but when we go through the process of recruiting a player, we look at his academic situation, we want to make sure he's a Northwestern kid."

CMU coach Rich Lackner claims there is an advantage to recruiting players who are successful academically. "They have the ability to digest knowledge, whether it be football or physics," he says. Northwestern's Sheridan, who hails from nearby Ebensburg, further makes the point that by recruiting players who are also good students, the program has players with "a great sense of discipline which they need as they spend so many hours not only in the meeting room, but in the classroom."

Sheridan also traces a big part of the Wildcat's dual success in academics and athletics to the coaches. "Our staff is unique with the way they take an active roll in our guys' academic careers," he says.

The effort Northwestern puts into their recruiting with academics in mind paid off as they recently were awarded the 2004 American Football Coaches Academic Achievement Award for graduating every member of their 1998-1999 recruiting class. As nice as the stories of academic and athletic success are at the highest level of NCAA football, they are still a vast exception to the rule.

Even though they may not be at the highest academic level, the struggle between academics and athletics seems to have finally found a peaceful end at the University of Pittsburgh. There seems to be a harmony between the administration and the athletic department that had not existed before Pederson came aboard. While maintaining a winning program, Harris was reportedly tough on players who didn't perform academically. In a story in the *Pittsburgh Post-Gazette*, writer Milan Simonich wrote that players claim he is an ogre when it comes to academics and that if a Panther performs poorly in the classroom he makes them do brutal exercises such as wind sprints and bear crawls. Former star receiver R.J. English claims that the only reason he graduated was because of Harris. This disciplined manner was evidenced during the 2004 fall training camp, when two of the team's top players for the upcoming season, Josh Lay and Jawan Walker, were held out of practice because of academic difficulties.

Has this newfound harmony meant success in the classroom as well as the football field? While it's true that the school is no longer an embarrassment on the gridiron (as it had been in the early to mid '90s), it's still on the outside looking in as far as the top 25 football programs in the country are concerned. In the classroom, they have improved on their dismal 16 percent graduation rate for the 1996 recruiting class. When the ratings for the 1997 recruiting class are announced, Pitt will move up a little to 31 percent, but in two years they may project as high as 65 percent.

There will be further reason to celebrate down the road, according to Pitt sports information director E.J. Borghetti. "Pitt's most recent senior class (2003 season) had 18 scholarship players," he says. "As of today, 14 of those players graduated... an impressive rate of 78 percent." The reason for the success, according to Simonich's article, was that Harris was reportedly so focused on his athletes academically that he even knew how many credits they needed to graduate. Improvement can also be found in the amount of award-winning scholar athletes the team has had. In 2003, they featured 10 All-Academic Big East selections and tied for most in the conference for the fourth straight season. They also had two first-team Academic All-Americans in Vince Crochunis and Dan Stephens.

Even with these impressive stats, what exactly should the coaches' and an athletic department's responsibilities be toward the academic success of an athlete? A coach should certainly not embarrass the university with recruiting violations and should treat his players within the legal framework of the NCAA legislations. But there is only so much he could and should do. If a player legally qualifies for admission to a university and a coach gives the player ample opportunity to study toward a degree and requires him to practice no more than the law allows, isn't it up to the athlete to take advantage of the free education he has been afforded? Coaches take too much responsibility for the lack of players' academic success. The young adult athletes—and we stress ADULT—take too little. A coach's main responsibility is to win football games.

Whether or not the NCAA, university presidents, athletic departments or football coaches ever admit it, schools play Division I football for the big money that's involved. They may preach academic standards, but if that was all that was important, Paul Hackett would still have a job. Bottom line: Hackett was fired because he couldn't win. Even after leaving Pitt and taking the top coaching position at academically stringent Stanford University, if Harris doesn't win on the field, he will be gone too—no matter how good he has been with academics. There's no problem with trying to win at the Division I level. It brings important money into the university. And when the team wins, it provides a public-relations coup that no advertising campaign could rival.

The problem with Pitt over the past six-plus decades has not only been a struggle for dominance between the administration and the athletic department, but a confusion as to what the main goals should be. During its tough stands, the administration not only wanted to be of Ivy League quality with their academic standards, but win national championships. The two rarely meet. That's why Ivy League schools don't play major college football. It's a philosophy that reeks of failure.

When the president of Carnegie Tech (now CMU) Robert Doherty decided to de-emphasize the football program in 1947, he said the school would not ever be a major college program again. "The only way to maintain a class A team is to sacrifice education," he said. The school remains an academic power today with a very successful Division III football program. Following that reasoning, if Pitt was so hell-bent on high academics in the past, it shouldn't have been in the Division I football business.

It's nice to see things at peace now within the academic-athletic structure at Pitt. It's also nice to see Heinz Field filled with rabid college football fans rooting for a successful Division I football team. The school must continue to understand what it needs to be successful at the highest possible level of college football—and, yes, achieve success without prostituting itself by doing things such as bringing in convicted criminals (as Miami did) or recruiting athletes who couldn't pass a kindergarten entrance exam. Hopefully, the administration at Pitt will never be embarrassed to have a winning football program at Pitt again. More importantly, the university will have lost its thirst for a good tug of war match.

Section IV

On Campus: Western Pennsylvania's College and High School Heroes

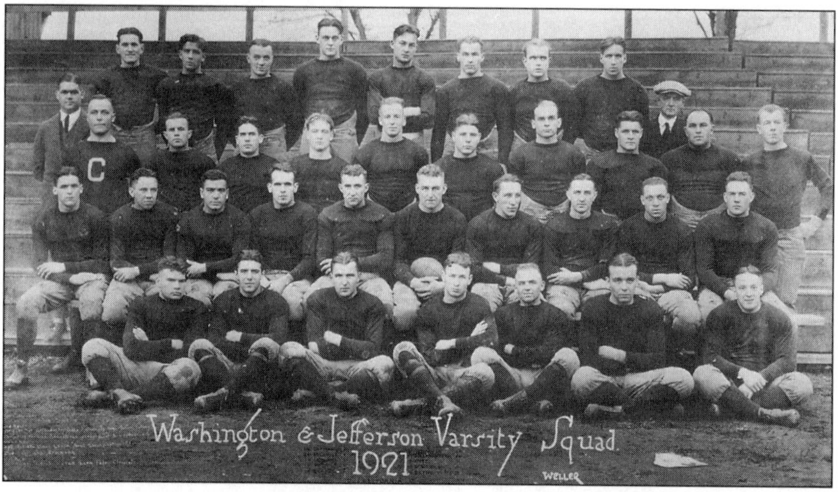

Washington & Jefferson College shocked the college football world in 1921, holding the powerful California Bears to a 0-0 tie in the Rose Bowl. (Courtesy of Washington & Jefferson College.)

TWENTY NINE

An Introduction to Small College Football in Western Pennsylvania

At one point in time, the city of Pittsburgh was one of the hot spots on the major collegiate football map. Travel down Fifth Avenue and not only did you find three top schools, but three top-ten football programs. While the story of the University of Pittsburgh is well known, eight national championships by 1937, Carnegie Mellon and Duquesne University also had their brushes among the elite of the sport.

In 1938, CMU, or Carnegie Tech as it was known at the time, was ranked 6th in the country in the Associated Press Poll, two spots above Pitt, while being invited to play in the Sugar Bowl. The Tartans lost to Texas Christian University 15-7 that day, but it was the high point in the history of their proud program. The Dukes of Duquesne had national success over a longer period of time, winning the Festival of Palms Bowl, the predecessor to the Orange Bowl, 33-7 over Miami (FL) before defeating Mississippi State 13-12 in 1937 when the game was officially known as the Orange Bowl. Three times in a five year period, the Dukes cracked the AP top 20, finishing 14th in 1936, 10th in 1939 and 8th in 1941. Along with the impressive tales of the Pittsburgh schools, we should not forget nearby Washington and Jefferson College who had a memorable "upset," a scoreless tie against the powerful California Golden Bears in the 1922 Rose Bowl or tiny Saint Vincent College out of Latrobe, which emerged victorious in the 1950 Tangerine Bowl.

Because of World War II and then the eventual de-emphasis of football at various universities, Pitt was the only school to remain at the major college football level in Western Pennsylvania. CMU went to a minor football status while Duquesne dropped the program altogether following 1950, after unsuccessfully trying to contend at the major level for five seasons after the war.

Today both schools compete very successfully at their individual levels, with CMU one of the winningest Division III programs over the past 30 years and Duquesne coming off a Division I-AA Mid Major national championship in 2003. As successful as those two schools are, there are many more flourishing programs that make this area something special when it comes to NCAA football. Robert Morris joins Duquesne as two of the strongest Mid-Major schools in the country while Slippery Rock and Indiana University of Pennsylvania are annually among the Division II powers. Add to the mix Washington & Jefferson, which has qualified for 15 of the last 18 NCAA Division III playoffs, and you can see the depth of football power in Western Pennsylvania.

While there are many other fine collegiate football colleges in the area, it's these six prominent and historical programs that will be featured in this section along with one that although successful in the past no longer exists, Saint Vincent College (although that is to change soon).

THIRTY

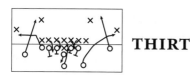

Shoo shoo rah rah: The History Of Duquesne University Football

Duquesne aficionados are well familiar with the chants of the most vocal Dukes fan, the late Mossie Murphy. For years, when the Duquesne basketball team would go on a run, the portly legend would stand up and stir the fans with his familiar chant... *shoo shoo rah rah*, and the building would go nuts.

Now that the basketball program has taken a tumble and the football team has risen to the status of Division I-AA power, we can only imagine Murphy extolling the campus' new favorite team on to victory at Rooney Field.

While the school is enjoying success on the gridiron it is nothing new for the university. There was a time long ago when the words Duquesne University football not only meant championships on the small college landscape, but that of the major college level. The following is a recap of a team that once tried to rule the college football world from high atop the Bluff.

Beginnings

The beginnings of football at Duquesne were in 1891 but because of incomplete records, the first recorded seasons did not occur until 1893, when they went 0-2, defeated by W & J 22-10 and the famous Pittsburgh Athletic Club 20-0.

In 1897, the school finally fielded a team that was made up specifically of students, but success on the field was still a long time coming. Between 1902 and 1926, the university produced not one winning team, going a combined 19-58-8 in 11 seasons (there were no teams between 1904-1912 and 1915-1919).

Probably the most interesting player in the time period was a quarterback in 1920 by the name of Art Rooney. In describing his play in a 35-0 win against Muskingum, the *Duquesne Monthly* magazine described his performance this way. "Stellar plays predominated, but none of the spectacular flashes counted for more efficiencies than the all-around work of Art Rooney, the resourceful little quarterback for the victorious eleven."

The losing would come to an end in 1927 when the great Elmer Layden, the former member of the four horseman at Notre Dame, took over and led the school into the upper echelon of college football.

The High Life

When Layden took over as head coach in 1927, the fortunes on the gridiron for the Dukes changed hands almost instantaneously. The lovable losers were now transformed into an overnight success story.

Following his 4-4-1 inaugural campaign, Layden led the Dukes to an 8-1 mark in 1928 under the direction of halfback and future Duquesne Hall of Fame member Ganzy Benedict. The season would mark the school's first steps into major college football when a Benedict to Joe Guerrier pass connected as time ran out to give the Dukes an upset win in their first victory against a major opponent, Washington & Jefferson, 12-6. The victory was more meaningful as W & J hadn't lost on their home turf since 1917.

The next year, future coach Buff Donelli quarterbacked Duquesne to the school's first undefeated campaign. The only blemish in the otherwise perfect season was a 7-7 tie against West Virginia. Probably the highlight of the 9-0-1 campaign was a 27-7 win against Geneva College that was the first football night game ever played in the Steel City. The school had printed up only 10,000 tickets in anticipation of what they thought would be a big crowd. Little could they have predicted that the final count to stroll through the turnstiles was an unbelievable (for the time) 27,000 fans. The game had originally been set for November 2nd but was moved a day earlier to Friday night as the men from the Bluff crushed their opponents under the bright floodlights in Forbes Field.

As the winning continued, the powers that be at the school were scheduling tougher contests. In 1931, Duquesne made their first foray into postseason football playing nearby Carnegie Tech in a game that would benefit the local unemployed. A crowd of 42,359 showed up at Pitt Stadium, raising $30,000 for the relief fund, and they were greeted with a hard-fought, scoreless tie. Tech went into the game as a prohibitive favorite, but the Duquesne defense was more than up to the challenge. The Tartans threatened on a few attempts, twice early in the game when they ventured as close as the Duquesne 21-yard line before tuning the ball over on downs and once late in the contest when they moved to the Duke's three following a fumble recovery on the 26. A Carnegie Tech halfback by the name of George Kavel carried the ball on the next play and was crushed by a Dukes' tackler, causing him to fumble. The ball went through the end zone, Duquesne got it back at the 20-yard line, and their scoreless tie against the more powerful Carnegie Tech club was preserved.

The following season, Duquesne would add another power to their schedule, the nationally ranked University of Pittsburgh Panthers, beginning one of the most bitterly fought rivalries in Western Pennsylvania history. While Pitt crushed them 33-0 in 1932, the next season things got a whole lot closer.

Duquesne started out the 1933 season 8-0 before facing their new rivals at Pitt Stadium. 60,000 were there braving a sleet storm as the Panthers' Izzy Weinstock shot in from nine yards out in the third quarter for the game's only score in a 7-0 loss.

The defeat proved to be the only blemish on an otherwise perfect year as the school finished out its 9-1 campaign with a convincing 26-0 victory against Geneva. As a reward for perhaps its finest season ever, Duquesne was invited to play Miami (FL) in a postseason contest called the Festival of Palms Bowl, a game that a couple years later would be more commonly referred to as the Orange Bowl. Playing what was a home game, the Hurricanes from Miami were not prepared for the onslaught they would receive by Layden and his boys.

Miami, who was undefeated going into the game, held Duquesne to a scoreless tie as both teams went into the locker room at the half, not knowing the deluge that was to greet them in the next 30 minutes. Layden brought in a substitute halfback by the name of Ed Zaneski who bolted in for the Dukes' first two scores before Miami cut their lead to 13-7. It was at that point the future Saint Vincent coach Al DeLuca had a fourth quarter to remember. DeLuca threw a 22-yard scoring toss and then was on the other end of a 44-yard bomb to put the exclamation point on a 27-point fourth-quarter outburst in the 33-7 victory.

Layden quit after the season when his alma mater came calling and the former member of the four horsemen went back to Notre Dame to take over their football program. After Steeler coach Joe Bach led the Dukes to an 8-2 mark in 1934, Christy Flanagan took the controls of the program, continuing the school's winning ways posting a 6-3 mark in 1935 that included wins over Washington, West Virginia and Carnegie Tech. Flanagan chose to leave after one season as athletic director and coach entering the oil business with his father instead.

Losing three coaches in three seasons, the administration turned to John "Clipper" Smith, an assistant to Flanagan, former head coach of North Carolina State and third former Notre Dame player (Layden and Flanagan were the others) to try and keep the newfound winning tradition going.

Smith seemed to be the right man for the job as he led the Dukes on a 8-2 run that included their first victory ever against Pitt, 7-0, and a trip to the Orange Bowl where they defeated Mississippi State 13-12 (a more in-depth look on the 1936 season can be found in chapter 23, "The Greatest Day in Pittsburgh Collegiate Football History"). 1936 was the first year of the Associated Press Poll, with Duquesne finishing 14th in the country. The students were ecstatic about their nationally ranked team as this description from the *Duquesne Duke*, the school student newspaper, exclaimed. "The welcome celebration climaxed one of the most successful seasons in the athletic history of Duquesne. Loyal followers cheered wildly and sang the school songs as the train bearing the squad pulled into the train shed a few minutes late."

Unfortunately for the former Knute Rockne disciple, the Dukes could not continue their winning ways, going 10-10 over the next two seasons and turning over the mantle of the Duquesne football program to a former alumnus, Buff Donelli.

The incredible Steel City football rivalry was diminishing as new tougher academic standards were severely hurting the recruiting efforts of both Pitt and Carnegie Tech. Duquesne seemingly had a clear road to dominance of the Pittsburgh college football scene. Both Pitt and Duquesne entered their contest in 1939 unbeaten, with the Panthers the No.1 team in the nation. The Dukes emerged victorious 21-13 and went on to beat Texas Tech, North Carolina State and Carnegie Tech, before tying another undefeated team from Detroit in the season's final game 10-10. With an 8-0-1 mark, Duquesne cracked the top-ten poll in the Associated Press, finishing 10th.

After the season, head coach Jimmy Hagan from Pitt and Donelli met to discuss the future of the classic city series between the two. Unfortunately, the meeting ended with a final decision to end the series, with the Dukes winning the last ever game between the two schools.

Donelli was able to keep things going the following season, losing only to Mississippi 14-6 before their marquee season in 1941. During that year, Donelli also got the opportunity to coach the Steelers when Bert Bell stepped down. He did so on the agreement he could stay on the Bluff, too. Layden, who was NFL commissioner at the time, gave him an ultimatum to stay at Duquesne or coach the Steelers. Luckily for the Dukes, he chose the collegiate brand of football.

The 1941 season turned out to be special, as the Dukes were dominant from the beginning. They rolled over all eight opponents by a combined score of 141-21, finishing the campaign with Duke and Minnesota as the only undefeated teams in the land. Their impenetrable defense not only led the nation in scoring defense but rushing defense and total defense, too. Their efforts not only secured them a No.8 rating in the final Associated Press poll, but years later when the Massey computer rankings came into being, their calculation showed the Dukes to be the 1941 national champions.

With the Americans' participation in World War II imminent, the Dukes played one more season of varsity football in 1942 before disbanding for the duration of the war. The squad finished another fine campaign at 6-3-1 thus ending an outstanding streak where they were 71-22-2, a .762 winning percentage, between

1933 and 1942, the sixth best in the country. It would also be the end of Duquesne University as a potent force in major college football as the squad that represented the university for the four seasons after the war bore little resemblance to the powerhouse they had before.

The Low Road

While there were bad times in their first 11 years of existence and a time period between1984-1991 when they went 22-49-3 under Terry Russell and Dan McCann, probably the lowest point in the annals of Duquesne University football occurred after the end of World War II.

Before the start of the great conflict, coach Buff Donelli had Duquesne University among the elite of the collegiate football world, finishing undefeated and in the top ten in 1941. When the war came, the school decided to disband the sport until after the hostilities ended. When it came back, Donelli had left for the NFL and the good times had come to a screeching halt.

Kass Kovalcheck led the post-war Dukes into action in 1947 with decidedly different results. After victories over Geneva and Western Reserve to start the new era at 2-0, the floor fell from underneath them as they hit the meat of their schedule.

Seven consecutive losses to the likes of Alabama, Wake Forest, Maryland, and Clemson left the school limping into the next season. The same sequence happened a year later, beating West Virginia Wesleyan and Alliance College in their opening two games before losing their final seven.

With matching 2-7 campaigns, the powers that be called on Phil Ahwesh to turn the tide; he could not. Following a 3-6 season in '49, seven of the nine games in 1950 were on the road with Duquesne going to Chattanooga for the final game of the season sporting a 2-5-1 mark. A 32-20 thrashing by Chattanooga ended yet another disappointing campaign, and as it turned out, the end of Duquesne University as a major collegiate football program.

Not long after the defeat, school president Reverend Vernon F. Gallagher announced the school was giving up the program for the fourth time because of the impending Korean War and more importantly the financial bath the school was taking because of the team.

"In the view of the impending draft of young men into the

armed services and the history of Duquesne for the past four years, we feel it would not be practical for the school to continue fielding a team," Gallagher stated. He further went on to tell of the financial losses the school had endured with football and the loss of Ahwash to the program, who had been called to active duty in the Pennsylvania National Guard. "Prior to the national emergency we and Mr. Ahwesh had hoped he would be able to continue as head coach. Now it is apparent he will be on active duty for an indefinite period."

While promising the loss of varsity football would be short, "We do not contemplate a permanent abandonment of football nor do we plan to make Duquesne a 'basketball school'" (in reference to the Dukes nationally ranked basketball program at the time... my how things have changed) the loss was for all intents and purposes permanent. Football on the Bluff didn't return until 1969 and it did so at the club level, the lowest form of collegiate football.

Eventually the school returned to the NCAA in 1979 at the Division III level before going to I-AA Mid Major, which is non-scholarship, but the sport was never again played at the highest level as it had been before 1950.

Current state of affairs

After a 19-year hiatus, college football returned to the Bluff in 1969 at the club level, but the results were much the same, going 2-4 under new head coach Joe Nicoletti.

However, 1969 would turn out to be Nicoletti's lone season as Dan McCann came aboard the following campaign and immediately turned the Dukes into club football powers, becoming the No. 15 team in the country his first season before taking the club on a ride that saw them in the top 10 in 1972-1974. The pinnacle came in '73, when McCann led Duquesne to an undefeated 10-0 season that was capped with a national championship tilt against Mattatuck Community College at the Dukes' home field in the early '70s, Three Rivers Stadium. It was a close contest, but in the end Duquesne emerged victorious and captured the national championship 13-7.

Three more top 10 rankings, (1974, 1976, 1977), highlighted their short stay at the club level in the 70s. In 1979, the program would finally return to the NCAA, although not at the major college level as they had been accustomed to, but at Division III.

Not expecting much their first season, Duquesne surprised many people in their inaugural contest by thrashing Assumption College out of Worchester, MA, 38-0, in a game where running backs Ed Mantich and Bobby Roche combined for 172 first-half yards. It was the springboard to a very successful 5-4 mark in 1979.

Probably the highlight of the first few seasons of Division III ball was a game against Carnegie Mellon September 3rd, 1981. CMU had long been the local Division III power and this contest would be the barometer to see how far the Dukes had come. The game would be televised by WPXI-TV from Three Rivers Stadium and Duquesne would not disappoint, thumping their local rivals 27-10.

Unfortunately, however, with the win did not come prosperity. Dreams of NCAA playoffs were replaced with mediocre to bad football, as a 6-3 record in 1982 was the high-water mark for the program at this level between 1979-1992.

With not much momentum behind them, Duquesne was faced with a dilemma when the NCAA passed a rule that said if schools had a Division I basketball program, and wanted to play football, they had to do it at the Division I-A or I-AA level. Rather than once again give up football, they opted to compete in I-AA at the Mid Major or non-scholarship level. The administration at the school chose to add a former nose guard for the legendary Joe Paterno at Happy Valley to direct the ship—Greg Gattuso.

Gattuso would have the benefit of playing in a facility on campus for the first time since the days of Buff Donelli in 1929, as the school constructed a football stadium in the parking lot that stood between the Towers dormitory and Mellon Hall. They named their new stadium after their former quarterback Art Rooney. The Dukes lost to St. John's, 37-12, in their first game there. That first year at I-AA saw the Dukes win only four of ten games. It was at that point the losing stopped.

Success would soon follow the Dukes as they moved into a new conference in 1994, the Metro Atlantic Athletic Conference (MAAC). It was a big step for Duquesne that has paid big dividends. "We've gone through a lot of transitions here," Gattuso reflects. "From club football to the jump to Division III where we spent some time floundering around, and then finally Division I-AA, where we hired full time coaches and built the wonderful facility that we have on campus. There was a lot of money spent upgrading the program in the process, but it is a successful program now."

That first season in the MAAC saw the Dukes go 6-4 with the highlight being a nationally televised game on ESPN2 from Rooney Field on Halloween night where Duquesne defeated Iona 16-12. The campaign would turn out to be a precursor to their first MAAC Championship season.

After falling for the second consecutive season to local rival Robert Morris, 38-20, in the second game of the season, the Dukes rattled off eight wins in a row, capturing the MAAC crown and a spot in the ECAC Bowl, which was to be played at Rooney Field. The game would be against the successful I-AA team from Wagner. Duquesne would not only beat Wagner, but crush them 44-20 in a win that let Gattuso know his program had arrived. "I look back at the early teams," he says. "When we moved up from Division III, we patterned ourselves after Wagner College, who had successfully made the move a few years earlier than Duquesne. In 1993, they crushed us, in '94 they had a late kickoff return to beat us and in 1995, we played them in the ECAC bowl and beat them by a couple of touchdowns. That win showed that we turned the corner."

The game was a springboard for MAAC dominance, as the school reeled off 10 more victories in a row in 1996, bringing their

The Duquesne Dukes capture the sixth of their eight Metro Atlantic Athletic Conference titles won during former coach Greg Gattuso's tenure in 2002. (Courtesy of Duquesne Athletics.)

school-record winning streak to 19 before losing to Robert Morris once again, this time in the ECAC Bowl 28-26.

After a two-year mini slump, finishing second and third in the MAAC, the Dukes recaptured the crown in 1999 and have not let go, winning it each time between 1999-2004. As Duquesne kept winning, Brian Colleary, the schools' recently departed athletic director, continued to upgrade the schedule, dotting it with many teams from the Patriot League, an upper echelon I-AA scholarship conference. He even included the nationally ranked University of Pennsylvania squad from the Ivy League in 2003. Yet despite playing tougher opponents, the Dukes continue to win.

In 2002, the Dukes thrashed 11 consecutive opponents. That streak included upsets of Bucknell, Dayton and Lafayette. Going into the ECAC Classic against Albany, they were ranked 1st among Division I-AA Mid Major schools in the nation and even made the ESPN top 25 poll that included all I-AA schools, peaking at 21st. If they emerged victorious at Albany, they not only would win their first Mid Major national championship, but had a real shot to become the first Mid Major selected to participate in the I-AA playoffs. Weather and a fired-up Albany club prevented that with a humbling 24-0 defeat, but they went into 2003 with hopes of rectifying that loss.

Losing to Bucknell and Penn in the first three weeks of 2003, the Dukes took a 1-2 mark into LaSalle, where they came away with a 62-14 victory that set up the rest of the season. Duquesne proceeded to run undefeated through their MAAC portion of the schedule (a feat they have done 33 consecutive times, losing their last MAAC tilt in 1999, 62-50 to Iona) losing only to Morehead State 15-10 in the process. That brought the school to a season-ending game against their nemesis Robert Morris. Duquesne defeated the Colonials 33-28 to end the year and was to face Monmouth in a return to the ECAC Classic, this time back at the friendly confines of the Bluff.

The Dukes came away with a dramatic 12-10 win and, doubled with a Morehead State loss in their last game of the season, saw themselves crowned the unanimous Division I-AA Mid Major national champions. They followed their championship season with a fine 7-3 mark in 2004 that included victories over two Patriot League opponents and a No. 5 national ranking.

The program is at a level where Gattuso feels it can be competitive with anyone they play. "We have stepped up over the years and played a tough schedule; teams from the Patriot League and now Ivy League," he says. "People thought we would be crushed when we first started this, but we were competitive to start and now we have beaten some Patriot League schools. We are not afraid to over achieve and that's why we are successful."

With the success, Gattuso seems most proud of the fact the school is not considered just a basketball school any more. "We've converted a lot of basketball fans at Duquesne," he notes. "They now care about football, too. We are not only a one-sport school any more. I think we inspire other programs on campus to succeed. I take a lot of pride in that."

While the Dukes may be considering taking their football juggernaut to the higher levels of Division I-AA football, they have committed to nothing at this point. Colleary says simply about a move up, "Not at this time but we continue to evaluate each level of 1-AA football."

According to the former Dukes athletic director, there are also plans in the works to upgrade Rooney Field although there is no date for the renovations yet. "There are preliminary plans to renovate Rooney Field, it is one component of the University's 10-year plan. No timetable has been set."

Through it all, after half a century of trying to field a successful football program, the coach seems satisfied where the team has eventually come. "The school has had an incredible past in football and I'm proud to be part of it. There had been a spread of 60 years between bowl games and now we've gone to five in the past nine years"

With perhaps an eventual move up the Division I-AA level in the future, the Dukes will have to move on without Gattuso, who took a position in spring 2005 at Pitt as a recruiting coordinator and tight end coach.

The greatest coach

In the long history of football on the Bluff, there are many fine coaches who have walked the sideline. Dan McCann, the second winningest coach of all time with 91 wins who revived the program twice, first as a national club team power, then bringing it back into the NCAA fold for the first time in 29 years in 1979, and Clipper Smith, who guided the Dukes to the 1937 Orange Bowl come to mind. When talking about the best though, the talk begins and ends with Greg Gattuso, Elmer Layden and Buff Donelli.

Gattuso recently guided Duquesne to the 2003 NCAA Division I-AA Mid Major national championship. After beating Georgetown 45-7 the third week of the 2004 campaign he became the all-time leader in wins with 92. The former Nittany Lion has enjoyed ample success in his 12 seasons, going a spectacular 97-32 through the '04 campaign that's included eight MAAC titles and two ECAC Classic championships to boot.

While proud of his accomplishments, Gattuso gives the former record holder McCann his due for building the program that flourishes today. "You really never break a record set by a man like Dan McCann. He took over a program that was in a lot different condition than it was when I started. To win 91 games under those circumstances was quite an accomplishment. It really isn't fair to compare. In my mind, Dan is still 'the Man' at Duquesne."

He also credits a good part of his success to the support he receives from the folks on the Bluff. "I'm a big believer that everybody has been a part of the success, from the coaches to the administration, who has committed to us not only financially, but with their support. With all this, ultimately we have gotten great kids to play here throughout the years."

In the Division I glory years there was Elmer Layden, one of the famous Four Horsemen at Notre Dame. Layden first put Duquesne on the map with a 48-16-6 record that included a victory in the 1933 Festival of Palms. After a successful seven-year run, Layden left the school to take over the program at his alma mater.

While Gattuso and Layden certainly can be proud of their accomplishments, Donelli gets the nod as the best coach ever at Duquesne. Originally the captain of the Dukes' first undefeated team in 1929, Buff, who picked up the nickname for his fascination with "Buffalo" Bill Cody became, oddly enough, one of the greatest male soccer players ever to don the Stars and Stripes for this country. Donelli was passed over for the memorable 1930 World Cup team that finished third, but became a star for the USA club four years later.

In a qualification match before the '34 cup, Buff scored all four goals in a victory against Mexico that propelled them into

Duquesne honors its departed coach Elmer Layden in 1934 after his alma mater Notre Dame called to have him take over their legendary program. (Courtesy of Duquesne Athletics.)

the tournament. He then had the only goal in the country's lone World Cup match that year, a 7-1 shellacking at the hands of Italy. For his efforts he was named to the U.S. Soccer Hall of Fame in 1954.

As strong as he was on the soccer field, he was that and more on the Bluff. Coming back to lead his alma mater after Smith, Buff took the school to heights never before seen, going 29-4-2. During his tenure he twice led Duquesne to undefeated seasons. His Dukes finished 10th and 8th respectively in the 1939 and 1941 Associated Press final polls. In retrospect, his 1941 team was named national champion by a computer ranking system called the Massey ratings, which works along the same lines as several of the Bowl Championship Series (BCS) computer polls. After the a stint in the pros, Donelli returned to the college game after the war where he directed Boston University to a 46-34-4 record in 10 seasons that included a No. 16 ranking in the 1951 Associated Press poll. He ended his coaching career leading the Columbia Lions to a very rare Ivy League championship in 1961.

Notable players

In the golden era of Duquesne football, the first half of the 20th century, probably the most notable player was center Mike Basrak. Basrak was a powerful blocker and became probably the school's greatest player, being named as its first, and only, consensus Division I All-American in 1936. He had the honor of not only being the first player ever from the Bluff to be drafted by an NFL team, but was chosen in the first round, fifth overall, by the Steelers.

Other players to lead the Dukes to prominence in the Division I days were Donelli, who was captain of Duquesne's first undefeated team in 1929, and. Nick DeCarbo and Ray Kemp, the first two Duke players to play in the NFL in 1933. Also on the list are John Rokisky, an end who was a Walter Camp All-American in 1941; Boyd Brumbaugh, the highest Duquesne player ever to be drafted (first round, third overall, by the Brooklyn Dodgers in 1938); Ralph Longmore, the last man from Duquesne to be drafted (in 1951, by the New York Yanks in the 19th round); and finally Al Demao, who played with the Redskins for nine seasons before ending his career in 1953. Demao was the last Duke to play in the NFL until Leigh Bodden. While Basrak might have been the greatest Duquesne player ever, Demao made the biggest impact in the NFL, being named one of the 70 greatest Redskins of all-time in 2002.

From the modern Dukes there was Pedro Bowman, the fireplug who ran for 3,830 yards in the early Division III days; Donte Small who broke his school record 17 years later with 4,260; the current quarterback Niel Loebig, who holds the school's passing yards record and became only the fifth Division I-AA quarterback and 21st overall in NCAA history to surpass 10,000 yards and 100 touchdowns in a career; Mike Hilliard, the school's third all-time leading rusher and first-team Academic All-American in 2003; and Dave Loya, the first great quarterback in the current I-AA Mid Major dynasty.

As great as those players have been, there are three names that come to mind when Gattuso thinks of Dukes who have made the biggest impact during his tenure.

First there was Tony Zimmerman, the blue-chip recruit who transferred from Pitt after a disappointing career. "Nobody was a bigger influence than Tony Zimmerman. Coming to Duquesne from Pitt, he legitimized our program. Tony was very heavily recruited out of high school and when he left Pitt, a lot of scholarship schools were recruiting him but we got him. He helped us beat some teams that we couldn't have beaten in the past." Zimmerman passed for 7,313 yards, breaking Loya's all-time record (his record was later broken by Loebig). He eventually became a star quarterback in the Arena Football's developmental league (AF2), where he was the 2003 Offensive Player of the Year, setting the league all-time mark with 93 touchdown passes. Last year he signed on in the Arena League as a backup with the Indiana Firebirds.

Gattuso's second pick was linebacker Trent Wisner. "Trent Wisner, who was a linebacker, was a talented freshman recruit who slipped through the cracks and came here. Getting him helped convince other recruits they could play here."

Finally, there was Leigh Bodden, probably the greatest player at the Bluff in the past 50 years. Bodden, a defensive back, was a two-time Division I-AA first team All-American and became the first Dukes' player to reach the NFL since Demao made the Cleveland Browns roster as a free agent. "Leigh Bodden is the greatest athlete to play football here," says Gattuso. "He made the Cleveland Browns last

Once considered the next coming of Dan Marino at Pitt, quarterback Tony Zimmerman took his disappointing career down Forbes Avenue to Duquesne, becoming perhaps the greatest signal caller the school ever produced. (Courtesy of Duquesne Athletics.)

year and gave us credibility that players could come here and succeed at the next level." Bodden grabbed 28 interceptions in his Duquesne career, 13 more than Dave Pucka, who is second on the list. Leigh was one of only two Duquesne alums to play in the NFL in 2003 along with fullback Josh Rue, who was with Arizona.

All-time record

285-226-18 (NCAA Varsity seasons only)

340-251-19 (including club football seasons 1969-1978)

Championships

Metro Atlantic Athletic Conference Championships: 1995, 1996, 1999, 2000, 2001, 2002, 2003, 2004.

ECAC Classic Champions: 1995, 2003

Festival of Palms Champions: 1933

Orange Bowl Champions: 1936

NCAA Division I Final Season Rankings (Associated Press poll): 14th-1936, 10th-1939, 8th-1941

Collegiate Club Football National Champions: 1973

NCAA Division I-AA Mid Major National Champions: 2003

NCAA Division I National Champions: 1941 (by the Massey ratings)

THIRTY ONE

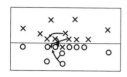

No Ordinary Joe

Former NFL and Pitt legend Joe Walton is the only football coach Robert Morris University has ever known. He has led the Colonials to two NCAA Division I-AA Mid Major national championships. (Courtesy of Robert Morris University.)

Joe Walton is taking a break from getting ready for his team's match-up against a tough rival. When Walton was coaching the New York Jets, the Buffalo Bills might have been such an opponent. That was in the '80s. In 2004, the game he's preparing for pits his Robert Morris University Colonials against the Duquesne University Dukes. On the line is small-college-power bragging rights in Western Pennsylvania.

Assistant head coach Dan Radakovich comes into the office lamenting the state of the practice field. "Did you ever play football in a rice paddy?" he asks Walton. "We're not practicing outside today."

"I bet the field's dry at Duquesne," Walton counters with a half a smile. Even when it's dry, Robert Morris' field offers a challenge. It's only 80-yards long. A temporary issue, and one that Walton has been able to overcome in his 11 years at the school. Away from the bright lights of the NFL, Walton has become a beacon at Robert Morris University, the NCAA Division I-AA school. He's the only coach the Colonials have ever known, building the program from scratch 11 years ago.

Walton had built a reputation as a teacher in the NFL. As a quarterbacks coach for the Washington Redskins, he tutored a raw Joe Theismann, turning him into a polished All-Pro. As head coach of the New York Jets, he brought two other signal callers along—Richard Todd and Ken O'Brien—both of whom had productive careers. His last stop on the NFL tour was with the Steelers, where his two-year stint as offensive coordinator ended sourly and abruptly. With young and immature quarterback Bubby Brister unable to grasp the nuances of the offense (but then again Brister couldn't grasp the meaning of the word nuance), Walton was shown the door as part of the coaching regime change from Chuck Noll to Bill Cowher. But such is the life of a professional coach. They're hired to be fired.

Contrast that with his position now at Robert Morris. You can't imagine a scenario where it would end that way. Walton has the job as long as he wants it. And at the collegiate level, he's able to continue his approach that coaching is, in essence, teaching, although there's a little different wrinkle to it. Now Walton is working with student athletes at a level where that phrase still means something. Unlike teams at the NCAA's Division I, Walton's players are students first, athletes second. And they're pretty good students, he's proud to report. Of the 105 students in the program, 101 had grade points above 2.0, with the majority logging 3.0 and better. And then there's the effect that the program has had on Robert Morris beyond football. It's put a name on the campus. While many small colleges—and even larger ones, for that matter—are cutting back on the number of varsity sports, Robert Morris is expanding. Division I ice hockey dropped the puck for the first time in 2004. There's even talk of adding a baseball program. Then there is the biggest sign of all, a brand new, on-campus football field set to open in 2005. It will initially hold 3,000, with the potential to expand to 10,000. And, appropriately, it will be named Joe Walton Stadium.

"This is probably the most meaningful job in football I've ever had," Walton says, sitting behind the desk of his office in Jefferson Hall on the Robert Morris campus. Looking tanned and fit beyond his 68 years—a slight limp notwithstanding—he beams when talking about small college football life.

Following his departure from the Steelers in 1991, Walton found himself out of football for the first time in more than 20 years. "I didn't want to get back in [the NFL], because I thought, 'been there, done that.' So, I took my coach's retirement. I'd been in the moving business, and I did some work there, and I played a lot of golf."

But he missed football. Moreover, he missed teaching football. He also liked being home, just over the hill from his native Beaver Falls. So it would seem his options were somewhat limited. A friend who was a member of the Robert Morris board of trustees called and suggested that Walton meet with Dr. Edward Nicholson, the school's president. "I had actually started thinking about small college football, when the call came, so the timing was good."

RMU was without a program, and Nicholson wanted to start football as something to add to the campus life. For Walton, who had no previous college coaching experience, it was an intriguing proposition.

"Three things really got me interested," Walton explains. "One, it was close to home. Two, I had never coached college before, so it was something new and different from the NFL. And three, it was a helluva challenge, building this from the ground up."

Armed with a small budget and a one-year timetable to set things up, Walton decided to add "architect" to his list of skills. Early on he placed a call to a former staffer and coaching buddy from Walton's New York Jet days who, like Walton, had lost an NFL job. Radakovich had a similarly strong coaching pedigree. He had been with a number of NFL teams, including the Steelers (1974-77) and was looking for a new challenge.

"Rad came to see me at the old office, if you could call it that, in the Sewell Center," Walton smiles, and then, as if on cue, Radakovich comes into the office. "No windows, just a desk and a phone," Radakovich chimes in.

Walton continues, "He looks at me and says, '*This* is your office?' So we talk for a while and he's getting interested, and he says, 'Let's go look at the locker room and the field,' and I look at him and say, 'We don't have any.'"

"I said, 'I'll see you,'" laughs Radakovich, almost as if it's an act that the two have rehearsed and performed many times.

But Radakovich was hooked and became Walton's first hire, serving as assistant head coach and defensive coordinator. The two had a lot to get done to get a program up in running for the 1994 season. It was truly building from scratch—with every aspect from the most minute detail to be established. It was a blank sheet of paper from which to start. The football architects headed out on a series of road trips, visiting other small college programs at Slippery Rock, Bethany, and Duquesne.

"I wanted to get a feel for the atmosphere," Walton says. "And we checked facilities to see what the others had. One of the things we came away with was that everything seemed kind of small, so we decided that we would try to make things a little bigger—a bigger locker room, more office space, that sort of thing. We had to convince the school into giving us the office space we have now, and we were able to cut down on the costs by doing a lot of the work ourselves."

Welcome to the college world. In the NFL, those kinds of cost concerns don't come into play. Neither does fundraising, which Walton tackled by setting up charity golf outings for which he tapped his friends in professional football—coaches and players—to get together to benefit the program. Among those teeing off at the Beaver Valley Country Club were Franco Harris, Joe Namath, Jack Ham and Theismann. It's grown into an annual fundraising event.

And in the NFL there are equipment managers. For a new

college team just starting out, that isn't the case. Walton had to take charge of securing equipment, and for that he turned to another of his NFL associates—former Steelers' equipment manager Tony Parisi. "He was a huge help," Walton says. "Take helmets, for instance. He taught me how to pick them out, introduced me to the vendors and helped get the best prices."

The school worked out a deal to play the RMU games at nearby Moon High School. However, the squad would not be able to practice there. That's when the 80-yard field came into play. The former softball field is the weekday home for the Colonials, the place where Walton, Radakovich and the rest of the coaches were set to kickoff the new football program in August 1994. There was another small snag, however. The school had budgeted for 60 players on that initial team. But the excitement level for the program lured 159 kids to show up. "I said to Rad, 'We're going to need more equipment,'" Walton smiles. "Thankfully, the president was just as excited as we were, so we were able to go out and buy the things we needed."

Camp was a short two and a half weeks before the Colonials would kickoff their inaugural season. The team loaded up the buses and traveled to Waynesburg for the opener, and the football nerves were back for Walton. An improbable last-minute goal line stand allowed Robert Morris to leave with a 24-19 victory. "Maybe the best victory I ever had as a coach," Walton says. "To come out, fresh out of camp, with a new program and get a win like that... amazing." So too was the rest of that season, culminating in a 7-1-1 record.

"One of the things we sold about this place is that you're going to learn all things about football," says Walton. "We use NFL blocking schemes, Rad does the same thing on the defense—it's all NFL schemes."

The players have responded well. The Colonials have claimed five Northeast Conference titles and a pair of national mid-major crowns. They've also placed two players on NFL rosters—Tim Hall, the running back with the Oakland Raiders who was killed in a tragic drive-by shooting, and Hank Fraley, a free agent center who was cut by the Steelers and is now a fixture on the offensive line of the Philadelphia Eagles. Rob Butler, a defensive back/wide receiver, made the Chargers' taxi squad. Not a bad decade's work. But that success has its roots in the

NFL. Following his collegiate days as a two-time All-American at the University of Pittsburgh, Walton spent seven years as an NFL player, first as a Washington Redskin in 1957, before coaching.

It was in D.C. where he met his wife, Ginger, a former Miss Washington, D.C. After four years, he moved to the New York Giants. He was an end on a pretty good Giants team, along with such names as Andy Robustelli, Y.A. Tittle and Pat Sumerall, that played in three NFL championship games. After spending more time in the moving business, Walton returned to the NFL as a coach, first working with the Giants as wide receivers coach (1969-73). Then it was on to the Washington Redskins (first as running backs coach '74-'77; then as offensive coordinator '78-'80). While with the Redskins, Walton learned from one of the most successful coaches of all time, George Allen. "He never had a losing record at any level," Walton says of his mentor. (Interestingly, Allen ended his coaching career by taking a path much like his protégé. Allen came back to resurrect a Long Beach State football program that hadn't won in years and led them to a winning record.)

From Washington, it was back to the bright lights of New York, this time as a member of the Jets' coaching staff. After two years ('81-'82), he was promoted from offensive coordinator of the Jets to head coach ('83-'89). But Walton was under the microscope in New York, the media capital. The fact that the Jets hadn't won a championship since the greatest upset in league history, Super Bowl III, only added to the pressure.

His '86 Jets came within an overtime field goal of advancing to the conference championship game. "We had a lot of injuries that year," he recalls, "but we still came pretty close."

After being fired by the Jets, Walton joined Noll's last Steelers staff as offensive coordinator. Unfortunately, the offense never gelled, despite his proven success in moving the ball while with the Jets.

So if the Brister-led Steelers had trouble with his offense, what changes did he make in coaching college students? "You have to concentrate more on teaching good fundamentals," Walton says. "We're teaching them a lot of the same things and plays that I used to use in the pros. The difference is that you have to spend more time on drills and teach them how to play the position. The pros usually come in with that knowledge."

He also says his approach at Robert Morris wouldn't be that

much different if he coached at the Division I level. "The players here aren't as big or as fast, but their minds are the same," he says. "It's the same challenges. They're learning football at a very high level."

It's a strong brand of football played in the Northeast conference, he adds. "It's funny that there's this perception that NFL coaches are smarter than any other coaches, and that's not necessarily true," Walton continues. "We've got some good coaches here [Division I-AA Mid Major] like Greg Gattuso [Duquesne], Bob Ford [Albany] and Kevin Callahan [Monmouth]. If you don't make sure you have everything covered, you're going to get beat. That's no different here than it is in the NFL, believe me."

One thing that is different, however, is the time requirements. That's a big plus for giving up the NFL lifestyle. "In the pros, you have the players all day for meetings and practice, so if you're going to be doing your game planning, you need to do it at night when the players are gone," he explains. "Here, we get in around 9 and get the players from about 3:30-6:00, and then it's time to go home for dinner." That leaves more time for being with his three children and six grandchildren.

Walton also enjoys the relationships that he's developed with his college players. It's a different dynamic. "You get to meet kids' families and get them involved," he says. "You talk to the kids about a lot of things like girlfriends or grandparents being sick, and you get involved with their lives. It's a nice feeling."

Part of the job also entails enforcing academic requirements. "In the early years, we had some Prop 48 students, but we don't do that anymore," Walton says. "Hank Fraley was one, but he ended up leaving here a 2.8 student. We've got a lot of great students here, and I'm very proud of that."

Walton also takes pride in developing coaches. With three full-time coaches, Walton depends on part-time coaches and graduate students to round out his "staff." The part-timers tend to be coaches looking to land a job as a head coach in the high school level or to break into college coaching. "We do have a lot of turnover," he admits, "but these guys have done well since leaving here. We have one who is an assistant AD at Michigan, another, Jeff Beltz, who is coaching at Beaver, and one of our film guys is at ESPN."

The lack of outdoor practice turned out to not have an effect. The Colonials manhandled the

Dukes, who came into the game as the No.1-ranked team in the NCAA Division I-AA Mid Major division, 34-14. And the game wasn't even that close. Robert Morris quarterback Drew Geyer took control of the Walton offense and riddled Duquesne for 302 yards and two touchdowns.

It's a satisfying win, with Robert Morris winning the crown of best local small college team. And that future can only be brighter with the opening of Joe Walton Stadium. The on-campus venue will feature artificial turf, new offices for the coaching staff and workout facilities for the players. "It's going to be a big help in recruiting," says Walton. "There's no question about it." And that's not limited to football. The growth of the university coincides with the launching of the football program.

"When we got here, the dorms were about 50 percent full," says Walton. "It was basically a commuter school. But now we're having to build more dorms. And we've grown from being known just as a business school—there's a new engineering program. It's a great atmosphere."

At age 68 and with John Banaszak, the former Washington & Jefferson coach on his staff as a possible successor, it's natural to wonder how long Walton will remain a coach for Robert Morris. "John's a helluva coach," Walton says. "He had some interviews at Eastern Michigan, but it didn't work out. We're lucky to have him."

As for how long he'll coach, Walton's a bit cryptic. "Hell," he says. "Compared to Joe Paterno, I'm still a young man."

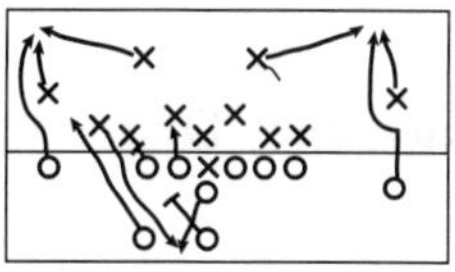

THIRTY TWO

How to Build a Powerhouse in One Easy Step: the History of Robert Morris University Football

When Robert Morris College (now University) decided to start a varsity football program on the Division I-AA non-scholarship ranks, it wanted to do so with a bang. The administration sought out to not only hire a coach, but to grab a local legend, Joe Walton.

Success was expected eventually, but not immediately. Within six years, the Colonials had success beyond their widest dreams, capturing back-to-back titles. No one could have imagined building a powerhouse could be done in one easy step, the one they took when they brought Walton on board. Here's the story of the Colonials rapid rise in college football.

Beginning

For Robert Morris, in 1993, it was time to take their athletic program to another level, and football seemed like the perfect sport to take it there. According to Jim

Duzyk, the Robert Morris sports information director, "We began things in 1994. Actually, the whole athletic department had a huge expansion since 1990. We had so much success since we took our program to a Division I level and adding football was a natural."

It began with a fortuitous friendship on July 27, 1993, and quickly turned into a success story as the school hired Joe Walton to direct its new varsity sport, football at the newly created Division I-AA Mid Major level (for schools that don't give scholarships).

Duzyk remembers, "Joe Walton was friends with one of the members of the board of trustees and (this friend) called Joe and asked him to apply. Joe didn't seem like he wanted to get back in the NFL so he applied and it was a big win for our program getting such a big name." It was a big win indeed.

Walton, who was considered an offensive innovator in the NFL, brought that philosophy to his new job and the results were immediate and astounding.

Not knowing what to expect, the Colonials surprised Waynesburg in the opener of the '94 campaign 24-19 and kept it going, reeling off five successive wins, the most impressive a 28-6 shellacking of the team that would become their most bitter rival in Division I-AA Mid Major, Duquesne University. The win against the Dukes turned out to be the one that put the program on the map. "We knew we had something special when we beat Duquesne in 1994," says Duzyk. "We were both undefeated when they came here to play and we knocked them off. When you beat a school that has enjoyed such success, especially one at our level, it was a big moment. After that we proved we couldn't be taken lightly."

More important than the 7-1-1 mark they would fashion that season was the fact Walton had recruited their first genuine superstar, Tim Hall. Hall ripped through opposing defenses to the tune of 1,336 yards in '94, including a school-record 278 yards against Bethany.

The 1994 campaign was the groundwork for the phenomenal decade the team was about to embark on. While surprising, in retrospect, Duzyk found reasons why they succeeded so early. "It was a shock to win so quickly, but Walton has helped that process. He talks of how important team chemistry is and then he points the kids in the right direction. It also helps that he has been able to recruit such great players as Tim Hall."

The High Life

With all their success in the Northeastern conference (NEC) since first joining in 1996 (winning titles five in a row between 1996 and 2000) probably their two best campaigns were in 1999 and 2000, when Robert Morris captured two NCAA Division I-AA Mid Major national championships.

It all started in 1999, coming off their first sub .500 season and losing two of their first three games. It was at that point Walton and quarterback Tim Levcik put things all together and won the last eight games of the season.

Levcik was awesome, completing 56 percent of his passes for 14 touchdowns and a 182.6 passer rating that saw him named the NEC's Newcomer of the Year.

Probably their two most memorable wins of the season came at Albany, winning 30-20 while ascending to the No.1 ranking for the first time in school history and finishing with a 51-19 drubbing at Stony Brook, where Walton and his club could officially celebrate the National Championship.

As the 21st century came into play, the Colonials were defending their first national crown. They started off in fine fashion, beating Buffalo State 30-20, a game where kicker Jeff Carlo hit a school record 55-yard field goal.

The wins kept coming as Levcik and a running back with a legendary Pittsburgh name, Sam Dorsett, led a devastating offense to a perfect 10-0 mark. While Levecik threw for 1,925 yards, Dorsett led a well-balanced offensive attack on the ground with 1,219 yards.

On the way to their school-record 10 wins were

Robert Morris' first feature running back turned out to be their best ever as Tim Hall rushed for 2,908 yards in two seasons. (Courtesy of Robert Morris University.)

victories against Division powers Dayton and St. John's, along with a thrilling contest at Wagner. That day, RMU was down by 14 points with only 14:09 left in the game. They fought back to tie it and won 38-31 in overtime, the school's first venture in OT, on a Nick Daniel six-yard run.

For their incredible undefeated season the Colonials were rewarded with a second consecutive NCAA Division I-AA Mid Major national championship.

Other than those two memorable championship seasons, probably the best moments in school history were their two consecutive ECAC Bowl titles, 28-26 against Duquesne in 1996, and 35-13 versus Georgetown the following season.

The Low Road

This would have to be their two sub .500 seasons. Despite finishing 4-6 in 1998, Robert Morris went 4-1 in the NEC, capturing a piece of the championship with Monmouth.

In 2002 they weren't so lucky, as the 3-7 record marked the low point in RMU football history.

Current State of Affairs

The Colonials rebounded with a 6-4 mark in 2003 before falling to 6-5 in 2004. Despite two mediocre seasons, the future seems extremely bright. According to Duzyk, there are no plans to move up a notch to Division I-AA scholarship football, although he sees a boost to the program when the team moves into their first on-campus facility in 2005. "The new stadium we are building, Joe Walton Stadium, will be a big boost in recruiting," Duzyk says. "It will be great to have an on-campus stadium instead of playing in a high school one, although Moon Stadium is an outstanding facility."

Building a new stadium is another step in the success of their program, success that came in such a remarkably short time. Duzyk puts in all into perspective. "We've won five Northeastern conference titles, won two ECAC Bowls and two Mid Major national championships in 1999 and 2000. Add it all up and even though we've slipped a little over the past couple years, it impresses a kid when they see all that we've accomplished in only 10 years and they want to come here and be a part of it."

The Greatest Coach

There is a simple answer to this question as there has only been one man to stroll the sidelines for Robert Morris, former

Pitt and NFL great, Joe Walton. (See Chapter 31, "No Ordinary Joe.")

In Walton they got a coach with impressive credentials: seven years the head coach of the New York Jets in the 1980s, twice leading them to the playoffs. A memorable offensive coordinator with the Pittsburgh Steelers as well as with the Jets and Washington Redskins, Walton came aboard in 1994 and never looked back, leading Robert Morris to the status of Division I-AA Mid Major Power, a title it enjoys a decade later.

Notable Players

Probably the greatest player in Robert Morris history was also its saddest tale. Running back Tim Hall was a star from the get-go, rushing for 2,908 yards in his short, two-year career, the first two seasons in the program's history.

He would go on to be a sixth-round draft pick of the Oakland Raiders in 1996, leading the club with a 5.7-yards per carry average in 1997, and second on the team in rushing to Napoleon Kaufmann.

Robert Morris celebrates on bitter rival Duquesne University's home turf as they defeated the Dukes in the 1996 ECAC Classic. (Courtesy of Robert Morris University.)

Unfortunately, while in his hometown of Kansas City, Missouri, on September 30, 1998, Hall was shot and killed instantly by a drive-by shooter.

Duzyk remembers him fondly. "Tim Hall is the face of the program, by what he did in terms of rushing for so many yards in only two years and the playing in the NFL," he says. There is now a Tim Hall scholarship that is awarded annually at RMU in memory of their fallen hero.

Other notables include Hank Fraley, starting center for the Philadelphia Eagles.

"Hank Fraley has to be a big part of the program," Duzyk notes. "He was a center, a non-glamour position, but fought hard, made the Philadelphia Eagles and now he's a starter." The SID also points to Sam Dorsett, the school's all-time career leading rusher with 3,847 yards, as a huge, inspirational contributor. "Sam Dorsett was the all-time leading rusher at Robert Morris, although it took him four years to break the record Hall set in two. Dorsett was never the strongest or fastest player, but he worked very hard to get where he did. He blew out his knee in the opening game in 2002 against Buffalo State. He was a senior and didn't have to come back, but he worked hard, rehabbed his knee and came back in 2003 to set the record."

With everyone else, the greatest quarterback in school history, Tim Levcik should also be included on this list. Levcik led the club to both national championships, tossing a school-high 7,222 yards for 76 touchdowns, also an RMU record. A two-time NEC Offensive Player of the Year, Levcik went on to play with the Philadelphia Soul of the Arena Football League.

All-Time Record

73-37-1

Championships

Northeastern Conference Championships: 1996, 1997, 1998, 1999, 2000

ECAC Classic Championships: 1996, 1997

NCAA Division I-AA Mid-Major National Championships: 1999, 2000

THIRTY THREE

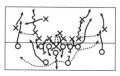

What's in a Name: the History of Slippery Rock University Football

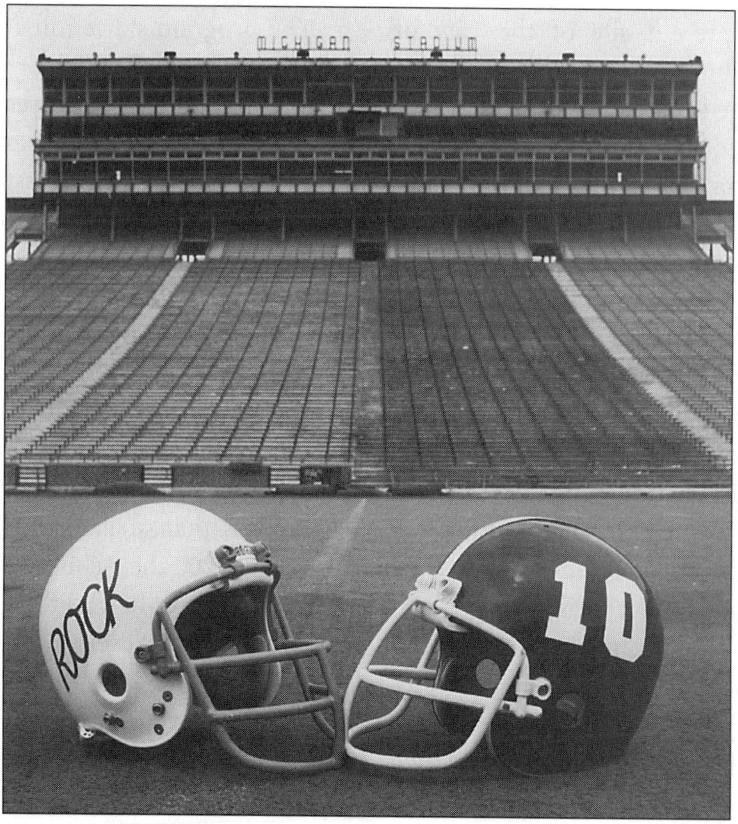

What's in a name? Because of Slippery Rock's unique name, fans at the House in Michigan would cheer wildly every time their score was announced at the 100,000-seat stadium. In 1979, the powers that be at the University of Michigan brought their adopted team to Michigan Stadium where Slippery Rock faced off against Shippensburg. More than 60,000 fans, a Division II record, saw the Rock lose 45-17. (Courtesy of Slippery Rock University Sports Information Department.)

What's in a name? For Slippery Rock University's football program, a name has meant everything. No one really has a concrete story as to where the unique name came from, but according to the team's 2004 media guide, the most popular tale goes like this: "In 1779, a certain Colonel Daniel Brodhead was in command of Fort Pitt at the present site of the City of Pittsburgh. Colonel Brodhead begged General George Washington to allow him to lead an expedition against the Seneca Indians, who were raiding settlements in the area. The troops encountered the Indians and were forced to flee for their lives. In the pursuit, the soldiers crossed a creek at a place where the stream bed was composed of large, smooth rocks. Wearing heavy boots, the soldiers were able to cross the creek safely, but the Senecas—wearing smooth moccasins—slipped and fell, which enabled the cavalry to make its escape. Historically, the Indians called the stream 'Wechachochapohka,' which means 'a slippery rock.' Since the location of the stream is in the heart of land once occupied by the Delawares, many believe the authenticity of this legend. Shortly after the Slippery Rock Creek was christened, the adjoining town also became known by the catchy name."

Great 18th century war stories aside, the unique name has given the school more opportunities on the football field than any other lower division college football program in the country.

Beginning

The program started in 1898, defeating New Castle High School in its only contest of the season 10-0. For the next seven seasons they competed unsuccessfully against local colleges and high schools mustering up a meager 9-17-5 mark.

A group of five coaches then came along—John Price, Harry Snyder, Emil Miller, Arthur Gant and Loyal Marshall—with much better success, although still against less-than-stellar competition. In 1920, the school hired N. Kerr Thompson, who took the school to the next level.

The High Life

Under Thompson's guidance, the school immediately became a power going 18-1 between 1923 and 1924, while winning the Pennsylvania State Championship the latter year over Shippensburg 39-21.

Colleges replaced high schools, some as good as Division I power Duquesne University, and winning became a habit. The victories weren't enough to make Slippery Rock a famous place—its unique name had something to do with it, too.

In 1936, the Rock went 6-3, including a 14-0 victory against Westminster. Why was that game so important? Because it was that victory, along with the strange-sounding name, that prompted a sportswriter to name them the 1936 national champions. The reasoning goes like this: Slippery Rock defeated Westminster, who defeated West Virginia Wesleyan, who beat Duquesne, who defeated Pitt, who won against Notre Dame, who beat Northwestern, who topped Minnesota, who was then named the Associated Press national champions.

It was done in jest, of course, but people loved the name. Because of it, Slippery Rock was invited to Fenway Park in Boston in 1937 to play Boston University. The Rock was thumped by Boston that day, 20-0, but it would become the first of many appearances in strange places over the years as college football fans all over the nation wanted a glimpse of the school with the strange name.

Success followed Thompson in 1939 with an undefeated season and his second state title before mediocrity ensued, sending the Rock to a 10-9-2 mark the next three seasons before the school suspended the program in 1943 and 1944 due to World War II.

The 1972 Slippery Rock Rockets celebrate winning the Pennsylvania State Athletic Conference championship. (Courtesy of Slippery Rock University Sports Information Department.)

After 20 seasons that were not exactly the most successful in school history, Charles Godlasky took over in 1959, returning the Rock to its winning ways. Godlasky took the Rockets to three successive Pennsylvania State Athletic Conference (PSAC) championship games between 1961 and 1963 winning the state title in 1962, 13-6 against East Stroudsburg State.

In '63, following a 36-6 loss to West Chester in the PSAC finals, the vaunted Slippery Rock name came to the forefront again as they were invited to face off against Northeast Oklahoma State in the All-Sports Bowl. 8,500 fans turned out in Oklahoma City to see the home school score 38 unanswered 4th quarter points en route to a 59-12 destruction of Slippery Rock.

The folks at the Rose Bowl came next, in 1964, calling on the sideshow that was Slippery Rock football to come out west to play California State in front of 15,000 fans at the famed venue. The team may have been a little jet-lagged. They were crushed by LA State 62-6.

The school fell on hard times again in the mid '60s until Bob DiSpirito came to the rescue.

The Low Road

When it comes to the successful Slippery Rock football program, the low point would have to be the 1950s. While the school did enjoy some success, Chester Stackhouse and William Meese resided over some of the worst teams in school history going 17-27-2 in a six-year period between 1953-1958.

Current State of Affairs

DiSpirito presided over losing teams in three of his first four campaigns as head coach, but the program took off both on the field and off in 1971. After winning the state title in 1972, the Rock was invited to play in the Knute Rockne Bowl. Back then, in lieu of a playoff system, the lower divisions played regional championships of which the Knute Rockne Bowl was the championship of the east. The game against Bridgeport was exciting all the way, with the Rockets pulling to within one 21-20 on a Tim Nunes to Ron Layton nine-yard touchdown pass. A two-point conversion put the Rock up by one. Bridgeport unfortunately scored a winning TD late in the game to eke out a 27-22 victory.

While winning the state championship again the following two seasons, Slippery Rock's star was growing nationionwide. Every school wanted to hear the Slippery Rock score announced at half time of their games. Beano Cook, famed sports announcer with ESPN says, "A presidential candidate in the New Hampshire primary would love to have the name recognition of Slippery Rock." Cary Walker of UCLA adds, "Slippery Rock is as much as part of the national folklore as the Land of Oz. But there are about as many people who know the whereabouts of Slippery Rock as there were Munchkins who befriended the Wicked Witch." Michigan sports information director Bruce Madej notes "They could be called America's Small College Team."

Even though their scores excite many, it's Michigan fans that have a special place in their hearts for the small Western Pennsylvania school. Their loyalty was so rabid

Coach George Mihalik's players give him a Gatorade shower following a Pennsylvania State Athletic Conference divisional championship. Mihalik led Slippery Rock to four consecutive divisional titles between 1997-2000. (Courtesy of Slippery Rock University Sports Information Department.)

that they invited Slippery Rock to the big house, the 100,000 seat Michigan Stadium, in 1979 to play Shippensburg. Why in the world would fans half a country away turn out to see a minor Division II tussle? Because it was the school with the strange name coming to play. What still stands as a national Division II record of 60,000 fans came, witnessing the Rock get crushed 45-17, but it didn't dull their enthusiasm. Two years later they went again with 30,000 people showing up to see them lose to Wayne State 14-13.

Dr. George Mihalik came aboard in 1988 and kept the program going, winning 111 games in 16 seasons, sending three consecutive teams to the NCAA Division II playoffs between 1997 and 1999, and going to the semifinals in '98 (a 47-21 loss to to Carson Newman).

As the winning continues, so does the mystique of Slippery Rock University. They were invited to play in the very last game at Tampa Stadium (against South Florida in 1998), before becoming Florida Atlantic's first opponent ever in 2001, playing at Miami's Joe Robbie Stadium. It's a tradition that goes on and on, born not only of winning, but by the strange name people seem drawn to.

The Greatest Coach

So far, 15 men have roamed the sidelines over the years as head coach of the Rock. But when it comes to talking about the best of all time, the list only includes three: N. Kerr Thompson, Bob DiSpirito and current boss Dr. George Mihalik. Thompson may have the honor of having the stadium named after him, along with more wins than any other coach. DiSpirito may have the field named after him as well as taking the Rockets to three state championships (as well as a spot in the NCAA Division III Eastern Championship). But the vote here goes to Mihalik.

Dr. Mihalik, who received his doctorate in safety management from West Virginia, has been associated with Slippery Rock football since 1970, when he was a quarterback on the three state-title teams in the early '70s.

He took over the program in 1988, winning 114 games (only 15 behind Thompson) and four PSAC Division titles to date. He also took the Rock to the NCAA Division II semifinals in 1998. Mihalik has five coach-of-the-year awards on his resume as well as election into both the Slippery Rock Hall of Fame and the Butler County Hall of Fame.

With Mihalik at the helm, success in Slippery Rock football should continue well into the future.

Notable Players

Perhaps the greatest player ever to don a Slippery Rock uniform was running back Chuck Sanders. Sanders rushed for 2,671 yards between 1983-1985, winning All-American honors his last two seasons. Sanders led Division II in rushing in 1984 and was talked about as a candidate for the Heisman Trophy in 1985.

Other notables are Greg Paterra and Randy McKavish, both finalists for the Harlon Hill Award, given to the Division II player of the year. Paterra finished 5th in 1988 while McKavish was 7th in 2000. Bob Schrantz and Greg Hopkins also make this list as they were each three time All-Americans.

All-Time Record

495-338-42

Championships

Pennsylvania State Athletic Conference Championships: 1924, 1939, 1962, 1972, 1973, 1974

Pennsylvania State Athletic Conference Divisional Championships: 1997, 1998, 1999, 2000

NCAA Division II Playoff Semifinal Appearances: 1998

NCAA Division III East Regional Championship Appearances (The Knute Rockne Bowl): 1972

Chuck Sanders (Courtesy of Slippery Rock University Sports Information Department.)

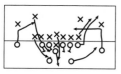

THIRTY FOUR

Coming Home: the History of Indiana University of Pennsylvania Football

Homecomings can make classic tales: Boy makes good. Boy comes home. Boy brings success with him. More often than not, however, homecomings are filled with unreal expectations and often lead to failure. Just ask Foge Fazio what it was like to come home again at Pitt.

Luckily for the Indiana University of Pennsylvania football program, the homecoming storyline is much better. In 1986, Frank Cignetti came back to coach at the school where he made his mark as a college football player.

While Cignetti has made IUP a Division II power, they have had much more success through the years.

Beginning

Even though the modern era of the program began in 1927, with IUP losing to Muskingum 6-0 before tallying their first win the next game against Saint Vincent 12-6, there is a connection between the school and the birthplace of professional football.

In 1895, the manager of the brand new Latrobe football club, Dave Berry, was looking for a quarterback to replace his starter, who had a prior commitment to play baseball on the same day they were to play their first game against nearby Jeannette. Berry had remembered seeing a 16-year-old quarterback, John Brallier, and paid him $10 plus expenses to play in the game. Until the 1960s, when an expense sheet proved Pudge Heffelfinger to be the first paid professional player of all time, it was believed this $10 payment made Brallier the first pro player ever.

Why is this story significant with IUP football? Because when Berry signed him, Brallier (even though in high school, he played at a time when eligibility restrictions were not at their tightest) was playing for Indiana Normal School, the precursor to Indiana University of Pennsylvania.

There was another famous alum for Indiana Normal who played with Brallier at the turn of the 20th century—none other than actor Jimmy Stewart's father.

The origins of the program actually began in 1890 with a 32-0 victory against Kiskiminetas. They would go undefeated their first two seasons (although that only encompassed four games) before succumbing to Western University of Pennsylvania (more commonly known as the University of Pittsburgh) in 1892, 8-6. While it would be unthinkable that IUP could ever defeat Pitt today, back in the 1890s that's exactly what did happen when Indiana Normal turned the trick 44-0 in 1894, the first of a successful (2-1-1) four-game series against the Panthers.

Playing a combination of high schools, colleges and the semi-professional club teams, perhaps Indiana Normal's biggest win of the decade was in 1895 when they crushed the famous Latrobe YMCA team 28-0.

In the early part of the 20th century, before the team entered the modern era in 1927, there were four notable undefeated teams. The first was in 1902 when they were 8-0-1, limiting the opposition to a mere 16 points while once again defeating Pitt 22-6. There was the team in 1912 that ran the table in all nine contests, before the 1915 version where the squad had only one blemish, tying the freshman Penn State club 0-0 in a 9-0-1 campaign.

The best of the group may have been the 1924 IUP football

team, winning all eight games under Coach Ruffner against the likes of Kent State, Saint Vincent, Grove City and Edinboro by the combined score of 289-6 (Conemaugh breaking the scoreboard in an opening season loss to IUP 7-6). It was two years later when George P. Miller took over as head coach, taking them to an 8-1 mark in 1926, leading them into the modern era of the program.

The High Life

Without a doubt, the football that is being played today at George P. Miller Stadium on the campus of IUP is truly the golden age of Indians football. Before that, they had two decent eras that certainly were successful.

In the nine seasons between 1934 and 1942, Miller led the club to a 44-17-5 mark that included two undefeated campaigns in 1934-1940. The second great run occurred between 1962 and 1975. It started with Chuck Mills guiding the Crimson and Silver to a 12-3-2 mark in '62 and '63 before a Pittsburgh legend, Chuck Klausing, took control. Klausing, who later took Carnegie Mellon to glory in the late '70s and early '80s, brought the school its first championships of any kind, capturing the Pennsylvania State Athletic Conference (PSAC) western division crown in his first two seasons, 1964 and 1965. Unfortunately, the team lost each time to East Stroudsburg in the PSAC Championship tilt.

The Indians would go 47-10-0 under the leadership of Klausing, who eventually was elected to the collegiate football Hall of Fame for his coaching prowess. His best season came in 1968, when his club went undefeated at 9-0 and was invited to play Delaware in the Boardwalk Bowl for the college division's Atlantic Coast championship.

IUP broke on top 21-10 at the half, but the Blue Hens fought back taking a 23-21 lead late in the contest. Klausing's troops would not be outdone, coming back on strength of a blocked punt and an 8-yard Wally Blacas to George Stark pass that set up Bob Tate's 33-yard field goal with less than a minute to go. Blacas, who didn't have the greatest game, 6 of 17 for 97 yards, hit the clutch pass when he needed to, the Stark completion as well as a 62-yard TD toss to future Steeler Dave Smith in the second period, gaving IUP the 21-10 half time advantage.

The Blue Hens dominated IUP this day, though, outgaining them 482-203, and came down the field quickly after the field goal, capping a 57 yard drive with a Tom DiMuzio to Ron Withelder pass at the 15 second mark for the 31-24 Delaware victory. The contest, which was played indoors at Atlantic City's Convention Hall, drew 9,849 fans.

Following an 8-1 mark in 1969, Klausing gave way to Bill Neal, who continued the winning ways into the mid '70s, highlighted by an 8-1 record in 1972 and a 8-1-1 one three years later.

The Low Road

There is no real drought era in IUP football history, although there were a couple of less-than-stellar seasons. The program had been discontinued during World War II in 1943 and 1944. When it came back, it was winless in two affairs in 1945 and suffered its worse season ever, 1-7, under Peck McKnight. A two-year stretch where the club was 4-11-2 in 1960 and 1961 were the only real down years in this highly successful program.

Current State of Affairs

When the administration made the decision to bring aboard Frank Cignetti, the former West Virginia University coach who replaced George Chaump in 1986, it proved to be one of the great moves in the annals of Division II football.

Cignetti, who was an NAIA All-American at the school in 1960, immediately took the program to places it had never seen before, the NCAA Division II playoffs, and took them there often, 13 times to be exact in his 18-year career.

Following a couple of first-round losses in 1987 and 1988, IUP made it all the way to the semifinals in 1989, losing to Mississippi College 26-14 in '89. The following season, Tony Aliucci and Jai Hill helped Cignetti exact his revenge as IUP crushed Mississippi College 27-8 in the semis on the strength of Hill's 5 catches for 117 yards and Aliucci's 184 yards passing. While North Dakota State crushed the Indians in the championship game, scoring 37 unanswered points in the second half that made a close 14-11 tilt at the half a laugher, it was an experience that IUP would enjoy once again in the not too distant future.

They finished the 1991 campaign ranked No. 1 in the nation in Division II with a 12-0 mark before being upset by Jacksonville State 27-20 in the semifinals. Two years later, the No. 4 ranked IUP Indians hit nirvana again, rolling to a 13-0 record, all the way to the Division II championship game against North Alabama, at North Alabama's Braly Municipal

Stadium. On the way to the title contest, the Indians beat New Haven 38-35 in the quarterfinals, holding the ball for the final three minutes of the game with New Haven frantically trying to get the ball back, and defeated North Dakota rather easily, 21-6, in the semis at George P. Miller Stadium.

While in enemy territory, the championship was a classic match-up in front of 15,631 rabid North Alabama fans and a national audience on ESPN. Everybody got their money's worth in this back-and-forth tilt. North Alabama broke on top 14-3, before IUP scored three unanswered touchdowns, the last on a 24-yard scoring toss from Scott Woods, who had 299 yards in the game, to Theo Turner, making it 24-14.

North Alabama shot back on the strength of a blocked punt and a touchdown run by Brian Satterfield, who ran for 180 yards, giving the host team a 34-24 advantage with only 3:17 left in the contest.

Cignetti's troops charged back with three nice passes by Woods and a one-yard run by Micheal Mann, cutting the deficit to three at the 1:54 mark. After recovering an onsides kick, IUP remarkably tied the score at 34 with a 34-yard Mike Geary field goal.

Unfortunately, offense was the name of the game this day, as both teams combined for 970 yards, 537 coming from North Alabama. Completing two long passes with time running out, quarterback Cody Gross finished a 69 yard drive in the game's final 45 seconds to give North Alabama the championship 41-34.

While not getting as far in the playoffs again, Frank Cignetti nevertheless has kept the program at the top of the Division II charts, winning nine PSAC western division crowns outright and four co-championships with 10 Lambert Trophies as the division's best team in the east. Cignetti's 170 wins are not only far and away the most in school history, but rank fourth among all active coaches in Division II. His .730 winning percentage is 7th. Since 1977, IUP has compiled a .723 winning percentage that ranks 24th in the nation out of all NCAA teams, regardless of division.

With Cignetti mixing the squad with talented freshman recruits as well as successful transfers, especially from the University of Pittsburgh in running back Mike Jemison, Tyre Young and Khiawatha Downey (the talented center who was signed as a free agent by the San Francisco 49ers this past offseason and whose inspirational story is featured in Chapter 16 "The Feel-Good Football Story of 2004"), the continued successful run of the IUP Indians appears to be a foregone conclusion as long as Frank Cignetti strolls the sidelines.

The Greatest Coach

There was the school's first coach in the modern era, George P. Miller, who lasted 21 years, went 86-45-9, and has the honor of having the school stadium named after him. And who can forget Chuck Klausing, who was a sparkling 47-10-0 before becoming a Steel City legend at Carnegie Mellon?

When speaking of the greatest coach, though, to grace the field at IUP, the argument begins and ends with Frank Cignetti. Cignetti is not only the school's winningest coach with a 177-45-1 mark (Miller is second), but he's won 10 PSAC West Division Titles, two PSAC Titles, 13 NCAA Division II playoff appearances in 18 seasons, six semifinal appearances and two excursions to the national championship game. A phenomenal coaching career for sure. But it all didn't start out so rosy for the 1960 NAIA All-American end.

He got his first opportunity to be a collegiate coach at West Virginia, where he went an unremarkable 17-27 mark before stepping down following the 1979 campaign. It wasn't anything on the football field that Cignetti will be known for in his short tenure at WVU, but his inspirational victory over cancer.

After being out of the business for six years, his alma mater came calling and Cignetti answered the call, a call that has certainly been fortuitous for all involved with the IUP football program.

Notable Players

Many fine players have donned IUP uniform over the years: Mike Jemison, the transfer from Pitt who ran for 1,311 yards his first season at Indiana; Michael Mann, the school's all-time leading rusher with 4,805 yards; super quarterback Rich Ingold as well as Brian Eyerman, whose 8,409 yards is tops at the school; Tony Aliucci, first-team All-American QB in 1991; and the school's first-ever, first-team All-American, quarterback Lynn Hieber. Those who played in the NFL include: John Jones, Leander Jordan, Chris Villarrial and finally the unforgettable wide receiver Dave Smith, the future Steeler who would become famous for spiking the ball before he crossed the goal line in a nationally televised Monday Night Game.

As great as those players were, when we think of IUP football, the first player to come to mind is linebacker Jim Haslett. Haslett was a two-time, first-team All-American who not only became the 1979 Defensive Rookie of the Year with the Buffalo Bills, but had a standout nine-year NFL career. In 2000, Haslett became the first IUP player to become an NFL head coach, where once again he promptly rose to the head of the class, being named Coach of the Year. He recently was elected to the College Football Hall of Fame in 2001.

All-Time Record

614-280-37

Championships

Pennsylvania State Athletic Conference West Divisional Championships: 1964, 1965, 1984,1985, 1986, 1987, 1988, 1990, 1991, 1992, 1993, 1994, 1996, 2000, 2001, 2002, 2003, 2004

Pennsylvania State Athletic Conference Championships: 1986, 1987

NCAA Division II Playoff Semifinal Appearances: 1989, 1991, 1994,1999

NCAA Division II Playoff Championship Game Appearances: 1990, 1993

THIRTY FIVE

A Higher Calling

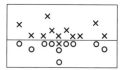

You hear the heroic and tragic story of former Arizona Cardinal Pat Tillman many times over, the NFL player who left his lucrative football career at its peak to go fight and unfortunately die for his country in the war against terror. It's an inspirational tale that should be told and celebrated. While we remember Tillman for his sacrifice and bravery, there are many more we don't hear about who have given up everything they have built in their lives to answer a higher calling, fighting for this country in the armed services during these troubled times. Former CMU linebacker Jesse Grapes is without a doubt one of those heroic figures.

Grapes, a Canevin High School graduate, is described by Tartans head coach Rich Lackner as intense and extremely committed in everything he did. "When you're not getting any [scholarship] money to play, you get different degrees of commitment," Lackner explains. "With Jesse, it was total commitment."

Lackner was one of the primary reasons Grapes came to CMU. "I picked CMU for two reasons," Grapes notes. "One, the academic reputation is on par with the top schools in the country, especially in technological areas in which I was interested. Two, Coach Lackner's recruiting. He came to my high school, and to one of my games. He called... but never pestered me. He told me if I didn't choose CMU that was okay, and that if it didn't work out at another school that I could always call him for a look. That endeared me to him. I came for an overnight visit... loved the campus, the environment, the players. It was perfect."

Perfect indeed. Grapes got everything he wanted out of his Tartan experience and more. "A few things highlighted my CMU career," he says. "First and foremost was the closeness of the team, especially my defensive unit. No one at CMU is paid to play football. We are all there for an outstanding academic experience and played because we loved football and continued to love playing for the Tartans. Also, due to the nature of the student body at CMU [very egalitarian and often arrogantly affluent] athletes, especially football players, tended to stick together even more so than at other schools. In fact, 8 out of the 11 guys on our starting defense and approximately 70 of a 120-man roster were in the same fraternity, Beta Theta Pi. This closeness led to extremely cohesive and fluid play, especially on defense, where our 3-4 style squad, affectionately nicknamed the 'Red Dogs' broke numerous school defensive records and formed lifelong friendships. I had the honor of being named the defensive captain of this unit. I loved my guys. On weekdays we were students, but come 4:30-6:30 every day, we were warriors."

"My career highlight was our final game together, a 21-7 victory in an ECAC bowl game," he continues. "Our opponent had just dropped from Division II with scholarship players still on their roster. They were decidedly larger and faster than us... but we sent them packing in style. It was a great defensive performance and a perfect finish to a career loving football."

Grapes not only left Carnegie Mellon in 2000 as a three-time All University Athletic Association selection at linebacker (with 131 tackles, 5 sacks, 2 fumble recoveries and 3 interceptions in his career), but he also earned a degree in Information systems and business. Jesse had interned for Arthur Andersen the two summers before he graduated and impressed them so much he was able to secure a contract with the company before he began he senior year. It was a job that the content CMU alum really

Jesse Grapes (back row, third from left) celebrates an ECAC Bowl victory with his CMU teammates. A couple years later Grapes' life would change dramatically when he joined the Marines shortly after 9/11. (Courtesy of Rich Lackner.)

seemed to enjoy. "With Andersen, I specialized in supply chain consulting, and worked all over the place—Chicago, Boston, Pittsburgh, London," he says. "It was a fun job with incredible people. Everyone was young, enterprising and energetic. It was a good team and I thoroughly enjoyed my time there." It was a job that he loved to the point that he went even when he was not feeling his best, never calling off sick in two years.

Appreciative of his dedication, Grapes' boss told him to go home early one day and to take the next one off. That day, ironically, was September 10, 2001; his day off would be the 11th, the day that not only drastically changed the way the world looked at things, but would forever change the course of Jesse Grapes' life.

"I watched the attacks on the World Trade Centers from my living room in live action with my mother," he recalls. "I was horrified, sorrowful, injured and angered. A sleeping patriotism surged through my body. I decided that day I was quitting my job to do 'something.' I knew there would be world-changing consequences of this day. I had to be a part of it... to matter... to make a difference."

That difference was to join the Marines and get right in the middle of the action. "I met my first active-duty Marine at a recruiting post the next day and was committed to the Marines within three days. Ronald Reagan said, 'Some people go their whole life wondering if they've made a difference, Marines don't have that problem.' What better place could I go?"

His next move was to seek out Lackner, his mentor at CMU, for a recommendation to the Corps. Lackner has always been someone Jesse admires and not only from a football standpoint. "Coach Lackner is a great man," he explains. "He is a Christian man true to the values that men aspire to. He loves his job, his family and his players and puts everything into them. He has left me with a warm feeling for CMU and for football. If I walked in his office tomorrow, I know we would have a great conversation. His steadfastness and strength to continue with his demanding job, while supporting his wife through cancer, has shown me the quality of his heart and will. He is a role model and a true leader. He came to my wedding last year, and during both of my tours to Iraq, he sent me CMU football memorabilia to give out to Iraqis. Imagine a 150-pound Iraqi soldier wearing a triple X-large football pullover an offensive lineman would wear. . . I have some hilarious pictures of this. He has shown me a man happy with life in all its nuances. A true role model."

Lackner remembers that meeting, stunned in the life his former linebacker was about to embark on. "I was floored," he recalls. "I remember it was in the gymnasium. He had called and said he needed to see me in private. We went to the gym because there were people in the office and he told me that 'I need you to do a favor' and not to say anything to anybody. I had no idea; it came from left field. Jesse said he was signing up for the Marine Corps and leaving his job and he needed a recommendation. I asked him if he was sure about it and he told me he was never so sure about anything in his life."

With the support of his coach in hand, Grapes went out on a much tougher journey, one that would see him have to tell his family, employers and friends of his decision, conversations that were not going to be easy. "Oh yeah," he laughs, "My best friend said it was insane. He thought I was giving up a promising career. My mother was petrified. She would have tried to talk me out of it had I not waited to tell my family until four weeks before I had to report for OCS. Some cried, some praised me. I just wanted to get away from talking about the Marine Corps and get busy inside of it."

The people at Arthur Andersen were also very stunned, yet after initially thinking Jesse was out of his mind, they supported him 100 percent. "At first, they thought I was insane and told me to wait a while till my head cooled down and I had thought more about it," he says. "They didn't understand my resolve. But after they saw I was serious, they were incredibly supportive. They even put me on hiatus... essentially continuing to pay me while I was in Officer Candidate School [the demanding boot camp for officers]."

With some people, a decision such as this would continue to be about themselves; to Grapes' credit, once he entered the Marine Corps, it became about his men. Jesse became a lieutenant, leading a squad of 43 infantrymen as a platoon commander in the 3rd Battalion, 1st Marines. It is that role that both inspires Lackner and shows just what type of special individual Jesse Grapes is. "We are proud of what he's done so far and what he will continue to do," his former coach says. "Our thoughts and prayers are with him. The captains of our football team and some of the staff sent some items to him in Iraq. When we asked Jessie's family what they should send him, they told us he wanted things for his men, not for him. That makes a big difference. It shows how he was raised and that perhaps football had a major influence on his life. He thinks of the team first. It makes us feel great that we may have had an effect on his life."

The CMU coach further went on to speak about an inspirational e-mail Grapes sent him shortly after he left for the Marines. "He said 'I have a platoon of 45 men that I am leading and I am confident they are the best trained in the Corps. I think they are going to do things to the best of their ability.' He went on a little more and just showed what a great leader he was and just how inspirational a person he can be. I wished he had given that speech to our players. The team would have busted through walls."

It was those members of Jesse's platoon that he would lead into battle right in the heart of the Iraq conflict. "My experience in Iraq has been a positive one," he says. "I've gotten to work for and lead some of the best men I've ever known. I have 43 infantry

Marines under my charge, and they can accomplish amazing things when presented a challenge and permitted some ingenuity and authority. We have killed some 'no-shit' bad guys in Fallujah and protected countless more innocent Iraqi civilians in the towns on the outskirts of this terrorist hotbed. There are a lot of boring times, capped with brief intervals of pure exhilaration. When you feel the adrenaline rush leading up to and during a gunfight, it's incomparable to anything else. When you bring smiles to a group of Iraqis by trading mixed phrases and conversation in Arabic and English... you know you are an ambassador of peace." It's a quote that can be explained by Lackner's assessment of Jesse's personality: "Jessie is the type of person, when he commits to something, he goes all out."

When he's done with his tour of duty, the plan is not for Jesse Grapes to return to his old way of life at Arthur Andersen, but to stick in the Marine Corps. The Marines are in his blood now. Their motto is Semper Fi, short for Semper Fidelis or "Always Faithful," which thoroughly explains Jesse's love for his new life. "After my initial tour is up in the infantry, I will attempt to cross-deck to the aviation side of the Marine Corps," he says. "I will become a pilot, hoping to fly F-18 Hornets... to drop bombs instead of shoot rifles. I love the Corps... its values, tradition and the quality of its men. I cannot see myself getting out now."

Through it all, it's not been retribution against the terrorists that Grapes was so horrified to see on 9/11, some four-plus years ago, that drives him in his new endeavor. "In the end, it's the challenge and success of leading men, Marines, in combat that is the most rewarding," he says. "They give up their lives for their country and more so for their fellow Marines, and they get little in return. That is the reward of this job, working with these young men. I pity anyone who never gets the chance to be a Marine." Semper Fi, Lieutenant Grapes.

Football Smarts: CMU's Legacy

When talking to Coach Lackner, one of the unique things he expresses about his football program is not what his young men have achieved on the field, but what they have achieved in life. To him, this is what the legacy of Carnegie Mellon football is all about. The following is a list of some players that Lackner feels epitomize his program.

Tony DiGioia: "Tony played tight end for CMU when I was here. He graduated with a degree in civil engineering and is now an orthopedic surgeon where he helped develop a computer-aided navigation system for guiding hip replacement surgery. He was a great football player and a great human being."

Bobby O'Toole:"Bobby was the captain of the 1990 team from Columbus and was named the 1990 College Division Academic All-American Player of the Year. He graduated in 1991, No.1 in his class here in mechanical engineering, got his Masters in mechanical engineering from Stanford and deferred his medical school acceptance while he worked for Dr. Tony DiGioia." O'Toole graduated magna cum laude from Harvard Medical School in 1999 and is in residency in orthopedic surgery there.

Mike Campie: "Mike is from Comanche, Iowa, and is the school's all-time leading rusher. I think he only got one B in his time at CMU, graduating with a 3.98 QPA in 2000. In the second semester of his senior year, where he was a civil engineering student, a time when most students are just coasting looking forward to graduating. Mike took 27 credits and got nine As."

While at CMU, Campie broke Scott Barnyak's all-time career rushing record with 2,910 yards and was named the University Athletic Association's player of the year in 1999.

Chris Haupt: An excellent linebacker and an architecture graduate of CMU. He was one of the primary architects on PNC Park.

Nick Zitelli: Zitelli transferred to CMU from Purdue after his freshman year and was named the MVP of the Aztec Bowl (Division III All-Star Game) in 2000. He was an excellent student who also earned a master's degree from the Heinz School of Public Policy and Management at CMU.

Kenny Murawski: Murawski was an All-American linebacker who graduated from the renowned CMU School of Business. Today he is very successful in the commercial real estate field in Cincinnati.

THIRTY SIX

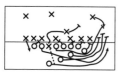

The Techsters: the History of Carnegie Mellon University Football

While the Carnegie Mellon Tartans have been a Division III power for the better part of 30 years (they haven't had a losing season in that time period), there was a time when the school was known as Carnegie Tech and had a top-ten, Division I varsity football team.

Through the years it has been an institution that puts academics in front of athletics. Yet it has found a way to succeed on the gridiron. Carnegie Mellon's long and proud tradition dates back to a time when the Techsters made the Notre Dames and Pitts of the world fear getting on the football field with them.

The Beginning

The first few years of intercollegiate football at the Carnegie Institute of Technology, or simply "Carnegie Tech", were not exactly years to brag about. After tying

California Normal 0-0 in their first game ever in 1906, and then defeating the Kiskiminetas Academy 5-0 in the next contest, Tech went on to drop five of their next six games, tying only Shadyside Academy 0-0 and never scoring another point the rest of their inaugural campaign.

Things didn't get much better over the next decade, recording only one winning season in 1909 with a 5-3-1 mark. Their all-time record was a dismal 24-46-6, under eight different coaches, their first 10 seasons before Walter Steffen put an end to the bleeding.

Steffen led the club to a 7-1 record in 1915, a year that included a record setting 88-0 thumping of Waynesburg, losing only to their powerful neighbors from the University of Pittsburgh, 28-0. They had another winning record in 1916 before the program was discontinued two years later because of World War I. Tech came back in 1919 with a meager 3-4 mark before turning the program around on the final contest of the 1920 campaign. That day they defeated Washington & Jefferson 6-0, marking their first ever win against what was considered a major college opponent. It would open the door for the golden era of Carnegie Tech football.

The High Life

Steffen added stability to the football program at Carnegie Tech; he also would soon add a reputation as one of the best teams in the sport.

Following their historical win against Washington & Jefferson in 1920, the Tartans reeled off five consecutive winning seasons going 26-14-3 in the process, two of the victories coming against Pitt, 7-2 in 1923 and 6-0 the following season.

That led Carnegie Tech into the 1926 campaign, a year where the school proved they were a force in major college football. The Tartans started out the season 2-1 after a loss to W & J before reeling off four wins in their next five games, three of them coming against Pitt, Detroit and West Virginia. That led Tech into its last game of the regular season against the legendary Knute Rockne and the Notre Dame Fighting Irish.

The Tartans had played the Irish the past four seasons, losing each time by a combined score of 111-19. Notre Dame had won its first eight games of the season going into the tilt, and while many thought it would be closer than the previous four seasons, they would still enter the contest as prohibitive favorites.

There was a rumor going around that the confident Irish would send in their second team against Tech, saving their first team to play at Southern California the following week. It was a rumor that the Hall of Fame coach would deny vehemently. In a telegram to Carnegie Tech officials, Rockne wrote, "We are pointing to your game and will give you all we have." While he made the statement, Rockne appeared to have little respect for the Steel City school, choosing to scout the Army-Navy game instead while he turned over the reins of the team to assistant coach Mills for the contest. It was a bad mistake.

Tech dominated from the get-go, stunning their Indiana guests. After battling to a scoreless tie in the first quarter, Mills, who in fact had the second team in, rushed in his first team to try and stop the Carnegie offense; it was not to be. Howard Harpster tossed a long pass to Bill Donohue at the 18 before Donohue rambled in from 15 yards for the opening score. A confused Irish were never the same as two Harpster field goals, from 42 yards (which the *Chicago Tribune* claimed would have been good from 10 more yards) and 35, put the icing on the cake for a 19-0 win that goes down as the biggest victory in the history of the school.

The wins kept coming, including a 7-1 mark in 1928 that saw the Tartans clip W & J, Pitt and Notre Dame, before an end-of-season 27-13 victory by NYU cost Carnegie Tech an undefeated season and a possible shot at the Rose Bowl.

After two mediocre seasons, Harpster took over the program in 1932 and could not turn things around, going 12-19-3 before giving way to a Pitt alum and Jock Sutherland disciple, Bill Kern, in 1937. Following a disastrous 2-5-1 campaign, Kern led Tech to a magical season in 1938. The Tartans captured the Eastern collegiate title, going 7-1 with wins over local rivals Pitt and Duquesne, before ending the season with a 14-0 victory against North Carolina State.

It was the victories against the two local schools that made this season special. Imagine having three top Division I collegiate schools separated by only a couple of miles on the same road. "The 1930s were a different time and a great time to be a college football fan in Pittsburgh between Pitt, Duquesne and Carnegie Tech. You could walk to each other's campus," current coach Rich Lackner stated.

With the spectacular campaign in hand, Tech accepted

a bid to play in the 1939 Sugar Bowl against Texas Christian. 50,000 fans jammed the stadium as Tech scored a touchdown late in the first half on a 50-yard bomb from Peter Moroz to George Muha giving the Tartans a 7-6 lead going into the locker room. The touchdown was Tech's only bright moment, as TCU scored 9 unanswered points in the second half enroute to a 15-7 win. The foundation of the school's major college status was about to come tumbling down.

The Low Road

Kern quit after the 1939 campaign, going to WVU as Carnegie Tech was about to enforce the tough academic requirement on football that Pitt had done a year earlier. The program slipped incredibly over the next five seasons and when Pitt crushed the Tartans 45-6 to end a winless 1943 season, it marked the last game in major college football for the school.

Tech discontinued the program throughout the duration of World War II, citing a lack of players and a loss of two varsity coaches to the Navy. During the hiatus, the school would lose football and baseball star Whitey Loos in a plane wreck while in the service over Dutch Guinea.

When they finally brought the program back in 1946, they did so in a minor collegiate status, moving their games from Pitt Stadium to a smaller Forbes Field. President Robert E. Doherty made the move because he knew he could not impose strict academic requirements and have a winning program. "We cannot have both a Class A football and professional education unless we set up football as a sideshow and set up special education programs for the squad. This we will not do!" To Doherty's credit, it was a noble move and one that the university maintains to this day, but it was one the students at the time were very much against.

The team had gotten so inept that they were in the midst of a 21 game losing streak prompting protests from the campus. They first began a fund raising effort, hoping to raise $1,000 to donate to the team in hopes of bringing top-notch players back to the school. It was thought that the donation would begin an alumni fund drive to revive the now moribund program. Afterward, it turned ugly.

Protest began after a 26-20 loss to Case Western in 1948. Signs were plastered everywhere on campus, including one that read "Here lies college spirit: Born 1909, Died 1939." Three thousand Pitt students joined their 2,000 brethren from Tech in a raucous riot outside Doherty's office, rambling, "Down with Doherty, de-emphasize Doherty." The president stayed firm, shooting back "Some of you may have come to the wrong school. We're trying to make this place an institution where a student can get a fine professional education. Unfortunately, if you do that, you can't have football to the extent you want."

The throng then screamed that an alumnus had offered $50,000 to fund the program, a rumor Doherty vehemently denied.

The president held his position. The team eventually defeated Grove City 7-0 in 1948 to end the 23-game losing streak. While the team never returned to major college status, it began winning at the minor level. They finished their first undefeated season in 1954, going 7-0-1 under the tutelage of Ed Baker, who returned to the school after leaving in 1942. Baker, unfortunately, would die at the young age of 50 in 1959.

Current State of Affairs

The school's football fortunes resurrected to heights previously unseen since 1938 when they tabbed former IUP coach Chuck Klausing in 1975 to take over the program. Klausing made the Tartans Division III powers within a couple of years, leading them to back-to-back semifinal appearances in 1978 and 1979.

While the Hall of Fame coach directed them to a remarkable 77-15-2 mark before taking a job at Pitt in 1986 as an assistant under Mike Gottfried, the constant during this new renaissance has been current coach Rick Lackner.

Lackner, who played for the school between 1975-1978 (he was named Presidents' Athletic Conference defensive player of the year in 1976), became an assistant coach under Klausing following his graduation. Lackner now stands as the school's all-time winning coach with 127 victories. While the coach certainly gives credit to Klausing for his success, he also remembers the man who started to lay the foundation before Klausing came aboard. "Prior to Coach Klausing coming to CMU, a man named Joe Gasparella was the head coach between 1963-1975," he says. "He deserves a lot of credit for keeping things going here. He was just a part-time coach, but worked hard to keep the program going. When the university decided to make a commitment to the program, they brought in Chuck Klausing as the full-time coach."

Rich remembers those two classic playoff runs in '78 and '79. The first year was his senior season at CMU when the Tartans upset top-ranked Dayton in the first round, 24-21, before losing to Baldwin Wallace, 31-6. "I was a senior on that team and it was a real Davey and Goliath story [the first-round game against Dayton]," Lackner recalls. "The top eight teams back then were invited to the playoffs and Dayton was No.1 and we were No. 8. They had a choice of whether or not to play the game at home. They were so confident that they chose to play here so that they were guaranteed of a home game in the second round. They were so good. I think they still had juniors and seniors that were still under scholarship. The atmosphere at the stadium was great. The theme was go bananas, there was a student dressed as a gorilla passing out bananas. We played hard and the game went to overtime. Their fullback hadn't fumbled all season and our defense hit him so hard that the ball popped out and Greg Galley recovered, winning the game for us."

The next season was Lackner's first as an assistant. CMU was a little better, capturing the Lambert Trophy, emblematic of being the best team in the east at the minor collegiate level. The club went into the playoffs with a 9-0 mark, capturing the first Presidents' Athletic Conference crown. After beating a stubborn Minnesota Morris team 31-25 in overtime in the first round of the playoffs, they went to Ithaca, where they held the lead late in the game amidst a horrible fog that had rolled into the field. They unfortunately fell apart late, losing the contest 15-6. "Anytime you come that close it's frustrating," Lackner says. It got so bad that when we were trying a field goal, one official stood where the ball was marked, two others stood on either side of the goal posts, while one went to see where the ball landed. Through that all they deduced it was good. We had the lead late and then lost it."

It was a game where the former Pirates announcer Bob Prince was broadcasting the contest. Lackner remembered the Gunner that day adding to the Prince mystique. "Bob Prince announced our games that season. In the fog at Ithaca during the playoff game, it was so thick that the field coaches had to call up to the coaches' box in the stands to tell them what was going on. Prince couldn't see a thing and was trying to listen to the coaches to see what was going on. He ended up just making up the play by play."

CMU continued the good times in the '80s winning five PAC titles before making the move to the University Athletic Association (UAA) in 1990 where they continued to dominate. The Tartans captured seven UAA titles in their first eight seasons in the league, including a 10-0 mark in 1990 where they made the NCAA playoffs once again (losing to Lycoming 17-7 in the first round). The move to the UAA was one that made sense for CMU going into the 21st century. "We moved because we felt we should be in a conference with schools who held our philosophies. The UAA was formed with schools that were research schools in major cities and were committed to Division III athletics. They felt that since they were competing for the same students and faculty, they should compete in sports as well. It's certainly worked well for us."

Through his tenure at the school, Lackner has had stability within his coaching staff that has helped keep the ball rolling, as well as players who excelled both on the field and off. "I guess the continuity within the coach staff is the most important (reason for his success)," the coach explains. "My coordinators Rich Erdelyi [offensive] and Terry Bodner [defensive] have been with me for an extended period of time, from the beginning in 1986. The number two reason is our kids have incredible brainpower; they have the ability to digest knowledge, whether it be football or physics. These kids have an incredible competitive spirit that translates well to football. They have an incredible burn to excel."

As does the university, which is committed to winning on the football field. "A lot of the credit for our success over the past few decades should go to Dr. Richard Cyert, president of the university," Lackner says. "The administration made a commitment to take the program to the next level. Dr. Cyert wanted the university to excel in everything it did, including on Saturdays."

Through it all, though, they have never wavered from President Doherty's proclamation some 50-plus years ago to never compromise academics over athletics. "As good as that time was [football at the school in the 1920s and 1930s], we are proud what we have accomplished at the Division III level today," notes Lacker. "Our administration's philosophy is to play by the rules and give everybody the tools to succeed. They will never compromise academically, though. We have real student-athletes and that's the way it's supposed to be." It's a philosophy they have been proving throughout the last 30 years, or more to the point 30 consecutive seasons without a losing record.

The Greatest Coach

There have been two golden eras of Carnegie Mellon football, one in the late 1920s and 1930s when they were a force in major college football, and one starting in the late '70s, when they became a Division III power. When considering the greatest coach the school ever produced, each era needs to be examined equally.

In the major college era, the nod goes to Steffen, who was there for 18 years (1914-1932) and presided over some of the greatest victories in school history. While Bill Kern took them to their best season ever and a berth in the Sugar Bowl, he finished his career at .500 with only 12 wins, while Steffen was 88-53-8.

In the modern era, Chuck Klausing was the one who made them great, presiding over four teams that went to the NCAA playoffs, the first postseason ventures since the 1939 Sugar Bowl appearance. Klausing, who was a star center for Penn State before World War II (where he was a second lieutenant in the Pacific theater) and for Slippery Rock afterward, started his coaching career at IUP before ending up at Carnegie Mellon in 1975. There he compiled a 77-15-2 record, making two consecutive NCAA Division III semifinal appearances in 1978 and 1979. Over the course of Klausing's 16-year collegiate coaching career he compiled a record of 124-25-2, landing him into the College Football Hall of Fame in 1998.

It was his intense preparation that made Klausing great. According to Coach Lackner, who is the winningest CMU coach of all time at 133-54-2, "Chuck Klausing always had a plan. He studied film like nobody's business, a real student of the game. He was always looking to find a way to win."

If the choice is between Steffen and Klausing, the nod would have to go to Steffen, as he compiled his record against the likes of Pitt and Notre Dame and helped make the school a power at the major college level.

Notable Players

Probably two of the most dominant players during the early golden era are the only two players to come out of the CMU program elected to the College Football Hall of Fame, Lloyd Yoder and Howard Harpster.

Yoder was a star tackle with Carnegie Tech in the late '20s. He was part of a Tartan team that not only defeated Pitt three out of four seasons, but scored their biggest upset ever in 1926 against Notre Dame. That year, Yoder was named All-American. In 1982, he was given the highest honor a college football player could be given, enshrinement in the Hall of Fame.

Harpster was the school's one and only consensus All-American who was elected to the College Hall of Fame in 1956. While most of his fame came as one of the top quarterbacks in the east between 1926 and 1928, Harpster was also a renowned safety and punter. He eventually took over the reins of his alma mater in 1933, presiding over four fairly unsuccessful teams. Today, the Football Hall of Fame at CMU is named in his honor.

On top of those two, there have been several other modern players (see Chapter 35, "A Higher Calling") who have made a difference in the program, including Scott Branyak, Richie Squires, Bobby Kennedy, Mike Beresford, Bill Snyder, Chris Dee and the coach himself, Rich Lackner, who was the PAC defensive player of the year in 1976 as a linebacker, received a Dapper Dan Award in 1978, was a two-time Academic All-American and was recently enshrined in the Western Pennsylvania Sports Hall of Fame.

All-Time Record

456-334-28

Championships

Presidents' Athletic Conference: 1979, 1981, 1983, 1985,1989

University Athletic Association: 1990, 1991, 1993, 1994, 1995, 1996,1997

ECAC Bowl Championships: 1999

NCAA Division III Playoff Semifinal Appearances: 1978, 1979

NCAA Division I Final Season Rankings (Associated Press Rankings): 6th - 1938

THIRTY SEVEN

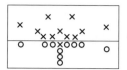

The Rise and Fall—and Rise Again: The History of Washington & Jefferson Football

Today Washington & Jefferson College football is a symbol of one of the great Division III programs in the land. Coming off of a record-setting season where the Presidents went 10-0 in 2004 (before losing in the quarterfinals, see Chapter 41 for more details), W & J continued a tradition that not only saw them once play in the Rose Bowl, but featured a strong team with players that helped shape the face of professional football in the 1890s.

This story will not only celebrate the unmitigated success the team has enjoyed since 1980, but that of their historical place in the great game of football.

The Beginning

The tradition of Washington & Jefferson football is one of the oldest and most successful of all

Western Pennsylvania colleges. Its beginnings coincide with that of the rich history of the birth of professional football in southwestern Pennsylvania.

While the program began with an auspicious debut in 1890, a 34-0 shellacking of Western University (later on known as the University of Pittsburgh), during its first decade it played many of the legendary club teams in the area that were the roots of the professional version of the sport.

Games against the powerful Pittsburgh Athletic Club (PAC) and the Allegheny Athletic Association (AAA) generally were met with much success. Perhaps one of the most impressive victories came against the AAA in 1892, when they beat the Pittsburgh-based club 8-0 to cap an undefeated 4-0 campaign. 1892 was also the year that Pudge Heffelfinger became the first ever professional player, when the AAA gave him $500 for a game against their bitter rivals, the PAC.

Success followed W&J through the 1890s, as they were one of the few collegiate teams to find success against the club teams of the era, sporting an overall 9-5-1 mark against the four best teams of the day: the AAA, the PAC, the Duquesne Country and Athletic Club, and the famous Latrobe Athletic Club, whom they defeated 11-0 in their only matchup in 1911.

Perhaps the reason for much of their success came in the fact that many of the great club players of that era were also W&J alums. The list includes John Brallier, the Latrobe quarterback who had been considered the first professional player until the early 1960s. Other notables from the early years included Ross Fiscus, Big Bill Hammer, W.D. Inglis (head coach of the 1898 Presidents), Edwin Lang, Tex Matthews, Tiger McFarland, W.B. Seaman and Ed Wood.

The High Life

While the first two decades of the 20th century were certainly stellar for the W&J football program, it wasn't until the 1920s that it became among the best in the country.

Bob Murphy was the graduate manager of the school at the time, a position that would be equal to a current-day athletic director, and he brought several fine collegiate players, coaches and teams to his small college with an enrollment of only 500 students.

Before that, the highlights included a 10-2-1 mark in 1908,

a year that the Presidents defeated the powerful University of Pittsburgh Panthers 14-0, before running off a 36-4-2 mark between 1913-1916 under the direction of Robert Folwell and Sol Metzger, whose first season was 1916. During that run, they defeated Pitt and West Virginia twice each. Two years after their fine '08 campaign, the school almost had to shut down the program with no money to pay for it. Murphy convinced the student body to pay $1 each in a levy, which was enough to save the program. The glory days were about to begin.

Among the players at W&J during that streak included one that stood high among the rest, tackle Wilbur Henry. Henry, also known as "Fats" and "Pete," was a tackle for the Presidents between 1915 and 1919, making the first team All-American squad in 1917, 1918 and 1919. On top of being a devastating tackle, Fats also was one of the premiere punt blockers in the nation as well as a fine place kicker, drop kicker and punter, with a 94-yard punt and 45-yard drop kick to his resume.

Pete was described as a jovial man off

A three time All-American at Washington & Jefferson, Wilbur "Fats" Henry has the distinction of not only being a member of the inaugural class in the College Football Hall of Fame, but that of the first class ever to be enshrined in the Pro Football Hall of Fame. (Courtesy of Washington & Jefferson College.)

the field. Apparently, when the whistle blew on the field, his personality changed. He is described on the Pro Football Hall of Fame Web site as having "the swift reflexes of a man-eating tiger. Good-natured, easy-going and prone to laughter off the field, he was an uncompromising competitor on the gridiron."

Henry, who went on to a stellar NFL career, had the distinction of not only being elected to the charter class of the College Football Hall of Fame in 1951, but also the inaugural class at the Pro Football Hall of Fame in 1963.

Following Fats at W&J was Ed Garbisch. Garbisch was a center and guard at the school between 1917 and 1920 before going to West Point, where he played four more seasons, graduating 17th out of a class of 245. Garbisch became the President's second player to be enshrined in the College Football Hall of Fame, receiving the honor in 1954.

The high point of the 1920s proved also to be the greatest moment in the history of the school: the 1921 campaign. The Presidents ran through their slate unblemished, beating the likes of Syracuse, 17-10; Carnegie Tech, 14-0; Pitt, 7-0; and WVU, 13-0.

The 10-0 mark put them in a position to be the eastern representatives in the Rose Bowl, along with Penn State, Cornell and Lafayette, the region's other unbeaten squads.

While Vanderbilt and Centre College were unbeaten and possibilities from the south, their candidacy was not being considered seriously against these teams from the east.

Penn State was the first to be knocked out, as their record included two ties. Cornell's administration did not permit the team to travel to California, marking the end of their run. While Lafayette had a fabulous season, they also had some people doubting the integrity of some of their players. That left Greasy Neale's squad, (the same Greasy Neale who was the Hall of Fame coach of the Philadelphia Eagles) as the winner of the Rose Bowl sweepstakes.

The Presidents were taking on the heavily favored California Bears in this contest, and Neale took a very controversial move in his approach to the game. It had been the practice to bring clubs out to California 10 days before the game, to better acclimate them to the time zone. Greasy decided he'd bring them out only three days in advance and throw them into the fire.

With the move, Neale would be a goat or a hero. Fortunately, hero was the order of the day. The Presidents put on a great show, pulling off what is considered one of the greatest Rose Bowl "upsets" in history, tying the 1921 recognized National Champion California Bears 0-0. The *Los Angeles Times* claimed they outclassed their western opponents, and this wasn't far from the truth. W&J had the game's only real opportunity to score and in fact, they did just that. Half back Wayne Brenkert ran the ball 35 yards in the opening quarter for an apparent touchdown. Unfortunately, All-American tackle Russell Stein was offsides, and the score was negated.

The Presidents' defense was awesome and held their stronger opponent off the board. With the tie, the school received the honor of being named National Champions by several selectors.

Success followed the Presidents throughout the decade, including a 6-1-1 mark in 1923 under the direction of John Heisman—yes, the same man who not only was elected to the College Football Hall of Fame, but has the greatest award in sports named after him.

Tragedy hit the campus in 1925 when the one constant with the program through the early part of the 20th century—Murphy—died unexpectedly at the age of 48 of pernicious anemia.

The school remained competitive over the next few years, eventually falling to a minor level of collegiate football in the late 1930s.

The Low Road

There were several low roads for W&J after their run as a major college team, the worst between 1954 and 1961, when they were winless on four occasions. It got so bad that between 1957 and 1961 they were a combined 3-32-2. The unfortunate architects of those clubs were Charles Nelson, who was 0-15-1 in 1954 and 1955, and Edward Chupa, 5-23-3 between 1956 and 1959,

Chuck Ream came on board in 1960 and while he suffered through some miserable campaigns that included a 5-24 run between 1969-1969, he did lead the Presidents to their first Presidents' Athletic Conference (PAC) title in 1970.

The Presidents also won a title in 1975, but continued to muddle through the bottom of the conference until John Luckhardt came on board in 1982 to change the fortunes of this small Western Pennsylvania school.

Current State Of Affairs

Since the arrival of Luckhardt, Washington & Jefferson College has become among the most successful Division III programs in the land. Under the leadership of Luckhardt, former Steeler John Banaszak, and current coach Mike Sirianni, the Presidents have reeled off a string of 18 PAC championships in the past 20 years, qualifying for 15 of the last 18 NCAA Division III playoffs.

"There's a great recruiting base in Western Pennsylvania and Eastern Ohio," says Sirianni. "You have to have good players to make a good program, and we certainly have a lot of good players around the area. I've only been here six years, the last two as head coach, so you also have to give credit to the other head and assistant coaches over the last 20 years not to mention the great support we've gotten from the administration. Our long standing goal is to win a national championship, something that despite all the success, we've never done here."

The great recruiting base Sirianni refers to helped Luckhardt pile up a school-record 137 wins against only 37 defeats in his 17 year tenure at the school. Probably the highlights of his career, as well as the program's since the 1922 Rose Bowl, were his two appearances in the NCAA Division III championship games in 1992 and 1994. While the Presidents lost both (a 16-12 heartbreaker to Wisconsin-LaCrosse in '92 before a 38-15 thrashing by Albion two years later) the appearances helped mark W&J as a true national power.

Since Luckhardt came aboard, Washington & Jefferson has reeled off an impressive 184-47-25 record in 22 years, a feat that that is mind boggling when we consider the tough recruiting standards that exist at the school.

Brian Dawson was one of the school's most successful quarterbacks. The Washington & Jefferson product is fifth all time in Division III passing efficiency with a 201.5 rating. (Courtesy of Washington & Jefferson College.)

A candid Sirianni points out that "Lets face it, we are a Division III school so we aren't going to land too many kids who are going to play in the NFL, but this is a great place to play and get on with your life. We get some kids who turn down scholarship offers from other schools to come here and get a top-notch education. We always ask a kid, 'where do you want to be in four years?' With a W&J education, they can be successful in life."

"W&J had 4,000 kids apply here last year and only 1,800 got in, that's less that 50 percent," he continues, "so it's a very tough place to get in and our coaches have to work a little harder to recruit. That being said, we have seven coaches recruiting in a football-rich area like this so we have to be doing something wrong if we can't get quality football players."

While successful in the classroom, they have also been successful on the field under the leadership of Sirianni, who came from the greatest lower division program in the land, Mount Union College in nearby Alliance, Ohio. "You bring things you learned from your mentor and the coach at Mount Union was certainly my mentor," Sirianni says. "We'd certainly like to be as successful as Mount Union, but you can't keep stuffing Mount Union, Mount Union, Mount Union down the kids' throats here. W&J has a successful tradition and program and every one is proud of the tradition here."

A great tradition indeed. Sirianni came to W&J after the short, but successful, reign of Banaszak, who went 38-9 in four seasons between 1999-2002, including four consecutive playoff appearances. Banaszak did not have his contract renewed following the 2002 campaign, as he had been actively looking to pursue a better coaching opportunity, being a finalist for the job at Cal (PA), a Division II program and Mercyhurst. Athletic director Rick Creehan said simply that the decision not to renew Banaszak's contract put an end to any uncertainty about the future of the program. But there were still rumors abounding.

The main one was that the program was being de-emphasized and when a program is de-emphasized at the Division III level, it's going down to the bottom of the barrel.

Sirianni quickly put an end to those rumors, as the new coach who had been an offensive guru as a coordinator made the statement that "My career record as a player and a coach at Mount Union was 88-4. People know that I do not like to lose. My answer to people who ask about these untrue rumors is 'Why would I have taken the job if I didn't think I was going to get full support from our administration?' I have been given 100 percent support from both President Brian C. Mitchell and Director of Athletics Rick Creehan. Both of them want us to be the very best in Division III in the classroom and on the field. I definitely wouldn't have taken the job if I thought otherwise."

They more than put the rumors to rest, with a 9-2 season that included a 41-19 win over Wilkes College, where Sirianni began his coaching career as an offensive coordinator, in the season-ending ECAC Bowl game.

Following the impressive ECAC Bowl performance, Coach Sirianni took W&J up to the level of his alma mater (Mount Union) by leading the Presidents to an undefeated 10-0 regular season in 2004, finishing third in the final division III national poll. This campaign, Washington & Jefferson would not have to settle for an ECAC Bowl berth but a spot in the Division III playoffs.

The Greatest Coach

They have had a lot of top quality coaches in the long and successful history of football at the school: Neale; Heisman; Clinton Woods, who was 18-1-1 in two seasons; and Banaszak. But the best has to be John Luckhardt. Luckhardt not only won a school record 137 games (the next highest is D.C. Morrow with 52), but he also resurrected a moribund program, taking it to 11 NCAA playoff appearances, including two championship games. He built the foundation on which the program continues to flourish.

Notable Players

Probably the most notable players in school history are John Spiegel, the school's first consensus All-American in 1914, and Wilbur Henry. While Henry is the best the school has ever produced, there are some more modern players that have been extremely successful in the current era. In Sirianni's eyes, they are the best who have come down the road in recent years:

"Joey Nichols is our second leading all-time rusher and is a great story. He didn't have much when he came here and worked extremely hard and gave his heart not only to become a great football player, but he got a W&J education and is going to be a successful accountant."

"Brian Dawson is a Western Pennsylvania kid and could have gotten a scholarship to play at many schools, but came here. He was our starting quarterback for four years. We've always had a reputation as a defensive school. He helped change that and helped us become known as an offensive, high-finesse passing school." Under Sirianni's leadership, Dawson became the fifth-best passer in Division III history with a passing efficiency rating of 201.5.

"T.J. Srsic and Geno Vacca are both Western PA kids born and bred. They are hard-working offensive lineman, gritty, and would run through a wall for you. T.J. went on to be a teacher at Pine-Richland, while Geno is a pharmaceutical rep."

All-Time Record

616-361-40

Championships

PRESIDENTS' ATHLETIC CONFERENCE: 1970, 1975, 1984, 1986, 1987, 1988, 1989, 1990, 1991, 1992, 1993, 1994, 1995, 1996, 1998, 1999, 2000, 2001, 2002, 2004.

ECAC BOWL CHAMPIONSHIPS: 2003

NCAA DIVISION III PLAYOFF SEMIFINAL APPEARANCES: 1993, 1995

NCAA DIVISION III PLAYOFF CHAMPIONSHIP APPEARANCES: 1992, 1994

DIVISION I NCAA NATIONAL CHAMPIONS: 1921 (By the Boand System, Earl Jessen, Jim Koger, Patrick Premo), 1926 (By the Soren Sorenson system)

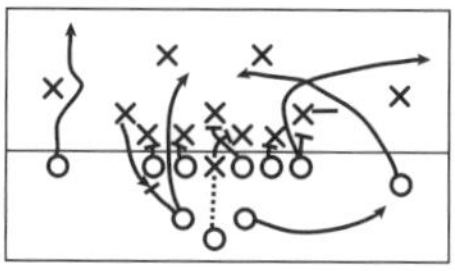

THIRTY EIGHT

There Used to Be A Football Team Here: The History Of Saint Vincent College Football

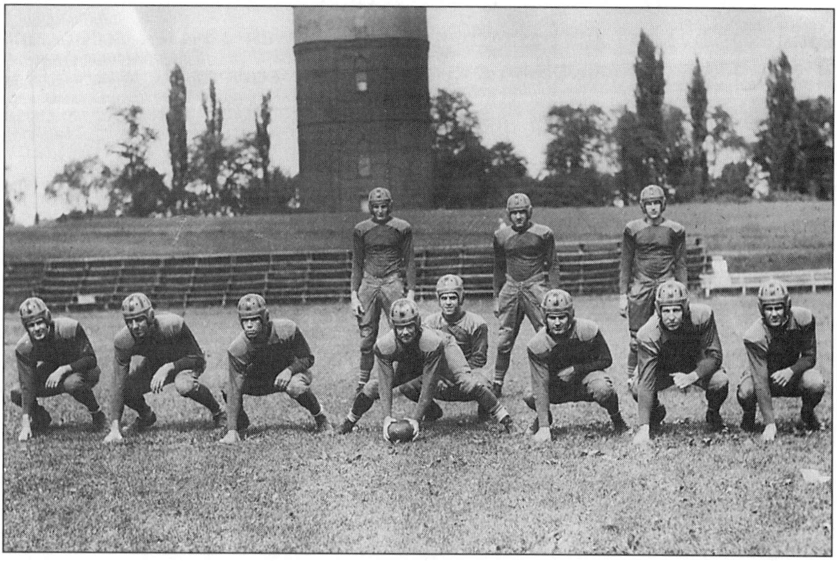

For St. Vincent College, 1950 began the downfall of their football program following their dramatic undefeated 1949 campaign. (Courtesy of Saint Vincent College.)

It was only fitting that a city so full of football history, Latrobe, PA, would field a strong varsity football club in the town's local institute of higher learning, Saint Vincent College. While they never really competed much at the major college level, they still slew their fair share of major college teams.

Football at Saint Vincent's was a proud community event on fall Saturdays at Bearcat Stadium, but unfortunately the reality of trying to financially establish a winning team reared its ugly head in the early 1960s. The college disbanded its club after the '62 campaign.

There was an attempt to return in a club football format in the late '60s. Despite the fact Saint Vincent remains a school without a team, the powers that be recently decided to revive the program at the NCAA Division III level in 2007. Hopefully the team of the future can live up to its past, when the football team was king of the campus.

The Beginning

From a schedule made up of three high school teams and Duquesne University, who thrashed Saint Vincent 27-3, the small private school from the football-rich town of Latrobe began its foray into collegiate football. Led by coach Marion Cleary, Saint Vincent began that season with an 18-0 victory over nearby Ligonier High, enroute to a 3-1 campaign.

Over the next eight seasons, they sputtered to a 29-35-4 mark with a schedule mixed with colleges and high schools. Probably the highlight of their first nine seasons was a 6-1 win against St. Francis College, which was considered one of the top teams in the east, on opening day of 1930.

In 1932 they hired "Genial" Gene Edwards, the quarterback of the 1926 Notre Dame Fighting Irish squad, to lead their forces. It was a move that took Saint Vincent up another level of intercollegiate football. Edwards had the pedigree, playing in the 1924 Rose Bowl before leading Knute Rockne's '26 club to a 9-1 record.

Under Edwards, the Bearcats became much more competitive, rolling to an 18-11-4 record his first four seasons. It was at that point, in 1936, that the school finally built a facility for the team, Bearcat Stadium, which was called by the school administration at the time, "a stadium equal to any arena of its kind in the country".

The High Life

The golden era of Saint Vincent football began in 1938 when Edwards led his Bearcat squad to a dominant 8-1-1 mark, including wins over Youngstown and St. Bonaventure. The Cats outscored their opponents 187-58 in the process that year.

After that phenomenal campaign, Saint Vincent went on a fine, four-year run under Genial Gene, going 20-8-5 that included a 7-1 mark in 1942, the last season of football at the Westmoreland County school until the war ended in 1945.

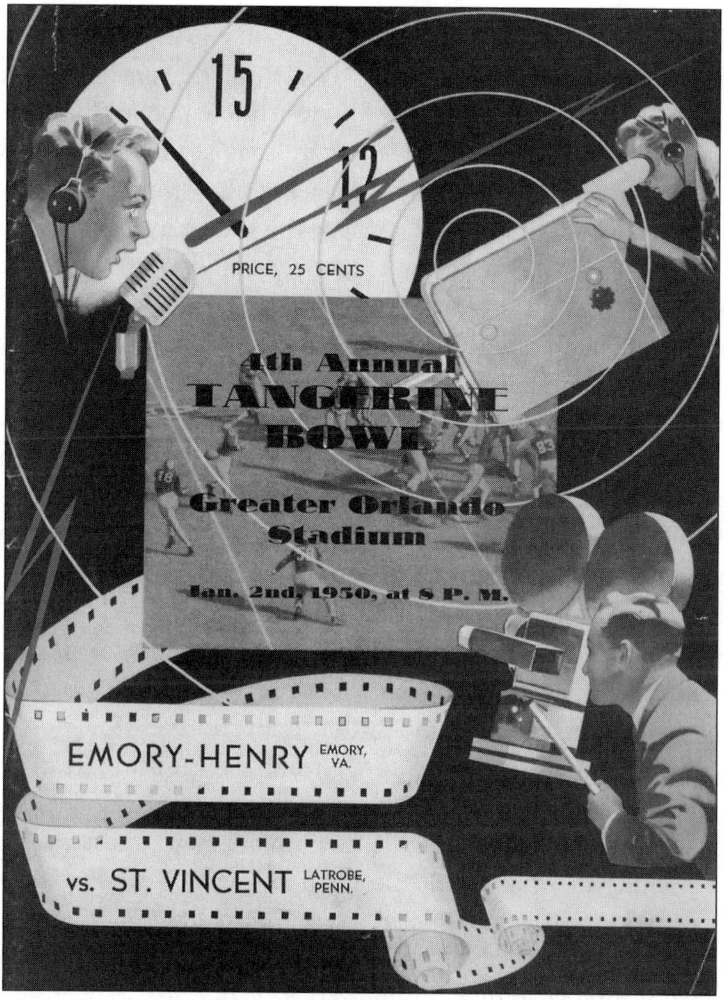

St. Vincent College began the 1950s by playing in their one and only bowl game, an exciting 7-6 victory against Emory-Henry College in the 1950 Tangerine Bowl capping a perfect 10-0 season. (Courtesy of Saint Vincent College.)

A year later saw a return of collegiate football to Latrobe under the direction of new coach Bap Manzini, captain of the 1941 Bearcats. Manzini, who had the unique hobby of keeping bees, played center in the National Football League with the Philadelphia Eagles in 1944 and 1945, before accepting the post as new headman of Saint Vincent. Manzini could not replicate Edward's winning ways and headed back to the NFL in 1948, making way for Duquesne's Al DeLuca to step in.

DeLuca was the star of the Dukes' Festival of Palms (the precursor to the Orange Bowl) victory in 1933, 33-7 over Miami (FL). He had spent time at his alma mater as an assistant coach, as well as head coach of Johnstown Catholic High. Al brought an enthusiasm and a new offensive philosophy to his job and had immediate results. His offensive system was called the "Adaptable T," which smartly took the best of the various formations of the time: the single wing, the T-formation, the "Notre Dame Box" and the short punt formation and made them into one. Its effect was astounding as the Bearcats rebounded quickly from 3-6-1 mark in Manzini's last season to a reverse 6-3-1 record in 1948 in DeLuca's inaugural campaign. It was a prelude to what would be the finest season in Saint Vincent football history.

Led by captains Frank DiMilio and Dave Hart, a Bearcat halfback better known as the future, albeit unsuccessful, coach of the Pitt Panthers in the 1960s, Saint Vincent barreled through its first six opponents to the tune of a combined 111-0 score before meeting West Virginia Wesleyan at Bearcat Stadium.

The only real significance of that contest came when Wesleyan's Charles Shepard went over from the one-yard line for a touchdown, marking the first score against the vaunted Bearcat defense all season. Unfortunately for the West Virginia school, they were behind 33-0 at the time, enroute to a 52-6 shellacking.

Saint Vincent ended up the regular season routing Mount Saint Mary's and Westminster 30-0 and 34-0, respectively, ending the Cats' 1949 campaign with its first and last undefeated mark in school history—outscoring the opposition 227-6.

As a reward for its banner season, the Bearcats had plenty of opportunities for postseason encounters, turning down such memorable events as the Smokey Mountain Bowl and a postseason game against New England College for a contest in Orlando, Florida, by the name of the Tangerine Bowl. While the Tangerine Bowl eventually developed into one of the best bowl games of its kind 50 years later, it was only in its fourth season then and pitted the undefeated 10-0 Emory-Henry College Wasps from Virginia against Saint Vincent.

The Bearcats rung in the new decade on January 2nd, beating the Wasps in an exciting tussle in front of 9,500 fans. Saint Vincent got on the scoreboard for the only time that evening in the second quarter, when Vince Sundry took a punt return 46 yards to set up a one-yard plunge by Don Henigin. Jack Heimbuecher knocked through the extra point, which proved vital, as it was the winning margin in a 7-6 victory.

While great things were expected following the 1950 Tangerine Bowl triumph, it unfortunately was the beginning of the end for Bearcat football.

The Low Road

After the 10-0 mark in 1949, Saint Vincent slid back to mediocrity before tumbling all the way down the ladder to their lone winless season in 1954. There was a small resurgence between 1956-1958, when the team combined for three consecutive winning seasons and a 14-5-3 record. But the times were coming to an end for varsity football at the school.

Before the 1960 season, the administration compiled a report that showed the football program was hemorrhaging money. In those three last winning seasons the losses for the program doubled—losing $10, 459 in 1956 compared to $21,660 in 1956. It was a huge amount at the time, considering the fact the school spent close to $32,000 in '56, taking in only $10,200 in revenue.

Cuts were made in an effort to save the program, but they were to no avail as the Bearcats won only eight games in the next three seasons. Finally, in 1962, following a 28-12 loss to King's College that capped a 1-6 campaign (the only win coming against Carnegie Tech, now Carnegie Mellon), the administration shut down varsity football at Saint Vincent College.

Current State of Affairs

Despite playing club football for a short time in the late '60s and early '70s, varsity football has remained dormant at the Latrobe campus since the end in 1962.

With their closest rivals from Seton Hill University beginning a football program in 2005, Saint Vincent decided it would not be outdone, unveiling plans to join local powerhouse Washington & Jefferson College in the Presidents Athletic Conference beginning in 2007. It's a move that will bring back the Bearcats to the college football landscape after an all too long 45 year absence.

Greatest Coach

While DeLuca brought the school to its greatest moment in 1949, he presided over some clunkers, too, finishing his 15-year coaching tenure with a 60-47-9 record. The vote here is for Edwards, who was 56-25-12 in his career at Saint Vincent.

Notable Players

Other than Manzini and Hart, some other Bearcat greats include All-American Harry "Sticks" Johnson, Bill Giel, Jack Rudge, Dino and Gino Amanati, Chippy Flauto, Bill Rafferty, Dick Detzel, Mickey Puskar, Al Pishioneri, Phillip Masciantonio, and Paul Giegerich as well as many other solid performers too numerous to mention.

All-time Record

148-108-25

Championships

Like Slippery Rock (unless it claims the 1936 national championship in which some scholar deduced that since the Bearcats defeated West Virginia Wesleyan, who beat Duquesne, who beat Pittsburgh, who beat Notre Dame, who beat Northwestern, who beat Minnesota, the recognized national champions, therefore making Saint Vincent the "Round-a-bout" national champion) the only title here is the 1950 Tangerine Bowl champions.

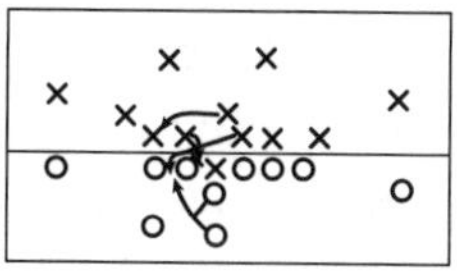 THIRTY NINE

The Quarterback Factory

Growing up, we were always taught about Pittsburgh's industrial might. The mills here churned out steel at an incredible rate for bridges, for skyscrapers and for the war effort. It was steel that gave this region and identity.

Students of football learn of the area's heritage of turning out quarterbacks. Like the steel produced in the mills, the quarterback factory that is Pittsburgh-area football has defined the sports landscape. What does it say when, arguably, three of the top four quarterbacks in NFL history have Western Pennsylvania roots? Statistically, that shouldn't happen. But signal callers here defy logic. They just seem to be bred for success.

"It makes sense," says Steelers' chairman Dan Rooney. "The way football is cherished here, generation after generation, you can understand why the guys who play the most important position on the field get to be so good in Western Pennsylvania. It makes sense to me at least."

Such questions of nature versus nurture may make interesting sociological fodder over beers at the local tavern (but then again, what doesn't?). But how can anyone explain 75 percent of the all-time, summa cum laude quarterback class lining up under center on Western Pennsylvania gridirons?

In no particular order, consider the qualifications of Joe Montana, who won four Super Bowls as a member of the San Francisco 49ers, three times capturing the MVP honors in the big game. That ability to play his best when the stakes were highest showed on the football field whether it was in high school at Ringgold or in college at Notre Dame. Montana was known for the great comeback, directing his team to 31 fourth-quarter comebacks in his NFL career. He is one of only five quarterbacks in league history to pass for 40,000 yards.

When it comes to passing yardage, no one compares to Dan Marino. The Oakland native and former signal caller from Central Catholic High School and the University of Pittsburgh holds 24 NFL records—including most passing yards and most touchdowns—and is tied for three others. His 1983 totals are among the best ever: 5,084 yards passing, 48 touchdowns and a passer rating of 108.9. Those are monster numbers.

Johnny Unitas was the man who held many of those records Marino broke. The Brookline native (later Mt. Washington and Bloomfield) brought the NFL into the consciousness of the American public by leading the Baltimore Colts to a sudden-death victory over the New York Giants in a nationally televised game that is often called "the greatest game ever played." It was one of three NFL championships Unitas won. He also holds football's equivalent of Joe DiMaggio's consecutive hit streak. Unitas threw touchdown passes in 47 consecutive games, a record that may never be broken.

Besides the Big Three, there have been a number of stellar Western Pennsylvania quarterbacks to make their mark in the NFL.

Joe Namath made his mark *against* the NFL, leading the American Football League's New York Jets to a 16-7 win over the Baltimore Colts in Super Bowl III. It's often called the greatest upset in football history. What made it even better was that the Beaver Falls native guaranteed it before the game. Joe Willie had some serious balls. Other quarterbacks may have had better stats but few influenced the style of the game as much as "Broadway Joe" did. The shame of it is that Namath never was able to showcase his ability as a pro after suffering serious knee injuries in high school and at college at Alabama. Namath's signing by the Jets was one of the forces that led to the merger of the two leagues. (See Chapter 8, "Huddle Diplomacy".)

Jim Kelly may not have ever won a Super Bowl, but the East Brady native did something unprecedented. He led his Buffalo Bills to four consecutive Super Bowl appearances. Kelly was a master of the no-huddle offense and played quarterback with a linebacker's mentality. His 35,647 passing yards in 11 NFL seasons ranked 10th in NFL history.

Until recently, no one had played more games than the seemingly ageless George Blanda. The Youngwood native spent 26 years in professional football. He came out of retirement in 1960 to lead the Houston Oilers to the inaugural AFL championship. He decided to stick around for

Beaver Falls product Joe Namath hit the zenith of his career leading the New York Jets to an improbable Super Bowl III victory.

(Courtesy of Graule Studios.)

another 15 years, gaining a reputation as a clutch quarterback and kicker. In 1970, at age 43, he had a magical season for the Oakland Raiders. In five games he led the Raiders to four wins and one tie with last-second touchdown passes or field goals.

Not all of our quarterbacks made the Hall of Fame. Still some had and are having nice NFL careers.

Babe Parilli had a solid professional career. His best years were with the Boston Patriots of the AFL, including 1964 when he led the league with 3,465 passing yards. The Rochester native finished his career as a backup to Namath on the Jets.

Although it's early in his career, Marc Bulger is starting to build some Hall of Fame-type credentials with the St. Louis Rams. The Central Catholic grad had six come-from-behind wins in his first season and a half and made Kurt Warner, a two-time NFL MVP, expendable. Keep an eye out for his development.

There have also been quarterbacks who were stars at the college level but didn't quite have that success translate to the NFL. For some reason, three of them ended up at Notre Dame.

Johnny Lujack was a Heisman Trophy winner for Notre Dame in 1947, leading the Irish's famed T-formation attack. A native of Connellsville, Lujack quarterbacked Notre Dame to a 26-1-1 record and three national championships. He's also remembered for the tackle on Army's Doc Blanchard that preserved a scoreless tie in 1946. Lujack spent four years in the NFL with the Chicago Bears. His best season was in 1949, when he led the league in passing yards (2,658) and touchdowns (23).

Butler's Terry Hanratty was also a strong quarterback for the Irish. A three-year starter, he led the 1966 championship team to an 8-0 record before injuring his shoulder. Hanratty was a consensus All-American in 1968 and finished third in the Heisman voting. The Steelers selected him in the second round of the 1969 draft. Unfortunately, he could never duplicate his college success, although he did manage to hang on for eight seasons in Pittsburgh and one with the expansion Tampa Bay Buccaneers.

The next Western Pennsylvania signal caller to make the trip to South Bend was McKees Rocks' Tom Clements, a three-year starter who led the Irish to a national championship in 1973. Clements never played a down in the NFL, choosing instead to play in the Canadian Football League. There he won two Grey Cups (our Northern neighbors' version of the Super Bowl) for the Ottawa Rough Riders. He was inducted into the CFL Hall of Fame in 1994. Currently, he serves as quarterback coach for the Buffalo Bills.

Tony Zimmerman was supposed to be the next Dan Marino. At least that's what the folks from NFL Films thought when they traveled to shoot his senior season at Penn Trafford High School. Like Marino, Zimmerman made his way to Pitt. But things didn't work out for him there. He transferred to Duquesne University and virtually rewrote the passing records at the school.

Zimmerman hasn't given up on his dream to make it to the NFL. He was the top quarterback in the Arena2 Football League at Quad City, setting the league record for touchdown passes in a season with 92 in 2003, and has moved up to the top Arena Football League with the Indiana Firebirds. Zimmerman's coach at Quad City was none other than the former IUP standout signal caller and his offensive coordinator with the Dukes, Rich Ingold.

Speaking of dreams, Uniontown's Sandy Stephens didn't let racism stop him from reaching his goals. Stephens was one of the first major college African American quarterbacks, leading the University of Minnesota to two Rose Bowl appearances and a national championship in 1960. He was drafted

Oakland's Dan Marino made a city happy when he decided to stay home and take controls of the offense at the University of Pittsburgh. Marino was a big part of the Panthers 33-3 run between 1979-1981. (Courtesy of the University of Pittsburgh.)

by the NFL's Cleveland Browns and the AFL's New York Titans. However, since neither franchise was willing to start a black man at quarterback, Stephens headed to the CFL and the Montreal Alouettes. He led them to a Grey Cup appearance in 1962.

Not all great quarterbacks are born. Some are made. As head coach for the University of Pittsburgh, Walt Harris did a great job in molding quarterbacks. Pete Gonzales was an ordinary quarterback at best, toiling for Johnny Majors before Harris arrived on the scene in 1997. Under Harris, Gonzales prospered and earned a shot in the NFL with the Steelers. Matt Lytle had similar success playing for the Carolina Panthers in 2001. Harris also turned Rod Rutherford, a raw recruit, into a polished college quarterback who went on to make the Carolina Panther practice squad this year. With the way Rutherford's successor, Tyler Palko, has performed above and beyond the call of duty in 2004, it looks like Harris will be able to add another page to his impressive resume.

There's no question that Harris has a way with quarterbacks. In fact, we considered doing a chapter on him, but given the overall coaching job he'd done with the Panthers, we weren't sure he'd still be employed in Oakland when this book came out. Turns out we were right, with Walt taking his ability to mold young quarterbacks to the West Coast as the new head coach at Stanford.

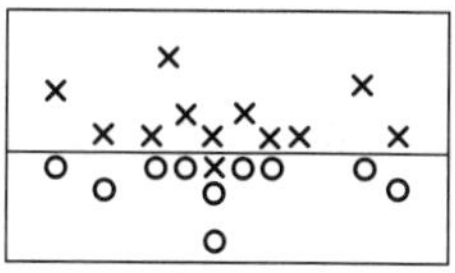

FORTY

Football Over the Bridge

It was heralded as a marvel when it was completed—the first time—back in 1896. The Monaca-Rochester suspension bridge was a beauty, just 10 feet short of the record for the longest such span of its kind. It was the first passenger bridge between Pittsburgh and Wheeling, and its effect on the two communities it joined was immediate. Both Monaca and Rochester prospered, and both towns were connected in a way not possible before. Residents walked across the 780-foot bridge over the Ohio River, and new friendships were forged.

The suspension bridge would finally give way to a newer, more modern cantilever design in 1930 and then finally a refurbished truss bridge in 1986 (for you bridge fans scoring at home), and the link between the two towns remained strong.

Rochester and Monaca were also connected by the high school football fever that burns on both sides of the Ohio throughout the Beaver Valley. The two teams had played each other since 1913, but the newly refurbished bridge brought an interesting twist to the rivalry. In 1988, the towns' mayors and managers made a friendly wager that turned into a tradition. They decided that the winner of the annual football game between

Monaca and Rochester would officially determine the name of the bridge. If Monaca won, you would be crossing the Monaca-Rochester bridge. Should Rochester be victorious, it would be the Rochester-Monaca bridge.

And just to add to the spectacle, Monaca mayor John Antoline and Rochester mayor Gerald LaValle lined up in the middle of the bridge opposite each other in a three-point stance as a photographer from the *Beaver County Times* snapped away. Both men knew a good photo-op was a boost for their political careers. The late Antoline parlayed his term as mayor to being a Beaver County commissioner. LaValle serves now as a state senator.

The debut "Bridge Game" helped grow the hype. Both teams entered the contest undefeated at 9-0 and more than 8,000 fans jammed into Rochester Stadium—unofficially the largest crowd to watch a game there. Monaca crushed Rochester 31-8, with Matt Raich, now an offensive assistant with the Pittsburgh Steelers, taking over the game as a two-way star. His 15-yard touchdown that put the Indians up for good is still talked about among local football historians—as he completely reversed his field and broke a number of tackles on his way to the end zone. That run turned a tight game into a laugher.

Monaca had possession of the first bridge trophy. And the rivalry grew. And both teams became powerhouses in Class A. Monaca made three straight WPIAL championship game appearances from 1998-2000. Rochester was even better, capturing five WPIAL crowns and winning the PIAA championship in 1998, 2000 and 2001. Now, flash forward to 2004 and the 17th edition of the bridge game. On paper, it didn't look to be much of a match-up. Rochester entered the game with a 5-3 record and a spot in the WPIAL playoffs on the line. Monaca came in at a lowly 1-7.

But the fans didn't pay attention to the records. This contest was the high school version of Army versus Navy, where the rivalry transcends the actually ability of the teams. It didn't matter what their records were, we were told over and over again. This was going to be a close game, they kept telling us. And we believed them.

"In 35 years, I haven't missed a game," says Rochester's Don Hatt. "This rivalry is a big one. It's always a close game." Hatt calls himself the top Rochester fan. The Rochester Quarterbacks

Club agreed, bestowing that title on Hatt one year. He not only goes to the high school games but also to the midget and JV contests, as well. "It's important to support the kids," he notes, "but it's also a cheap time out. You don't spend a lot of money at these football games."

Standing nearby the fence where the Rochester squad will enter the field is his compatriot Samuel Pedlaine. "I've been coming to games since I was 10, and I'm 79 now," he says. "It's a good team this year." Like Hatt, Pedlaine also is a former Fan of the Year. Looking down the row that lines the fence are more winners of the award, guys who gather each Friday night—but this bridge game is the big one.

On the other side, it's not quite as cheery as it is among the Rochester rooters. "It's been a tough year," says Monaca resident Rick Vaccarelli. "The crowds don't seem to be traveling with the team that much. It's a little lighter than usual." Indeed, on this night, when the marching band gets up to do its on-field performance, the Monaca section of the grandstands is sparse. One fan, however, does have a vested interest in the game. Dennis Bickerstaff played against Rochester in the pre-bridge game years of the early '70s. Now he's here to watch his son Colin, a senior quarterback/defensive back for the Indians, follow in his football footsteps.

"It's a great rivalry, and it really doesn't matter about the records. You can throw them out," says the elder Bickerstaff. "And it's fun. I have a lot of friends in Rochester, and we all see each other at this game. It's the best of the year."

The game also has a special meaning for Monaca's head coach, Shawn McCreary. "I played in the game, so I know what it's like," he says. "As a coach you try not to approach it in a different way, but the atmosphere makes it hard. Plus 95 percent of the time it has playoff implications."

This particular year, however, the bridge game would fall into that other 5 percent. The game was over in the first half, with Rochester building up a 34-0 lead. The Rams' defense forced three turnovers; running back Brent Whiteleather ripped through the Indians' defense for 79 first-half rushing yards and two touchdowns; and Rochester quarterback Cory Schleyer directed a potent passing attack that executed its playbook more on the level of a college squad than a high school team. Monaca, on the other hand, managed only 28 total yards in the first half. It wasn't pretty. You couldn't just throw records out the door, after all. Those heady fans who had predicted a close contest suddenly found themselves in the midst of a laugher. The fence men on the Rochester side talked of it being one of the most impressive performances in memory against the rivals from across the river. The Monaca fans quietly hit the refreshment stands, few of them opting to buy a raffle ticket for a game ball. This would be a game to forget. And quickly.

Yet despite the bad contest on the field (the final after a merciful second half was 34-6 Rochester), the game was a celebration of the best that high school football can embody.

It was an inviting atmosphere as we walked the sidelines during the game. At one point the referee tossed a football our way, asking us to hold it while another ball was rotated into play. We were welcomed into the fray, which is not surprising, given the closeness that played out even amongst rivals.

The two communities mingled together, even with some good-natured ribbing and lots of "wait until next years" flying back and forth. Police from both towns were on hand, talking to the families they served (by the way, the Monaca police uniforms have the Indians' emblem on their sleeves—an indication of the deep connection between the community and its high school football team). Not that the police are called upon to do much other than socialize during a bridge game.

"The great thing about this rivalry is that we've never had a problem," coach McCreary says. "It's not bad blood. At the end of the game, everybody shakes hands. There are a lot of good friends on that field."

Come back next year, we were told. The game would be more competitive. And we might make the trek to the other side of the river next year to see what it's like. Would there be Monaca's version of the fence men? And who is the Monaca Fan of the Year? And then there is the game itself. When two programs that have had such success meet for the bragging rights and the bridge trophy it's most likely going to be a compelling story. There was too much of a talent gap to bridge in the 2004 edition. For Monaca this year, it was simply a bridge too far.

Monaca runs onto the field in hopes of ending a disappointing season with a victory over their closest rival from Rochester. It was not to be as the Rams humbled them 34-6.

Every fan who entered Rochester's home field for the 2004 version of the bridge game led the authors to believe that you can throw out the records when these two schools lined up; apparently they were wrong.

Section V

2004: A Pigskin Odyssey

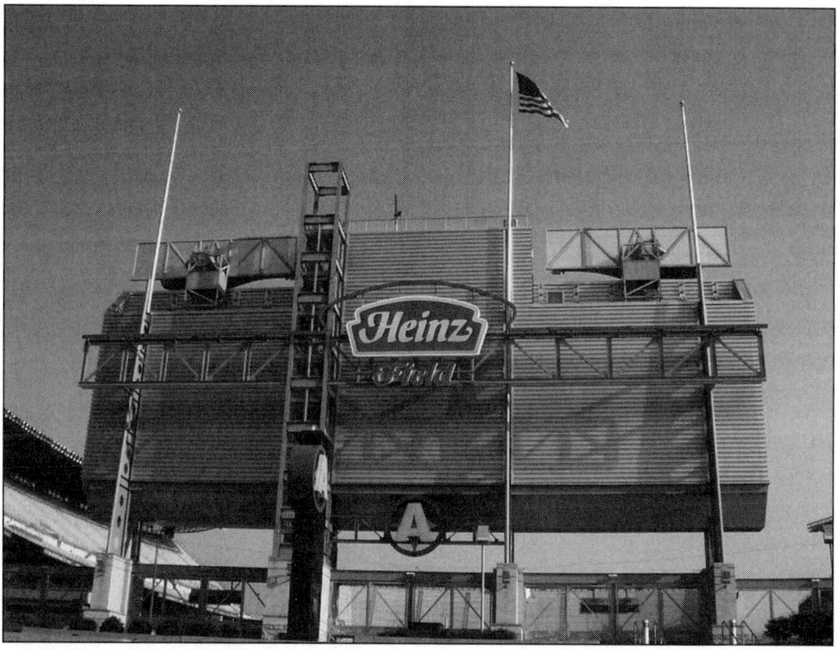

Heinz Field was the site of many a football miracle in 2004.

It was not easy being a sports fan in Western Pennsylvania as August blew its sultry winds across the Allegheny Mountains. The Pirates were in the process of finishing yet another sub-.500 season, their 12th in a row. The Penguins, Pittsburgh's boys of winter, had recently finished a chase for the top pick in the NHL draft by having the most pathetic campaign since the days before the arrival of Mario. Worse off, the passions of the Steel City, the Steelers and the University of Pittsburgh football team, were going through very disappointing training camps that brought hopes of a shining season to a crashing and sudden halt.

Following a 30-13 thumping in the second game of the season at the hands of the hated Baltimore Ravens, a game when veteran quarterback Tommy Maddox went down with a serious elbow injury that prompted the sudden acceleration of rookie Ben Roethlisberger's career, thoughts of a playoff spot were exchanged with those of high first-round draft picks.

The fortunes of Pitt were not much better after a disorganized loss to the upstart Connecticut Huskies. Quarterback Tyler Palko looked lost, coach Walt Harris sounded like a man who wanted to be fired, and a 3-8 season threatened to throw the program back into the dark days of the Paul Hackett regime.

Things were certainly bleak around here. The only real positive was the NHL strike would spare beleaguered Pittsburgh fans another win-starved season.

Just when we were poised for an all-time sports low, something strange happened. It was as if the voices of Steel City sports aficionados stood up in unison and shouted "We're mad as hell and we're not going to take it anymore." (Or maybe we just saw a rerun of the movie *Network*.) Someone heard the cry for help and the football gods came down in winged force, changing this putrid year into something magical. How else can you explain a coach on the verge of extinction finding a way with a sieve of a defense to flip a tragic campaign to a winning one to give his team their first Big East title and BCS (Bowl Championship Series) bid? Stranger yet, enlighten us on how a team with horrendous injuries, led by a rookie quarterback and a broken-down, past-his-prime running back become the scourge of the NFL and crush two undefeated teams in back to back weeks to shoot out to a 10-1 record. You got us.

As confused as we both are, we will do our best to try and explain the year that was in 2004, a year where the football teams took the city from the depths of depravity to exultation and finally a hope for the future.

FORTY ONE

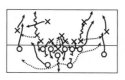

Battle of the Titans: Recapping the 2004 WPIAL and City League seasons

From the beginning of the season it was only about two teams, one the defending Quad A champion and the other a former powerhouse from decades past that was attempting to resurrect its former glory.

They met in the opening contest of the season, with the 2003 AAAA champions from Pittsburgh Central Catholic defeating the Gateway Gators 28-20 in an exciting contest. Many thought the difference was the loss of Justin King, perhaps the greatest player ever to don a Gator uniform, because of cramps and dehydration in the first half. Had King played the whole game, they thought, the men from Monroeville would have defeated the Vikings—and it would have been Gateway and not Central Catholic that garnered a top 10 national ranking. If "could haves" were reality, perhaps Neil O'Donnell would have hit a streaking Ernie Mills for the game-winning TD in Super Bowl XXX. Such what-ifs are not reality, though. (O'Donnell threw the ball into the waiting arms of the Cowboys' Larry Brown, costing the Steelers their elusive "one for the thumb," but we'll get back to this later.) In the real world, the Gators were 0-1 and dreamt of a rematch, one at Heinz Field in November, one where they would have Justin King for the whole game, proving once and for all they were the rightful heirs to the AAAA throne.

While the Quad A championship seemed to be a two-team race, Penn Hills and Upper St. Clair also quickly set themselves apart from the pack. The Indians ripped through the Quad East conference losing only to—you guessed it—Pittsburgh Central Catholic, 39-25, on their way to an 8-1 regular season mark. Running back Ed Collingwood, who ran for 1,700 yards, and wide receiver David Harvey, who was expected to choose to continue his career at either West Virginia or Penn State, led a potent Penn Hills offense into the playoffs. Upper St. Clair ran the table in the Quad North, going 9-0 on the heels of their heavily recruited, standout running back Sean Lee. Despite his prowess as both a running back and safety, Lee was being recruited as a linebacker by the likes of Penn State, West Virginia, Iowa and Georgia Tech.

Despite the success of the Panthers and Indians, it was Gateway and Central Catholic that quickly set the tone. In the second week of the season, Gateway hosted a football classic at their newly named football shrine, Pete Antimarino Stadium. It was there that the two schools showed their muscle. The Gators ripped apart their rivals Woodland Hills 47-6 as King rambled for 84 yards on his first carry. Central Catholic did Gateway one better, destroying St. Joseph's of Philadelphia, who came into the contest with a 35-game win steak, 38-12.

As the season ended, the four Titans, Pittsburgh Central, Gateway, Penn Hills and USC entered the WPIAL AAAA tournament as the top four seeds. Odds were great that one of them would fall in the 16-team playoffs before the semifinal round. After all, it had been since 1995 that all four top seeds made it that far. This was not a normal year, though, with the four titans dominating their way through the first two rounds, outscoring their opponents by a 283-54 margin and setting up the dominant final four.

Even with Penn Hills and USC playing so well, destiny was not on their side. The Vikings did their part for a Gateway rematch with a 20-12 victory over the Panthers. For the Gators, the road would be a little more difficult. Penn Hills thought it had the game plan to stop King and Gateway dead in their tracks and did so for all but two minutes of the exciting contest. Unfortunately for the Indians, champions find ways to win and Justin King is just one of those players. Bottled up all night in this defensive affair, King broke loose for a 32-yard run with only 1:34 left to give the Gators a 10-7 victory, sending them to their first final in 18 seasons.

1986 was the last time Gateway smelled the rarified heights of a WPIAL championship match. Back then their current coach, Terry Smith, was their quarterback. That squad was led by Pete Antimarino, at the time the only coach the school ever had, leading the Gators since 1958 to a 236-80-12 record over the course of his 32 years on the Gateway sidelines. The team was a fixture in the WPIAL playoffs winning or sharing five championships. CMU coach Rich Lackner has fond memories of Antimarino, who came to the Tartans staff after retiring from Gateway in 1989: "He was a good coach... and always had his kids prepared and ready to play on Saturday. Pete also had a great sense of humor. He had some good one-liners in the coaches' locker room, and he kept us loose."

Antimarino had his team prepared that day in 1986 as they took on the nation's top-ranked team, the North Hills Indians. Smith, who would go on to a stellar career at Penn State as a receiver, led the Gators that day to an upset 7-6 victory; a day that would turn out to be the last day in the sun the successful Gateway program would have for almost two decades.

For the most part the school floundered after Antimarino's retirement—that is until Smith returned to his alma mater to return the school to its former glory days. Gateway's climb to the mountaintop of the WPIAL looked to be at hand, even with a little deja vu. The Gaters entered the Heinz Field on November 20 to take on another highly ranked national opponent, just like they did 18 years earlier.

While the Gators were ranked No. 20 nationally in the USA Today High School Poll, the Pittsburgh Central Catholic Vikings were No. 7. Despite the fact both teams had competent passing games (Aaron Smith threw for more than 1,000 yards for Gateway and the Vikings' Shane Murphy topped 1,200 yards passing with 17 touchdowns) this battle of the titans looked to be a tussle between the WPIAL's two most dominant running backs.

For Gateway, it was King, who ran for 1,900 yards. Central Catholic countered with Eugene Jarvis, who came in at 1,686 yards.

There have only been five rushers in WPIAL history to eclipse 4,000 yards in a career, and two of them would now face each other for the area's biggest prize.

King was thought of as Western Pennsylvania's most promising prospect (for defensive back and not running back, though) eliciting scholarship offers from around the nation. His recruitment had been an odyssey. The finalists were Florida, which was the top choice until coach Ron Zook was dumped, Michigan and Penn State. Eventually, before the WPIAL championship tilt, he picked the Nittany Lions, school of his coach and stepfather Terry Smith. With that decision done, the talented running back could now concentrate on bringing the title and the glory back to his school, where it belonged.

This time, there would be no cramping or dehydration to prevent King from bringing the championship back. He was healthy and ready to go. But a funny thing happened on the way to Gateway's coronation. The defending WPIAL champion Central Catholic team decided they would show up and play a little football of their own. As so often happens, the game never lived up to its hype. The Vikings routed the Gators 28-0, with Jarvis having a little something to say about who the best back in Western Pennsylvania was by outgaining King 221-105. It was another case of the could-have-beens.

Despite the loss, it was still a dominant year in high school football, not because of the great play and talented players, but because every team we came in contact with had a very successful season. "The Midas touch" if you will.

Both our alma maters made it to their respective semifinal rounds, losing by almost exact scores. Fletcher's Blackhawk squad made it to the AAA semifinals before falling to Thomas Jefferson 21-17. Finoli's beloved Greensburg Central Catholic Centurions dropped a tough one to Seton-LaSalle, 21-16, in the AA semi's. The school districts we currently live in, Woodland Hills and Gateway, also made the playoffs with the Gators crushing Woodland Hills 31-12 in the quarterfinals. Let us also not forget the magic we brought to Rochester as we went to cover the bridge game there between Rochester and Monaca. It was our first high school game since 1980 and our aura helped the Rams capture the A title with an exciting 15-14 victory over Clairton.

As good as it was at the quad A level, it was also just as fine a year in local high school football in the lesser divisions too as they had titans of their own. Rochester, of course, won their fourth WPIAL title in five years. Seton-LaSalle survived an AA tournament that saw all four semi-final participants enter the finals undefeated. Seton-LaSalle's impressive passing game, led by quarterback Bill Stull (the first WPIAL player ever to eclipse the 3,000-yard plateau—and that's up against the likes of Marino, Montana... ah we know the list) and receiver Carmen Connolly (who caught a state-record 112 passes, the 10th most ever in high school football history) helped cap off a perfect 13-0 campaign with a 42-35 win over a tough Aliquippa squad. The year's only true Cinderella, West Mifflin, knocked off top-ranked West Allegheny 23-22 in the semis, but lost the AAA championship tilt to a tough Thomas Jefferson team 20-0.

The Pittsburgh City League also had its own titan, Perry Traditional Academy, which was led by quarterback Desmond Brently and captured its fifth straight City League title with a 16-12 win over Peabody.

Yes, 2004 was a year where we could truly say only the strong survived, keeping the fabled Western Pennsylvania high school tradition alive; a tradition that has endured proudly for well over 100 years.

Failure At The PIAA Altar

When the New York Yankees go to the World Series and lose, George Steinbrenner doesn't order the most expensive champagne on the menu and celebrate a good season, he gets angry and plots how he will overrun the baseball world 12 months later. That's how great teams act. They accept nothing but the pinnacle of success, a championship. Nothing else is acceptable. This is why when it comes to the PIAA (Pennsylvania Interscholastic Athletic Association) state football championships, the men from the WPIAL consider their history there nothing short of a failure.

Let's look at the record coming into this season. Out of 64 possible championship appearances in the 16-year history of the tournament, Western Pennsylvania schools (the WPIAL and the City League) have been there 48 times; an incredible 75 percent success rate. Yet with all of those appearances in title clashes, the WPIAL has managed only 19 state championships, while Perry captured the City League's only crown in 1989, a meager 39 percent winning percentage. Thank god for all the schools involved that Steinbrenner does not lead their charges.

Western Pennsylvania has long been considered one of the bright spots of high school football in the nation, and the region should certainly be the dominant force in football throughout the commonwealth. But according to the state championship clashes, that dominance is missing, although two of the 2004 WPIAL titans did bring back a measure of respect to the area.

In looking at it by class, A ball has been by far the most successful. WPIAL squads have been in 12 of 17 championships, winning seven—including three by Rochester. But the Rams were nothing more than fodder for Southern Columbia in 2004, losing in the final 35-0 to give the victors their third straight championship.

Jumping up one class, AA has captured a similar amount of championships, 12. But these schools have only captured four state titles, as this year's District 8 (WPIAL) representative Seton-LaSalle and its high-flying offense was crushed by Tyrone 26-7 in the quarterfinals.

Despite the fact teams from AAA historically have been the least successful (winning only three times before this year) Thomas Jefferson made it four with their first state championship in 2004. The Jaguars won the western championship with a 21-20 thriller over Erie's Strong Vincent before thrashing eastern winner Manheim Central, 56-20, on the strength of quarterback Brad Dawson's 11 for 16, 190-yard performance in the final.

With all the other divisions having a disappointing track record, perhaps the worst was the kingpin of them all—Quad A. After dominating the early days of the state championship tournaments (they won six of the first eight championships between 1988 and 1995), no WPIAL school has won a title since Penn Hills destroyed Lower Dauphin in '95. Pittsburgh Central Catholic threatened to break their record of futility, one that has seen Western Pennsylvania squads lose six title matches in a row, by tossing into the mix one of the strongest teams in the area in many years.

The Vikings pummeled their way to the western championship

by stuffing what was considered a strong Bishop McDevitt team like a turkey, 44-0. Coming into the contest McDevitt boasted one of the greatest running backs in the country, LeSean McCoy, who had 2,788 yards to that point including an average of 343 a game in his previous five encounters. The Steel Curtain-like Viking defense showed him no respect, holding the previously unstoppable McCoy to 39 yards on 22 carries.

It would be this club from Oakland that brought back the Yankee-like swagger to Western Pennsylvania high school football. Breaking the nine-year hex over AAAA teams from the area, Central Catholic not only captured the state's highest crown, but did so in a way that humiliated the way they play the game in the east. The Vikings, who are ranked sixth in the country according to *USA Today*, shot out to a 35-0 first-half lead against Neshaminy and never looked back, putting the icing on a 16-0 season. Their superstar back Eugene Jarvis rambled for 192 yards and five touchdowns. So dominant was the Central Catholic defense that through three quarters it only gave up 43 yards before the eastern champions scored two meaningless touchdowns against the Viking backups in the fourth quarter to make the final 49-14.

While the WPIAL schools cannot be proud of their performance at the altar of the PIAA in the past, there are perhaps a couple of reasons why they have not been able to fulfill their destiny. The first may be that they have the longest road to travel in the tournament, having to win seven playoff games (including the WPIAL championships) to secure the state championship; no other district is asked to win more than six. Seven of Pittsburgh Central Catholic's 16 victories came in the postseason. A second reason may be the WPIAL itself. Its tournament is so grueling and tough (perhaps teams there are fighting tooth and nail against better competition than in the state playoffs) that sometimes the PIAA championships can be anticlimactic. It doesn't figure to get easier as WPIAL squads are now asked to play one extra game in the state championships than they used to. Even though it makes things more difficult, give credit to Central Catholic and Thomas Jefferson. They found a way to bring the swagger back, a feat that would make George Steinbrenner proud.

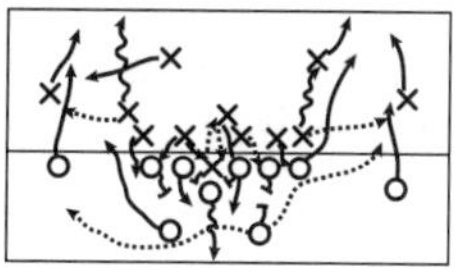

FORTY TWO

THE WALT ZONE: RECAPPING THE 2004 YEAR THAT WAS IN WESTERN PENNSYLVANIA COLLEGE FOOTBALL

Welcome to a world where things don't make sense. It's where bad football teams become champions. Where left-for-dead, seemingly poor coaches become geniuses, leading their teams to incomprehensible victories. And where mistake-prone quarterbacks become great field leaders. Welcome to... The Walt Zone... Do do do doooooooooo!

While Walt Harris' tenure at the University of Pittsburgh was filled with more ups and downs than a roller coaster gone bad, nothing could have prepared Pitt fans for what they were to experience in 2004. To quickly recap his time in Oakland: he took a moribund program and made them winners if not champions, had impressive victories making nationally ranked Virginia Tech Pitt's daddy on more than one occasion and beating Joe Pa 12-0 in 2000, the last meeting between Penn State and Pitt in the foreseeable future. Harris has become renowned in taking bad-to-average quarterbacks and turning them into successes, as well as molding bad receivers into good ones, average ones into greats and greats into legends.

Despite the fact that his resume here was filled with things he can be proud of, there was also the other side—the one that made the Panther faithful bang their collective heads against the wall. There were the defenses that, for the most part, resembled Swiss cheese. Opposing running backs tended to amass unbelievable yardage against defensive players who were out of position. There was the whole 2004 recruiting debacle where four major recruits changed their minds and went to other schools on national letter of intent day. Add the many big games that could have sent the program to the upper echelon of college football that ended with bitter defeat. And worse, there were the inexcusable losses to the likes of South Florida and Toledo, the top 10 team in 2003 that crumbled in front of them, the thrashing at the hands of their biggest rival West Virginia. And the days that will live in infamy: the swinging gate play against Texas A&M and the decision to use the best receiver in college football history as a decoy in a bowl game.

For every good thing that happened to Walt, there was an equal and ultimately bad thing that came up, too. Even so, nothing could have prepared fans for what unfolded in 2004. Nothing!

It was a cranky Walt Harris who began fall training camp for the University of Pittsburgh Panthers. While many often criticized every breath he took in August, it was no wonder why the Pitt coach seemed so irascible every time he seemingly opened his mouth. The last 12 months of his head coaching career had been one bump in the road after another.

The 2003 campaign began with so much promise. The team rose to the top 10 for the first time since the Danny Marino days, and a Big East championship and spot in the BCS seemed real possibilities for the Panthers. Harris had seemingly brought the program back to the level where it belonged. A funny thing happened on the way to the national championship: the defense forgot how to actually stop someone from scoring. Many opposing backs ran for miles and miles against the formerly impenetrable Pitt defensive line, as the club struggled to an 8-5 record garnering a meaningless Continental Tire Bowl bid instead of the long awaited BCS shot.

Despite the fact the team did not live up to their lofty expectations, Harris was in the process of recruiting his most successful freshman class, one that promised to put the University of Pittsburgh back in the upper echelon of college football. He had gotten the prime picks from the fertile Western Pennsylvania high school harvest, Anthony Morelli from Penn Hills, perhaps the top signal caller in the nation, and stud running back Andrew Johnson from Pittsburgh Central Catholic. Fate, unfortunately, was unkind to the Panther coach (as was the Atlantic Coast Conference) when the money-grubbing presidents of the ACC grabbed the two jewels of the Big East crown, Virginia Tech and Miami, to join their circuit. The reverberation was heard throughout the land, but it especially stuck a dagger in the heart of Oakland.

Unsure of the perilous future of the Big East and the Pitt football program, Morelli bolted for Penn State, and Johnson went to Miami. If that wasn't enough of a slap in the face, star wide receiver Johnny Peyton, who would vie to fill the large shoes of the departed Larry Fitzgerald, reneged on his verbal commitment to stay closer to home and went to South Florida, and fellow Florida prep star Alphonso Smith opted for Wake Forest.

When things looked like they couldn't get worse for the faltering program, they did. An irritated Harris was at odds with both his players and the press constantly during training camp and the seemingly annual quarterback controversy took an unexpected and ugly turn.

Injuries took their toll on the young squad, one that was littered with nine new starters on offense. The maladies caused little sympathy from the Pitt head man. By August 21, 17 players had missed practiced for the day, the strangest being the new starting wide out Greg Lee, a player whose grip on a starting position was now tenuous at best. At first he claimed his hamstring was injured, then his quadriceps, which elicited the following response from Harris: "It's not a hamstring now, it's a quad. It was a hamstring for a while, but now his quads are hurting. I don't know what his problem is. But if he can't practice, he isn't going to start. You don't just show up around here, you have to practice."

He showed little patience for any other Panthers who couldn't suit up. "I don't want to talk about all those guys," Harris said. "Let's talk about the guys who work their butts off practicing, getting triple time in workouts. The problem is they get worn out." Walt further went on to grumble, "It does concern me (the injuries). Some of those scholarship guys need to wake up or transfer if that's the way it's going to be."

When the Emperor himself, Chuck Noll, used to make such claims, the media and fans alike would understand where he was coming from and back the coach up. But when Walt Harris made them, it was a different story. After all, Walt didn't win four Super Bowls and worse yet, these were kids and not grown men. The media had little patience for Harris. Despite the fact his conference was disintegrating and his team seemingly was falling apart in front of him, the press had enough of his grumbling. On another front, some of the alumni base seemingly had enough of the Harris excuses for not bringing Pitt to the forefront of the college football world. If you thought that things couldn't get any worse for the coach, think again.

Academics took one of his brightest running backs in Juwon Walker as well as a potential offensive lineman on what was already a painfully thin area on the club in Troy Banner. Seemingly the only position where he had some promise was at quarterback, where heralded sophomores Tyler Palko and Luke Getsy were in the midst of a spirited battle for the starting nod. When he finally named Palko as the starter, things once again backfired. Getsy decided if he couldn't start for the Panthers, he didn't want to be here at all. What hurt most of all was Getsy's choice to transfer to Akron, where Harris' former offensive coordinator J.D. Brookhart was now the head honcho.

The young quarterback's decision was also damaging in the fact that he choose to transfer so late in the year that Harris did not have a chance to properly prepare Palko's replacement. Any injury to Palko would now be devastating. Because of the timing of the transfer, the Pitt coach used his prerogative and denied Getsy's transfer, meaning if the quarterback left and went to Akron, Getsy would be ineligible to receive a scholarship until the 2005-2006 school year and would have to pay his own way this year. Getsy did leave, and once again the city was up in arms. "Why would you do this to a young kid" many felt as Walt was once again painted as the bad guy. Never mind the fact that Getsy, a young ADULT, mind you, chose to slap his teammates in the face and pick up his ball and go away because he couldn't start. No, it was cranky Walt's fault.

Luckily for the beleaguered Pitt coach, training camp finally came to a long awaited end. As the team prepared for its opening game in Tampa against one of the soon-to-be Big East's new brethren, South Florida, on Labor Day, we looked at the club's scorecard. On defense, the Panthers were returning a club that was one of the most pathetic defensive units in Division I football in 2003; on offense it was even worse. A spanking new quarterback was to be put behind an offense line that, while it included a solid performer in Rob Petitti, had four new starters with little experience (including red-shirt freshman Mike McGlynn and converted defensive tackle Charles Spencer). The running back corps was unspectacular, and the receivers—at one time thought to be the team's strength before season-ending injuries to Terrell Allen and Princell Brockenbrough—were now being manned by the maligned Lee and walk-on Joe Del Sardo. So troubled by this was Harris that he said "When you have walk-on, Joe Del Sardo, who looks like he is going to have a tremendous chance to start, that's not the grand plan... We have a lot of picking up to do."

The only break the Panthers seemingly got was when Hurricane Charley rolled into South Florida, postponing their tough season opener until December 4th. This meant that Pitt would commence their 2004 campaign with a much easier test against Ohio of the Mid American conference in the friendly confines of Heinz Field.

While the 24-3 win looked like a comfortable victory to the naked eye, a closer look suggests trouble was brewing. Offensively, Palko's debut as a starter was less than stellar. He completed only 6 of 19 passes for 49 yards. For the contest, the seemingly undermanned Ohio squad outgained the Panthers 290-217.

Next up was the long-awaited matchup against former athletic director Steve Pederson's new employer, Nebraska. Over the past decade, the Cornhuskers had one of the most storied programs in college football history, but no one was sure what to expect with this new version of Big Red, one that promised to eschew their power running game for a more open offense. As the morning of the game finally came, the contest was not the primary story on the minds of the city—a record-setting rainfall the day before caused catastrophic flooding everywhere in Western Pennsylvania. Whether or not the game would go on was still a consideration, as the floodwaters not only overcame the parkway around Heinz Field but were cresting ever so close to the facility itself. The game went on as planned. Pitt wished it wouldn't have. Three interceptions and a fumbled punt led to 17 quick points, with Nebraska sporting a 24-10 firsthalf lead. The oft-maligned defense stepped up to the plate and shut down the Huskers in the second half as Palko also came to life. He hit Lee with a 34-yard pass and drove the Panthers to Nebraska's 14-yard line before throwing an incomplete pass into the end zone with five seconds left to leave the home team just short of a spectacular comeback.

Would this contest be a sign of a surprise season, or was Nebraska just not as good as advertised? Even though Nebraska finished the campaign with their first losing season in four decades, the answer to the more important questions about Pitt would come when the Panthers played their third consecutive home game, this one against division I-AA power Furman on September 25.

Let's make this clear: a Division I school should never lose or play a close game against a Division I-AA team, no matter how good the lesser division club is. That being said, when Furman shot out to a 31-14 thirdquarter lead and maintained it at 38-24 midway in the fourth, it looked like this could be the lowest point Pitt football ever endured. Thankfully, Palko showed grit, completing 30 of 36 passes for 380 yards that included two fourth quarter drives to tie the game at 38. Pitt escaped with their hides in overtime 41-38 and were going on to face the upstart Connecticut Huskies in their first away match of the season.

The close win against Furman had to be the low point of a forgettable season. Not quite. The Panthers went into East Hartford to play a Husky team that was new to the Big East and should not have provided Pitt with much of a challenge. While Lee was beginning to look like a star, catching two passes for 129 yards, precious few others from the blue and gold did. Not only was Pitt being outplayed and committing incomprehensible dead ball penalties as the Huskies were up 10-7 late in the first half, but Harris was about to be assailed as never before. With the Panthers driving to either tie or go ahead late in the half, Palko took the snap on a third down deep in Husky territory. Instead of going for paydirt on a third and goal at the Connecticut 12, the sophomore signal caller inexplicably ran to the center of the field and slid down, setting up a field goal instead. While Josh Cummings' connected kick tied the game at 10, Harris' strange call left many wondering if he was just looking to be fired. To make matters worse, UConn took the kickoff back to set up a 49-yard field goal that sent the teams to the locker room with the Huskies up 13-10.

Down 16-10, Palko hit Lee with a 77-yard bomb and then took the ball in from one yard out, putting Pitt ahead 17-16 early in the third quarter. At that point the offense and defense both disappeared. UConn dominated the remainder of the game, winning 29-17. This had to be the lowest point of the season, right? Even after linebacker Clint Session admitted after the game that the team came out in the second half complacent because they thought they had the game in the bag—even though they were behind 13-10. "We thought we had the game wrapped up at half, so we came out flatter than we should have," he said. Harris tried to defend his senseless Palko sliding call. But this was not the low point.

In the week following the Husky debacle Harris' agent, Bob LaMonte, was quoted in the papers with several derogatory comments about the University of Pittsburgh, including "Pitt is better than it has been in decades. He [Harris] has the program strong again. And unless people are living in La-La Land, they have to realize what he's up against. It's not like there was an outcry by the big conferences [Atlantic Coast and Big Ten] to bring Pitt in. People think Pitt should just be this major power, but the teams the ACC wanted were Virginia Tech and Miami. It wouldn't matter if Walt Harris or Vince Lombardi coached there, you have to deal in reality." With everything that had gone on with Harris this season, this was the icing on the cake prompting many, including the school's most revered former player Tony Dorsett, to call for Walt's head. Was this to be the low point? Not yet, Panther fan.

Pitt went into the following contest against the single most pathetic Division I team available, the Temple Owls. As bad as the Owls were, Pitt was that much worse. The Panther defense was being shredded by Owl quarterback Walter Washington who not only threw for 314 yards, but ran for 82, as Temple held a 16-6 lead in the third quarter and was at the Pitt one with five minutes left in the frame. The Pittsburgh defense was holding, but Temple wanted to go for the knockout punch with a fourth down at the one-yard line. This, my friends, was the lowest point of Pitt's season.

With the possibility of a 23-7 deficit, the Panthers were in real trouble. The defense was playing poorly, the offense was sporadic and if the Owls scored, the game for all intents and purposes would be over. A loss would have been humiliating. The question now was not if Harris would be fired at the end of the year, but would he last the week? If the Panthers lost, there was a real possibility they would not win another game, sending the program into the depths of depravity it had not felt since the Paul Hackett days. It all depended on this one play.

Session would not let it happen. He made up for his strange comment following the UConn loss, as he and academic All American Vince Crochunis stuffed Washington short of the goal, giving the Panthers life. They responded with three fourth quarter touchdowns to stave off an embarrassing upset with a 27-22 win—a victory that no one could have imagined would be the springboard to a Big East championship and BCS berth.

A funny thing happened on the way to Walt Harris' execution. Against the powerful Boston College Eagles, the team not only woke up, but a football version of "Angels in the Outfield" was about to take place. The grouchy head coach must have made a pact with higher beings, as the fictional curmudgeon of a Pirate manager, Guffy McGovern (played by Paul Douglas), did in the 1951 screen classic.

The Eagles had come into the game with a potent running attack, but it was the Panther defense that controlled the line, limiting BC runners to a mere 56 yards on the ground. Time and time again Boston College would threaten, and each time Pitt came up big, including stopping the Eagles on a fourth and goal from the one midway in the fourth quarter to preserve a 17 –10 lead.

What the Pitt stop troops couldn't control was quarterback Paul Peterson who lit up the secondary for 367 yards and two scores, including one to Grant Adams with 3:26 left in the contest, knotting it up at 17 apiece.

After 60 minutes, the clubs went to overtime despite the fact Boston College dominated the game, outgaining Pitt 423-308 and holding the ball for over 34 minutes. With BC limiting Pitt to a 27-yard Josh Cummings field goal in their possession, the Eagles had the opportunity to finally put away the Panthers and control their own destiny in the Big East. That is until defensive back Mike Phillips stripped the ball from an Eagle receiver. The ball was recovered by Thomas Smith, giving Pittsburgh the improbable victory.

What was happening here? Could a season of discontent turn into something special? After a 41-17 thumping of Rutgers in a game where the Panthers were outgained 407-397 by the Scarlet Knights, they were all of the sudden within one game of fighting for the Big East championship on Thanksgiving evening. All it would take would be going into the Carrier Dome and beating the Orange of Syracuse.

Apparently Harris must have angered the angels that seemed to be watching over him. The Panther defense became invisible, allowing two Syracuse backs to gain over 100 yards. Despite that fact, Pitt somehow came back from a 21-6 firsthalf disadvantage to sneak ahead, 24-21, in the fourth quarter thanks to the arm of their quarterback. Palko passed for 342 yards and three TDs, and their emerging superstar receiver Greg Lee snatched nine receptions for 188 yards.

Syracuse tied the game at 24 with only 1:11 left before Palko drove the team down the field, giving Pitt the opportunity to escape with another win. Perhaps one of the biggest improvements in the club in 2004 was that of their kicking game. Punter Adam Graessle had been magnificent with an average of 44 yards per kick, while Cummings had become the very reliable kicker they had been missing. All he had to do was hit from 51 yards out with time running out to make the Panthers bowl eligible with six wins. Cummings missed horribly to the left. And Syracuse won in the second overtime, 38-31.

The roller coaster campaign took a downward twist as the Panthers would now have to travel to South Bend to face Notre Dame before hosting West Virginia Thanksgiving night and traveling to Tampa to play South Florida in the makeup game. Never mind a Big East title, the Panthers were now in severe danger of not winning enough games to get a bowl bid.

South Bend had not been kind to the University of Pittsburgh, as they had lost six consecutive games at Knute Rockne Stadium dating back to 1986. The nationally televised contest saw the Panther defense looking very bad for the second consecutive week, as much like the Syracuse loss, the contest was resembling a pinball game.

Palko was once again on fire, and he would garner several national player of the week awards for his 334-yard, five-touchdown performance—the most TD passes ever thrown by an opponent in the long and storied history at South Bend. Every time the sophomore QB came up big, so did the Irish. The back-and-forth contest was tied at 38 after Notre Dame hit a 45-yard field goal (at ironically 1:11 of the fourth quarter, just like the Orange did a week before).

Also like the Syracuse game, Palko drove them down the field, not letting the Panthers give up on themselves and putting Cummings in position to make amends for his failure in the Carrier Dome. Thankfully, the junior kicker nailed a 32-yard field goal to give Pitt the win, their fourth in five weeks, despite being outgained once again. For the sophomore quarterback, the only mistake he made in this fine performance was dropping the "F bomb" to a national audience on NBC in his postgame euphoria.

At 6-3, the Panther club was having a remarkable season that was indescribable when you factor in the controversy, sloppy play, weak defense and everything else that made this moment unthinkable only a month before. They would go into their final Big East game of the year against WVU in the "Backyard Brawl" on Thanksgiving night for a possibility of playing in a BCS game. Yes, the team that almost lost to Furman and was one play away from being blown out by Temple was all of the sudden in a position to play in the BCS—an opportunity that was helped by the fact Temple inexplicably defeated Syracuse while the Panthers were taking care of the Irish. This storyline would certainly make Rod Serling proud.

In the Brawl, the Mountaineers, the preseason conference favorites who were beaten badly by BC the week before, found a way to control Palko, limiting him to 165 yards. They also controlled the game, but could only muster up 13 points, thanks to an undisciplined performance that netted West Virginia 89 penalty yards and two missed field goals. Regardless, the Mounties were driving early in the fourth to put the game away when super frosh Darrelle Revis picked off a Rasheed Marshall pass at the Panther 27-yard line.

Palko had certainly proved himself to be a winner, but could he finally figure out the tough

WVU defense? Of course he could, after all when it came to football in the 'burgh in 2004 the unexpected was expected. Four times Tyler was faced with third down situations, and four times he came up big, hitting Lee on three occasions and tight end Eric Gill on one. Harris called an ill-advised halfback option from the 10 yard line with Pittsburgh down by four, 13-9. The angels were watching the Panthers, all right, as WVU was hit with a pass interference penalty in the end zone, giving Pitt the ball at the two.

Justifiably Tyler ran it in from two yards out to culminate a 14-play, 73-yard drive to give Pittsburgh their first lead of the day, 16-13, with 4:06 left.

Marshall, a Pittsburgh City League alum, took matters into his own hands, leading the Mountaineers down the field. The Panther defense finally held at the 32-yard line, with 55 seconds left giving WVU a shot at the tying field goal. Mountaineer coach Rich Rodriguez had no faith in his kicking game and decided to go for it on fourth and five. A reincarnation of the Indianapolis Colts offense WVU ain't, as Marshall tossed an errant pass to give Pitt the ball and the win.

Now in a position to win the Big East, the Panthers had to rely on another miracle, a win by Syracuse at Chestnut Hill against BC on the following Saturday. The Orange were beaten and humiliated after the Temple loss. And, with a win, Boston College would get the Big East bid in the BCS before they packed up and joined Miami and Virginia Tech in the ACC. While 99 times out of 100, Syracuse would lose to the Eagles, this was 2004, so bet on the unexpected. Sure enough, the Orange not only beat the Eagles but embarrassed them, 43-17, forcing a four-way tie for the Big East title and the BCS berth.

Boston College and West Virginia were eliminated immediately for the BCS bid, as both were 1-2 in head to head games against the four co-champions. This left Syracuse and Pitt to battle it out. In theory, the Orange should have gotten the shot because of their win over the Panthers during the season, but this was 2004 and things were going our way. The rules state that the head-to-head winner gets the bid—except if the losing team is five spaces up in the BCS standings. Syracuse at 6-5 was unrated, while Pitt was now ranked (pinch me, we must be dreaming) No. 21. Barring a loss at South Florida, which by the way was the kind of game that Harris always seemed to lose in the past, the Panthers would go to a BCS bowl for the first time since the 1983 Cotton Bowl.

Fortunately this was not a game that Harris would lose in 2004 as Pitt finally outgained an opponent, 475-352, with the Panthers playing their most complete game of the season to thump South Florida 43-14. Palko had a career-high 422 yards on only 19 completions for five more TDs. It was the finishing touch on a remarkable campaign, one that saw him go from being a mistake-prone quarterback in the first half of the year, to a savvy leader with future Heisman hopes by season's end.

The next day, Pitt accepted a bid to the Fiesta Bowl against the undefeated Utah Utes. On the BCS show on ABC Walt Harris looked anything but happy. He seemed uncomfortable and stiff with his answers, but who could blame him after what he went through this season?

To grasp it completely, he had a very inexperienced QB, who became the latest in the legacy of great Pitt quarterbacks because of his last-minute heroics. His battered receiving corps ended up being one of the strongest in the land, as Lee went from the dog house in training camp to having the third highest receiving yard total in Pitt history (behind only Larry Fitzgerald and Antonio Bryant). Add to that Del Sardo, who went from a walk-on to a very reliable possession receiver whose remarkable grabs included a spectacular one-handed touchdown against Rutgers. His weak link offensive line, by the end of the season, was probably the best he had in his tenure. And his defense, while not a strength, made one big play after another in the clutch, producing the best freshman defensive back the school had seen in ages in Revis.

As for Harris himself, he went from one of the most inept coaches in school history to the Big East Coach of the Year in leading this young squad to its first Big East crown. Opportunities that were nowhere to be found in September were now plentiful for the Panther coach.

Winning the Big East and securing a spot in the BCS should be enough to settle any controversy as to whether or not Harris should have been retained, right? Unfortunately for Walt the administration had a long memory and his agent's comments and his refusal to dispute them still seemed to be ringing loud and clear in their heads.

Despite the controversy, Harris had his supporters. Fans

like Pitt expert Joe "The Titleman" Huber were in his corner. "Walt Harris has rebuilt a wreck of a football program and has produced a true Heisman candidate in Larry Fitzgerald. The crown jewel of his career may be Tyler Palko. He must stay," Huber proclaimed. While some were beginning to paint a rosy Walt Harris picture, one must also remember why he was criticized in the first place. His teams could be sloppy, his defense and offensive lines were rarely where they needed to be and he had the reputation that while he could lead a team to eight wins, he made too many glaring game-day mistakes ever to compete for a national championship. Add to the mix that he was in a slump in landing quality Western Pennsylvania recruits and we can see why the school was unhappy with him. All this is not to suggest that Walt did a less then stellar job at Pitt, but to show it's an argument where there were definitely two sides.

When Stanford let coach Buddy Teevens go following a poor 2003 season, the Cardinal administration came calling on Harris for the vacant job. He met with the Northern California school only a couple days after the zenith of his coaching career and reportedly came back to Pitt to see if the University administration was interested in keeping him by giving him a raise and contract extension. Despite the word that Harris reportedly wanted to stay in the Steel City, the administration was apparently not as interested. They reportedly refused to extend Walt's contract.

In this ever-growing soap opera, Harris left the University of Pittsburgh to become the coach of the Stanford Cardinals only a week after receiving his first-ever BCS bid. The only question that remained in this warped campaign was if he would be allowed to coach the Panthers in the Fiesta Bowl, making this a BCS contest of two lame duck head coaches (Utah's Urban Meyer had also accepted another job, this one at Florida).

Losing Harris brought back some unfortunate memories for Pitt coach fans. The move felt like a similar maneuver in 1989 when the administration let Mike Gottfried go right before the John Hancock Sun Bowl. Like Harris, Gottfried was a coach who had resurrected the program from the doldrums of the Foge Fazio era. His replacement was Paul Hackett, a man who took Pitt into the bowels of major college football, a place it hadn't been since the late '60s.

There are distinct differences between the two situations, though. While both Harris and Gottfried had fallen out of favor with the University of Pittsburgh administration despite their success on the field, the reasons stemmed from two diverse philosophies. In Gottfried's case, it seemed to be more from the administration's desire to upgrade the academic aspects of their athletic program and in major college football, that philosophy can be wrought with failure. At least at Pitt it was. With Harris, the philosophy might not be just of a personality conflict but that of an aggressiveness to compete in the upper echelon of college football. Alumni and fans alike seem to be frustrated that the program has not taken the step that would bring Pitt football back to the glory days of the '70s and early '80s. Not to mention the fact that the university has spent a lot of money upgrading its facilities in an attempt to get the school to that level. To that point Walt has not delivered. Despite their success this year, this team has too many holes, especially defensively, to be considered potential national champion contenders in the near future.

Is it a gamble to let Walt Harris go? Absolutely. With Walt a shot to go to a bowl every year, even though it's not competing for a national championship. Pick the wrong man to succeed him and the team could return to the days when the University of Pittsburgh was spoken in the same breath with the Temple and Rutgers of the world.

Regardless of the controversy, there was still a Bowl game to play in the midst of this soap opera and Pitt was a prohibitive underdog, with Utah opening as a 16-point favorite.

Pitt athletic director Jeff Long decided that it would be in the best interest of the university to let Walt coach the game rather than an amalgamation of assistants who were also now lame ducks. While Long did this, he would go on a quick, aggressive search for the replacement.

The odds-on favorite was Dave Wannstedt, former Pitt player and assistant—and, oh yeah, former head coach of the Chicago Bears and Miami Dolphins. Dave had just been through a very stressful run with Miami and decided the time was not right for him to jump back into the college coaching mix and quickly withdrew his name from consideration. That left Long to choose among several experienced coordinators such as current Pitt defensive guru

Paul Rhoads, Oklahoma defensive coordinator Bo Pellini and two former Panther players and coaches, Matt Cavanaugh and Sal Sunseri.

Long had set a Christmas Day deadline for himself to name the man who hopefully would lead Pitt to the promised land. That decision seemed to finally come down to Cavanaugh and Rhoads (although some claimed Pellini was the choice along with the former Pitt QB). This was Pitt football 2004 and the only thing that seemed to be expected was, in fact, the unexpected. Reenter Dave Wannstedt.

It's a former NFL coach's prerogative to change his mind, and that's exactly what Wannstedt did. Following the sweetening of the financial parameters by the university, the Pitt alum was announced as the official new coach of the Pittsburgh Panthers, replacing the beleaguered Walt Harris.

Despite the fact he was replaced, Harris still prepared the club for the Fiesta Bowl, reminiscing only long enough about his eight-year tenure to say, "I do love these football players. I have told them how much they mean to me. But life goes on."

Life indeed does go on, and the hope was that the heavy underdogs would want to prove all those who said they didn't belong in a BCS bowl wrong and also win one for the Gipper, or in this case their exiting coach.

Utah seemed to give their Big East counterparts little respect, as did their fans. They were busy printing up Fiesta Bowl Champions shirts and "We'll Beat the Pitt Out of Pittsburg" shirts (notice the lack of spelling skills by certain Utah fans) before the game actually began.

In the end, apparently the Panthers didn't deserve any respect, as the Utes pummeled Pitt 35-7. Perhaps the game was a microcosm of all that the Walt critics claimed was wrong in the Harris regime—a poor defensive line that seemingly lacked aggressiveness and physical play, a lack of a quality offensive line (although two starters were not up to par) as Palko was flattened so often he began to resemble Muhammad Ali after the Larry Holmes fight (for those non boxing fans Ali was beaten to a pulp in that fight) and failure to defeat a big opponent when it appeared the program would take a big step forward with a win.

Even with the loss to Utah and all that might have gone wrong over the past eight years, Walt Harris' tenure at Pitt certainly has to be considered a success. After all, six bowls in eight years and bringing the program up from the ashes are certainly nothing to sneeze at. It was his apparent lack of seeing the potential of a brass ring (a national championship) at the end of the rainbow that was his downfall, though. His silence after his agent's bizarre comments (an agent who Harris ironically fired following his appointment at Stanford) in mid season spoke volumes. Contrast Harris with his replacement. Wannstedt truly believes there's a championship down the road, and he has set getting there as his main goal for the program. He said so loudly and clearly in the press conference announcing his hiring. It's a goal all Panther fans have been waiting 20 years to hear again, and one that took the bizarre year they call 2004 to bring to light.

The Small College Experience In 2004

A season that began with so much promise for the area's local division I-AA squads ended with disappointment—although that's not to say that the campaigns were debacles.

Robert Morris shot out to a 2-0 start with impressive wins against Buffalo State and a 34-14 crushing of the Duquesne Dukes. But the dream of a third national championship soon ended with a thud, as a 4-5 finish put the Colonials at 6-5 for the season.

For Duquesne, it's tough to say whether or not a No. 6 national ranking, yet another MAAC title and a 7-3 mark (that included two wins against the higher ranked Patriot League) is a disappointment. The downside included the 34-14 loss against a very average Robert Morris team, a 41-34 defeat at the hands of Fordham (that included six Dukes interceptions) and a 30-20 loss to Bucknell at the end of the season where the Dukes committed five more turnovers than their opponents. Taking those missteps into account, you can see why the men at the Bluff must be kicking themselves at what should have been a successful defense of their 2003 national championship.

In the lower divisions, Slippery Rock had a poor 4-7 mark, while IUP had a mid season slump that led to a un-IUP like 7-3 record. CMU also had a fine, if unspectacular campaign, at 6-4, which moved their non-losing streak to 30 years.

While it wasn't a banner year for most small schools in Western Pennsylvania, Washington & Jefferson restored the area's pride with an undefeated 10-0 mark that found the Presidents ranked third in the nation at the end of the regular season and qualifying for a playoff spot. The Presidents defeated Bridgewater, 55-48, and Christopher Newport, 24-14, in the first two rounds and advanced to a quarterfinal matchup at Cameron Stadium against Mary Hardin-Baylor. The Texas school quickly derailed W&J's national championship hopes, scoring early and often in a 52-16 blowout.

Despite the disappointment that losing to a school named Mary isn't exactly the thing memories are made of, the Presidents finished the season with a school-record 12 wins and hopes of completing the task of a national title in 2005.

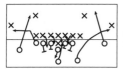

FORTY THREE

The Football Gods must be Smiling: Recapping the 2004 Steeler campaign

A Super—Not Quite Super Bowl—Year.

Seven and nine. That was our prediction for the Steelers' 2004 season. We weren't alone. Nearly every sports publication had predicted Pittsburgh to be in the lower echelon of its division. Most picked the team to finish third behind the defending champ Baltimore Ravens and Marvin Lewis' retooled Cincinnati Bengals.

It stood to reason. The Steelers were coming off a disappointing 6-10 year. The once-vaunted defense had become suspect, giving up big plays and not creating the turnovers that had been a staple during Bill Cowher's coaching tenure. This latest edition of the team had seemingly eschewed the clock-controlling running game in favor of a high-powered, yet high-risk, aerial attack. Most tellingly, in the offseason, the team had not made the sweeping personnel changes that might be expected following a 6-10 year.

Then there was the schedule. Even in a parity-driven league, the Steelers had drawn some difficult opponents. The schedule featured two tough games against the Ravens, plus match-ups against perennial powers the New England Patriots and the Philadelphia Eagles. On the bright side, there were still two games each against Cleveland and Cincinnati. (We still weren't convinced the Bengals were a big-time team yet.) So, yes, 7-9 seemed like a safe prognostication for the year.

And if that weren't enough adversity, add a slew of injuries at key positions. First there was starting guard Kendall Simmons, who tore up his knee in training camp and was gone for the season. Then backup quarterback Charlie Batch suffered a season-ending injury on the eve of the team's preseason opener, leaving the Steelers with a suddenly suspect quarterback corps—Tommy Maddox, a former journeyman signal caller who only four years before was selling insurance; Brian St. Pierre, a third-string signal caller with little actual game-time experience; and rookie Ben Roethlisberger, a highly touted first round draft pick, but whose college experience came in the Mid American Conference. (Those were only the first injuries. It seemed like the entire squad became red shirt-wearing extras in *Star Trek* episodes. And we all know what happens to those guys.)

Maybe 7-9 was a little ambitious, but that didn't take into account the best job done by a Steelers' coaching staff in recent memory, the depth and determination of this squad and, frankly, the stars lining up in just the right way. Week by week, expectations grew for a bunch of guys who epitomized "team" in every sense of the word. One player would go down and another would take his place. There were great story lines: The rookie quarterback, expected to be a clipboard holder at best, who takes the city—and country—by storm. The running back, forced to take a hefty pay cut to stay with the team, who proves to all doubters that there is still something left in his tank. Add to that the return of the defensive coordinator to the place where his considerable reputation for creating an attacking defense was born. And there were thoughts of a return to grandeur of the halcyon days of the Steel Curtain and the best regular-season run in franchise history. This is how 7-9 became 16-2.

Actually, it started before training camp, and it started on the coaching staff. The offseason was a tumultuous one for Bill Cowher's staff. Offensive coordinator Mike Mularkey was hired away to become head coach of the Buffalo Bills. It seemed his departure was another chapter in the ongoing battle between Cowher and Bills' team president Tom Donahoe. (Donahoe, the former Steelers' general manager, had lost out to Cowher in a much-publicized power struggle, and their relationship continued to be quite frosty as Donahoe settled into his job with the Bills.) Adding to the intrigue, both the Bills and the Steelers were in the market for a new defensive coordinator (the Steelers dumped Tim Lewis after the disastrous 6-10 season), and both had made Dick LeBeau their top candidate. LeBeau had built his reputation in an earlier stint with the Steelers. As their defensive coordinator, he was the architect of the so-called Blitzburgh Defense—an attacking style of play—and inventor of the zone blitz that other NFL teams scurried to copy. LeBeau left the Steelers in 1997 to become head coach of the Cincinnati Bengals but had little success (like anyone has success there). At the time, there were reports that the Cowher-LeBeau relationship had deteriorated, which would have made it difficult for him to remain as defensive coordinator for the demanding Steelers coach. It came as a surprise, then, when LeBeau chose to return to Pittsburgh instead of heading to Buffalo to join Mularkey's staff. (Dom Capers, another former Cowher coordinator turned head coach, had a similar opportunity but chose not to return to Pittsburgh.) However, it would come as no surprise that he would toss out his predecessor Lewis' read-and-react style of defense.

On the other side of the ball, Cowher had to fill the vacant offensive coordinator position. Mularkey had at one time been seen as a visionary among network analysts who marveled at his bag of tricks—a seemingly endless stockpile of gadget plays designed to keep opposing defenses off balance. But by his third season as coordinator, Mularkey also kept *his* offense off balance. The Steelers, long known for their power running game that set up the pass, had reversed their balance. In 2003, the pass was used to set up the run. In fairness to Mularkey, it would be tempting to go in that direction, thanks to a deep, play-making receiving corps of Hines Ward, Plaxico Burress and Antwaan Randle El. Even the head coach signed off on the strategy.

So it was surprising that in seeking to replace Mularkey, Cowher looked to promote from within, elevating former tight ends coach Ken Whisenhunt to offensive coordinator. But any questions were quickly dispelled as Cowher returned to his roots. "When he interviewed me for the job, the first question out of his mouth was, 'How do you feel about the run game?'" Whisenhunt recalled.

But who would be carrying the ball, and could the offensive line clear a path for him? In 2003, the Steelers sported a makeshift line. Poor health inevitably led to poor play. Before the season even started, guard Kendall Simmons was diagnosed with diabetes and was never a factor. Other injuries had forced mass substitutions, and there was no continuity as offensive line coach Russ Grimm was forced to create lineups on the fly.

That affected the Steelers' ground attack as much as the play calling did. Running back Jerome Bettis didn't have those gaping holes to run through. And even on those occasions when creases opened, the once-effective Bus seemed to be running on fumes. Although he is arguably the greatest big running back in NFL history, 11 years of pounding had clearly taken their toll on Bettis. Nagging injuries and snipes about his weight left many to ponder how effective he could be. Among those with concerns was Steelers management. For Bettis to come back to the team in 2004, it would mean taking a substantial pay cut of $2.7 million. The team also went shopping via free agency in the offseason, signing former Philadelphia running back Duce Staley. Despite concerns about Staley's durability—he had missed parts of four seasons because of injuries—Bettis was relegated to a backup role but remained perhaps the most popular player in the Steelers' locker room.

For the most part, the Steelers held pat in terms of roster changes. Cornerback Dwayne Washington was released, as were linebacker Jason Gildon, tight end Chris Bruener and running back Amos Zereoue. Punter Chris Gardocki was signed to replace Josh Miller, a frequent occupant of Cowher's dog house. Staley was the lone high-profile free agent signing. Cornerback Willie Williams, a fixture on the last Steelers Super Bowl team in '95, was also brought in to add some depth after Washington's release.

Though by all accounts the Steelers had a nice draft class, featuring Roethlisberger at No. 11, rookies just didn't impact Cowher teams. Rookies were worked gradually into the lineup. Such was the case for the previous year's No. 1 pick, Troy Polamalu. The Steelers made the rare move of trading up in the draft to be able to select the safety from USC. And then they promptly placed him on the bench, working him into dime defense situations by midseason and then as a starter as the season waned. But Polamalu gained some game experience that would prove particularly valuable for 2004.

As the Steelers headed to training camp in Latrobe, Cowher promised a much different experience. "It's going to be a very physical camp," he told me a week before heading to St. Vincent College. "We're going to set the standard from the very beginning. This is going to be a very physical football team." Apparently, Whisenhunt was listening. In a goal line drill early in camp, the new coordinator gave a glimpse of what would be expected for the season. Four straight plays the offense played smash-mouth football, with goal line plunges. No passes here. The running game was back.

The offensive line appeared to be healthy, at least until Simmons' injury. Alan Faneca, perhaps the best offensive lineman in the league, was able to return to his natural position, center Jeff Hartings' knees were stable while Keydrick Vincent, a solid backup, would step up for Simmons at right guard. There were only two question marks—tackle Oliver Ross had not shown much the previous year, finally losing an anointed starting job to Todd Fordham, who turned out to be equally ineffective in 2003. And, there was the question of depth. Losing Simmons meant there wasn't a lot of room for error on the offensive line. Another injury could be devastating and could spell a repeat of 2003.

The health of the line became even more of an issue when Batch went down. Batch was a good backup quarterback who had tasted some success with the Detroit Lions as a starter. Because the Steelers' starter, Tommy Maddox, was neither the most mobile nor the most durable of quarterbacks, having a strong backup like Batch was important. Brett Favre not withstanding, it's very rare for a quarterback to go an entire season without missing a snap these days.

But depth would prove to be a positive for this Steelers team. While there may not have been a lot of roster moves, there were significant changes made to the starting lineup, particularly on defense. The safeties were new, with Polamalu and Chris Hope taking over for an injured Mike Logan and Brent Alexander, who was no longer with the team. Clark Haggans, who proved himself as a backup, replaced the departed Gildon at left outside linebacker. With Kendrell Bell hobbled once again by nagging injuries, Larry Foote saw time at right inside linebacker, with the hopes that a healthy Bell would be back. James Harrison was brought in as a backup in the linebacking corps and would prove to be a special-teams demon. At right corner, Deshea Townsend replaced Washington. In making the moves, the Steelers got younger and faster on defense. Coupled with a more aggressive style of play, where opposing quarterbacks could no longer exploit the Steelers' cornerbacks, the pieces were quietly put into place for a defense to be reckoned with.

In the season opener, at home against the Oakland Raiders, there were some shades of 2003—moments of brilliance and instances of frustrating inconsistency. The Steelers took the opening kickoff and drove 67 yards. Bettis came off the bench to join the goalline offense. His one-yard touchdown run opened the scoring, pacing them to a 7-0 lead. The Steelers added another touchdown on another Bettis plunge and appeared to be cruising. Right before the half, the specter of the big play surrendered on defense came back to haunt them. With 1:46 left in the half, Polamalu bit on Raider receiver Doug Gabriel's double move, and Oakland quarterback Rich Gannon fired a perfect 58-yard bomb to put his team back in the game. In the second half, the Steeler lead grew to 21-13. But much like the previous year, the Steelers had a difficult time putting an opponent away. On fourth and 12 late in the game, the defense allowed Raiders receiver Alvis Whitted to get behind them—a cardinal sin—and once again Gannon tossed a touchdown pass, this one from 38 yards. A two-point conversion tied the score at 21.

The offense had been inconsistent since the opening drive, but Maddox took charge. He coolly moved the team down the field, completing three of four passes for 38 yards in the team's march into field goal range. From there, kicker Jeff Reed converted on a 42-yarder as time expired for a 24-21 win.

At times the Steelers resembled their championship squads, sacking the quarterback and forcing turnovers. The offense looked efficient, with Staley moving the ball between the 20s and Bettis punching it in. (Bettis had a statistically strange day: five carries, three yards, three touchdowns.) But there was no consistency. There was, however, a 1-0 start, although not a performance to build upon.

"On a fourth-and-12 play you have to get off the field," Cowher said at the post game wrap-up. "That was probably the most disappointing play of the game because you work hard to get off the field. We got some turnovers, we got some pressure, and we had some big plays. And to me that would have translated into a pretty good day, but then they hit the one big play and got back into the game. But we showed a lot of resilience in coming back and we never panicked."

Maddox was less positive. "We have to play better when we have teams on the ropes," he said. "We can't play like this and expect to win." But in the opener, the Steelers showed a trait that would last all season long—the ability to come back.

Game two provided the first test to the team's psyche. They traveled to Baltimore for an important division game against the Ravens. It was ugly. The Ravens took the opening drive and ran through the Steelers' defense. Running backs Jamal Lewis and Chester Taylor put up big runs. Quarterback Kyle Boller scrambled to convert a second and 19. The Steelers offense, on the other hand, could not move. The half ended 13-0, and if it weren't for some timely defensive stops, the Ravens' lead could have been much more.

The Steelers opened the second half with the ball but shortly lost their starting quarterback. Maddox was creamed on a blitz and tore ligaments in his elbow. To add insult to the injury, he fumbled on the play and the Ravens set up shop at the Steelers' one on their way to a 20-0 lead.

Welcome to the NFL, Ben Roethlisberger. Your team is down by three touchdowns on the road, and you're facing one of the league's top defenses. Now go out there and have fun. Amazingly, that's what he did. Although it didn't start off that way. In his first series, Big Ben simply handed the ball off three times. In his second possession, it wasn't much better—an incompletion to Burress and then an interception. But then Steelers fans got their first look at this remarkable rookie's amazing ability to shake off adversity. Roethlisberger calmly took the field again and tossed a 58-yard pass to Ward to set up a short touchdown pass to Randle El. On his next possession, the rookie quarterback engineered a 70-yard drive that closed the gap to 23-13. A defensive stop put the offense back on the field, but all hope for a comeback was dashed when Raven defensive back Chris McAlister picked off an errant pass and returned it 50 yards for a touchdown. Final score: Ravens 30, Steelers 13.

Cowher tried to put a positive spin on the defeat in his post-game comments and on the prospects of having a rookie starting quarterback the following week in Miami. "Not the ideal scenario to come into a game on the road and down 20-0," he told the media. "But he came in and did some good things, and most of that was in the hurry-up offense."

Asked if a rookie quarterback can keep a team in the playoff hunt, Cowher replied. "We will certainly find out. I don't see any reason why he can't."

Some of his players weren't quite as gracious. Faneca started a little controversy when a reporter asked if it was exciting to have Roethlisberger come in and see what he could do. Faneca, one of Maddox's closest friends, didn't quite see it that way, and in the heat of the moment referred to the team's new starting quarterback as "some little kid out of college." Clearly among Steelers and among those in the Steeler Nation, there was concern that this could turn out to be even worse than last year's 6-10.

But just as this team could have splintered, a force of nature brought them together. Hurricane Jeanne crashed through Florida, the site of the Steelers' game against the Dolphins. With the devastation, the league decided to delay the game until Sunday evening, and the Steelers found themselves holed up in the eighth and ninth floors of the Westin Hotel in Ft. Lauderdale. With the power out, their boyish natures shined. Some groups played flashlight tag. Others hung around telling stories. Yet out of this seeming disaster, a team bonded. "There's no question that this became a close team that weekend," Ward would say later.

There was still a game to play. Roethlisberger, having just faced one of the league's top defenses in his professional debut, had another tough task in going up against the Dolphins. Although Miami was reeling from the defection of its star running back, Ricky Williams, the Dolphins still featured one of the best defenses in the league. Weather conditions didn't make it any easier, with torrential rains making the football difficult to grip and the footing poor.

Roethlisberger had a tough start. After a Dolphin turnover set the Steelers up at the Miami 30, the rookie quarterback's first pass was intercepted, halting a scoring opportunity on a night when points would be difficult to get. But Roethlisberger again showed the ability to come back. He led the team on a late touchdown drive, and the defense limited the Dolphins to only 169 yards on offense in a hard-fought 13-3 win. Polamalu made a key interception as the Steelers defense set the offense up in field goal range.

"The weather in the first half was not conducive to doing anything," said Cowher. "It was difficult to hold the ball, and both teams couldn't throw for a while. The quarterback played well. He never lost his composure."

It helped that the running game took off much of the pressure. "You know we're going to run the ball," said Staley. "We're going to line up and we're going to point in the direction we're going. I thought because of the conditions, I thought it was imperative that we run the ball."

Suddenly a pattern began to emerge. The next week against the Bengals, Roethlisberger continued to show great poise. The rookie quarterback led the team on a late 89-yard touchdown drive after the Bengals had taken the lead. The game was iced by another key Polamalu interception, this one off of his college roommate Carson Palmer, returned for a touchdown that sealed a 28-17 victory. With everything else, the running game was firing on all cylinders, with Staley rushing for 123 yards.

The game plan continued the following week against the Cleveland Browns. A confident Roethlisberger began to create believers in the Steeler Nation. He moved calmly out of the pocket to connect on some big plays in a 34-23 win at Heinz Field. Rookie quarterbacks were not supposed to be this polished. Big Ben was drawing rave reviews across the league and quite a stir in his adopted city. Soon, restaurants were naming sandwiches after him. (By the way, we authors have just finished digesting the gargantuan "Roethlisburger" from Peppi's that we had in November.)

Staley turned in his third consecutive 100-yard performance, and the Steelers were sitting atop the division with a surprising 4-1 record.

Just as Miami proved to be a seminal stop in the Steelers' season, the following week in Dallas showed that this black and gold squad just might be for real. Trailing 20-10 late in the third quarter, Roethlisberger led his team back. He started off with a nine-yard run. Then after two short completions to Ward, Big Ben avoided a sack and found his tight end Jay Riemersma on a brilliant shovel pass to keep the drive alive. He finished with a seven-yard touchdown toss to his other tight end, Jerame Tuman, to bring the Steelers within three.

Then the defense made a game-turning play. The Cowboys were just about to put the Steelers away. A third-down conversion would have enabled Dallas to run out the clock. But Farrior forced Cowboys' quarterback Vinnie Testaverde (he of the bad luck against the Steelers) to fumble, and Kimo Van Oelhoffen picked up the loose ball and rumbled to the Cowboy 24. From there, Roethlisberger drove them the rest of the way. He completed two clutch passes to Burress and to Tuman before designated closer Bettis ran it in from two yards out. The Steelers escaped Dallas with a 24-20 win and had an extra week to prepare for the New England Patriots at Heinz Field.

Sizing up his team before the bye Cowher said, "I'm not totally surprised that we're 5-1 going into our off week. We have great momentum, and momentum can create confidence. Sometimes I think we are more confident than we are good. The guys believe in each other, and to tell you the truth, I really don't know how good we are."

The Patriots would provide a good gauge from which to judge. The defending Super Bowl champs came into the game undefeated and riding an NFL-record 21-game winning streak. Their coach, Bill Belichick, was hailed as a modern-day Vince Lombardi (although it's hard to imagine Lombardi prowling the sidelines wearing a hooded pullover). Despite Cowher and his players spending the bye week downplaying the importance of the game, this would be a chance for the Steelers to show that they were among the league's elite teams on a nationally televised game. Even though they entered the game with a 5-1 record, many of the Steelers' victories had come against the NFL's middle-of-the-pack teams. Were the Steelers a force, or had their schedule to this point allowed them to be a farce?

As it turned out on this Halloween game, the Steelers proved there was no masquerade. They took apart the Patriots 34-20 after spotting the world champs a 3-0 lead. The defense forced key turnovers, including a Deshea Townsend interception returned for a touchdown, and harassed Patriots quarterback Tom Brady all day. The offense was even better. The new, old-style Steelers dominated the game by controlling the line of scrimmage. The Steelers rushed for 221 yards, with Bettis again converting in a goal line situation. The big back added 15 carries for 65 yards, as he came off the bench to spell Staley, who had injured his hamstring. Roethlisberger had another efficient day, completing 18 of 24 passes for two touchdowns. Perhaps most impressive, the Patriots knew the Steelers, having gotten a big lead early, would be running the ball to try to keep the clock moving, but they were unable to slow down the black and gold's rushing attack.

The team was also brimming with confidence. "We can play with anybody," said receiver Ward. "Right now Ben [Roethlisberger] is doing a great job. He shows no rattle. He shows a lot of poise in the huddle. The whole time, he felt like we could take it every drive and go down there and score."

But there would be not a lot of time to celebrate the win. Next on the docket were the Philadelphia Eagles, who like the Patriots the week before, came into Heinz Field undefeated. They left the same way New England did, beaten badly by the Steelers, 27-3. Bettis filled in for an ailing Staley, carrying the ball 33 times for 149 yards.

"[Jerome] is the Pittsburgh Steelers," Ward said after the game. "He's an ultimate All-Pro. When he's not starting, he's still encouraging guys to go out there. And when he got his opportunity, he took full advantage of it. It couldn't happen to a greater guy."

Bettis wasn't the only sub to fill in admirably. Chris Hoke found himself in the starting lineup after all-pro nose tackle Casey Hampton was lost for the year against the Cowboys. Cornerback Willie Williams stepped in for Chad Scott (also a victim in Dallas) as the Steelers were proving to be a team with depth.

They were also giant killers. It was the first time in NFL history that a team had knocked off previously unbeaten teams in consecutive weeks so late in a season. All was going according to plan for Cowher. His run-first offense was battering opponents. The defense was forcing opponents' mistakes and creating turnovers. The Steelers had already reached our predicted win total. And there were still eight games left in the season.

At the season's midpoint, Roethlisberger had all but sewn up NFL Offensive Rookie of the Year honors. It was a great story. The quarterback who was drafted out of the so-called second tier Mid American conference was virtually rewriting the rookie record book and it would only get better. By season's end, he would break Dan Marino's rookie records for completion percentage (66.4) and passer rating (98.1). Most impressively, though, he broke Mike Kruczek's NFL record for most consecutive victories to start a career (13). In fact, including college, Roethlisberger hadn't lost since a 21-3 defeat at the hands of Iowa on August 30, 2003—26 games before.

Pittsburgh loves a winner and so does the Steeler Nation. By season's end, Roethlisberger's jersey would be the hottest seller in the NFL. Big Ben T-shirts became all the rage, with stores selling out of them as soon as they were delivered. And the fans began to connect this quarterback and his team to the Steelers of the '70s. There were some parallels. In both eras, the city was facing turmoil. Thirty years ago it was the collapse of the steel industry. In 2004, it was the city's bleak financial state and Act 47 proceedings that taxed the confidence and spirit of its residents. In both eras, the Steelers provided great solace from the news of the day. Increasingly, the fans were cheering the exploits of a new quarterback who had not tasted defeat as he started his pro career.

"I don't ever want to remember what it feels like to lose," he said. "I want to continue to win football games. We take it one game at a time. We are a selfless team and that's why we have had the success we have had."

Perhaps no player was as selfless as Bettis. The former starter relished the chance to prove his critics wrong when he became the starter because of the injury to Staley. "It was real good to get out there and just show that my ability is still there," he said. "The opportunities are not there, and that was my choice to stay here and be in the role that I am in. I understood what was going on. It was one of those situations where the franchise has to think about the future. I understand that. I just wanted to be a part of this team and this city, and I did not want to leave."

The Steelers were also glad that Bettis stayed and didn't test the free-agent market (though admittedly given his 2003 numbers it would have been difficult to find an opportunity to start with another team). The Bus responded with a breakout year, rushing for 100 yards in each of his starts on his way to 941 rushing yards, good for 12th in the league. Along the way he reached some milestones. He passed Eric Dickerson for fifth on the NFL's all-time rushing list and probably ensured his enshrinement in Canton once his career is over. Bettis also heaped praise upon his offensive line. "A lot of people have a tendency to put the running game on the running back," he explained. "The running back is not super man. He cannot go out there and run over 10 people. You need those guys up front to pound the football and give you an opportunity."

The second half of the season was all about seizing opportunities. Against the Browns, linebacker Porter was tossed before the game even started following a nasty on-field fistfight with running back William Green. Harrison stepped in to fill the void and had a big day, pressuring Browns quarterback Jeff Garcia into key mistakes—including another clutch Polamalu interception. Roethlisberger had another efficient day, managing the offense in a 24-10 win. One week later against Cincinnati in another division rematch, the Steelers recipe for success continued: Roethlisberger's efficiency combined with a steady dose of the Bus and an opportunistic defense added up to victory (19-14).

However, some cracks were beginning to show, despite the team's 9-1 record. The Bengals, not known for their ability to bring pressure, sacked Roethlisberger seven times. Some of those sacks were caused by the rookie holding onto the ball too long. Against the Washington Redskins the following week, it was another ugly win. The Redskins brought a lot of pressure on Roethlisberger and held the offense in check for much of the game. The special teams—with Reed going three for three on field goal attempts, punter Chris Gardocki (he of the NFL-record 1,045 consecutive punts without a block) keeping the Skins in poor field position and a 60-yard punt return by Randle El—keyed a 16-7 victory.

The winning continued in Jacksonville in one of the more physical match-ups in the NFL season. Roethlisberger led another late drive as Reed's field goal sailed through the uprights with 23 seconds. The Steelers continued to find ways to win, and their rookie quarterback kept adding to his mystique, while drawing praise from his head coach after the 17-16 win.

"He is resourceful," Cowher said in describing the latest Roethlisberger-led victory. "He sees the field, he's accurate and he scrambles. After they kicked the field goal [to go up 16-14], I told him this is like training camp. It was a two-minute drill with 1:47 left and no timeouts left, and we need a field goal, and that's what it was."

Coming off the Jacksonville win, Roethlisberger showed he was a rookie for one of the few times against the New York Jets. The Jets confused the Steelers quarterback, not letting him get comfortable and forcing him into bad decisions. But the coaching staff adjusted the recipe for success, leaning more heavily on Bettis, who broke the game open with a well-executed halfback option pass. And again fate seemed to be on the side of the Steelers. The play hadn't worked all week in practice, but in a crucial fourth quarter situation against the Jets, Bettis found Tuman open in the end zone, and the Steelers escaped with a 17-6 victory. Despite the score, the Jets proved to be one of the toughest opponents for the Steelers, and the game foreshadowed a difficult playoff showdown.

With the Jets win, the Steelers clinched the AFC North division title. But Cowher reminded his team at every opportunity that they had not accomplished anything yet. "This is only the first step," he stressed to them and to all of the Steeler Nation. He also noted that the team would have to step up its performance—particularly on offense. His team responded with an exciting 33-30 win over the New York Giants in a battle between the two highly touted rookie signal callers, Roethlisberger and New York's disappointing (at least until that game) first round pick Eli Manning. The offense opened up with Randle El enjoying his best receiving day, catching five passes for 149 yards and a touchdown as he moved up the depth chart for the injured Burress. He even contributed a touchdown score of his own on a nifty shovel pass. Bettis also had a big game, carrying the ball 36 times—the most in six years—for

140 yards. The game ended with what was becoming a familiar sight: Roethlisberger taking a knee to run out the clock.

With two games remaining, Cowher's team was 13-1, and more importantly by virtue of their victory over New England, holding onto the AFC's No. 1 seed, which would guarantee home field advantage throughout the playoffs. When New England was upset by Miami, the Steelers would only need to win one of those games to clinch the top spot. The first opportunity came against Baltimore, the only team to beat them. In the rematch, it was a complete role reversal. This time, the Steelers dominated. The offensive line forced its will on the Ravens defense, opening up big holes for Bettis, who rushed for 117 yards. The highlight was the opening drive of the second half. The Steelers strung together 12 consecutive running plays on what center Hartings called "our best drive of the season." The Steelers exacted revenge on the Ravens with the 20-7 victory, but the team held its collective breath as Roethlisberger was knocked out of the game by a borderline cheap shot by the Ravens' linebacker Terrell Suggs. Perhaps the most impressive stat of this divisional match-up came from the leg of Gardocki, or more clearly the lack of Gardocki's leg. Amazingly enough, the Steeler punter was not called on to punt for the second consecutive game.

In the season finale, a meaningless game for the Steelers but one that had playoff implications for the host Buffalo Bills, Cowher chose to rest many of his starters, including Bettis and Roethlisberger. There was some speculation that since the game was against nemesis Donahoe's team, the Steelers' head coach might go for the throat. He didn't, but his subs did. Little-used running back Willie Parker zipped through the Bills' defense for 102 yards on 19 carries. Randle El had another big game, hauling in seven passes for 81 yards and reserve linebacker Larry Foote recovered a fumble in Pittsburgh's 29-24 victory. The loss kept the Bills out of the playoffs and finished the Steelers' regular season at 15-1, the best record in AFC history.

The Steelers would have a week off to prepare for the playoffs. Home field advantage had not been kind to the team in the past. There was the loss against San Diego to end the '94 season, as the Chargers hit a bomb late in the game and stopped the Steelers three yards away as the clock expired. In 1997, the Steelers led the Denver Broncos at half time, but quarterback Kordell Stewart threw devastating interceptions. And more recently, in 2001, a kickoff return and a blocked field goal return led to an upset by the New England Patriots. Ever cognizant of that history, Cowher took the opportunity to keep his team focused. “It was a nice way to end the regular season,” he said, “but we recognize now the real journey begins for those rings.”

To be 15-1 requires a certain amount of good fortune in addition to talent. The offensive line managed to avoid major injuries, and when players did go down in other positions, there are always seemed to be someone ready to fill in. Great teams also make a lot of their good fortune, whether it comes from strong coaching and depth or the ability to make plays in key situations. But as the Steelers played their opening division round game against the New York Jets, plain old luck couldn't be discounted.

Just like in the regular season game, the Jets provided matchup problems for Roethlisberger. Although the Steelers shot out to what looked to be a blowout, jumping on top 10-0, the quarterback had another bout of ‘rookie-itis’. His first half stats: 4 of 12 for only 48 yards. He tossed two interceptions, including one that safety Reggie Tongue returned 75 yards for a touchdown to put the Jets ahead 17-10 in the third quarter. New York had scored their other touchdown on a Santana Moss punt return, as the big special team's play seemed to be a harbinger for yet another home playoff disappointment.

Still, the Steelers fought back. As he had all season, Roethlisberger shrugged off a disappointing start. His shovel pass to Ward tied the game at 17 with six minutes left. Then for the first time, the Jets began to move the ball and found their way into field goal range late in the game. For the Steelers to advance, they would need to be lucky. And that luck was delivered by Jets placekicker Doug Brien. A week earlier in the wild card round, Brien kicked a key overtime field goal to eliminate the favored San Diego Chargers.

Brien had the chance to do the same thing to the Steelers, but his 47-yard attempt missed only by inches and clanged off the lower left corner of the goal post. After the miss, the Steelers took over at the Jets' 37 with under two minutes to play in regulation. Unfortunately on first down, Roethlisberger overthrew Burress, and cornerback David Barrett intercepted the pass. The Jets had a second chance, and so did Brien. As the clock ticked down in regulation, luck was with the Steelers. The 43-yard attempt floated wide, and the Steelers were still alive.

New York won the coin toss and received the ball first in overtime. The Steelers' defense was up to the task and forced a punt. This time the offense would click. In a bit of role reversal, Staley came off the bench to fill in for Bettis, who had suffered leg cramps. Staley, still shrugging off the effects of a hamstring injury, was brilliant. He carried the ball six times for 28 yards. Roethlisberger directed a clutch 14 play, 72-yard drive setting up Reed's 33-yard field goal attempt. Unlike Brien, Reed, taking full advantage of knowing his home field, delivered a game winner as the Steelers advanced to the AFC championship game, 20-17.

They were lucky to be advancing, but they also proved to be survivors, blowing a 10-point lead and overcoming three turnovers and two returns for touchdowns. Were the Steelers a team of destiny? "No question," said Staley. "I have faith and believe in God. He truly blessed us tonight."

Does destiny trump dynasty? That was the question as the Steelers prepared to host the Patriots in the AFC championship game. The Pats had little trouble in dispatching the Indianapolis Colts in the division round, making record-setting quarterback Peyton Manning look like a rookie in the process. Who knows what the mastermind Belichick would have in store for the rookie Roethlisberger, who was coming off his worst game as a pro. So despite riding a league-best 15-game winning streak, the Steelers came into the championship game as slight underdogs.

This rematch followed a similar script to the Halloween game, only this time the nightmare was one for the Steelers. The carnage started early. Roethlisberger was intercepted on his first throw, as he missed an open Randle El. The defense held the Patriots to only a field goal on that drive and appeared ready to make a move of their own, moving to the Patriots' 39. Cowher made an early gamble, going for a fourth-and-1, but Bettis was stopped in his tracks and fumbled. On the very next play Patriot quarterback Brady beat Townsend with a 60-yard pass when the Steelers' safeties failed to provide deep help. (Earlier in the week, Belichick's staff had noticed a flaw in the Steelers' coverage and exploited it on the big play.) Trailing 10-0, the Steelers nonetheless had a chance to get back in the game. They moved the ball to the Patriots' 27 but had to settle for a Reed 43-yard field goal.

But Brady didn't let the Steelers create any momentum. He hit receiver Deion Branch for another long gainer, this time for 45 yards. Two plays later he found David Givens after cornerback after Williams fell down, and the lead was stretched to 17-3. As he had all year long, Roethlisberger looked to rally his offense. Big Ben moved his team to the Patriots' 19, where a touchdown would have put them back in the game right before half time. His second interception of the day was a killer, though, when New England safety Rodney Harrison stepped in front of Tuman and dashed 87 yards for a touchdown. The Patriots headed to the locker room, secure with a 24-3 lead.

Even though the Steelers scored on a long touchdown drive to open the third quarter, the game was never really in question. Each time the Steelers would score the Patriots would answer. Burress dropped a pass in the end zone that would have closed the gap to 14 to start the fourth quarter, and the Steelers had to settle for a field goal. That was as close as they got. A late touchdown reception by Burress ended the scoring, with the Patriots routing the home team 41-27.

"When you look at the game, we had three turnovers," Cowher said in his postgame comments. "We gave up some big plays on defense, and we got ourselves into a hole that we really couldn't get out of—the things that we really have not done all year. And certainly the turnovers we overcame last week, but we were not able to overcome it today.

"Ben did some things well," he continued, "but you can't throw three interceptions, not in a game of this magnitude—and not one for a touchdown." A magical season in which the Steelers exceeded all expectations was over.

But what a season it was, although to listen to the sports talk shows in the days following the championship game loss fans would think the Steelers had gone 2-16 instead of 16-2. Certainly, it was a disappointing loss, the second time in four years that it was the Patriots hoisting the Lamar Hunt Trophy as AFC champs in the middle of Heinz Field, and there will be fallout. The barbs of Cowher being unable to win the big one will continue, even though most teams don't even get the opportunity to make it to the championship round with the frequency that he has directed the Steelers.

Emotions ran rampant.

Perhaps Ward was most visibly upset by the loss. He broke down in tears the next day, the source of which was the thought that the team had failed to deliver Bettis to a Super Bowl, and there might not be another chance. Bettis offered that he needed time to mull over a return to the Steelers.

Burress, an unrestricted free agent, told the media his days in Pittsburgh were over and that the coaching staff had failed to get the ball into his hands enough. (Never mind that he had dropped a key touchdown pass late in the game.) He soon signed with the New York Giants.

And in this salary-cap era, more change was in the wind. Scott and Riemersma were salary-cap casualties. Defensive tackle Clancy joined Burress in New York as a free agent. Tackle Ross got a great offer and moved to Arizona, while guard Vincent signed with the Baltimore Ravens. As for additions, the Steelers picked up tight end Marco Bettaglia, a free agent who didn't play in 2004, and wide receiver Cedrick Wilson. The team had what analysts call a strong draft, but its impact is yet to be seen.

Yet there is a strong nucleus in place, with depth at key positions and a relatively young squad. Unlike in previous years, Cowher's coaching staff will remain in place. Roethlisberger, even with the possibility of a sophomore slump, looks to be a franchise-type quarterback.

"The kid will learn," Cowher said of his young quarterback. "He is going to be a good quarterback."

It's unlikely the Steelers will repeat their 15-1 performance. But then again, it was unlikely that they would be better than 7-9 this season.

As we were putting this book to bed, there was a seismic shift in the Steeler Nation. Myron Cope, long-time voice of the Steelers, announced he was stepping down after 35 seasons in the booth. A generation of football fans has known only the flamboyant Cope as the color man for Steelers broadcasts. Some might even have to turn up the volume on their sets and listen to the network broadcasts for the first time.

Like Bob Prince did for Pirates games, Myron (no last name needed) transcended the game for Pittsburghers. We tuned in to hear his stories, his commentaries and his quips. Who else would compare Rocky Bleier with famed dancer Nijinsky? He was a homer, for sure. But he was *our* homer. And he was not above letting us know when the Steelers were stinking up the joint. Above all he made football fun and created a lasting bond between fans and the organization. His invention, the Terrible Towel that looks so regal in NFL Films when twirled by 50,000-plus lunatic fans, ensures his place in local football history long after he heads to the great huddle in the sky.

His voice weakened, Myron bade farewell to the local media in midsummer after Joe Gordon, a fixture in the club's PR staff for years, honored a long-time request and told the Steelers' broadcaster that his skills were eroding. We should all have friends who can be that honest with us. Myron processed the information and simply shrugged, "I'm done."

Still, there was a void as training camp approached. We wouldn't get Myron's annual pick for the sleeper—that late-round draft pick who would surprise everyone by making the squad. There would be no more Cope's Cabana after the games (and thankfully no more music videos starring Myron).

Fittingly, the Steelers will honor him during a nationally televised Monday night game on Halloween (a coincidence?). We actually feel sorry for the visiting Baltimore Ravens. They don't stand a chance with the emotion that will be pulsing through Heinz Field on that night. Quoth Myron on the Balt Ravens: *Nevermore.*

Timeline

Evolution of Western PA football, 1890-2004

YEAR	EVENT
1890	Pitt, then known as the Western University of Pennsylvania, plays its first game, a 38-0 loss to the Allegheny Athletic Club.
1892	Pudge Heffelfinger receives $500 for a game, making him the first professional player.
1895	Latrobe manager Dave Barry pays John Brallier $10 plus expenses for a game against Greensburg. Until Heffelfinger's contract was found in the '60s, Brallier was thought to be the first pro.
1897	Latrobe plays at Greensburg's Athletic Field (now Offutt Field) against Greensburg in what could have been the first all professional game.
1901	Art Rooney, Sr. was born on January 27th.
1902	The Pittsburgh Stars defeat the Philadelphia Athletics 11-0 in what is billed as the championship of the first National Football League.
1908	Pitt becomes the first collegiate team to wear numbers on their uniforms.
1910	The Panthers have their first undefeated season going 9-0. That year Pitt outscored their opponents 282-0.
1914	Wilkinsburg captures the first WPIAL championship.
1915	Pitt hires Glen "Pop" Warner and wins first national championship. They also win in 1916 and 1918.
1920	Quarterback Art Rooney leads the Dukes.
1921	On October 8th, Pitt beats West Virginia 21-13 in the first ever college football game to be broadcast on the radio. KDKA does the honors.
1922	Washington & Jefferson pull one of the great "upsets" in Rose Bowl history tying the mighty Bears of California 0-0.

1924	Jock Sutherland is hired as coach of Pitt.
1925	On September 26th, Pitt beats Washington and Lee 28-0 in the first game ever played at Pitt Stadium.
1926	Carnegie Tech defeats Knute Rockne and Notre Dame 19-0.
1927	Duquesne hires Elmer Layden.
1927	Despite the fact they have won the second most games in WPIAL history, Greensburg-Salem captures their only WPIAL crown this season.
1927	On October 8th Pitt's Gibby Welch returns a kickoff 105 yards against West Virginia.
1929	Despite a 47-14 shellacking at the hands of USC in the Rose Bowl, Pitt wins the national championship.
1929	Duquesne plays first night football game ever in Pittsburgh, beating Geneva 27-7.
1932	Dan Rooney was born on July 20th.
1933	The Steelers, then called the Pirates, play their first game, a 23-2 loss to New York.
1933	Duquesne defeats Miami (FL) 33-7 in the Festival of Palms Bowl, a game that soon became known as the Orange Bowl.
1933	Martin Kottler rambles 99 yards with an interception on September 27th against the Cardinals. The score came in the 2nd game in Pirates franchise history; it's never been eclipsed.
1934	After defeating Carnegie Tech 20-0, Pitt wins third national championship.
1936	Emerging victorious in the Rose Bowl, a 21-0 shutout of Washington, Pitt wins a share of the national championship.
1936	Duquesne beats Mississippi State in the Orange Bowl 13-12.
1937	The Panthers tie Fordham 0-0 for the third consecutive year, but capture the school's eighth national championship.

1937	Pitt's Marshall Goldberg rambles 77 yards for the game's only score as the Panthers gain revenge for a 1936 defeat, beating Duquesne 6-0.
1938	The Pirates sign Supreme Court justice Byron "Whizzer" White.
1938	Carnegie Tech goes to the Sugar Bowl, losing to TCU 15-7.
1938	Sutherland resigns at Pitt in a dispute with the administration.
1939	Duquesne hires Buff Donelli who leads his alma mater to an 8-0-1 mark and no. 10 ranking.
1940	The Pirates officially change their name to the Steelers.
1941	The Dukes finish undefeated at 8-0-0 with a no. 8 ranking.
1942	The Steelers have their first winning season ever at 7-4.
1943	The Steelers combine with the Philadelphia Eagles to form the Steagles due to a shortage of war-time players.
1944	Pittsburgh joins forces with the Chicago Cardinals and combine to go 0-10. Many called the configuration the Car-Pitts.
1945	Pitt changes its colors from blue and gold to red and white.
1946-1948	Art Rooney hires Jock Sutherland to coach his team. Sutherland leads the Steelers to their first ever playoff encounter, losing to the Eagles 21-0 in 1947. He dies suddenly on April 11th, 1948.
1949	Bobby Gage runs for a Steeler record 97 yards on one play in a game against the Bears on December 4th.
1949	Joe Geri blasts a team record 82-yard punt in a game November 20th against the Packers.
1950	Duquesne discontinues its varsity football program. It would remain dormant until coming back at the club level in 1969.
1950	St. Vincent College in Latrobe defeats Emory & Henry 7-6 in the Tangerine Bowl.

1951	Pitt plays its first ever nationally televised game at the Rose Bowl in Pasadena on September 29th against Duke.
1952	The Steelers rout the Giants 63-7.
1956	Bobby Grier integrates the Sugar Bowl becoming the first African American to play in the contest.
1957	Former Detroit Lions head coach Buddy Parker takes over the Steelers.
1962	John Henry Johnson becomes the first Steeler to eclipse the 1,000-yard barrier rushing.
1963	Pitt finishes third in the nation with a 9-1 mark. Because of delaying their game with Penn State a week due to the assassination of President Kennedy, the Panthers lost out on a bowl bid.
1964	Pittsburgh's John Henry Johnson becomes the first Steeler runner to eclipse 200 yards in a game as he rambles for 200 on the nose in a game October 10th against Cleveland.
1964	Brady Keys returns a punt 90 yards against the Giants on September 20th. The run still remains a Steeler record.
1968	On November 3rd Steeler receiver Roy Jefferson catches a team record four TD tosses in a game against Atlanta.
1969	Pittsburgh hires Chuck Noll as coach. He goes 1-13 his first season.
1969	Noll drafts Joe Greene with the first pick of his tenure in Pittsburgh.
1969	Don McCall sets a team record with a 101 yards kickoff return for a touchdown against the Vikings on November 23rd.
1970	The Steelers win a coin toss with the Bears for the rights to draft Terry Bradshaw.
1970	The Steelers move into Three Rivers Stadium.

1970	Nerf Football was developed by former Pitt kicker Fred Cox and an associate, John Mattey.
1970	John "Frenchy" Fuqua rushes for a team record 218 yards against the Eagles on December 20th, 85 of them came on a single play. The record still stands today.
1970	Pitt comes back from down 35-8 at the half to beat West Virginia 36-35 on October 17th.
1972	Franco Harris arrives and leads the Steelers to their first championship of any kind, the AFC central division. He is the key player in the Immaculate Reception game against Oakland, Pittsburgh's first postseason win.
1973	Duquesne wins the National Club championship.
1973	Johnny Majors comes over from Iowa State to lead the moribund Pitt program.
1974	The Steelers draft four Hall of Famers in the first five rounds (Lynn Swann, Jack Lambert, John Stallworth and Mike Webster).
1974	Pittsburgh wins their first Super Bowl, 16-6 against the Vikings in Super Bowl IX.
1975	The Steelers win Super Bowl X, 21-17 against the Cowboys.
1975	The Panthers ramble for a school record 530 rushing yards in a game against Army on October 18th.
1975	Tony Dorsett runs for a school record 303 yards in a 34-20 upset of Notre Dame on November 15th.
1976	Rocky Bleier and Franco Harris become the second running back tandem in NFL history to both rush for 1,000 in one year.
1976	Johnny Majors completes the greatest turnaround in college football history, leading the undefeated Pitt Panthers to the national championship. Tony Dorsett captures the school's only Heisman Trophy.
1976	Tony Dorsett sets the all-time NCAA rushing mark in a 45-0 defeat of Navy on October 23rd.

1976	Pitt retires the number 33 in honor of Tony Dorsett.
1978	The Steelers win their third championship in Super Bowl XIII, 35-31 against the Cowboys.
1979	Pittsburgh becomes the first team to win four Super Bowls with a 31-19 win against the Rams.
1979	Duquesne returns to the NCAA at the Division III level.
1979	Jackie Sherrill recruits Danny Marino from Central Catholic to Pitt.
1980	Pitt captures the New York Times Poll national championship. Hugh Green also captures the Maxwell and Walter Camp Awards.
1980	Pitt retires the number 99 in honor of Hugh Green.
1981	John Brown makes the "Catch" in the Sugar Bowl to cap the Panthers third consecutive 11-1 season.
1981	In a game at the Kingdome in Seattle on November 8th, two quarterbacks hook up on a team record 90 yard touchdown pass as Terry Bradshaw hits Mark Malone for the score.
1982	The modern golden era of Pitt football ends when Jackie Sherrill resigns.
1982	Pitt retires the number 13 in honor of Danny Marino.
1984	Pittsburgh upsets Denver 24-17 in the first round of the playoffs before losing to Miami in the AFC championship.
1984	The Pittsburgh Maulers are born as a USFL franchise, making a splash by signing Heisman Trophy winner Mike Rozier and having the first sell out in USFL history. The team goes 3-15 in its only season.
1984	Pitt retires the number 79 in honor of Bill Fralic.
1985	The Panthers beat Purdue 31-30 on August 31th in the first night game at Pitt Stadium.

1985	Mark Malone completes a team record five touchdown passes in an opening-day win September 8th against the Colts.
1986	Gateway finishes third in the nation on the USA Today Poll by defeating top ranked North Hills 7-6 in the WPIAL championship.
1987	The Pittsburgh Gladiators play in the first Arena Football League game ever at the Civic Arena in front of 12,117 fans. Pittsburgh beats Washington 48-46.
1987	The Gladiators play in the first Arena Bowl, losing to Denver 45-16.
1987	North Hills captures the USA Today High School National Championship.
1987	Gateway's Curtis Bray wins the Gatorade National Player of the Year.
1988	The PIAA establishes the first ever state football championship playoffs. The WPIAL musters up only one championship as Pittsburgh Central Catholic wins the AAAA crown.
1989	The Gladiators play in Arena Bowl III, losing to Detroit 39-26.
1989	Pitt beats Texas A&M in the Sun Bowl 31-28 as Paul Hackett wins his first game as coach of the Panthers.
1989	Steeler quarterback Bubby Brister sets a team record by completing 15 consecutive passes in a game October 1st against the Lions.
1990	Chuck Noll wins his 200th game.
1990	Allegheny College defeats Lycoming 21-14 to capture the NCAA Division III championship.
1990	Indiana (PA) loses in the NCAA Division II championship game 51-11 to North Dakota State.
1990	The Gladiators move to Tampa Bay following a 61-30 loss to Detroit in the playoffs.

1990	On October 14th against the Broncos, Bubby Brister hits Dwight Stone for a team record-tying 90-yard toss.
1991	Chuck Noll retires.
1992	Pittsburgh hires Bill Cowher and wins their first Division title since 1984.
1992	Barry Foster breaks the all-time Steelers single-season rushing mark with 1,690 yards.
1992	Duquesne moves to Division I-AA.
1992	Washington & Jefferson makes the Division III championship only to lose 38-15 to Albion.
1993	Duquesne builds on campus facility with Rooney Field.
1993	Robert Morris begins playing NCAA varsity football; they hire former NFL coach Joe Walton to lead them.
1993	Indiana (PA) loses once again in the NCAA Division II championship game, this time 41-34 to North Alabama.
1994	Pittsburgh returns to the AFC championship game, losing to the Chargers 17-13.
1994	Washington & Jefferson loses once again in the NCAA Division III Championship game.
1994	Gary Anderson nails a team record 19 consecutive field goals.
1994	Robert Morris plays their first varsity game ever, a 24-19 win against Waynesburg on September 3rd.
1995	The Steelers win the AFC championship 20-16 against the Colts. They go on to lose Super Bowl XXX to Dallas 27-17.
1996	North Hills Lavar Arrington wins the Parade National Player of the Year.
1996	Kordell Stewart takes off on an 80-yard touchdown run in a game against Carolina on December 22nd.

1997	Kordell Stewart takes over at quarterback and leads Pittsburgh to the AFC title game, losing to the Broncos 24-21.
1997	After seven seasons of futility, new coach Walt Harris leads Pitt to the Liberty Bowl.
1997	Pitt honors its greats retiring the number 89 for Mike Ditka, 42 for Marshall Goldberg and 65 for Joe Schmidt.
1997	Pete Gonzalez tosses a school record seven touchdown passes for Pitt in a 55-48 win over Rutgers.
1998	On Thanksgiving Day the Steelers go into overtime against the Lions tied at 16 and lose 19-16 in part due to a controversial coin toss. Steelers go on to lose their last four games of the season.
1998	Steelers' Courtney Hawkins sets a team record by catching 14 passes on November 1st in a game against the Titans.
1999	Pitt plays its last game at Pitt Stadium beating Notre Dame 37-27.
1999	Robert Morris wins the NCAA Division I-AA national championship.
2000	The Steelers close the door after 30 years at Three Rivers Stadium with a 24-3 win against the Redskins.
2000	Robert Morris wins their second consecutive national championship.
2001	Heinz Field opens up as Pittsburgh wins the Central Division but eventually loses the AFC championship to New England.
2001	Pitt opens the Heinz Field era as David Priestley rambles 85 yards for the first score in a win over East Tennessee State.
2001	Pitt retires Mark May's jersey on September 27th.
2001	Quarterback Kordell Stewart rambles for a season record 5.8 yards per carry, breaking Franco Harris' 1972 mark of 5.6.
2001	Kordell Stewart hits Bobby Shaw on a 90-TD strike, tying a team record in a game against Baltimore on December 16th.

2002	The Steelers win the first ever North Division championship then rally in the divisional playoffs down 24-7 to beat the Browns 36-33.
2002	Steeler kicker Jeff Reed nails six field goals in a game against Jacksonville, tying Gary Anderson's team record.
2002	Tommy Maddox throws for a Steeler record 473 yards in an overtime tie against the Falcons on November 10th. Receiver Plaxico Burress also sets a team record by piling up 253 yards receiving in the game.
2002	Hines Ward becomes the first Steeler ever to eclipse the 100-reception barrier by catching 112 passes for the year.
2003	Duquesne U. captures the I-AA non-scholarship national championship.
2003	Larry Fitzgerald captures the Walter Camp Award as a Pitt sophomore, following a season where he led the nation in catches, (92), and touchdowns (22.)
2004	Despite numerous injuries, rookie quarterback Ben Roethlisberger wins his first 12 NFL starts leading Pittsburgh to a surprise North Division championship and a record 15 wins.
2004	After a poor start, Pitt rebounds to capture its first Big East championship and a spot in the Fiesta Bowl.
2004	Pittsburgh Central Catholic wins the first state championship for a WPIAL AAAA school since 1995 by going 16-0.
2005	Robert Morris opens their first on-campus facility, Joe Walton Stadium.
2005	Seton Hill University begins their first season of varsity football.

b i b l i o g r a p h y

Media Guides

CMU Media Guide
Duquesne Media Guide
IUP Media Guide
Northeastern Conference Media Guide
Penn State Media Guide
Pittsburgh Panthers Media Guide
Robert Morris Media Guide
Slippery Rock Media Guide
Steelers Media Guides
Washington and Jefferson Media Guide

Books

Blount Jr., Roy. *About Three Bricks Shy of a Load*. Boston: Little Brown Publishing, 1974.

Bynum, Mike, Larry Eldridge Jr., and Sam Sciullo Jr. *Greatest Moments in Pitt Football History*. Nashville: Athlon Sports Communications Inc., 1994.

Carroll, Bob and Bob Braunwart. *Pro Football from AAA to '03*. North Huntingdon, PA: PFRA, 1990.

Carroll, Bob, Michael Gershman, David Neft, and John Thorn. *Total Steelers*. New York: Harper Perennial, 1998.

Didinger, Ray. *Great Teams, Great Years Pittsburgh Steelers*. New York: Macmillan, 1974.

Elias Sports Bureau (compilation). *2004 NFL Record and Fact Book*. New York: Time Inc Home Entertainment, 2004.

Finoli, David and Tom Aikens. *The Birthplace of Professional Football: Southwestern Pennsylvania*. Mount Pleasant, SC: Arcadia Publishing: 2004.

Fulks, Matt. *Super Bowl Sunday: The Day America Stops*. Lenexa, KS: Addax Publishing Group, 2000.

Hoppel, Joe, Mike Nahrstedt, and Steve Zesch. *College Football's Twenty-Five Greatest Teams*. St Louis, MO: The Sporting News, 1988.

Johnson, Lloyd and Miles Wolff. *The Encyclopedia of Minor League Baseball.* Durham, NC: Baseball America, Inc, 1997.

Mule, Marty. *Sugar Bowl: The First Fifty Years.* Birmingham, AL: Oxmoor House Inc, 1983.

Neft, David and Richard Cohen. *The Football Encyclopedia.* New York, NY: St Martin's Press, 1991.

Roberts, Randy and David Welky. *The Steelers Reader.* Pittsburgh, PA: The University of Pittsburgh Press, 2001.

Web sites

American Renaissance: www.amren.com
Baseball America Online: www.baseballamerica.com
Cal Poly Pomona University: www.csupomona.edu
Classic Mythology Online: www.classicalmythology.org
College Football Data Warehouse: www.cfbdatawarehouse.com
College Football News: www.collegefootballnews.com
Columbia University: www.columbia.edu
The Daily Star: www.thedailystar.com
Division I-AA Football: www.i-aa.org
Division II Football: www.d2football.com
Division III Football: www.d3football.com
Donnan.com: www.donnan.com/murphy.htm
Football@ JT-SW.com: http://www.jt-sw.com/football/
ESPN: www.espn.com
The Knowledge Rush: www.knowledgerush.com
The Mail Archive: www.mail-archive.com
The Massey Ratings: www.mratings.com
Nashville City Paper: www.nashvillecitypaper.com
National Football League: www.nfl.com
The Official Duquesne Athletics Web site: www.goduquesne.com
The Official Pittsburgh Steelers Web site: www.steelers.com
The Official Pro Football Hall of Fame Web site: www.profootballhof.com
The Official University of Pittsburgh Athletic Web site: www.pittsburghpanthers.com
Philly.com: www.philly.com

The Pittsburgh List of Champions Web site: www.nosecatbooks.com/pittchamps.html
Pittsburgh Live: www.pittsburghlive.com
Pro Football Reference.com: http://www.pro-football-reference.com
The Pro Football Research Association, www.footballresearch.com
Pro Football Weekly: www.profootballweekly.com
Pulp: www.pittsburghpulp.com
Slam Sports: www.canoe.ca
United States Football League: www.thisistheusfl.com
USA Soccer: www.ussoccer.com
Steelerettes: www.steelerettes.com

Newspapers and Magazines

Beaver County Times
Chicago Tribune
Los Angeles Times
New York Times
Pittsburgh Post-Gazette
Pittsburgh Press
St. Petersburg Times
Sporting News
Sports Illustrated
Tribune Review
Washington Times

acknowledgments

With a book of this undertaking, support is essential. Luckily we had that and more from:

- One of the most legendary Pittsburgh sports figures of all-time, Hall of Fame Steeler owner, Dan Rooney
- The great Steeler head coach, Bill Cowher
- The former NFL great and current Robert Morris coach, Joe Walton
- Former Steeler director of player development and the "best" get back coach in the NFL, Anthony Griggs
- Carl Mattioli of the Latrobe Historical Society for not only providing information, but also some photos in the project
- E. Kay Myers, Latrobe author and member of the Latrobe Football Committee to bring the Hall of Fame to the city, for his very informative interview and help
- Alex Kramer, former administrative assistant to many of the Pitt coaches from 1977 through 1995, including Jackie Sherrill, Mike Gottfried, Paul Hackett and Johnny Majors. Mr. Kramer is THE authority on Pitt football history and was very gracious in the time he spent with us answering any question we had pertaining to the program.
- EJ Borghetti, the sports information director at the University of Pittsburgh, and his wonderful administrative assistant, Celeste Walsh
- Former Pitt great, Bobby Grier
- Former coach of the 2003 Division I-AA Mid Major National Champion Duquesne Dukes, Greg Gattuso
- The highly successful coach of the CMU Tartans, Rich Lackner
- The inspirational Lieutenant Jesse Grapes
- CMU's sports information director, Mark Fisher
- Duquesne University sports information director, Dave Saba, for the wonderful photos he donated
- Duquesne athletic director, Brian Colleary

- Agent extraordinaire, Joe Linta
- Bob Carroll, head of the Professional Football Research Association, for not only his comments but also the information he provided us
- Joe Huber, more commonly known as "The Titleman" for his unique and very informative views on his favorite Steel City team, the Pitt Panther football squad
- The Pro Football Hall of Fame, especially information services manager, Pete Fierle
- Dwight White of the Steelers
- The fine people from the Monroeville Library, for all their help with the microfilm
- Saint Vincent College sports information director, Jeff Zidek, for not only the photos, but the wonderful information he gave us about the Bearcats now extinct football program
- Sports information director, Jim Duzyk, of Robert Morris
- Head coach Mike Sirianni of Washington & Jefferson
- Washington & Jefferson sports information director, Sean McGuinness
- Slippery Rock director of sports promotion & information, Bob McComas
- IUP sports information director, Mike Hoffman
- Northwestern director of football operations, Justin Sheridan
- Westmoreland Historical Society's executive director, James Steeley
- Westmoreland County football historian, Robert Van Atta
- Steelers equipment manager, Rodgers Freyvogel
- New Brighton High School athletic director, Joe Ursida
- All the people from Rochester and Monaca, who hosted us at their high school game
- Photographer Keven Cooke and Grande Sudios for the portrait and historical shots

David Finoli and Chris Fletcher

a u t h o r s

David Finoli (left) has authored four well-received sports books, three on baseball and one on football. *For the Good of the Country* chronicles baseball during World War II and was cited by *Diamond Angles* as "meticulous" and "an excellent record". He has done freelance work for *Pittsburgh Magazine* and contributes to Baseballspot.org.

Chris Fletcher (right) is a senior marketing, writing and strategic planning consultant. Prior to that he served as vice president of publishing and Internet services for WQED Pittsburgh where the magazine won numerous local and national awards during his tenure.

Both David and Chris live in Western Pennsylvania and are graduates of the Duquesne University School of Journalism where David served as the assistant sports editor of the *Duquesne Duke* and Chris was associate editor. David's wife and three children share his obsession with Western Pennsylvania football, while Chris's wife and son merely tolerate his.

Author photo by Kevin R. Cooke

The Dukes score again in the 51-14 thrashing of St. Louis during a disappointing 1949 campaign. Duquesne would drop varsity football a year later. The authors are both proud alums and fans of a re-instated program. (Courtesy of Duquesne Athletics.)

i n d e x

Page numbers in italics refer to photographs.

Background photo on pages 440-441: *Duquesne beating St. Louis University 51-14 at Forbes Field in 1941 was one of the few shining lights in an otherwise dismal 3-6 campaign for Duquesne. (Courtesy of Duquesne Athletics.)*

CHECK YOUR LOCAL BOOKSELLER FOR COPIES OF

STEEL CITY GRIDIRONS

by ***DAVID FINOLI***
and ***CHRIS FLETCHER***

(ISBN 0-9770429-1-X)

from Towers Maguire Publishing

(***an imprint of*** THE LOCAL HISTORY COMPANY)

www.TowersMaguirePublishing.com
sales@TowersMaguirePublishing.com
(or www.THE LOCAL HISTORY COMPANY.com)

If your local bookseller is not able to provide you with a copy of this title, visit our website above, or contact us at:

Towers Maguire Publishing
The Local History Company
112 NORTH Woodland Road
Pittsburgh, PA 15232-2849

Or—Call 412-362-2294
Fax 412-362-8192

QUANTITY ORDERS INVITED

This and other titles from Towers Maguire Publishing *and The Local History Company are available at special quantity discounts for bulk purchases or sales promotions, premiums, fund raising, or educational use by corporations, institutions, and other organizations. Special imprints, messages, and excerpts can also be produced to meet your specific needs. For details, please write or telephone at the address or phone number above:*